PRENTICE-HALL
HISTORY OF MUSIC SERIES
H. WILEY HITCHCOCK, editor

MUSIC IN LATIN AMERICA: AN INTRODUCTION

GERARD BÉHAGUE

Department of Music
University of Texas at Austin

PRENTICE-HALL, INC., ENGLEWOOD CLIFFS, NEW JERSEY 07632

Library of Congress Cataloging in Publication Data

BÉHAGUE, GERARD.
   Music in Latin America, an introduction.

   (Prentice-Hall history of music series)
   Includes bibliographies.
      1. Music—Latin America—History and criticism.
   I. Title.
   ML199.B44   780'.98   78-17264
   ISBN 0-13-608919-4
   ISBN 0-13-608901-1 pbk.

TO GILBERT CHASE
on his seventieth birthday

Printed in the United States of America

10 9 8 7 6 5 4 3 2 1

© 1979 by Prentice-Hall, Inc.
Englewood Cliffs, N.J. 07632

PRENTICE-HALL INTERNATIONAL, INC., *London*
PRENTICE-HALL OF AUSTRALIA PTY. LIMITED, *Sydney*
PRENTICE-HALL OF CANADA, LTD., *Toronto*
PRENTICE-HALL OF INDIA PRIVATE LIMITED, *New Delhi*
PRENTICE-HALL OF JAPAN, INC., *Tokyo*
PRENTICE-HALL OF SOUTHEAST ASIA PTE. LTD., *Singapore*
WHITEHALL BOOKS LIMITED, *Wellington, New Zealand*

CONTENTS

FOREWORD

Students and informed amateurs of the history of music have long needed a series of books that are comprehensive, authoritative, and engagingly written. They have needed books written by specialists—but specialists interested in communicating vividly. The Prentice-Hall History of Music Series aims at filling these needs.

Six books in the series present a panoramic view of the history of Western music, divided among the major historical periods—Medieval, Renaissance, Baroque, Classic, Romantic, and Contemporary. The musical cultures of the United States and Latin America, viewed historically as independent developments within the larger Western tradition, are discussed in two other books. In yet another pair, the rich yet neglected folk and traditional music of both hemispheres is treated; and, finally, one volume is dedicated to the classical music traditions of India. Taken together, the eleven volumes of the series are a distinctive and, we hope, distinguished contribution to the history of the music of the world's peoples. Each volume, moreover,

Foreword, continued

may be read singly as a substantial account of the music of its period or area.

The authors of the series are scholars of national and international repute—musicologists, critics, and teachers of acknowledged stature in their respective fields of specialization. In their contributions to the Prentice-Hall History of Music Series their goal has been to present works of solid scholarship that are eminently readable, with significant insights into music as a part of the general intellectual and cultural life of man.

H. WILEY HITCHCOCK, *Editor*

PREFACE

Since the publication in 1945 of Nicolas Slonimsky's *Music of Latin America*—the result of what he called a "Pan American fishing trip"—factual and interpretative data on all aspects of the so-called art-music tradition in Latin America have substantially increased, both in quality and quantity. The present volume attempts to present those data in broad perspective and to provide additional ones. Considering that a comprehensive view of the history of music in Latin America has never been proposed, a justification for this survey is unnecessary. Yet there are still so many gaps to be filled in our reconstruction of Latin American music history that the writing of a historical introduction such as this one may seem premature or even presumptuous. Thanks, however, to the efforts of several Latin American, American, and European scholars, the major outlines of this history can now be sketched with some degree of accuracy and cohesion.

This volume de-emphasizes vital statistics. Presentation of detailed information on the lives of composers, histories of musical institutions, or activities of musical associations has been avoided in favor of a closer examination of some of the main works by the most representative composers of the various periods, trends, and countries. To the degree warranted, a balance between description of the historical and cultural environment that produced a given music repertory and the stylistic analysis of that repertory has been sought. Thus this introductory book is addressed to historians as well as musicians.

Of necessity the three main parts of the book are organized differently. The substantial development of colonial music in Hispanic America since the sixteenth century prompted an individual treatment of sacred and secular music. A separate examination of Luso-Brazilian colonial music is amply justified historically. Part Two considers the various expressions associated with musical nationalism in several periods and countries. The nineteenth century is reviewed primarily from the nationalistic point of view, although I realize that not all the music of that century belongs to the nationalist current. As the most important motivating force in the creation of art music during the first half of the twentieth century, musical nationalism is studied in each of the following geographical and cultural areas: Mexico and the Caribbean (including Venezuela for both geographical and musical reasons), the Andean area, and Brazil and the River Plate area. Rather than taking this geographical approach, Part Three examines the non-nationalist stylistic trends since about 1910 in chronological order. The fact that six of the ten chapters of this book deal with the twentieth century simply reflects the fuller development and the considerable accomplishments of Latin American music of the period. I have endeavored particularly to provide as much information as possible on music since 1950, since such information is not readily accessible.

With so many composers and works to deal with, the selection of representative examples was not an easy one, and lack of space did not allow the inclusion of many musical examples. The success, or the lack of recognition, of the many composers active in the Latin American republics at various periods has been at times due to nonmusical reasons. Only the major figures could be considered here, but while I admit that other criteria for the choice of such figures might yield quite a different appraisal, my basic concern has been to reflect Latin American opinions in conjunction with my own assessment of the relative merits of composers' works, viewed from an essentially historical perspective. I have, therefore, given special attention to the three best-known composers of Latin America—Heitor Villa-Lobos, Carlos Chávez, and Alberto Ginastera.

A basic knowledge of Latin American history since the beginning of the colonial period has been assumed. The main facts of that history are readily available in numerous reference sources; I might point especially to the one-volume *Encyclopedia of Latin America* edited by Helen Delpar

(New York: McGraw-Hill Book Company, 1974), which provides concise, up-to-date information on Latin American history.

I cannot convey adequately my expressions of gratitude to all who have helped me in many different ways over the years to try to penetrate the unique and thoroughly exciting world of Latin American music. I am particularly grateful to Luiz Heitor Corrêa de Azevedo and Francisco Curt Lange for sharing with me their insights, arising from long experience and study of that music; to Robert Stevenson, who read the manuscript of Part One, for his very useful comments; to Juan A. Orrego-Salas, who made excellent suggestions on the whole manuscript; to H. Wiley Hitchcock, for his exemplary editorial skill and his encouragement; to the many librarians throughout the continent who spared no effort in my constant requests, particularly Mercedes Reis Pequeno of Rio de Janeiro; to the numerous composers who graciously supplied all sorts of material and discussed their activities with me; and to my colleagues and students at the University of Illinois and the University of Texas for providing me with meaningful dialogues on the music-making process the world over. To my wife and daughters I express my grateful love for their confidence and their understanding and patience during my many hours away from them in the preparation of the manuscript. To my teacher, constant well-wisher, and friend Gilbert Chase, whose help in the very conception of this study was fundamental, I dedicate this volume on his seventieth birthday.

G. B.

Austin, Texas, 1976

ABBREVIATIONS

StMP   Robert Stevenson, *The Music of Peru*. Washington, D.C.: Pan American Union, 1960.

StRBMS   Robert Stevenson, *Renaissance and Baroque Musical Sources in the Americas*. Washington, D.C.: Organization of American States, 1970.

SCAnt   Samuel Claro, *Antología de la Música Colonial en América del Sur*. Santiago de Chile: Ediciones de la Universidad de Chile, 1974.

StLACA   Robert Stevenson, *Latin American Colonial Music Anthology*. Washington, D.C.: Organization of American States, 1975.

part one

The Colonial Period

ONE

SACRED MUSIC
IN SPANISH AMERICA

Throughout the centuries religion has been a cultural focus in Latin America, but no other single influence was as important in colonial Latin America as that of the Catholic Church. As a political, social, economic, and cultural force the Church occupied a paramount position. Church organization in the New World was the crown's responsibility, and royal ecclesiastical patronage—the right of the crown to nominate clerical officials in America—was delegated in a series of Papal Bulls (1501, 1508). The first episcopal sees were established in Spanish America as early as 1511: two bishoprics in Hispaniola and one in Puerto Rico. All emigration of clerics to the New World was directed by the King through the Council of Indies. Clerics were required to go to a designated post and could not preach without a license. Royal authorities legislated on controversies between ecclesiastical councils and bishops or parish priests and bishops, and on virtually everything concerning the rights and prerogatives of both regular and secular clergy. Thus, both Spanish and Portuguese colonial empires in the New World were typically theocratic states.

Bishoprics were created in important towns as rapidly as their population warranted. Under Charles V as King of Spain (1516–1556) there were twenty-two bishoprics in addition to the archbishoprics of Santo Domingo, Mexico City, and Lima. By the end of the sixteenth century there were five archbishoprics and twenty-seven bishoprics. Regular clergy or members of ecclesiastic orders arrived in Spanish America before the seculars. In Brazil, monks began to increase in number and importance from the late sixteenth century. The most important of the orders were at first the Franciscans, Dominicans, and Augustinians, but later the Jesuits predominated, and other orders such as the Benedictines, Carmelites, Mercederians, and Capuchins participated actively in conversion; missionary work was primarily in their hands. In Brazil, the Jesuits were the first to arrive, and they soon became the leaders in educational and religious work, as well as in the defense of the Indians. However, Portugal felt that the Jesuits constituted a threat to its local and central government and eventually expelled them from its colonies in 1759; in Spanish America they were expelled in 1767.

By the second half of the eighteenth century, the political organization of Latin America had resulted in the following divisions of the territory into viceroyalties, each of which was subdivided into *audiencias* (presidencies or captaincies): the viceroyalty of New Spain, extending from Florida and the Western bank of the Mississippi to present-day Costa Rica and the Caribbean Islands; the viceroyalty of New Granada, comprising Venezuela, Colombia, Panama, and Ecuador; the viceroyalty of Peru, including the *audiencias* of Lima, Cuzco, and Chile; the viceroyalty of La Plata with the *audiencias* of Charcas (Bolivia, Paraguay) and of Buenos Aires (Argentina, Uruguay); and finally the viceroyalty of Brazil, divided into captaincies-general. The various capitals of these territories saw the most substantial musical development during the colonial period (early 1500s to 1820s).

MISSION MUSIC

Throughout the continent, missionaries paid special attention to music in the catechization of the native populations. They constantly praised the Indian aptitude for assimilating European cultural traits, above all music. Thus, Indian participation in church musical activities proved to be one of the most effective tools of conversion. Indians are reported to have been particularly skilled in the making and playing of musical instruments. In fact, the number of Indian musicians became so large in Mexico as early as the second half of the sixteenth century that in 1561 Philip II ordered a "reduction in the number of Indians who shall be permitted to occupy themselves as musicians." But the social structure of colonial Latin America never allowed Indians to hold positions of leadership in the musical life of the area. In Spanish America, only a few mestizo musicians, whose ancestry was Spanish and Indian, held significant positions during the middle colonial period (ca. 1650–1750). In Mexico and Peru, Indians of noble descent were singled out for special educational opportunities, including, frequently, training in music. In Quito, the Franciscans organized the Colegio de San Andrés (1550–1581) for sons of Indian chiefs; its music instruction consisted mainly in familiarizing the "natives" first with Gregorian chant and later with *canto de órgano*, or polyphony. Printed copies of motets by the famous Spanish composer Francisco Guerrero, published at Venice in 1570, are reported to have been acquired by the Colegio a few years later, indicating the degree of musical accomplishment of the Indian choirs.

The orders most closely associated with missionary work were the Franciscans and the Jesuits. The former had a stronger impact on native North and Central American cultures, while the latter worked in larger numbers in South America and, during the seventeenth and eighteenth centuries, developed their most celebrated missions in Paraguay, Bolivia, Argentina, and Brazil. Under Jesuit music instruction, the Indians or mestizos became knowledgeable enough to be formed into choirs and small orchestras. Serafim Leite reported the participation, for example, of four music ensembles in a procession in Olinda (Pernambuco) in July 1611.[1] Music instruction in Paraguay had reached such a high level by the mid-eighteenth century that Pope Benedict XIV mentioned in his encyclical *Anus qui hunc vertetem* (1749) that there was almost no difference between Europe and Paraguay in the singing of Masses and Vespers. According to the Spanish Jesuit José Cardiel, who began working in Paraguay around 1730, every *pueblo* (small town) had generally thirty to forty musicians, including *tiples* (trebles, upper voices), tenors, altos, contraltos, and instrumentalists. The latter included four to six violinists, six to eight bassoonists and oboists, two or three trumpet players, three or four harpists, and one or two organists. "We provide them," stated the missionary, "with [music] notations of the best musicians from Spain and even Rome, for singing and playing." Many mission musicians, in the opinion of the same monk, would have been thought excellent even in the best cathedrals in Europe. If the extant manuscripts in such places as Guatemala City and other Guatemalan localities (San Juan Ixcoi, San Miguel Acatan) or the Eastern region of Bolivia (former Jesuit missions of Moxos) are any indication of the "best" music from Spain, Italy, or France made available by the monks, these mission musicians knew such composers as Morales, Alonso de Ávila, Ceballos, Isaac, Mouton, Compère, and Claudin de Sermisy, as well as Juan de Araujo and Domenico Zipoli. (Most of the pieces in such manu-

---

[1] Serafim Leite, *História da Companhia de Jesus no Brasil* (Lisbon: Livraria Portugália, 1938), V, 421.

scripts, however, are unattributed. The codices also contain several pieces with native-language texts, which attest to the use of this music in the missions for conversion purposes. In addition, several parts still bear various types of inscriptions in Indian languages.[2])

Several accounts of mission life reveal the continued coexistence into the eighteenth century of indigenous and European music. Indian dances were allowed as part of religious services, especially in the various processions commemorating the most important feasts. As defenders of the Indians, the Jesuit missionaries assumed a conciliatory attitude toward them, and in Brazil, at least, "theirs was a liturgy social rather than religious, a softened, lyric Christianity with many phallic and animistic reminiscences of the pagan cults."[3] Thus, religious music seems to have exhibited syncretic traits. Besides the singing of antiphons, psalms, and hymns, Indians were taught in the schools to sing *alabanzas* and *alabados*, songs of religious praise that remained popular throughout the continent and were eventually retained as folksongs.

The reports of Indian history and culture of the early missionaries represent the primary source of information about Indian musical accomplishments during the colonial period. The many writings of sixteenth- and seventeenth-century Spanish missionaries provide data on the transplanting of European cultural values and very significant historical documentation on pre-Conquest native music, as well as European music in the New World. In Mexico, for example, the Franciscan monk Juan de Torquemada summarized in his *Monarquía Indiana* (1615) the accomplishments of Indian musicians and choirs, as reported in earlier accounts. We learn that Indians were able to execute excellent copies of polyphonic music ("beautifully done with illuminated letters throughout"); that "every town of one hundred population or more" had singers and instrumentalists proficient in polyphonic music; that instrument-making had become so widespread as to render imports from Spain unnecessary; and that there were many Indian composers whose "polyphonic music in four parts, certain Masses and other liturgical works, all composed with adroitness, have been judged superior works of art when shown to Spanish masters of composition."[4] In Peru, the first piece of vocal polyphony printed in the New World, *Hanacpachap* (to a Quechua text and without attribution to a composer), appeared in 1631 in the Franciscan Juan Pérez Bocanegra's *Ritual*. Also in Peru, the most important collection of secular music of the seventeenth century was compiled by the Franciscan Gregorio de Zuola, while the apogee of mission music was signified by the

[2]See Samuel Claro, "La música en las Misiones Jesuitas de Moxos," *Revista Musical Chilena*, no. 108 (July–September 1969), 7–31.
[3]Gilberto Freyre, *The Masters and the Slaves* (New York: Alfred A. Knopf, 1964), p. 97.
[4]Juan de Torquemada, *Veinte i un libros rituales i Monarquia Indiana* (Madrid: N. Rodríguez Franco, 1723), III, 214; as translated in Robert Stevenson, *Music in Mexico* (New York: Thomas Y. Crowell Company, 1952), p. 68.

presence in Argentina, from 1717 until his death in 1726, of the Jesuit Italian organist and composer Domenico Zipoli, as will be seen below.

CATHEDRAL MUSIC

The term "cathedral music" is here understood to represent the music used in the various Catholic religious services throughout the liturgical year, including not only Latin music (*officium divinum*) but also songs of praise in the vernacular (*villancicos*). Like most aspects of colonial life in Spanish America, cathedral organization adapted Spanish traditions to new conditions. Most cathedrals were modeled after those of Seville (Mexico City, Lima, La Plata) or Toledo (Puebla, Durango). In every major city the cathedral stood at the center of public life. The distinction of having the finest cathedral in the region was a matter of great civic pride. Normally located in the main city square, the cathedral was the focus of most religious fiestas and processions, as well as of political manifestations. The Church controlled education at all levels, and it fostered the great majority of intellectual and artistic activities. Just as many architects, sculptors, and painters worked directly for the Church throughout the period, so did composers and musicians. Cathedral musicians frequently supplied the musical needs of the viceroyal palaces as well, and thus they were often responsible for a city's first attempts at secular art music.

Each cathedral was governed by an archbishop and a council of clergymen known as the chapter (*cabildo*). The chapter supervised all activities of the cathedral, appointed musicians, set their salaries, determined the music budget in general, and drew up job descriptions. In all major cathedrals the chapter governed through a set of more or less strict rules known as choir constitutions. The most elaborate provisions of such constitutions, such as those for the Lima Cathedral (*StMP*, 73–75), included detailed instructions regarding the duties of the chapelmaster, the repertory to be sung and played at specific feasts, and the manner in which it was to be performed—with or without improvised counterpoint, in *fabordón* (parallel counterpoint), or as *canto de órgano* (polyphony). Professional musicians got most of their training in the music chapels that formed an integral part of the cathedral life. As opposed to the organizers of mission music, the cathedral authorities were not concerned with the training of Indian musicians. Thus, the most important positions in the cathedral—those of the chapelmaster and the organist—were filled mostly by Europeans or Europe-trained musicians, with notable exceptions during various periods. Many cathedrals, however, had to rely on Indian singers and instrumentalists, since Spanish musicians were not plentiful. In Mexico City, for example, Indian instrumentalists were entered on the cathedral payroll as early as 1543. Members of some Indian or mestizo families practiced the music profession for several generations, enjoying a definite monopoly in certain fields of performance.

In addition to selecting the music repertory, rehearsing the musicians, and conducting the music services throughout the year, the chapelmaster was responsible for writing original compositions and teaching the choirboys (known as *seises*). From the choir constitutions and chapter minutes (*actas capitulares*), we learn of the importance attached by the chapters to the formal instruction of the choirboys, and to the chapelmaster's ability for composition. Before entering the competition, a candidate for the post of chapelmaster had to give evidence of his knowledge of composition, an indication that creativity was considered an essential quality for appointment.

Although many chapelmasters were priests, they were not guaranteed their salaries by the cathedral foundation. Since they were at the mercy of the local chapter, when financial difficulties arose they and the musicians of the chapel were frequently cut from the payroll without prior notice. Most cathedrals lacked any provision for pension rights, and chapelmasters had to work until very late in life. Salaries varied a great deal from cathedral to cathedral, but in most places musicians could supplement their income by performing at such occasions as receptions, anniversaries, commemorations of sovereigns, farewells, funerals, and consecrations.

Next to the chapelmaster, the organist was usually the highest-paid cathedral musician, even though his salary also depended upon the financial status of the cathedral foundation. His principal duty was to accompany the liturgy and the choir, and in rare instances to compose music also. A number of colonial organists gained recognition as virtuosi on the instrument.

The level of musical competence and creativity in a cathedral depended essentially upon the benevolence of its chapter, and even to a greater degree on that of the archbishop. Throughout the colonial period, many archbishops in major centers fostered the musical life in their cathedral. Actions to improve cathedral music generally included recruitment of better musicians, with a consequent raising of salaries; enlargement of music libraries and archives, with the necessary repair and replacement of damaged or stolen manuscripts or prints; and the upkeep of musical instruments.

The main cathedral archives of Mexico, Guatemala, Colombia, Peru, and Bolivia still hold many original editions or manuscript copies of Spanish and Italian music (see *StRBMS* for details). As early as 1553, Morales's first book of Masses (published at Rome in 1544), together with six more collections of polyphony, belonged to the Cuzco cathedral library. A manuscript copy of the same Morales collection reached the Puebla cathedral in the very year of its publication. The best of Renaissance Spanish and Italian polyphony was known and used at the Bogotá cathedral in the sixteenth century. Part-books were copied throughout the continent, and some of the extant volumes attest to the excellence of local scribes. Such part-books, however, were generally copied on paper of poor quality, which wore out after extensive use;

only large plainchant books were of parchment. Thus an almost constant recopying of music sources in the libraries was necessary. But neglect and apathy prevailed most of the time, resulting in the total loss of numerous collections. Judging by inventories made at various times, the extant manuscripts and prints in library cathedrals and other church archives in Latin America represent only a very small proportion of the riches they once boasted.

The transfer of European musical styles to the New World was a slow process. Polyphonic music of the late Renaissance influenced the Latin music written in Hispanic America up to about the middle of the eighteenth century. During the seventeenth and eighteenth centuries, Baroque influences were felt in villancicos, solo cantatas, duets, and arias, with figured or unfigured basso continuo and separate instrumental parts. A homophonic, pre-Classic style prevailed in much of the sacred music written during the latter part of the eighteenth century. The church music of the colonial period does not exhibit any native stylistic orientation, since the European idioms were considered the only models suitable for Christian worship. Even forms such as villancicos, *chanzonetas*, *xácaras*, and *juguetes*, while often set to texts in indigenous languages or local dialects, maintained in general the European musical idiom.

Mexico and the Caribbean ("New Spain")

MEXICO CITY CATHEDRAL. When the traveler Thomas Gage referred in 1625 to the music he heard in Mexico City as being so exquisite "that I dare be bold to say that the people are drawn to their churches more for the delight of the music than for any delight in the service of God," sacred Latin music had been implanted there for almost a century. Founded in 1528, the Mexico City cathedral within only two years could rely on an Indian choir for Sunday services. This choir had received its training in the San Francisco school opened and directed by the Franciscan Pedro de Gante (ca. 1480–1572), a relative of Charles V. De Gante's success as an educator in New Spain was extraordinary. As early as 1532, he was able to suggest that Indian singers trained in his schools would do so well in the imperial chapel that the Emperor would have to hear them himself "in order to believe it possible." The missionary was speaking with authority, since he had lived in the surroundings (in present-day Belgium, and provinces of northern France) that produced the great Flemish masters of the Renaissance.

The first bishop of Mexico, Fray Juan de Zumárraga (1468–1548), appointed in 1528, devoted himself to an ambitious program for the cathedral, requesting special funds from Charles V for professional singers. He is reported to have hired musicians while in Spain, and to have purchased choirbooks for use in his cathedral. In 1539, he appointed Canon Juan Xuárez as *maestro de capilla* of the cathedral and Antonio Ramos as organist. Xuárez's chapelmastership lasted until 1556, when he was succeeded by Lázaro del

Álamo, whose education at the Salamanca University had included extensive music training and who had been a cantor in the cathedral since 1554. References to del Álamo's compositions appear in the *Tumulo Imperial* (1560) by Francisco Cervantes de Salazar, describing the ceremony of 1559 in Mexico City in honor of the memory of Charles V. The same source also mentions del Álamo's directing two antiphonal choirs in a performance of music by Morales. (The original compositions by del Álamo have not survived.) Del Álamo's successor in the Mexico cathedral post, one Juan de Victoria, from Burgos, Spain, was appointed around 1570, but was sent back to Spain a few years later after having staged a choirboy play mocking the viceroy's policies.

The leading composer of sixteenth-century New Spain, Hernando Franco (1532–1585), was chapelmaster at the Mexico City cathedral for the last ten years of his life. Born near Alcántara (Extremadura), Franco served from 1542 to 1549 as a choirboy in the Segovia cathedral, where he received the best training available. Though he must have emigrated to New Spain in 1554, he is first mentioned only in 1573, as chapelmaster of the Guatemala cathedral. Financial considerations may have been an important factor in his decision to move later to Mexico City. During his first seven years at the cathedral (1575–1582), the music chapel was well funded, with new singers and instrumentalists being hired, but need for extensive funds in 1582 to begin construction of a new cathedral led to the musicians' salaries being reduced, causing Franco to resign and the chapel musicians to strike. The chapter reconsidered and finally restored the former salaries, with a few exceptions. Probably because of his precarious health, Franco was relieved of teaching duties in 1584. He died the next year and was buried "in the main chapel, where the auditors sat," a place of honor decided upon by the chapter and recorded in its minutes.

Franco's extant works are found in the archives of the Guatemala cathedral, the Mexico City cathedral, the Carmen Codex (for location see *StRBMS*, p. 133), the Viceregal Museum at Tepotzotlán, the Puebla cathedral, and the Newberry Library (Chicago). They include psalms, hymns, responsories, *Salves* (antiphons), and an important codex with sixteen Magnificats, two for each of the eight tones.[5]

The "Franco Codex," which has been called "one of the most valuable musical monuments of the Americas,"[6] reveals the technical and expressive competence of its composer. These Magnificats belong to the golden age of

---

[5]First studied by Steven Barwick, who edited this collection of Magnificats as *The Franco Codex of the Cathedral of Mexico* (1965), the manuscript apparently lacks the third-tone settings. In the 1960s Lincoln Spiess identified the last of the even-verse third-tone settings, preserved in the recto of folio 26, facing the left-hand page of the second tone setting.

[6]*StRBMS*, p. 134.

Spanish polyphony in their smoothly imitative but quite formal counterpoint and their sober handling of dissonance and chromaticism. Franco follows the plainsong reciting tone, in generating his melodic subjects for the successive imitations. Example 1-1 illustrates this practice; here only the soprano is derived from plainchant. Though we find a skillful spacing of the parts, the voices frequently exhibit a restricted range. The rhythmic balance between voices is generally well achieved. To vary the texture Franco resorts to trio

EXAMPLE 1-1 Fernando Franco, *Magnificat primi toni:* "Anima mea Dominum," mm. 1–8. From Steven Barwick (ed.), *The Franco Codex.* Copyright 1965 by Southern Illinois University Press. Quoted by permission.

settings of individual verses, and he sets the twelfth verse for six voices, with a canon between two of them.

Franco uses both syllabic and melismatic treatments for text settings, and occasionally utilizes melismas for word-painting. Although there is no written indication, instruments were most likely used in the performance of this music; this would account for the extreme variety of the settings, and hence, to some extent, for their lack of consistency.[7] The Franco Codex reveals a somewhat archaic harmonic style, largely because of frequent use of incomplete triads and a large incidence of triads in root position. Cross-relations are frequent, while phrygian and plagal cadences appear occasionally. Although Franco's is not the most elaborate polyphony, it reveals nevertheless his frequently imaginative mastery of the technique of his period.

Two hymns to the Virgin, with Nahuatl texts, in the Valdés Codex (at Mexico City), have for a long time been attributed to Franco.[8] However, the Hernando Franco cited in the codex may possibly have been an Indian composer who took his sponsor's name at baptism; yet, while such a custom was indeed very common, there is no documentary evidence for it in this instance, yet the rather naive style of these hymns does not correspond at all to the other works of the Mexico City chapelmaster.

Of some 220 books printed in Mexico by the end of the sixteenth century, thirteen were liturgical books with monophonic music. An Augustinian *Ordinarium*, with plainsong, was published in Mexico City in 1556, the first music book to be printed and published in the New World. The remaining imprints consist of graduals, antiphoners, psalters, a passionary, a sacramentary, and a missal. Particularly notable in the history of music printing in New Spain was the publication of *Quatuor Passiones* (1604) by the Franciscan Juan Navarro (ca. 1550–ca. 1610), from Cádiz, because he was active in the province of Michoacán. His book (of 105 numbered folios) includes plainchant for the four Passions, eight Lamentations, and the prayer of Jeremiah.[9] Polyphonic music was not printed in Mexico during the colonial period. Probably the main reasons were the limited local demand and the monopoly exercised by the mother country.

During the late sixteenth and early seventeenth centuries, the Mexico City cathedral's music chapel enjoyed the services of Juan Hernández, chapel-

[7]For further comment, see Steven Barwick, "Sacred Vocal Polyphony in Early Colonial Mexico" (unpublished Ph.D. dissertation, Harvard University, 1949).

[8]For discussion and transcription of these pieces, see Robert Stevenson, *Music in Aztec and Inca Territory* (Berkeley and Los Angeles: University of California Press, 1968), pp. 204–19.

[9]The previous attribution of these works to the Spanish Juan Navarro "Hispalensis" (from Seville) was refuted by Gilbert Chase in 1945. See Gilbert Chase, "Juan Navarro *Hispalensis* and Juan Navarro *Gaditanus*," *Musical Quarterly*, XXXI/2 (April, 1945), 188–92.

master from 1586 to about 1620. He may have been identical with the Juan de Lienas whose works occupy some sixty pages of the Carmen Codex.[10] These works include a *Missa a 5*, a *Magnificat a 5*, a *Salve Regina a 4*, Lamentations *a 4* and *a 5*, an incomplete Requiem *a 5*, and a motet *Coenantibus autem illis a 4*. The Mass, of the cantus firmus type, uses the subject *fa, re, ut, fa, sol, la*, which does not, however, conform with the typically extended, self-contained cantus firmus of most Mass settings of this type. Here the subject appears as head motive and also functions within each movement as a real cantus firmus (Example 1-2). In its well-balanced counterpoint, its good voice spacing and rhythmic smoothness, this work belongs to the best tradition of sixteenth-century Spanish polyphony.

Hernández was followed as the Mexico City cathedral's chapelmaster by Antonio Rodríguez de Mata, who served from ca. 1620 to 1643; Luis Coronado from 1643 to 1648; Fabián Pérez Ximeno from 1648 to 1654; Francisco López Capillas from 1654 to 1674; José de Loaysa y Agurto from 1676 to 1688; and Antonio de Salazar from 1688 to 1715. Of these, López Capillas has been singled out as the "most profound and prolific composer of Masses in Mexican history."[11] His importance as a composer is suggested by the number of works ascribed to him in four of the nine choirbooks of polyphonic music in the cathedral archive, two of which are almost entirely of his composition. He is also the only colonial composer of New Spain represented by a full book (containing Masses and Magnificats) at the Madrid National Library. Born around 1615, López Capillas acted as assistant organist at Puebla from 1641 to 1648, before being elected chapelmaster at Mexico City. In the Puebla chapter minutes for early 1648, he is referred to as *licenciado*, which implies that he probably earned a degree locally, perhaps at the University of Mexico, which had been established in 1553. Recognition of his competence is attested by his being promoted to a full prebend in 1671. His works certainly attest to that competence as a composer. His concern for craftsmanship, especially for technical devices of polyphony, appears especially in his Masses (see *StLACA*, pp. 242–46). His Magnificat *a 4* in the Carmen Codex shows a sober, elegant polyphony which contrasts, at times, static parts (Superius in Example 1-3) with very active ones.[12]

[10]See *StRBMS*, p. 133. Hernández's name is mentioned once in the Codex, but it is known that he originated in Aragon, where the small village of Lienas exists. On the other hand, it is indeed strange that "Juan de Lienas," whose life is totally unknown, would have so many works copied in the Codex.

[11]Robert Stevenson, "López Capillas, Francisco," *New Catholic Encyclopedia*, VIII (1967), 986.

[12]For an analysis of López Capillas's Hexachord Mass, see Lester D. Brothers, "A New-World Hexachord Mass by Francisco López Capillas," *Yearbook for Inter-American Musical Research*, IX (1973), 5–44. For transcriptions of several works, see *StLACA*, pp. 235–46.

EXAMPLE 1-2 Juan de Lienas, *Missa a 5:* "Christe Eleison," mm. 1–10. From
Jesús Bal y Gay (ed.), *Tesoro de la Música Polifónica en México*, I (Mexico: Instituto
Nacional de Bellas Artes, 1952), 88.

FIGURE 1-1 Francisco López Capillas's *Missa Batalla a 6*. "Kyrie eleison." Tiple 2, alto and bass parts (Mexico City Cathedral Archive).

EXAMPLE 1-3   Francisco López Capillas, *Magnificat a 4:* "Gloria Patri," mm. 1–20. From Jesús Bal y Gay (ed.), *Tesoro de la Música Polifónica en México*, I (Mexico: Instituto Nacional de Bellas Artes, 1952), 48.

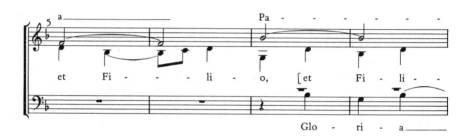

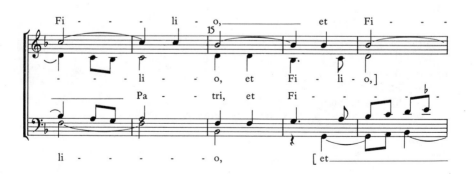

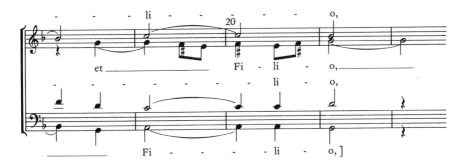

By the time of López Capillas's death, instrumental music at the Mexico City cathedral was flourishing, and by the end of the seventeenth century the cathedral orchestra included fifteen different instruments—strings, woodwinds, brass, and organ. In 1695 a new organ made in Spain was brought to the cathedral; its installation required more than two years of work. With seventy-eight stops and a monumental, locally-made case, it greatly enhanced the musical splendor of the new cathedral. A second organ, built entirely in Mexico by the master José Nazarre and considered in Spain as one of the wonders of the New World, was dedicated around 1735. Still in place, it had no fewer than 3,350 pipes and some 86 stops.

By the first years of the eighteenth century, the music chapel of the cathedral, then under the direction of Antonio de Salazar, had an orderly and updated collection of music in its archives. The chapter had ordered Salazar to deposit in the archives his own works and those of "other distinguished masters" in his possession. During his twenty-seven years of service as chapelmaster, Salazar not only wrote some of the best polychoral motets of his time[13] and set to music some of Sor Juana Inés de la Cruz's villancicos but had charge of music instruction. The chapter provided extra remuneration in 1700 for his supervision of the performance of polyphony at the city's "escoleta pública" (public schools). (Among his students was his successor at the cathedral, Manuel de Zumaya.) Salazar was able, in addition, to develop both the size and quality of the cathedral orchestra, which was to reach its apex under Manuel de Zumaya's chapelmastership (1715–1739).

Zumaya, the first Mexican-born chapelmaster, received his musical training in the cathedral with financial support from the *cabildo*. He learned composition from Salazar and organ from José de Idiaques, the remarkable first organist at the time. Zumaya was soon promoted to second organist and second chapelmaster and won the competition for the chapelmastership after

[13]Transcribed examples are to be found in Lincoln Spiess and Thomas Stanford, *An Introduction to Certain Mexican Archives* (Detroit: Information Coordinators, Inc., 1969). See also *StLACA*, pp. 274–79.

Salazar's death in 1715. Under his twenty-four-year administration the music chapel reached an unprecedented level of competence. Zumaya's numerous works (preserved at the Mexico City Cathedral, the Museo del Virreinato in Tepotzotlán, the Puebla Cathedral, the Oaxaca cathedral, and Morelia) include Vespers music, psalm settings, Misereres, sets of Lamentations, and many villancicos. Compared to that of his immediate predecessors, Zumaya's style tends to break away from the *prima prattica* of the seventeenth century. His villancicos in particular show a clear Italian Baroque influence in their use of concertato style, opening choruses, numerous arias, and choral finales. As had occurred in Spain earlier, the villancico in Zumaya's time tended towards the cantata, not only through its different structure (large proportions, long, elaborated choral numbers, and solo arias) but also in its overall performance characteristics, such as orchestral accompaniment with continuo. Zumaya ascribed an unusual importance to the melodies of his villancicos, but continued to write in a predominantly polyphonic texture (see *StLACA*, pp. 355–67).

Zumaya was also the author of the second opera to be produced in the New World. (The first was Torrejón y Velasco's *La Púrpura de la Rosa*; see Chapter 2.) On a libretto by Silvio Stempiglia, his *La Parténope* was given at the viceroyal palace on 1 May 1711. The new viceroy, the Duke of Linares, who had arrived earlier that year, was fond of and knowledgeable about Italian opera. Although the music of Zumaya's opera is not extant, it must have followed the Italian style, since it pleased the Duke.

The presence of several important Italian composers at the Madrid court around the mid-eighteenth century had repercussions in Mexico. In 1749, Ignacio Jerusalem (ca. 1710–1769) was appointed chapelmaster at Mexico City; he was the first Italian to hold the post. Called a "musical miracle" in his own time, Jerusalem, a native of Lecce, directed concurrently the orchestra of the Coliseo Nuevo theater, and his theatrical orientation had decisive influence on the church music of the time. For example, the cathedral orchestra saw during his tenure a predominance of strings. Jerusalem's output includes some two hundred Latin works (six Masses, five Magnificats, two *Te Deums*, fifteen Misereres, eighteen Vesper psalms, etc.), plus arias, pastorelas, loas, and villancicos preserved at Mexico City; about twenty sacred cantatas, arias, and villancicos at Guatemala City; a Christmas pastoral and a Latin motet at Morelia; and several motets, two Masses, and a *Te Deum* at Puebla. He cultivated a predominantly homophonic style, harmonically imaginative, with highly embellished melodic writing. He favored dynamic and textural contrasts, and his bravura-like violin passages in the orchestral accompaniment of his most elaborate settings are symptomatic of the secular character given to the cathedral music of the time.[14]

---

[14]Transcribed examples may be found in Spiess and Stanford, *An Introduction to Certain Mexican Musical Archives*. The villancico "A la milagrosa escuela" (1765) provides good examples of passages beginning with imitation and ending in homophonic texture.

FIGURE 1-2 Ignacio Jerusalem. Title page of "Motette a 4 con Ripienos VVs. i Trompas A la Ascención de Nuestro Señor. Compuesto Por el Sr. M.º Dⁿ Ygnacio Jerusa.ᵐ Mº de Capilla de la S.ᵗᵃ Ygle.ᵃ Cathe. de Mex.ᶜᵒ año de 1759" (Mexico City Cathedral Archive).

Jerusalem's successors, Matheo Tollis de la Roca (ca. 1710–1781) and Antonio Juanas (d. 1817), followed the church-music style of late eighteenth-century Italian composers such as Jommelli and Paisiello. This style tended to resemble that of opera, and thus operatic idioms and forms (da capo arias, accompanied recitatives, short homophonic choruses) penetrated the New World church repertory.

PUEBLA CATHEDRAL. Another important artistic center of New Spain, Puebla de los Angeles (founded in 1531), had developed a very active musical life by the end of the sixteenth century. Its main church became a cathedral as early as 1550 and, for a time during the next century, it was even to surpass Mexico City's in wealth and grandeur.

During the seventeenth century, Puebla boasted some thirty magnificent churches, several schools for middle and advanced studies, and, from 1646, the first public library in the New World, with a collection of five thousand volumes donated by the extraordinary bishop Juan de Palafox y Mendoza, a patron of the arts. Several painters and writers (Sor Juana Inés de la Cruz, for example) contributed also to the intellectual atmosphere of the city. In addition, Puebla included at one time some nineteen printers.

The first Puebla chapelmaster whose works are extant was Pedro Bermudes (=Bermúdez), born in Granada, where he is reported to have been *medio capellán* in the Royal Chapel choir in 1592. Before being selected as chapelmaster at Puebla (in February 1603), he worked in the same capacity at Cuzco, Peru, and had perhaps also been at the Guatemala City cathedral, which had several of his works copied in 1602. His compositions, which include four settings of the *Salve Regina*, a *Domine ad adjuvandum*, a *Missa de Bomba*, hymns, antiphons, and invitatories, exhibit a powerful rhythmic flow, a special concern for harmonic expressive devices, and a well-balanced counterpoint.

Bermudes was succeeded at Puebla by the Portuguese-born composer Gaspar Fernandes (=Fernández) (ca. 1566–1629), who came in 1606 from the Guatemala City cathedral. While the archive of the latter cathedral preserves a *Magnificat a 4*, a *Benedicamus Domino* in the eight tones, and some organ pieces by Fernandes, he is best remembered today for some 250 villancicos written for the Puebla cathedral from 1609 to 1620. (They are now in the Oaxaca cathedral archives.) The variety and liveliness of these pieces—to Spanish, Portuguese, and even Tlaxcala texts—attest to the dynamic musical life developed in the city, and they constitute an early corpus of vernacular polyphony. Fernandes's villancicos, of the *negro, guineo,* and *negrilla* types (differing from the normal type of villancico in drawing on Afro-Hispanic musical traditions), with picturesque effects in pseudo-Negro dialects, provide an early example (if only a pale one) of the Afro-American musical heritage of the area (see *StLACA*, pp. 120ff).

A new cathedral at Puebla, consecrated in 1649 by Bishop Palafox, followed the typical architectural plan of Spanish churches, with the choir bisecting the central nave and enclosed on three sides. On these side panels were located the organ pipes. The musicians sat within the choir, facing each other. This arrangement favored antiphonal effects, either by the alternation of plainchant and polyphony or by polyphony alone sung by double choirs. The composer who took best advantage of these conditions was Juan Gutiérrez de Padilla (ca. 1590–1664), chapelmaster at Puebla from 1629 and undoubtedly the most important composer of New Spain during the seventeenth century. Born at Málaga, he was first trained by the local chapelmaster, Francisco Vásquez, then at the collegiate church in Jérez de la Frontera. In 1616, already ordained, he became the chapelmaster of the Cádiz Cathedral, in which post his excellent services were recognized by the local chapter. The first written record of his presence in the New World dates from 1622, when he was officially named *coadjutor maestro* (co-chapelmaster) at Puebla. Shortly after the death of Gaspar Fernandes, Gutiérrez de Padilla succeeded him as chapelmaster, serving until death (with a one-month suspension in 1634 for alleged misbehavior). By the middle of the century, Padilla had succeeded in gathering around him very competent composers and performers: Francisco López Capillas (until 1654), the organist Pedro Simón, the bassoonist Simón Martínez, the harp virtuoso Nicolás Grinón, the cathedral succentor Francisco de Olivera, and Juan García (who was to be Padilla's own successor).

FIGURE 1-3 Juan Gutiérrez de Padilla. *Missa Ego flos campi, a 8.* Beginning of *Kyrie* (Puebla Cathedral Archive).

In addition, a large number of musicians formed part of the music chapel during his time. The instruments considered most important were the continuo instruments: organ, harp, and bass viol. Then came the recorders, shawms, sackbuts, cornetts, and the soprano, tenor, and bass *bajons* (bassoons), whose function was to double or substitute for the vocal parts. In most Spanish and Spanish-related churches of the time, instrumentalists were expected to be able to sing and singers expected to play, as occasion demanded. As at the Mexico City cathedral, the Puebla orchestra began to include violins, string bass, flutes, trumpets, and horns only by the early eighteenth century.

Gutiérrez de Padilla's extensive output survives in several sources, the most important of which is Choirbook XV at the Puebla Cathedral, which contains Masses, motets, hymns, psalms, Lamentations, responsories, antiphons, a litany and a St. Matthew Passion. His villancico cycles are found in loose sheets (also at the Puebla Cathedral), and other such pieces (for Christmas, Holy Trinity, and Assumption) are in the Jesús Sánchez Garza collection at the Instituto de Bellas Artes in Mexico City and in the Guatemala City cathedral archives.

Padilla's Latin music reveals a marked preference for double choir, and his treatment of it presents considerable diversity; both imitative techniques and antiphonal effects are combined (occasionally at the same time) very effectively. Actually, Padilla conceives of each choir as a four-part unit, using both choirs together as often as he alternates them, in both polyphonic and homophonic sections. His is a type of *stile antico* polyphony which remained in common use even in Spain until the end of the seventeenth century. Clarity of form and of polyphony enhances the mystical character of this music. There is no indication in the music of a basso continuo, but, as observed by Ray (Catalyne), the bass lines may easily be doubled by organ or harp (or both, in the Spanish tradition).[15] Example 1-4 illustrates some aspects of the expressive force and the techniques of Padilla's double-choir usage. According to Ray (Catalyne), these techniques are either polyphonic, homophonic (infrequently used), or homophonic-antiphonal, very common in polychoral works.

Padilla's Masses for double choir, such as the *Ave Regina* and *Ego flos campi* Masses, achieve formal homogeneity through the use of a motto phrase recurring in each movement, and of thematic material announced in the previous movement.

The polyphonic villancico reached the peak of its popularity in Mexico during Padilla's time, and he himself wrote many different villancico types, such as the *negrilla, calenda, gallego,* and *jácara,* all characterized by some

---

[15]Cf. Alice Ray (Catalyne), "The Double Choir Music of Juan de Padilla" (unpublished doctoral dissertation, University of Southern California, 1953).

EXAMPLE 1-4 Juan Gutiérrez de Padilla, *Exultate Justi In Domino*, mm. 1–8 and 16–18. Transcribed by Alice Ray (Catalyne), "The Double Choir Music of Juan de Padilla" (unpublished doctoral dissertation, University of Southern California, 1953). Used by permission.

Exultate, Justi in Domino

. . .

confitemini Domino
in cithara . . . .

(*Translation*): *Exult, O just ones, in the Lord*
Thank the Lord
on the harp. . . .

references to folk-music elements of various traditions. By the middle of the century, villancicos were composed especially for Corpus Christi and, even more, Christmas. They were also written for Matins on specific saints' days. As in seventeenth-century Spain, cathedral chapelmasters in Hispanic America had the responsibility of writing new villancicos each year, for which they had to find suitable poetry. Generally written in sets or cycles, the most famous examples are the villancicos of the poetess Sor Juana Inés de la Cruz,

FIGURE 1-4   Juan Gutiérrez de Padilla. *Exultate Justi in Domino, a 8.* Beginning of first-chorus parts (Puebla Cathedral Archive).

FIGURE 1-5 Juan Gutiérrez de Padilla. *Dies irae, a 8.* Beginning of first-chorus parts (Puebla Cathedral Archive).

whose Christmas sets of 1678, 1680, and 1689 were written for Puebla. These included literary imitations of dialects described as *gallego, portugués, indio, vizcaíno,* and *puerto rico.* Particularly important among the many variant types was the *negro* or *negrilla,* a narrative and devotional type in supposedly Black dialect. The standard musical traits of the seventeenth-century *negro* are a vivid rhythm in 6/8 meter with constant hemiola shifts to 3/4, F or C major as the almost exclusive keys, and the responsorial practice of soloist versus chorus.[16] While it is impossible to indicate a precise formal structure for each of the various types of villancico, the form presents in alternation an *estribillo* (refrain) and several *coplas* (couplets or stanzas), a *responsión* (a short choral refrain), or a *respuesta* (a solo refrain). One *negrilla* by Padilla, *A siolo flasiquiyo* (transcribed in Robert Stevenson, *Christmas Music from Baroque Mexico,* pp. 118–23), *a 4* and *a 6* (1653), illustrates the typical Christmas villancico cultivated in New Spain in the seventeenth century. The systematic syncopations throughout, in addition to the text itself, constitute the Black traits of the piece, which seems to follow the form known as *el canario,* a name reflecting the importance of the Canary Islands in the slave trade of the seventeenth and eighteenth centuries.[17] (For another example, see *StLACA,* p. 208.)

Another important Puebla chapelmaster whose villancicos won him wide recognition not only in New Spain but throughout the Spanish American colonies was Miguel Matheo de Dallo y Lana (ca. 1650–1705), who was appointed at Puebla in 1688 and served there until his death. He set four villancico cycles by Sor Juana Inés de la Cruz which were performed in the cathedral in 1689 and 1690. His Latin works, many of them polychoral, are now preserved at the Puebla cathedral, the Sánchez Garza collection, and the Mexico City cathedral. His villancicos are found in such widespread places as Bogotá, Guatemala City, Évora (Portugal), and Sucre (Bolivia). Another composer of villancicos was Francisco de Atienza y Pineda, chapelmaster at Puebla from 1712 to 1726: the Palafox Library at Puebla includes the texts (only) of thirteen villancico sets printed between 1715 and 1722, with the indication that they were sung at the cathedral with music by him.

During the eighteenth century the Puebla cathedral suffered a decline in the creative ability of its composers, but its orchestra, larger in size and families of instruments than during the seventeenth century, continued to assure splendid musical performances. Some of the liturgical works of Manuel Arenzana, chapelmaster from 1792 to 1821 and zarzuela composer as well, call for a large orchestra.

[16]Robert Stevenson, "The Afro-American Musical Legacy to 1800," *Musical Quarterly,* LIV/4 (October 1968), 496–97.

[17]E. Thomas Stanford, *El Villancico y el Corrido Mexicano* (Mexico: Instituto Nacional de Antropología e Historia, 1974), p. 20.

PROVINCIAL CENTERS. Among the Mexican provincial centers that deserve mention for their music activities during the colonial period are Morelia (formerly Valladolid), in Michoacán, and Oaxaca. The music archive of the Colegio de Santa Rosa de Santa María in Morelia preserves works by Spanish and local composers active especially during the eighteenth century.[18] The Colegio was a school for girls founded in 1738 in which daily music lessons were given until at least the beginning of the nineteenth century; this may explain the large number of music manuscripts in the school's archives. Two local composers represented among them are Francisco Moratilla (flourished ca. 1730), Valladolid cathedral chapelmaster, and José Gavino Leal, also identified as chapelmaster; he apparently also held a similar post at Oaxaca. The latter center's cathedral archive reveals the intense cultivation of music there. Especially noteworthy are Gaspar Fernandes's *chanzonetas* and villancicos, in a 284-folio volume, and manuscripts by two Mexico City chapelmasters, Antonio de Salazar and Manuel de Zumaya.

THE CARIBBEAN AREA. In the Caribbean area, colonial church music developed especially at the cathedral of Santiago de Cuba during the eighteenth century, with the composer Esteban Salas y Castro (1725–1803) in charge of the cathedral's music chapel from 1764. Salas studied organ and composition in Havana, his birthplace, and philosophy, theology, and canon law at Havana University. When he moved to Santiago, the cathedral included six singers, an organist, and a bassoonist. During his tenure he succeeded in increasing the quantity and quality of the music personnel: already by 1765, he had at his disposal eight voices, two violins, and a cello, besides the organ and a bassoon. Since some of his works call at times for flutes, horns, and violas, these must have been available outside the music chapel. Salas's extant output numbers 146 items; of them 52 are villancicos (some of the cantata and *pastorela* genres), which display a consistently high quality and represent Salas's best contribution to the Latin American colonial repertory. While most of his villancicos follow the traditional format (*estribillo-copla-estribillo*), those entitled "cantatas" or "pastorelas" include recitatives and arias, in which one may observe a direct influence of the Neapolitan school.[19] This is quite evident in the elaboration of the instrumental accompanying ensemble, particularly in the important melodic role assigned to the violins. Some of the instrumental preludes of the villancicos are structured like shortened Italian overtures. The Baroque style of these pieces is confirmed by the consistent presence of a basso continuo. At the same time, many

---

[18]The archive has been inventoried by Miguel Bernal Jiménez. Cf. Jiménez, *El Archivo Musical del Colegio de Santa Rosa de Santa María de Valladolid* (Morelia: Ediciones de la Universidad Michoacana de San Nicolás, 1939).

[19]Cf. Alejo Carpentier, *La Música en Cuba* (Mexico: Fondo de Cultura Económica, 1946), pp. 83–88.

villancicos and *pastorelas* contain melodic and rhythmic traits of a clear Spanish popular-music derivation. Salas's Latin music reveals a transitional style between late Baroque and early Classic styles, similar to that cultivated by the late eighteenth-century Venezuelan composers.

Venezuelan colonial music developed much later than in Mesoamerica, although the city of Caracas, founded in 1567, had several musicians on its cathedral payroll by the mid-seventeenth century. The position of chapelmaster at the Caracas cathedral was created and held by Father Gonzalo Cordero in 1671. The next chapelmaster we know of, Francisco Pérez Camacho (1659–ca. 1725), occupied the post from 1687 and also held the music chair at the University of Santiago de León (Caracas).

A more productive phase occurred during the latter part of the eighteenth century (and extended into the post-colonial period), when the fairly homogeneous group known as the *Escuela de Chacao* or *Escuela del Padre Sojo* developed around the composer Juan Manuel Olivares (1760–1797), under the active encouragement of Father Pedro Palacios y Sojo (1739–1799), the most notable patron of music in colonial Venezuela. In the early 1780s, Sojo founded the congregation of the *Oratorio de San Felipe Neri*, modeled after the original Italian order, where the *Academia de Música* functioned under Olivares. This music school developed the most significant group of church music composers in Venezuelan history. Notable in the group were José Francisco Velásquez (ca. 1755–1805), José Antonio Caro de Boesi (ca. 1760–1814), Pedro Nolasco Colón (b. ca. 1750), José Cayetano Carreño (1774–1836), Juan José Landaeta (ca. 1780–1812), and Lino Gallardo (ca. 1775–1837). The most celebrated figure of the Sojo School was José Angel Lamas (1775–1814). Lamas first worked in the cathedral as a soprano in the choir, then as a bassoonist. About thirty-eight works of his are preserved (four, however, of doubtful attribution), of which the best known are *Popule meus*, *Ave maris stella*, a Mass in D, and a Miserere. Usually, these works call for a four-part mixed chorus with a characteristic *settecento* accompaniment including two oboes, two horns, and strings, which mainly double the vocal parts. Choral homophony prevails, with little imitation. Short solos alternate with choral sections. Perfect formal balance and very sensitive melodic writing are the main qualities of Lamas's religious compositions.

As a result of the division of Venezuelan colonial society into whites (Spaniards and creoles, the latter of native birth but European descent) and mulattoes (*pardos*), slaves, and Indians, the majority of the younger composers of the *Escuela de Chacao* were free mulattoes, since the circumstance of exercising the music profession put them in a privileged social position. (Notable exceptions, as non-mulattoes, were Cayetano Carreño and Lamas.) The same situation occurred in colonial Brazil.

South America

COLOMBIA ("NEW GRANADA"). One of the most important areas of art-music activities in South America during the colonial period was the territory of New Granada (now Colombia). The coastal city of Cartagena de Indias was founded in 1533, and four years later the first musician, Juan Pérez Materano (d. 1561), settled there. He was an organist, an expert in plainchant, and the author of an unpublished treatise, *Canto de órgano y canto llano.* It was, however, the Bogotá cathedral that was to be the center par excellence of sacred music throughout the colonial era. In 1599 the archbishop Bartolomé Lobo Guerrero was transferred to Bogotá from Mexico. In addition to buying a new organ for the cathedral, he commissioned Francisco de Páramo, a local scribe, to copy out thirty-two huge books of plainchant, on parchment with precious illustrations. With the transfer of materials from Cartagena, the cathedral archives at Bogotá were to house—and still contain today—the richest repertory in the New World of European sixteenth-century polyphony and Baroque music. In addition to original editions of Francisco Guerrero and Victoria, and manuscript copies of Morales's works, the archive contains numerous Spanish and Italian publications of the period 1582–1632 (see *StRBMS,* pp. 3–28).

In 1584 the cathedral appointed to its chapelmastership the most significant sixteenth-century composer in South America, Gutierre Fernández Hidalgo (ca. 1553–1620), whose manuscript *Libro de Coro,* preserved in the archive, contains ten psalms, three Salves, and nine Magníficats of his own composition, together with works by Rodrigo de Ceballos, Guerrero, Juan de Herrera, and Victoria. Little is known concerning the early life and training of Fernández Hidalgo. The first notice we have concerns his entering into service at the cathedral in May 1584, when the archbishop Luis Zapata appointed him *maestro de canturrias* in the new Seminario Conciliar de San Luis, expecting him to prepare four to six seminarists to sing the canonical hours every day in the cathedral. This proved to be a difficult undertaking, and Fernández Hidalgo abandoned the seminary in 1586.[20] Several months later he left Bogotá and served at the Quito Cathedral until 1589. He finally found a more satisfactory and stable position at the cathedral of La Plata (the present Sucre, Bolivia), where he was chapelmaster until his death in 1620. None of the works that he wrote for the La Plata cathedral has survived.

Fernández Hidalgo belongs, in both technical competence and mystical

---

[20]Robert Stevenson (*StRBMS,* p. 3) indicates the years 1585–88 as corresponding to Fernández Hidalgo's chapelmastership at Bogotá.

FIGURE 1-6 Gutierre Fernández Hidalgo. *Salve Regina a 5*. Folio 103 bears the inscription "De Gutierre Fernandes Hidalgo. Maestro de esta Santa Iglesia, año de 1584" (Bogotá Cathedral Archive).

character, to the best Spanish tradition of Renaissance polyphony as developed by Victoria. His *Salve Regina a 5* and his *Magnificats sobre los 8 tonos* reveal clearly the reasons for his fame. His Magnificats *a 4* set the odd-numbered verses and reveal skill and imagination in the varied treatment of the sections. The chant formula may appear in any voice and is switched to different voices from one section to another. The settings do not proceed *a 4* continuously: varied texture is called for, especially for the Gloria verse, as in Tone II (*a 5*), Tone III (*a 5*), Tone IV (*a 6*), Tone VI (*a 5*), and Tone VII (*a 6*). Example 1-5, from the "Gloria Patri" of the Magnificat in Tone VII, illustrates a typical imitative opening, with canon at the fifth between the tenor and altus 1 (mm. 7–14). Such canonic passages are quite frequent in the Gloria verse settings of this composer's Magnificats. (For other examples, see *StLACA*, p. 152; *SCAnt*, p. 172.)

The two most important composers associated with the Bogotá cathedral during the seventeenth and early eighteenth centuries were José de Cascante, maestro from about 1650 to his death in 1702, and Juan de Herrera

EXAMPLE 1-5 Gutierre Fernández Hidalgo, *Magnificat* (Tone VII): "Gloria patri," mm. 1–14.

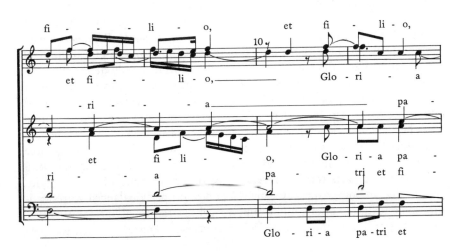

(ca. 1665–1738). Cascante served the cathedral for almost half a century, under the archbishops Sanz Lozano and Ignacio de Urbina, both known for their support of music. His extant compositions are mostly villancicos (an example in *StLACA*, p. 76). Juan de Herrera, a native of Bogotá, occupied the post after Cascante, from 1703 until his death. His numerous extant compositions, including Masses, psalm settings, Lamentations, villancicos, and others, make him the most prolific composer of New Granada. Son of a local army officer, he probably received a good education before his ordination. He may have received his music training at the Seminario Conciliar de San Luis. From about 1690 he acted as chaplain and chapelmaster of the nuns of the Santa Inés convent. Of his thirty-eight or so extant works at Bogotá, twenty-eight are to Latin texts; the remainder are vernacular works. While Herrera treats the liturgical compositions polychorally most of the time, his vernacular works call for only two or three voices with continuo (examples in *StLACA*, pp. 215ff.). His earliest dated piece, *Laudate Dominum omnes gentes* (1689), for three choruses and harp (as continuo), exhibits antiphonal treatment between the choruses, which come together only at the final cadences of the three sections. Strangely enough, the third chorus consists of two voices only; their high tessitura suggests that they were intended for boys' voices (see *SCAnt*, p. 168). Herrera's more mature Latin works were written after he took over as cathedral chapelmaster. They include six Masses, an incomplete *Officium defunctorum*, seven collections of Vesper psalms, three collections of Lamentations, and some villancicos. The Office for the Dead *a 8* (only seven parts remain) reveals some of the characteristics of his style: specifically, smooth, expressive, melodic lines, properly balanced voice-leading, some textural variety, and a simple, rather strict tonal harmony.

According to the cathedral chapter records, Herrera proved too permissive with the musicians under him at the Bogotá cathedral and was consequently reprimanded. The chapter record for 26 June 1711 reads, in part: "Recently the music of this Holy Church has deteriorated through the deficient voices as well as the lack of [musical] intelligence of most [singers] caused by the permissive nature of the Chapelmaster. . . ." Two years later, however, the choir had apparently overcome such difficulties with the selection of new musicians and singers.

Among some twenty-five names of Bogotá cathedral musicians who were active during the latter part of the eighteenth century, the significance of Salvador Romero's is due to his post as chapelmaster and his extant output including Latin compositions. During the last quarter of the century, however, the cathedral's musical life suffered a sharp decline. By 1781, for

FIGURE 1-7 Juan de Herrera. *Officium Defunctorum, a 8.* (1744). Beginning of the first *cantus* part of the first chorus (Bogotá Cathedral Archive).

example, neither of the two organs was playable. The arrival at Bogotá (1791) of Archbishop Baltazar Martínez Compañón, an eminent artist and intellectual of the period, and former cantor at the Lima Cathedral (1768–1778), could have contributed greatly to an improvement of the situation, but his early death in 1797 prevented him from achieving any significant change.

ECUADOR. Substantial documentation attesting to relatively important musical activities and production in colonial Ecuador has been uncovered and studied, but not a single polyphonic work by musicians active at Quito, Cuenca, or Guayaquil has been found in Ecuador. Considering, however, the splendid development of colonial architecture, painting, and sculpture related to the church (especially in Quito and Cuenca), similar accomplishments in the field of music undoubtedly existed. The transplanting of European music to Ecuador began with the establishment in Quito in 1535 of a Flemish Franciscan order by the monks Josse de Rycke of Mechlin and Pierre Gosseal of Louvain. As mentioned earlier, the Franciscans were responsible for training the first native musicians, especially at their Colegio de San Andrés. Diego Lobato (ca. 1538–ca. 1610), the son of one of the wives of the Inca Atahualpa, received such training and was appointed chapelmaster at the Quito cathedral in 1574. Documentary evidence indicates that he composed *motetes* and *chanzonetas*, but none has been recovered. Gutierre Fernández Hidalgo's sojourn in Quito (1588–1590) was too short to be of lasting significance in the cathedral's musical life. During the seventeenth century the chapter appointed another distinguished composer, Manuel Blasco, who served from 1682 to 1696. He also came from Bogotá, where his extant works are preserved (an example in *StLACA*, p. 67). He was replaced by José Ortuño de Larrea, whose relatives, Francisco (an organist) and Juan (chapelmaster), dominated music at the cathedral during the latter half of the century.

There is little information concerning church music in Ecuador during the eighteenth century. At that time, the city of Guayaquil seems to have taken the lead over Quito, but no primary sources remain. This lack of colonial musical sources is partly due to the financial difficulties of the church, repeated dissension between the musicians themselves, and other calamities, such as frequent earthquakes and fires.

PERU. Together with Mexico, Peru, which was until the eighteenth century the main administrative center of Spanish South America, occupied the most important place in the Spanish colonial empire. During this period, Cuzco, the city of the Incas, and Lima, the "City of the Kings," developed an extraordinary artistic and cultural life.

The Cuzco cathedral's music chapel had at its disposal by the mid-sixteenth century a substantial choral library including, besides plainchant books, several polyphonic books containing such works as Morales's Masses. By 1553, the cathedral had two organs placed at opposite sides of the choir. The first appointment of record in the sixteenth century was that of Pedro Serrano, a shawm and cornetto player, who was to teach counterpoint to clergymen and playing and singing to twenty-four Indian youths, sons of *yanacona* (those serving the Inca nobility and Inca-by-privilege). In addition, he had to teach the players of shawms, sackbuts, cornetts, cornemuses, and bassoons. However, Serrano did not fulfill his obligations and was dismissed two years later. Under Bishop Antonio de la Raya's government of the diocese (1598–1606), the cathedral music library improved both in quality and quantity, as did the music personnel of the chapel. La Raya also founded in 1598 the Seminario de San Antonio de Abad, the first in the New World in which polyphonic and instrumental music was regularly taught. The present music archive of the seminary contains a rich collection of post-1600 manuscripts of Spanish and Peruvian composers' works, including a large number of polyphonic villancicos, *tonadas*, *jácaras*, liturgical works (both with and without composer attribution), and dramatic works. By contrast, virtually nothing but plainchant books survives in the Cuzco cathedral archives; examples of polyphonic works are limited to a copy of Philippe Rogier's *Missae sex* and Philippe de Monte's *Missa ad Modulum Benedicta es sex vocum* (see *StRBMS*).

There is no evidence that such composers as Torrejón y Velasco, Fernández Hidalgo, or Juan de Araujo—music by all of whom exists in the seminary's archive—served the cathedral in any capacity. The only cathedral musician of the late sixteenth century by whom we have any music is Tomás de Herrera, appointed organist at the cathedral in 1611. A three-part *chanzoneta* of his, *Hijos de Eva tributarios* (transcribed in *StMP* and in *StLACA*, p. 234), was copied in the late seventeenth century in a commonplace book, *Libro de varias curiosidades, Tesoro de diversas materias*, by Fray Gregorio de Zuola (ca. 1640–1709), a Franciscan preacher active during the last years of his life at the San Francisco convent at Cuzco. Herrera's piece constitutes the earliest example of New World polyphony in the vernacular.

Lima, the capital of the viceroyalty of Peru, developed a musical life during the period unsurpassed by that of any other South American city. Founded by Francisco Pizarro in 1535, the city's first church was inaugurated in 1540, and the cathedral became an archbishop's seat as early as 1549. During the sixteenth century, the first groups of vocal and instrumental musicians in the cathedral were few in number, and even in 1612 the lists of musicians on the payroll include only five adult singers, five instrumentalists (who may have doubled as singers), and four choirboys. In all likelihood, the usual practice in performing polychoral works was to have one voice for each part, although Andrés Sas indicates also the frequent hiring of extra musicians for first-class (i.e., major) services.[21] It was only at the beginning of the seventeenth century that the music chapel was organized on a regular basis. The

[21]Cf. Andrés Sas, *La Música en la Catedral de Lima durante el Virreinato*, Part I (Lima: Universidad Nacional Mayor de San Marcos [and] Instituto Nacional de Cultura, 1971–1972).

chapter and the archbishop, Bartolomé Lobo Guerrero, felt the need at that time to formulate and issue choir constitutions; these were to regulate the music chapel until the end of the colony. The fourteen provisions defined the various responsibilities of the members of the chapel and revealed the very specific requirements for the singers and the chapelmaster. They also specified the liturgical repertory to be sung at various occasions, and in what manner. The second clause, for example, reads in part:

> For first- and second-class services the *capilla* shall start by singing in *canto de órgano* [i.e. polyphony] the [*Domine*] *ad adjuvandum*, and those who know how to improvise counterpoint [*echar contrapunto*] will do so [by adding counterpoint below or above the cantus firmus of] the first Vesper antiphon and the Magnificat. . . . The *Et misericordia* verse of the Magnificat shall be sung by three voices selected by the chapelmaster, from which the chosen singers shall not excuse themselves or they shall be fined. . . .

Another clause stipulates that "the chapelmaster shall compose new pieces every year, such as motets and some unusual things [*cosas peregrinas*], and the necessary *chanzonetas* for Corpus [Christi] day and its octave and Easter. . . ." Originality was thus demanded of the chapelmaster, and the supervision of the disciplinary behavior of the musicians remained his responsibility.

By 1623 the regular personnel of the Lima music chapel numbered nine singers (including six *seises*, or choirboys), two bassoonists, two cornettists, and two organists, in addition to one or two players of *chirimías* (chalumeaux) and a sackbut player, who was to be replaced in 1633 by a harpist. According to Sas, around that date shawms were substituted for the *chirimías*. The chapel orchestra underwent further transformation during the early part of the eighteenth century under the influence of Italian chapelmasters; in the 1730s it included two organists, two harpists, two violinists, two shawms, and two bassoonists. The vocal ensemble numbered thirteen singers and six *seises*. Later in the eighteenth century the shawms and cornetts tended to disappear in favor of oboes and flutes, which were to be viewed by the chapter during the early nineteenth century as the most important instruments, judging by the salaries granted their performers. The music personnel in 1815 was increased to eleven voices and six *seises*, two organists, six violinists, one double bass player, one harpist, two flautists, two oboists, one bassoonist, and two horn players.

The choral organization of the cathedral required the use of two choruses, each with its own organ accompaniment. Throughout the period, however, the chorus depended on the available voices. *Tiples* and tenors were always in demand (the *tiple* parts were generally sung by the choirboys). Most of the instrumentalists were Peruvian musicians, many of them Indians or mestizos, and, towards the end of the colonial period, Blacks and mulattoes. Entire families made a given instrument their specialty—for example, the Esparza family (four members of which served the cathedral as harpists during the late seventeenth and early eighteenth centuries), the singers of the Cervantes del Aguila family, and the organists of the Dávalos family in the eighteenth century.

The Lima cathedral chapter created a chapelmastership in 1612. The first appointee was Estacio de la Serna, an organist and composer who had worked at the royal chapel in Lisbon before his transfer to Peru. His successors were Miguel de Bobadilla (1616–1622), Cristóbal de Bersayaga (1622–1633), Pedro de Villalobos (interim 1630–1632), Manuel de Sequeyra (1633–1656), Pedro Jiménez (1656–1672), Pedro de Cervantes del Aguila (short interim period in 1668), Juan de Araujo (1672–1676), Tomás de Torrejón y Velasco (1676–1728), José de Orellano (short interim period in 1728), Roque Ceruti (1728–1760), José de Orejón y Aparicio (1760–1765), Cristóbal Romero (1765–1776), Ventura Marín de Velasco (1776–1798), Manuel Dávalos (interim 1798–1799), Juan Beltrán (1799–1807), Julián Carabayo (1807), and finally Andrés Bolognesi (1807–1823). Most of these left works that attest to their high competence in composition. In addition, they were able to gather the most substantial music library in South America. The present *Archivo Arzobispal* (inventoried in *StRBMS*) is but a pale reflection of what was once the repertory of the music chapel. In 1809, Bolognesi (then chapelmaster) requested an inventory of all the "useless papers" (made so by either excessive use or insect damage); these apparently included almost the total repertory of the chapel, for a few months later a list showed only some 220 "usable pieces."

Andrés Sas's statement that "Don Tomás de Torrejón y Velasco is the supreme figure offered by the history of the Music Chapel of the Lima Cathedral and the history of music in Peru"[22] is justified if one considers the length of Torrejón's career as a composer. The son of one of Philip IV's huntsmen, Torrejón y Velasco (1644–1728) was raised in Fuencarral, in the Madrid province of Spain, where he received a careful education in which music had an important position. Early in his life he became a page in the house of the Count of Lemos, the future viceroy of Peru, and in 1667 he arrived in Lima as a member of the Count's entourage. Until 1672 he held the important posts of superintendent of the Lima armory and magistrate and chief justice of Chachapoyas province. He was appointed chapelmaster on 1 July 1676; he served in that capacity until death. Judging by the extant documentation, he won wide recognition throughout this period. His works were known and praised not only in the viceroyalty but in Guatemala City as well. In 1680, on the occasion of the installment of a second grand organ in the cathedral and of the beatification of the late sixteenth-century Lima archbishop, Toribio

[22]Sas, *La música en la Catedral*, Vol. II, Part II, 395.

FIGURE 1-8 Tomás de Torrejón y Velasco. "Villancico a Duo. de Navidad. Si el Alva Sonora se zifra en mi voz. Maestro Don Thomas Torrejon y Velasco. Año de 1719." Title page (Cuzco San Antonio Abad Seminary Library).

FIGURE 1-9 Tomás de Torrejón y Velasco. *Magnificat.* Tone VI. First *tiple* part (Cuzco San Antonio de Abad Seminary Library).

Alfonso Mogrovejo, eight polychoral villancicos by Torrejón y Velasco, requiring thirty-two musicians, were performed. The texts of these pieces were published in Echave y Assu's *Estrella de Lima* (Antwerp, 1688). Concerning Torrejón's memorial Vespers music for Charles II, performed at the cathedral in 1701, his contemporary José de Buendía wrote in his *Parentacion Real al Soberano . . . Don Carlos II* (Lima, 1701):

> The chapelmaster Don Tomás de Torrejón had with very special care composed new polychoral music for the Invitatory, the Lamentations of Job in the three nocturnes, and for certain psalms such as the *Miserere.* . . . Having managed to assemble all the best voices of the city, he united them in such a moving ensemble that everyone present was reduced to tears during the more affecting canticles.[23]

Such praise and recognition continued throughout Torrejón's career. The chapters of the Cuzco and Trujillo cathedrals sought his advice on important matters concerning their music chapel. Perhaps the most important event in his career was a commission in 1701 from the Viceroy of Peru, the Count de la Monclova, for an opera; this resulted in *La Púrpura de la Rosa*, the earliest opera known to have been produced in the New World (see Chapter 2).

[23]As translated in *StMP*, pp. 82–83. Used by permission.

FIGURE 1-10 Tomás de Torrejón y Velasco. "A este sol peregrino." *Vailete a 4.*
First *tiple* part (Cuzco San Antonio de Abad Seminary Library).

Torrejón's extant sacred works are for the most part polychoral pieces.
They include an *Ave Verum Corpus*, an incomplete *Christus factus est*, two
settings of *Dixit Dominus*, a Lamentation for Holy Wednesday, a Magnificat,
a *Nisi Dominus*, a *Regem cui omnia vivunt*, and numerous villancicos. The fact
that fourteen of his works are preserved at the Guatemala City cathedral
(where they were sung until 1772) is indicative of his continent-wide fame. The
Cuzco San Antonio de Abad Seminary holds the remaining repertory. None
of his works, strangely, have been found at Lima.

An excerpt from Torrejón y Velasco's *Lamentación* for two choruses
and continuo reveals his rather austere polychoral style, characterized by
alternation of the choruses and a prevailing homophonic texture (Example
1-6). The shift from major to minor from one section to the next (mm. 16–17
and 86–87; the latter not shown in Example 1-6), used as an expressive device,
is characteristic.

The influence exerted by Italian composers at the Madrid court during
the early eighteenth century had obvious repercussions on the musical life of
the colonial capital in Peru, both at the viceregal court and in the cathedral.
Thus the new viceroy, Marquis Castell dos Ríus, appointed an Italian violinist
and composer as the musical director of his palace. This was Roque Ceruti
(d. 1760), who contributed substantially to the introduction of Italian music
in Peru, first at the palace, and, from 1728, at the cathedral, when he succeeded

Torrejón y Velasco there. Ceruti was the first Italian to occupy the chapel-master's post. During his tenure he introduced violins into the cathedral orchestra. Many of his sacred works remaining in the Archivo Arzobispal reflect the festive character of court music of the time, with solo and choral ensembles and a concertato treatment of voices and instruments. (Da capo arias

EXAMPLE 1-6 Tomás de Torrejón y Velasco, *Lamentación*, mm. 1–25. From *SCAnt*, pp. 165–66. Copyright Samuel Claro Valdés, 1974. Used by permission.

became standard for solo ensembles.) An example of such treatment is Ceruti's "sainete" (a theatrical genre), *A cantar un villancico* (see *SCAnt*, pp. 14–15). Written for two high voices (*tiples*), two violins and continuo, this villancico shows the influence of the Italian style of the early eighteenth century, particularly in its short instrumental introduction, the presence of a short recitative preceding the *estribillo*, and the dialogue between both the two voices and the voices and violins. This secularization of sacred music raised many objections from cathedral musicians throughout the century. For example, thirty-two years after Ceruti's death, Toribio del Campo, a cathedral composer, still blamed him for his neglect of melodic invention in favor of harmonic sequences and figuration, and opposed him to the talent of Orejón y Aparicio.

Born in Huacho, Peru, José de Orejón y Aparicio (1705–1765) is considered one of the most significant composers of eighteenth-century Peru. Most likely a pupil of Roque Ceruti and, from 1715 (when he became a choirboy in the cathedral choir), of Torrejón y Velasco, Orejón cultivated with great success the Neapolitan style of the period. In addition, many of his works are reminiscent of the sentimental and lyrical tone of much sacred Italian music of the time, like that of Pergolesi. In his own time, he was praised as a virtuoso organist, and in 1742 he won without difficulty the post of first organist, since no other candidate opposed him in the public competition, "in consideration of his skill and aptitude." On 8 December 1760, after Ceruti's death, Orejón was appointed interim chapelmaster, becoming titular maestro in 1764, a year before his death.

Orejón's high reputation was well summarized by his disciple, Toribio del Campo, writing in 1792:

> My beloved Aparicio . . . exceeded all others, particularly in the canticles of the Church. Left by him are hymns, Masses, psalms, and a canticle to the Sacrament, which begins: "I adore Thee, Truth Incomprehensible." Until we saw and heard the works of Terradellas and the immortal Pergolesi, none could be compared with him.[24]

His works, surviving at Lima and Sucre, Bolivia (see *StRBMS*), reveal a very mature talent and an unusual skill at melodic invention, compared to the rest of the colonial repertory of his time. His most imposing work is a *Passion del Viernes Santo* (St. John Passion) written in 1750; originally for triple chorus and orchestra, it was reduced to two choruses with added orchestral parts (flutes and horns) by Melchor Tapia, cathedral organist and composer, for a revival of the piece in 1810. The Passion story is divided here into thirteen sections, seven of which are set for full ensemble, three for the choruses with violins and bass accompaniment, two for soprano solo, and one for soprano

[24]Andrés Sas, *La música en la Catedral*, Vol. II, Part II, 295–96.

FIGURE 1-11 José de Orejón y Aparicio. "Passion del Viernes Santo a Dos Coros con Violines Flautas Trompas y Bajo por Don José Aparicio Presbítero." Title page of this Passion according to St. John (Lima Archivo Arzobispal).

EXAMPLE 1-7a José de Orejón y Aparicio, *Passion del Viernes Santo:* "Ecce adduco vobis," mm. 19–36.

nu - lam - in ve - ni - o in___ e - - o___ ca - u - sam,

duet. For the most part the setting is homophonic, with a large degree of voice doubling and voicing in thirds. Such doubling and voicing occur mostly between the same instruments, to a lesser extent between instruments and voices. Counterpoint is sparse, occurring generally for brief passages in the vocal lines. In Example 1-7c, from the "Et inclinato" section, the first choir has an imitative passage, but it soon dissolves into the more prevalent homophonic texture of the other parts. Antiphonal interplay between the two choruses (as in the "Tolle, tolle" passage of Example 1-7b) compensates very frequently for the lack of counterpoint, as does the common Baroque technique of textural thickening through the gradual addition of parts (as in the opening of the "Jesum Nazarenum" section). Melodically, both vocal and

EXAMPLE 1-7b José de Orejón y Aparicio, *Passion del Viernes Santo:* "Tolle, tolle, crucifige," mm. 4–9.

instrumental parts are generally related to each other. Notable exceptions are found in "Quam accusationem" (see *StMP*), "Si non esset hic malefactor," and "Ecce adduco vobis," the latter a *tiple* solo, part of which is transcribed in Example 1-7a. (This appears to be the only section with a relatively independent vocal line.)

EXAMPLE 1-7c José de Orejón y Aparicio, *Passion del Viernes Santo:* "Et inclinato," mm. 8–15.

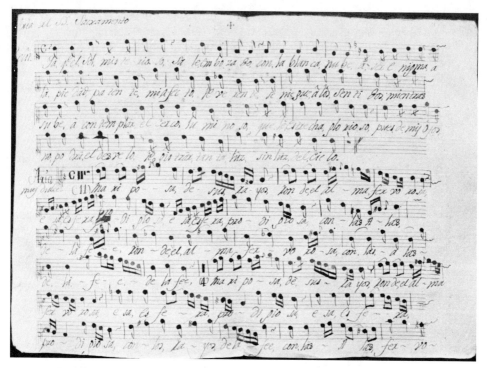

FIGURE 1-12 José de Orejón y Aparicio. *Cantada a sola al SS. Sacramento.* "Mariposa de sus rayos." Recitative and Aria (Lima Archivo Arzobispal).

Orejón y Aparicio's villancicos, duets (examples in *SCAnt*, pp. 30–45, and *StLACA*, pp. 247ff.), and solo arias ("cantadas") exhibit his effective use of melody, harmony, and form, as well as his concern for expressiveness. The *Aria al SS. Sacramento* (*Cantada a Sola Mariposa*) is perhaps the best example (transcribed in *StMP* and *StLACA*). The first section of this work is an accompanied recitative (with continuo only); the second is a da capo aria for soprano, two violins, and continuo. Particularly Baroque in style, in the recitative, are the short, ejaculatory, and irregular phrase lengths. The aria follows the standard form, with an eleven-bar instrumental introduction and four- or five-bar interludes; it also reveals the incipient cultivation of bel canto style among eighteenth-century Peruvian composers. The figuration on the word "alas" (wings) (Example 1-8) adds to the dramatic expression of the setting through word-painting. The vocal part in both sections of the aria is doubled most of the time by one of the violins. Parallel motion or imitation characterizes the concertante violins. Chromaticism, with a rather fast harmonic rhythm, occurs in this and other arias by Orejón. Modulations from the minor to the

EXAMPLE 1-8   José de Orejón y Aparicio, *Cantada a Sola Mariposa:* "Aria," mm. 44–50.

relative major (B minor to D major), or by thirds (e.g., D major to F♯ major), are found in the aria of the dramatic work *Guil guerillo,* for two *tiples,* two violins, and continuo. This cantata shows Orejón y Aparicio at his best, whether in his melodic writing, his use of modulations and form, or his smooth contrapuntal technique. Stevenson has ranked this piece as one of "the choicest items by any native-born Peruvian" (*StRBMS,* p. 124).

Orejón offered evidence of his technical scholastic knowledge in his *Contrapunto ala Consepsion de Nuestra Señora*; its intricate chromatic counterpoint has been compared, somewhat precipitately, to Gesualdo's chromaticism.[25]

The last chapelmaster represented in the Lima cathedral archives is Juan Beltrán, appointed to the post in 1799 and serving to the end of his life (1807). His only extant work is a *Passion para el Viernes Santo* of 1806, written in a classic harmonic vocabulary.[26]

The Genoese cellist Andrés Bolognesi, the last colonial chapelmaster in Lima, set out in 1809 to reorganize the music chapel and to rebuild the archive, which he found to be "entirely destitute." Throughout his tenure, however, Bolognesi faced opposition from the chapter and a reduced music budget, which eventually forced his retirement to Arequipa. This coincided with the period of Peruvian independence (1820s) and the obvious decline of cathedral music at Lima in favor of music in concert halls and opera houses (to which Bolognesi himself contributed substantially).

BOLIVIA ("ALTO PERÚ"). The Audiencia de Charcas (present-day Bolivia) was part of the Viceroyalty of Peru and was known as "Alto Perú" ("High Peru") until 1776, after which (to the time of Peruvian independence) it formed part of the Viceroyalty of Río de la Plata, with Buenos Aires as capital. Silver and other precious-metal mines of the Charcas (specifically from the Cerro of Potosí) made this *audiencia* one of the wealthiest provinces of Spanish America. The exploitation of the Potosí mines began as early as 1545 and lasted on a full scale for some 230 years, with the highest levels of production occurring in the period between 1572 and about 1630, and again in the mid-eighteenth century. The city of Charcas or Chuquisaca (founded in 1538), later known as La Plata, then Sucre, was the capital of the *audiencia* and developed into the most refined and graceful artistic center of High Peru. The San Francisco Xavier university opened in 1624 and soon became the most distinguished in Spanish America, after those in Mexico City and Lima. The La Plata cathedral, at first under the ecclesiastic government of Lima, became an archiepiscopal seat in 1609. The present-day archive at the Sucre cathedral (see *StRBMS*), even if only a mere skeleton of former holdings, is one of the richest of the continent in seventeenth- and eighteenth-century manuscripts and reveals the musical importance of the area.

Documents allowing us to trace the music history of La Plata go back to 1564, when Sebastián de León, a member of a famous family of organ builders, was transacting some business with local convents and churches. A school for teaching singing, instrument-playing, and dancing was opened in

---

[25] Andrés Sas, "La vida musical en la Catedral de Lima durante la colonia," *Revista Musical Chilena*, nos. 81–82 (July–December 1962), 45.

[26] Sas has mentioned the existence of a *Dixit Dominus* and several *Vigilias*, but these works were not to be found when I studied the Archivo Arzobispal in 1969.

1569, under the initiative of a Spaniard, Juan de la Peña Madrid, and Hernán García, a mulatto-*huaquero* (i.e., a dealer in precious objects robbed from Inca graves).

In the long list of chapelmasters who served the La Plata cathedral, the first celebrated one was Gutierre Fernández Hidalgo, whose appointment dates from 1597. After some unhappy experiences at Bogotá and Quito (see p. 29), and perhaps several years at the Cuzco cathedral (as a singer), he moved to La Plata as music teacher at the St. Elizabeth of Hungary Seminary. Fernández Hidalgo signed an agreement in 1607 with a Jesuit from Paraguay, Diego de Torres, entrusting the latter with the responsibility for having Hidalgo's collected works printed in France or Spain. These were to include a volume each for his Masses, Magnificats, hymns, Holy Week office, and motets. Although seemingly nothing came of it, the agreement reveals the extent of Fernández Hidalgo's production and the significance he attached to it.

Soprano castrati were not at all common in colonial Spanish American cathedrals; they were a luxury beyond the reach of most cathedrals. Nevertheless, the *capón tiple* Francisco de Otal was hired at La Plata and caused a sensation upon his arrival there in 1618. His starting salary was set at the astronomical figure of one thousand pesos annually, exactly twice as much as that of the chapelmaster, even one of the stature of Fernández Hidalgo.

Seventeenth-century chapelmasters of some consequence at La Plata included Pedro Villalobos and Andrés Flores. But it was under Juan de Araujo (1646–1712) that the cathedral chapel achieved its best. Born at Villafranca, Spain, Araujo moved to Lima at an early age and received his formal education at the San Marcos university. He may have been trained in music under Torrejón y Velasco (*StMP*, p. 189); he preceded Torrejón, however, as director of the Lima music chapel, after his ordination. He left the post in 1676 to take over that of the Panama cathedral. His appointment at La Plata was in 1680, at a time when the wealth of the cathedral was prodigious. This probably explains why, under Araujo, the cathedral music library increased substantially, with the acquisition of works not only from the Iberian peninsula but also from other Spanish colonies. This wealth also afforded Araujo the performing forces necessary for his numerous polychoral works. As opposed to many colonial chapelmasters, Araujo apparently took his teaching responsibilities very seriously; according to Stevenson, "his unusual success in training choirboys assured him throughout his career of an abundant stream of high *tiples*" (*StMP*, p. 189).

Araujo's extant output is dominated by his villancicos, which number over 140. His Latin works include a Passion setting, an incomplete *Salve Regina*, a four-part *Lamentacion 2ª del Miercoles Santo*, the hymn *Ut queant laxis* (in *StLACA*, pp. 52ff.), and a *Kirie Eleison padre exaudl nos*. Most of his works are preserved at the Sucre cathedral archive, which also contains manuscript copies of various other compositions from the late eighteenth or

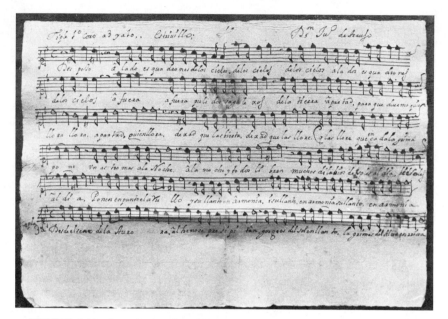

FIGURE 1-13 Juan de Araujo. Villancico "Despejo antorchas de los Cristalinos Orbes." *Tiple* of the first chorus (Sucre Cathedral Archive).

early nineteenth centuries with dubious ascriptions to him; one example is a *Dixit Dominus* for three choruses, with two-organ accompaniment supplemented by two violin and two horn parts (in *StLACA*, pp. 23ff.). Araujo's works are also found in the Cuzco San Antonio de Abad Seminary, the private collection owned by Julia Elena Fortún of La Paz, the San Ignacio de Moxos Church Archive (Beni, Bolivia), and the Museo Nacional Histórico of Montevideo (see *StRBMS*).

In many instances, Araujo favors a polychoral texture, especially for his villancicos, which he handles very effectively. He shows special partiality for the harp as the continuo instrument. His choral treatment is quite varied: at times, the choruses alternate rather regularly, or imitative entries are followed by full ensemble homophonic passages;[27] at other times, a solo voice (*tiple*) is set against three- or four-part choruses, or antiphonal imitations in pairs prevail (cf. *SCAnt*, pp. 5, 50, 62, and 153). Araujo's villancicos follow the standard structure of *estribillo*, *coplas*, and *estribillo*. The Spanish texts reveal obvious affinities with typically Baroque Spanish literature, such as that of the poet Calderón de la Barca. Araujo accomplishes his most original effects with pseudo-Negro and "gypsy" dialects in his villancicos and *jácaras*,

[27]See examples in Carmen García Muñoz and Waldemar Axel Roldán, *Un archivo musical americano* (Buenos Aires: Editorial Universitaria de Buenos Aires, 1972), pp. 99–107 and 129–62.

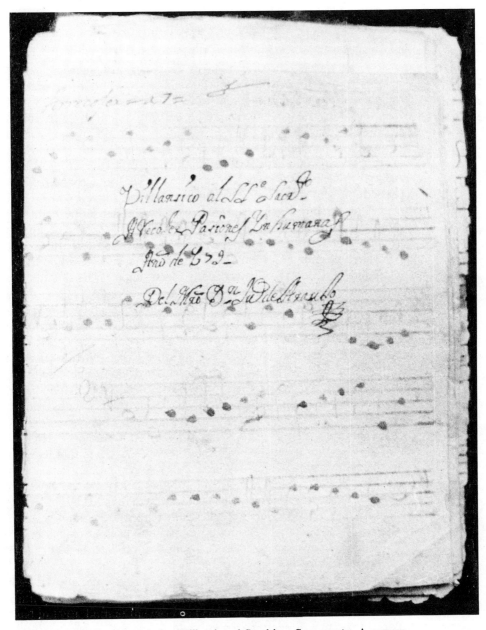

FIGURE 1-14 Juan de Araujo. "Villancico al Santísimo Sacramento. A recoger pasiones inhumanas. Año do 179-(1709?) Del Maestro Don Juan de Araujo." Title page (La Paz Private Collection of Julia Elena Fortún. Kind permission for microfilming the collection by the owner).

such as the Christmas villancico *Los Coflas desde la estleya*: Negritos (in *StMP* and *StLACA*), whose rhythmic drive results from the systematic use of the syncopation ♪ ♩ . Araujo knows how, through text accentuation, to make the most rhythmically of African-like or -derived words, such as "gulumbe, gulumbe, gulumba," with the last syllable stressed by its being set on the strong beat. In the copla section one cannot but marvel at the effective imitation of the typically Afro-American responsorial technique, by means of short reiteration by the chorus of the ending of the soloist's phrase. Although Stevenson's transcription of this piece puts it entirely into 6/8 meter, the real metrical structure reveals a hemiola rhythm (3/4 alternating with 6/8). Finally, if this piece was indeed written for a Black brotherhood (*cofradía*), its repetitiousness also stresses its "African" quality.

After Araujo, the most productive chapelmaster at La Plata in the eighteenth century was Manuel Mesa (y Carrizo) (d. 1773), who occupied the post from 1761 to 1772. His many works preserved at the Sucre archive and the Fortún collection at La Paz reveal a transitional style based on Baroque contrapuntal practices together with early Classic idioms. Mesa's Latin works include the hymns *Lucis Creator optime* and *Laeti colamus hanc diem*, a *Magnificat a 7*, and a *Misa a 3 Coros*. With an instrumental accompaniment of two violins, an oboe, two horns, and an organ, the last-named work belongs to the *Missa brevis* type (Kyrie and Gloria only). The Gloria section illustrates the most bravura violin writing since Ceruti. Mesa's villancicos, duets, *juguetes*, and *jácaras*, with their particularly vivid spirit of good humor and gaiety, have been found to have at times a "delightful folkloric flavour" (*StMP*, p. 191). Such a flavor is frequently the result of Mesa's buoyant melodic writing.

Río de la Plata (Argentina, Paraguay, Uruguay). High Peru joined the new Viceroyalty of Río de la Plata in 1776. Up to that date, however, the entire region comprising present-day Argentina and Paraguay was a political dependency of Lima. Such important colonial cities as Santiago del Estero, Tucumán, Córdoba, and Mendoza were founded by settlers from Peru and Chile. These centers were musically related to Peru, and especially High Peru, since the city of Buenos Aires began to prosper only after 1776.

Little is known or preserved of the musical production during Argentine colonial history. As elsewhere on the continent, the earliest efforts to establish a regular musical life were due to missionaries, especially the Jesuits. But the absence of conventual historians and the disappearance of the music archives of the Jesuits make difficult any objective assessment of music-making in the area during the sixteenth and seventeenth centuries.

The first reference to an organ, in the church of Santiago del Estero, dates from 1585. The first school of music was founded by Father Pedro Comental (1595–1665). Documentary evidence points to locally made European instruments prior to 1600. Among the best known music teachers active in the missions were the Belgian Father Juan Vasseau, or Vaisseau (1584–1623), the French Father Luis Berger (1588–1639), and the Austrian Father Antonio Sepp (1655–1733). Berger's activities and influence extended to Paraguay and Chile, while Sepp made the Guarani mission of Yapeyú one of the flourishing music centers of the area.

The early eighteenth century was dominated by the presence in the colony of the distinguished Italian organist and composer Domenico Zipoli (1688–1726), who arrived in Argentina in 1717. By the time he joined the Society of Jesus (1716), Zipoli had published his well-known keyboard collection, *Sonate d'intavolatura*. As a prospective Jesuit missionary, he was assigned to the Paraguay province. He settled in Córdoba, which had a Jesuit Colegio Máximo and Universidad, and concluded there the required studies of philosophy and theology. However, for lack of a bishop in Córdoba he could not be ordained.

Unfortunately, little is known about Zipoli's activities in the New World. Only if additional works of his are uncovered will we be able to assess

FIGURE 1-15 Domenico Zipoli. *Missa.* "Acompañamento para la Missa de Zipoli; a quatro voces. Se copió en Potossì, el Año de 1784" (Sucre Cathedral Archive).

the relative importance of his last years as a composer. A manuscript copy of a three-part Mass by him, with an instrumental accompaniment of two violins, organ, and continuo, was found at the Sucre cathedral archive in 1959. This copy was made at Potosí in 1784, attesting to Zipoli's lasting popularity in the viceroyalty. A request for copies of his works came from Lima, and two additional works, a *Tantum Ergo* and a *Letania*, were located at the San Ignacio de Moxos church archive (Beni, Bolivia) in 1966.[28] The Potosí Mass (whose tenor and first violin parts were mislaid in the early 1960s) lacks the Benedictus and Agnus Dei, which, according to Ayestarán, may reflect local liturgical practices. Some passages of the Mass reveal a solid contrapuntal organization. The "Cum Sancte Spiritu" and the "Et vitam venturi" of the Gloria and Credo, respectively, are three-part fugatos with well-balanced voice spacing. All four Mass sections, from Kyrie to Sanctus, are in F major, with a well-timed harmonic rhythm and modulations within the circle of fifths (see *StLACA*, pp. 298ff.).

With the expulsion of the Jesuits, musical activities in the Argentine and Paraguayan areas were considerably curtailed. Studies in the archives of various churches and convents (Humahuaca, Jujuy, Tucumán, Santiago del Estero, Rioja, Córdoba, Santa Fe, and elsewhere) have revealed but very few manuscripts of original works.

Sacred music in colonial Uruguay was limited to the San Francisco Church of Montevideo, and later its cathedral (consecrated in 1804). The earliest extant composition of sacred music written in Montevideo is the *Misa para dia de difuntos* (1802) written by Fray Manuel Úbeda, a Spaniard who settled there in 1801.

BIBLIOGRAPHICAL NOTES

The major bibliographical tool concerning Latin American music is Gilbert Chase's *A Guide to the Music of Latin America*, 2nd edition (Washington: The Library of Congress and the Pan American Union, 1962), which covers materials published up to about 1960. For items since that time, the music section of the *Handbook of Latin American Studies* should be consulted. For American doctoral dissertation dealing with Latin American music, see *Latin America and the Caribbean. A Dissertation Bibliography,* ed. by Carl W. Deal. Ann Arbor, University Microfilm International [1978].

In addition to the references given in the text and footnotes, the following items are useful: Gabriel Saldívar, *Historia de la Música en México: Epocas Precortesiana y Colonial* (Mexico: Editorial "Cultura," 1934); Lota M. Spell,

[28]The Mass copy was located by Robert Stevenson, the two additional works in Bolivia by Samuel Claro.

"Music in the Cathedral of Mexico in the Sixteenth Century," *Hispanic American Historical Review*, 26/3 (August 1946), 294–319; Lota M. Spell, "The First Music Books Printed in America," *Musical Quarterly*, XV/1 (January 1929), 50–54; Isabel Pope, "Documentos Relacionados con la Historia de la Música en México," *Nuestra Música*, 6/21 (1951), 5–28; Robert Stevenson, "Sixteenth- and Seventeenth-Century Resources in Mexico," *Fontes Artis Musicae*, 1954/2, 69–78, and 1955/1, 10–15; Stevenson, "Mexico City Cathedral Music: 1600–1750," *The Americas*, XXI/2 (October 1964), 111–35; Thomas Stanford, "Una Lamentación de Jeremías Compuesta en el Siglo XVI para el Uso de la Catedral de México," *Anales* (Instituto Nacional de Antropología e Historia), XVIII (1965), 235–70. Biographical data on Hernando Franco are also provided in Stevenson, "European Music in Sixteenth-Century Guatemala," *Musical Quarterly*, L/3 (July 1964), 341–52, and Stevenson, "The First New World Composers: Fresh Data from Peninsular Archives," *Journal of the American Musicological Society*, XXIII/1 (Spring 1970), 95–106. Also informative is Jesús Estrada, *Música y Músicos de la Epoca Virreinal* (Mexico: Secretaría de Educatión Pública, 1973). For Puebla and Juan de Padilla, besides Alice Ray Catalyne's studies, Stevenson's article "The 'Distinguished Maestro' of New Spain: Juan Gutiérrez de Padilla," *Hispanic American Historical Review*, XXXV/3 (August 1955), 363–73, provides a good introduction, which is updated in his *Christmas Music from Baroque Mexico* (Berkeley, Los Angeles: University of California Press, 1974).

The bibliography of the Caribbean area is well covered in Stevenson, *A Guide to Caribbean Music History* (Lima: Ediciones "CVLTVRA," 1975). Cuban colonial music is treated in Alejo Carpentier, *La Música en Cuba* (Mexico: Fondo de Cultura Económica, 1946), and is the subject of Pablo Hernández Balaguer's articles "Panorama de la Música Colonial Cubana," *Revista Musical Chilena*, XVI/81–82 (July–December 1962), 201–8, and "La Capilla de Música de la Catedral de Santiago de Cuba," *Revista Musical Chilena*, XVIII/90 (October–December 1964), 14–61. José Antonio Calcaño surveys the Venezuelan colonial period in *La Ciudad y su Música* (Caracas: Conservatorio "Teresa Carreño," 1958) and in "Música Colonial Venezolana," *Revista Musical Chilena*, XVI/81–82 (July–December 1962), 195–200. Also useful for English readers is Juan Bautista Plaza, "Music in Caracas during the Colonial Period (1770–1811)," *Musical Quarterly*, XXIX/2 (April 1943), 198–213.

Besides the music anthologies containing Latin American colonial music mentioned in this chapter, Arndt von Gavel's *Investigaciones Musicales de los Archivos Coloniales en El Perú* (Lima: Asociación Artística y Cultural "Jueves," 1974) provides a few transcribed pieces. Likewise, some Colombian choral works (Cascante for the Colonial Period) are available in Luis Antonio Escobar (ed.), *Obras Polifónicas* (Bogotá: Imprenta Nacional, 1972). A good survey of colonial music in Colombia is Stevenson's "Colonial Music in Colombia," *The Americas*, XIX/2 (October 1962), 121–36. José Ignacio Perdomo Escobar presents, however, the most comprehensive and detailed study of the Bogotá Cathedral Music Archive in his monumental work *El*

Archivo Musical de la Catedral de Bogotá (Bogotá: Publicaciones del Instituto Caro y Cuervo. 1976). His "Music in Quito, four centuries," *Hispanic American Historical Review*, XLIII/2 (May 1963), 247–66, is a historical account of music activity at the Quito Cathedral.

Chilean colonial music is treated succinctly in Samuel Claro and Jorge Urrutia Blondel, *Historia de la Música en Chile* (Santiago de Chile: Editorial Orbe, 1973). Santiago cathedral holdings are catalogued in Samuel Claro's *Catálogo del Archivo Musical de la Catedral de Santiago de Chile* (Santiago de Chile: Editorial del Instituto de Extensión Musical, Universidad de Chile, 1974). Argentine music in the colonial period is the subject of Guillermo Furlong's *Músicos Argentinos durante la Dominación Hispánica* (Buenos Aires: Ediciones Huarpes, 1945) and of Francisco Curt Lange's *La Música Eclesiástica durante la Dominación Hispánica* (Córdoba: Imprenta de la Universidad, 1956). Vicente Gesualdo gives a detailed account of the history of music in Argentina in his *Historia de la Música en la Argentina*, Vol. I (Buenos Aires: Beta, 1961). His article "La Música en la Argentina durante el Período Colonial," *Revista Musical Chilena*, XVI/81–82 (July–December 1962), 125–34, is a brief summary of the subject. Domenico Zipoli's activity in the area has been studied by Lauro Ayestarán, in *Domenico Zipoli: Vida y Obra* (Buenos Aires: Facultad de Artes y Ciencias Musicales, 1962) and "Domenico Zipoli y el Barroco Sudamericano," *Revista Musical Chilena*, XVI/81–82 (July–December 1962), 94–124, and by Francisco Curt Lange in "Der Fall Domenico Zipoli: Verlauf und Stand einer Berichtigung," *Festschrift Karl Gustav Fellerer* (Kassel, 1972), 327–55 and "O Caso Domenico Zipoli: Uma Retificação Histórica. A sua *Opera Omnia*," *Barroco* (Belo Horizonte, Brazil), 5 (1973), 7–44.

Uruguayan colonial music is studied in Lauro Ayestarán's *La Música en el Uruguay*, Vol. I (Montevideo: Servicio Oficial de Difusión Radio Eléctrica, SODRE, 1953), in his "Fuentes para el estudio de la música colonial uruguaya," *Revista de la Facultad de Humanidades y Ciencias*, no. 1 (1947), 315–58, and in his "La 'Misa para Día de Difuntos' de Fray Manuel Ubeda (Montevideo, 1802)," *Revista de la Facultad de Humanidades y Ciencias*, no. 9 (1952), 75–93. Brief mention is also made of colonial music in Susana Salgado's *Breve Historia de la Música Culta en el Uruguay* (Montevideo: Aemus, 1971).

Recordings of Latin American colonial music are scarce. *Salve Regina* (*Choral Music of the Spanish New World 1550–1750*) (Angel S 36008), *Festival of Early Latin American Music* (Eldorado S-1), and *Blanco y Negro* (*Hispanic Songs of the Renaissance from the Old and New World*) (Klavier Records KS-540) contain good performances of some of the pieces mentioned in this chapter.

TWO

SECULAR MUSIC
IN SPANISH AMERICA

The distinction between sacred and secular music is not always easy to establish. Classifications tend to be arbitrary, but in the present context the only workable criterion has to do with musical functions. As indicated in the previous chapter, a vernacular text cannot be the sole line of demarcation between sacred and secular repertories. Villancicos, *chanzonetas*, and other genres with Spanish texts functioned as religious songs of praises in the cathedrals, if often also as "dramatic" music. We shall deal now, therefore, with colonial Spanish-American music-making that is without known religious context; an exception is made for the popular religious theater of the early colonial period. There are numerous references throughout the period to commemorative festivities of all kinds for which stage and dance music and, less often, purely instrumental music was required. The actual extant repertory is, however, quite limited. Since the church supported the only truly well-organized musical life, it is not surprising that church musicians were in most cases also responsible for secular music-making.

MEXICO ("NEW SPAIN")

In the sixteenth and seventeenth centuries, dramas were written mainly to serve the didactic purposes of the Church. Such literary genres as *autos*, *coloquios*, and *entremés* were cultivated in New Spain and other Spanish colonies. Particularly important for the Franciscan missionaries were the *autos sacramentales*, religious plays, with music, whose central theme dealt generally with the Eucharist. A purely secular theater, however, did not develop until the late seventeenth century, when the dramatic works of Lope de Vega and Calderón de la Barca and the *zarzuela*, Spain's national theatrical genre, became known in the colonies. At first, these were performed for the courtly and aristocratic circles of the viceroyalties, but the eighteenth century saw them appearing in new theaters and opera houses in the larger cities—for example, the Teatro Coliseo in Mexico City, which opened in 1670 and lasted until 1722, when it was destroyed by fire. A larger theater, the Coliseo Nuevo, inaugurated in 1735, by the middle of the century had as director of its orchestra the cathedral chapelmaster Ignacio Jerusalem. The first known production of a full opera in New Spain, however, took place at the viceroyal palace on 1 May 1711, with *La Parténope*, on a libretto by Silvio Stampiglia, for which the future chapelmaster Manuel de Zumaya wrote the music. (Only the libretto, printed in Mexico City in both Italian and Spanish, remains.) In three acts, the rather convoluted plot presents seven characters, two of them rival princesses. Since the music apparently pleased the Viceroy (the Duke of Linares, an admirer and connoisseur of Italian opera), Zumaya must have been fairly well acquainted with the operatic style of the time. However, for lack of suitable conditions (regular troupe, audience) Italian opera did not develop in Mexico until the era of independence. Well into the beginning of the nineteenth century, *tonadillas*, *sainetes*, and zarzuelas of the buffa type prevailed in the local repertory. Even Italian operas tended to be presented as zarzuelas in Mexico—that is, with interspersed spoken dialogue. Such was the case with Cimarosa's *El filósofo burlando*, produced at the Coliseo Nuevo during the season of 1805. The Puebla chapelmaster Manuel Arenzana was also a composer of *comedias* and zarzuelas: the same 1805 season at the Mexico City Coliseo included Arenzana's *El extrangero*, listed in the *Diario de México* as a "comedy in two acts with music," and his "new duo," *Los dos ribales en amor*. During the 1806 season the Coliseo presented Paisiello's *Il barbiere di Siviglia*, in Spanish translation, as an opera buffa in four acts. On the day of the premiere the *Diario de México* made the following announcement:

The orchestra will be considerably enlarged in order to meet the instrumental specifications in this opera. The interludes will consist of short Mexican dances [*bailes del país*] in order not to lengthen unduly the whole evening's presentation. The admission price will be double the ordinary price in order to pay for the heavy expenses of this production.[1]

The popular Mexican songs and dances used as interludes seem to have represented the only original contributions to Mexican stage music of the time.

Purely instrumental music was cultivated in New Spain during the seventeenth and eighteenth centuries, but the extant examples are few. Three tablatures remain in Mexico. The first one, an organ tablature,[2] has been dated at about 1620; it is in the same notation as Francisco Correa's *Facultad orgánica* (1626) and carries the indication "Tiento de quarto tono, medio Registro, tiple del Maestro Fran.co correa y son muy elegantes sus obras de este Maestro" ("Tiento in the fourth tone, on an eight-foot stop, with the soprano part by Maestro Francisco Correa, whose works are very elegant"). The *tiento* is the Spanish counterpart of the Italian motet-derived, polyphonic *ricercar*; Spanish and Portuguese composers of the seventeenth century, such as Rodrigues Coelho, Francisco Correa himself, and Cabanilles were quite fond of this form. Despite the attribution to Correa, the soprano does not correspond to any of the fourth-tone compositions in that composer's *Libro de tientos* (1626). The second tablature is a *Método de Citara* (cittern instruction book), by a Sebastián de Aguirre, dating from the mid-seventeenth century. Dances constitute the main contents of the book, including examples of the *pavana, pasacalle, gallarda, branle, panamá, zarabanda, minuete,* and others. In addition to an Indian *tocotín* (an indigenous dance, with singing, used for religious expression during the colonial era), we also find one of the oldest references to a Negro dance, a *portorrico de los negros*. The book also provides an early example of an instrumental transcription of a *corrido*, a well-known Mexican folk song of the ballad genre. A *Tablatura de Vihuela* (ca. 1740), preserved at the Biblioteca Nacional in Mexico City, is the third one. Some fifty types of dance music are represented in it (*jota, fandango, folias españolas, sarabanda, paspied, rigaudon, tarantela, seguidillas,* and others), with some Negro dances and songs referred to as *cumbees*. This tablature also features vihuela transcriptions of seventeen movements from Corelli's chamber sonatas and a sonata attributed to a Samuel Trent.

The province of Michoacán developed during the eighteenth century substantial musical activities. As early as 1738–1740, a school of music was founded in Valladolid (today Morelia) as part of a convent for orphan girls, the Colégio de Santa Rosa. This "escoleta de música" was apparently a

---

[1] As translated in Robert Stevenson, *Music in Mexico* (New York: Thomas Y. Crowell Company, 1952), p. 174. At the turn of the nineteenth century, the Coliseo orchestra, under the direction of José Manuel Aldana, included strings, flute, bassoon, trumpets, and kettledrums.

[2] Described and reproduced in facsimile in *Revista Musical Mexicana* (July, August, September, 1942).

model of organization in the entire colony. During the latter part of the century, the school's fame extended beyond the limits of New Spain, for Pope Benedict XIV referred to it in a "Brevis," calling it "conservatorium mulierum et puellarum." Among the many works found in the archive of the convent are several pieces of instrumental music. Two overtures (*sinfonias*) for a small orchestra of typical *settecento* instrumentation (violins 1 and 2, viola, bass, oboes 1 and 2, French horns 1 and 2) represent the very best works of the genre in the Spanish colonies in the late eighteenth century. The composers, identified in the manuscripts as Antonio Rodil and Antonio Sarrier, remain unknown. Sarrier's overture in D major, in three movements (Allegro; Andante; Fuga, presto), reveals not only good melodic and harmonic writing but also good structural balance. The Allegro is a typical first movement of a pre-Classic symphony: a bithematic exposition (with the classic tonal relationship between themes), some thematic elaboration in a central section (by means of melodic sequence and some, admittedly timid, fragmentation), and an abbreviated recapitulation. The Andante, in binary form, is again a fairly characteristic cantabile movement. The closing Fuga, with a subject of Mozartian character in both melodic contour and rhythmic figuration, is a rather elaborate movement for a simple Italian-type overture. First presented by the second violins, the subject is supported by two countermelodies, one of which (the viola's) has the function of countersubject (Example 2-1). The first violins provide a real answer and bravura figuration at the end of the first exposition. Whether or not Rodil and Sarrier were local composers, the fact that these works were used at Morelia presupposes the existence of a local orchestra capable of performing them.

EXAMPLE 2-1   Antonio Sarrier, *Obertura:* Fuga, presto, mm. 1–5. From Miguel Bernal Jiménez, *El Archivo Musical del Colegio de Santo Rosa de Santa María de Valladolid* (Siglo XVIII) (Morelia: Ediciones de la Universidad Michoacana de San Nicolás, 1939), p. 29.

PERU

The origins of lyric spectacles in the viceroyalty of Peru go back to the first two decades of the seventeenth century. Rubén Vargas Ugarte's anthology *De nuestro antiguo teatro* (1943) provides eight examples of Peruvian colonial plays, including passages with music integral to the action. Five accompanied villancicos for solo voices recur in the *auto sacramental El dios Pan*, written between 1608 and 1621 for Potosí or La Plata by Diego Mexía de Fernangil, a Sevillian poet. Similarly, the three-act play *Amar su propia muerte*, written at Cuzco around 1648, calls for military instruments (for a victory march), a chorus, and offstage voices. Throughout the century, theatrical companies included singers and instrumentalists among their personnel; we have ample documentary evidence of various musicians employed by specific troupes during the viceroyal period.[3] And, after the arrival at Lima of the Viceroy, the Count of Lemos, in 1667, demand for stage music increased:

The simple accompaniment of guitars and harps that sufficed for stage music when the Lima stage was in its nonage had already in Lope de Vega's last years [d. 1635] and much more in Calderón's given way to a veritable orchestra comprising brass, woodwind, and strings. Marcelino Menéndez y Pelayo [1865–1912] claimed that whereas Lope conceived of drama in terms of the novel, Calderón did so in lyric terms. Simply to say that the two autos performed at Lima in 1670 were Calderón's is to assure ourselves that music intervened constantly. Because Torres's company alone could not manage so much music, José Díaz and "his boys" (which had already been singing around at many church affairs) were called to the rescue. Among his aides Díaz counted not only such Indians in cathedral employ as Francisco de Castro and Francisco de Valdés but also Indians from the Santiago del Cercado parish.[4]

The Count of Lemos had the comedy *El Arca de Noé* (written by Antonio Martínez de Meneses, Pedro Rosete Niño, and Jerónimo de Cáncer) presented nine times in the patio of his palace between 11 February and 2 March 1672. Staging ("as it is done in the Buen Retiro palace in Madrid") included the whole apparatus (lighting, machines, costumes, etc.) appropriate for a court spectacle, but new to Lima. Much of the play was presented in *música recitativa*, although the composer of the music is not mentioned. Torrejón y Velasco was most likely the composer, without rejecting the possibility of Lucas Ruiz de Ribayaz, who had also come to Lima with the Count of Lemos but did not remain there very long.[5]

The only opera written and produced in the New World during the colonial period for which the music is extant is Torrejón y Velasco's *La Púrpura de la Rosa*, premiered at the viceroyal palace in Lima on 19 October

---

[3] See Guillermo Lohmann Villena, *El Arte Dramático en Lima durante el Virreinato* (Madrid: Estades, 1945).

[4] Ibid., p. 271, as translated in Robert Stevenson, *Foundations of New World Opera* (Lima: Ediciones "CVLTVRA," 1973), p. 42. Used by permission.

[5] Lohmann Villena, *El Arte Dramático*, p. 276. For further data on Ribayaz, see Stevenson, *Foundations*, pp. 43–44.

1701 (see p. 39). This was commissioned by the Viceroy, Conde de la Monclova, to honor Philip V on his eighteenth birthday and the first year of his reign. The libretto, by Calderón de la Barca (the best known Spanish dramatist in the viceroyalty), had been used previously by Juan Hidalgo, whose opera had been produced in Madrid in 1660 and was undoubtedly known by Torrejón y Velasco. The libretto was appropriate for the occasion, since Calderón wrote it to celebrate the marriage of Louis XIV to the Spanish infanta. The plot deals with the myth of Venus and Adonis, but Calderón added to the main characters a soldier, a peasant, and his wife, who, in Stevenson's words, provide "a kind of comic relief, a mixing of the sublime and the ridiculous, not found in Italian baroque libretti."[6] A *loa* or complimentary ode, with different text from that of Calderón, precedes the opera itself. In two-part-form sections, the *loa* is set for solo, duet, and four-part chorus. Written in one long act ("Jornada única") in various scenes (including a wood, a garden, a grotto, gardens, a mountain, and the heavens), the opera comprises numerous solo pieces alternating with frequent short choral sections. Of the main parts, the role of Adonis is certainly the most demanding, from the point of view not only of range but of the length of the part and its melodic elaboration (large intervallic skips, chromaticism, motivic imitation, rapid figuration). Torrejón provides each of the main characters—Adonis, Mars, Venus—with a distinctive refrain-like theme; generally presented at the beginning of a scene, the theme identifies that character throughout the scene (see examples in *StMP*, pp. 125–27). These refrains also function as structural elements: "They are often so spaced as to build within scenes a striking architectural unity. Mars's first four repetitions are separated from the next set of four by an interval three times the length of a repeat. On occasion ... Torrejón so alters the vocal part at each repeat (meanwhile keeping the bass constant) that he writes a set of ground bass variations."[7]

The accompaniment consists of a single continuo line (lightly figured) written with a remarkable versatility for disclosing changes of mood. At times the bass imitates the vocal line; at others it tends to maintain a certain independence, as in the nymphs' choral number "No puede Amor." No one knows for sure what instruments realized the continuo; probably strings and harpsichord (or harp) were the most important ones. Rubrics in the score call for offstage trumpets and drums ("cajas") to announce the approach of Mars or Bellona.

Throughout the work, Torrejón sets the text carefully. Harmonic, melodic, and rhythmic devices symbolically stress the meaning of certain

---

[6]*StMP*, p. 121. For the main plot see *StMP*, pp. 120–21. Torrejón's manuscript of the work survives at the Lima Biblioteca Nacional and has been described in detail by Robert Stevenson. See Stevenson, *Foundations*, for facsimile and transcriptions.

[7]*StMP*, pp. 126–27.

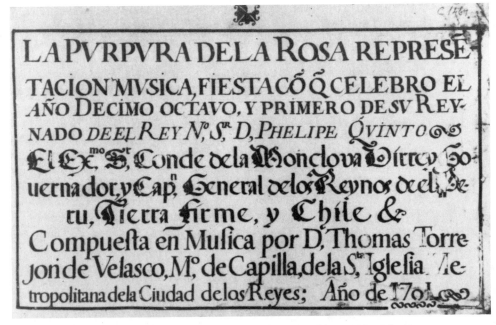

FIGURE 2-1 Tomás de Torrejón y Velasco. Title page of the opera *La Púrpura de la Rosa*. "La Purpura de la Rosa representacion musica, fiesta con que celebro el año decimo octavo, y primero de su Reynado de el Rey Nuestro Señor Don Phelipe Quinto. El Exmo. Sr. Conde de la Monclova, Virrey Governador y Capitan General de los Reynos de el Peru, Tierra firme, y Chile, & Compuesta en Musica por Don Thomas Torrejon de Velasco, Maestro de Capilla de la Santa Iglesia Metropolitana de la Ciudad de los Reyes; Año de 1701" (Lima National Library).

words—unexpected alteration on the word *bastardo*, false relation on *temor*, rests between each syllable of *suspensión*, etc. (See examples in *StMP*, p. 133.) To a lesser degree than Hidalgo's *Celos aun del aire matan* (1660), Torrejón's opera is marked by a popular flavor, especially in the choral ensembles— "Viva Philipo" of the *loa*, and "Arma guerra" and "Huid pastores" in the "jornada."

In 1708, Italian opera officially entered the viceroyalty, with the presentation of *El mejor escudo de Perseo*, its libretto by the recently arrived Viceroy himself, its music by Roque Ceruti. This period corresponds to the domination of Italian opera in Spain under Philip V. During most of the century the Lima stage was similarly dominated by Italian musicians: Roque Ceruti from Torrejón's death to 1760, Bartolomé Massa from about 1765 to the end of the century, and Andrés Bolognesi from 1810 to 1820. Many of Ceruti's villancicos are conceived as dramatic music. *A cantar un villancico* (see p. 43 and *SCAnt*, pp. 13ff), subtitled *Saynete a duo*, is set in dialogue form. From a structural viewpoint, the work is nearer to being a cantata, as it consists of a short instrumental introduction, a recitative, an *estribillo*, and two *coplas*. The text is made up of questions and answers in the *coplas* (First *tiple*: "Sacristan, when did you learn to sing harmoniously?" Second *tiple*: "In my native land the maestro slapped me around"); it has the jovial and rustic character of the *tonadilla escénica*, the Spanish genre of comic opera of the eighteenth century.

Bartolomé Massa (1721–1799), Italian-born, who had been active in Buenos Aires as manager of a local theater (producing in 1760 his own opera *Las Variedades de Proteo*), transferred to Lima, where he became the manager of the Lima Coliseo, for which his contract also required him "to compose all the music needed for the plays, operas, and other diversions offered in the Coliseo, and to teach and perfect all the actors and actresses in whatsoever they were to sing."[8] His stage music survives (although incomplete) in the private collection of the director of the Lima Teatro de San Marcos; it includes the "comedias" *El Monstruo de la Fortuna y la Bendera de Napoles* (1767), *La Presumida y la hermosa* (1773), and *Yo por vos y vos por otro* (1768) and the opera *Primero es la Honra* (1762), the latter given at the Coliseo.

The highland cities of Cuzco, La Plata, and Potosí in the viceroyalty of Peru also developed a significant theatrical life. La Plata (present-day Sucre) is reported to have had by 1639 a "sumptuous oval public theater with two balconies that cost 50,000 pesos to build."[9] The repertory presented there comprised the most recent successes of the Spanish theater, especially the plays of Lope de Vega, as well as those of local playwrights. The Sucre cathedral archive preserves part of the incidental music for Calderón de la Barca's play, *El monstruo de los jardines*, composed by Blas Tardío de Gusmán, the cathedral chapelmaster from 1745. The nearby Potosí opened its own "Coliseo" in 1616, while Cuzco's *corral de comedias* was replaced by an indoor theater in 1622. During the seventeenth century, troupes traveled every year from Lima to High Peru, performing from Cuzco to La Plata and Potosí. Most of the dramatic music that survives at the San Antonio de Abad Seminary in Cuzco was apparently written in connection with official celebrations such as the arrival of a new viceroy or the appointment of an eminent ecclesiastic.[10] In 1743 the newly appointed Cuzco bishop, Don Diego Morcillo Rubio y Auñón, was welcomed with a whole week of festivities,

---

[8]Lohmann Villena, *El Arte Dramático*, p. 431.
[9]From a contemporary document. Quoted in Robert Stevenson, *Foundations*, p. 63.
[10]See Samuel Claro, "Música dramática en el Cuzco durante el siglo XVIII y Catálogo de manuscritos de música del Seminario de San Antonio Abad (Cuzco, Perú)," *Yearbook*, Inter-American Institute for Musical Research, V (1969), 1–48.

including the performance of the play *Antíoco y Seleuco* by the well-known seventeenth-century Spanish writer Agustín Moreto. Incidental music for the play exists in some anonymous instrumental parts; it has been attributed to Fray Esteban Ponce de León (ca. 1692-ca. 1750s), cathedral chapelmaster. The first song, *Venid pastores de Henares*, gives a good illustration of the style cultivated at Cuzco. For *tiple* and continuo, and a pair of violins which enter into dialogue with the vocal line, the song reveals the typically Italian flavor that had been introduced to the area by Roque Ceruti.[11]

When the former rector of the San Antonio Abad Seminary, Don Fernando Joseph Pérez de Oblitas, was elected bishop of Paraguay in 1749, there were more festivities in Cuzco; they included the performance of an *Opera Serenata, Venid, Venid Deidades* (*SCAnt*, pp. 108ff.). According to Claro, "music and text of the *Opera Serenata* are indubitably the work of experienced professionals, versed in the latest techniques of Italian opera."[12] Indeed, the aria da capo "Con tal derecho bien disputo" confirms the statement. The dialogued presentation of the beginning of the melody between the voice and the violin, the dance-like rhythmic patterns, the melismatic, virtuoso singing, and the modulation to the relative key (mm. 27–30) are all typical traits of the late Baroque Italian aria da capo (see *SCAnt*, pp. 111–13).

Two dramatic-music scores by Fray Ponce de León, performed in 1750 and preserved in their entirety, bear evidence of frequent performance. These works represent the incidental music for a *Comedia de S. Eustachio*, for two choruses, two violins, and continuo, preceded by the customary *loa*.

Fray Gregorio de Zuola's commonplace book, known as the De Zuola Codex, includes seventeen items of colonial music.[13] Most of these are significant examples of the kind of music sung and played by the layman in colonial times (excepting, of course, folk music). The codex contains, with one exception, song settings in the vernacular. Besides Tomás de Herrera's three-part *Hijos de Eva tributarios*, mentioned in Chapter 1, and two four-part pieces, *Dime Pedro por tu vida* and *Por qué tan firme os adoro*, credited to a Correa (possibly Manuel Correa, who died in 1653), none of the remaining pieces is attributed. De Zuola himself may have been the composer of at least the version of the *Credo Romano* that appears in the book. Twelve of the pieces are simple monophonic songs, including three Spanish *romances* (entered as "Romances varios") whose texts derive from a printed source, *Romances varios de differentes authores* (Amsterdam, 1688). The popular flavor of some of the pieces—especially *Marizápalos* and *Yo sé que no ha de*

---

[11]Ibid., p. 24. The song is transcribed at p. 12.
[12]Ibid., p. 19.
[13]Carlos Vega, *La música de un códice colonial del siglo XVII* (Buenos Aires, 1931). See also Carlos Vega, "Un Códice peruano del siglo XVII. La música en el Perú Colonial," *Revista Musical Chilena*, nos. 81–82 (1962), 54–93.

ganar (*StMP*, pp. 153–54)—results from their buoyant rhythmic character, with numerous syncopations and dotted figures.

The last collection gathered in Peru and deserving attention because of the popular character of the music it contains is that of the bishop Baltasar Jaime Martínez Compañón (1737–1797), who visited the diocese of Trujillo in 1782–1785. The collection furnishes examples of Christmas carols ("round dances") and secular songs collected throughout the province. Martínez Compañón identifies the various places where the material was collected and presents the various songs in geographical order, in addition to providing alternate versions of each song.[14]

BIBLIOGRAPHICAL NOTES

The general histories indicated for Chapter 1 deal also with secular music. Most of the primary sources of colonial secular music in Spanish America are catalogued in *StRBMS*. Spanish popular theatrical genres popularized in Mexico are succinctly studied in Vicente T. Mendoza, *Panorama de la Música Tradicional de México* (Mexico: Imprenta Universitaria, 1956). An overview of theatrical activity and literature is given in José Juan Arrom, *El Teatro de Hispanoamérica en la Epoca Colonial* (Havana: Anuario Bibliográfico Cubano, 1956). Robert Stevenson, in *Foundations of New World Opera*, discusses thoroughly "Seventeenth-Century Spanish Musical Spectacle" and provides an excellent historical survey of the Peruvian lyric stage. Also valuable is the study by César Arróspide de la Flor, "La música de teatro en el virreynato de Lima," in *Revista Musical Chilena*, nos. 115–16 (1971), 39–51.

Chilean secular musical activity of the eighteenth century is documented by Eugenio Pereira Salas in *Los Orígenes del Arte Musical en Chile* (Santiago: Imprenta Universitaria, 1941). A good stylistic discussion of Torrejón y Velasco's secular works appears in Samuel Claro, "La Música Secular de Tomás de Torrejón y Velasco (1644–1728). Algunas Características de su Estilo y Notación Musical," *Revista Musical Chilena*, XXVI/117 (January–March 1972), 3–23. Pieces from the Mexican vihuela tablature are available in the record *Tablatura Mexicana del Siglo XVIII para Guitarra Barroca* (Angel SAM-35029).

---

[14]Examples in *StMP*, pp. 304–20, and Stevenson, *Music in Aztec and Inca Territory* (Berkeley and Los Angeles: University of California Press, 1968), pp. 318–19.

THREE

MUSIC IN BRAZIL

Compared to Spanish America, Brazilian cultural development during the first two centuries of the Portuguese colonial period was meager. In Brazil, church organization lagged. While a bishop was appointed to Bahia in 1551, additional bishoprics were not created until the mid-seventeenth century, and Bahia did not become the seat of an archbishop until 1676 (although by the end of the period, bishoprics had been established in Pernambuco, Maranhão, Pará, Minas Gerais, Rio de Janeiro, and São Paulo). Moreover, with the possible exception of the work of the Jesuits, the Church in Brazil was unable to develop the moral and political stature of its Spanish American counterpart. While it provided education for the privileged few, most artists and intellectuals had to rely on Portugal's educational institutions. No university was established in Brazil during the entire period, as opposed to those of distinction at Mexico City, Lima, La Plata, and elsewhere. Printing presses were unknown until 1808, and the colony imported few books. Nevertheless, colonial Brazil produced a significant literature, at first with the Jesuits Manoel da Nóbrega and José de Anchieta (sixteenth century) and Antonio de Vieira (seventeenth century), then with Gregório de Matos, Antônio José da Silva, Cláudio Manuel da Costa, and Tomás Antônio Gonzaga, to cite but a few authors.

Relatively little is known concerning art-music activities and production until about the middle of the eighteenth century. Throughout the colonial period the majority of music-making related directly to church services. The extant late colonial repertory is, therefore, mainly sacred music, with a few isolated exceptions. Substantial documentation attesting to musical activities in Pernambuco (Olinda, Recife) and Bahia (Salvador) has only recently been compiled and studied.

The regular clergy were responsible for organizing Christian religious life in Brazil. The Franciscans started using music in the conversion of the Indians, but the Jesuits had the strongest impact in bringing European musical practices to the colony. By 1550, the Jesuit Manoel da Nóbrega had initiated musical instruction at Bahia. Father Leonardo Nunes, another Jesuit, is reported as one of the directors of a choir comprised of "laymen of good voices" performing at the feast of Anjo Custódio in Ilhéus in 1549. On that same feast the procession was accompanied by "high music to which trumpets answered." We also have notice of festivity that took place in Pernambuco in 1576 and was described as "very solemn and with polyphonic music." Indeed, the earliest and most important centers of church music were Bahia and Pernambuco.[1]

BAHIA

Officially named São Salvador da Bahia de Todos os Santos, Bahia was the capital of the Brazilian colony until 1763. As the first episcopal see and the most active center of the slave trade, it was of paramount importance for early Brazilian music history. At the Bahia cathedral, music occupied a prominent place in daily services as well as on special occasions. Prior to 1559, a Francisco de Vacas, "great musician and singer," is reported to have offered his services in Bahia as music teacher and chapelmaster, having succeeded in being ordained and even in obtaining a prebend. The chapelmastership was created in 1559 and filled by Bartolomeu Pires from ca. 1560 to 1586; of his successors, the following have been identified: Francisco Borges da Cunha (from ca. 1608 to ca. 1660), Joaquim Corrêa (from 1661 to ca. 1665), Antonio de Lima Carseres (from 1666 to ca. 1669), João de Lima

---

[1]For further information, see Francisco Curt Lange, "A organização musical durante o período colonial brasileiro," in *Actas do V Colóquio Internacional de Estudos Luso-Brasileiros*, IV (Coimbra, 1966), 5–106.

(probably in the 1670s), Frei Agostinho de Santa Monica (1680s to ca. 1703), Caetano de Mello Jesus (ca. 1740 to ca. 1760), and Theodoro Cyro de Souza (from 1781). In Brazil the post of chapelmaster was not limited to cathedrals but extended also to parish churches (*matrizes*). The required qualifications and duties of the chapelmaster did not differ in either jurisdiction. Besides teaching, conducting the choir, and composing music, he had to be a good singer and be able to play one or more instruments. The chapelmaster acted as contractor for musical services in and out of the church, and he established artistic standards. He alone controlled all music matters in his jurisdiction; no one could conduct any group without his permission. This widely practiced system of control and monopoly, although illegal, precipitated a kind of musical stagnation ("*estanco*") in colonial Brazil.[2]

The first position of organist at the Bahia cathedral was established by royal decree in 1559; it was filled a year later by the canon Pedro da Fonseca, who was followed by Father Francisco da Luz. Of the previously mentioned cathedral chapelmasters, biographical information is available for Frei Agostinho de Santa Monica (1633–1713), who belonged to the Portuguese congregation, Ordem de São Paulo I Eremita. He studied music with João Fogaça, a favorite pupil of Duarte Lobo. According to a biography written in 1737 by a member of the Ordem de São Paulo,[3] Frei Agostinho's output comprised forty Masses (many of them polychoral), psalms, Lamentations, and several Offices for the Dead. The biographer states that the majority of the Masses survived in the Bahia cathedral archive; none, however, has been found.

The first archdiocesan council of Bahia took place in 1707. An account of its various sessions published at Lisbon in 1719 refers to the polyphonic music performed on the occasion and characterizes the cathedral as the "most sumptuous and magnificent temple of all of those in America." Later accounts mention the singing of a *Te Deum* in 1728 by "four music choruses including the best musicians and instrumentalists" and the practice of performing antiphonal psalms with "two polyphonic choirs alternating in two verses, the plainchanting clergy responding in the third verse."[4]

The oldest known music manuscript of Brazilian colonial music is in the central library of the University of São Paulo.[5] It contains a recitative and aria to a Portuguese text, written at Bahia and dated 2 July 1759, for soprano, two violins, and basso continuo. The original source gives no clue

---

[2]The term is Régis Duprat's; see Nise Poggi Orbino and Régis Duprat, "O estanco da música no Brasil colonial," *Yearbook*, Inter-American Institute for Musical Research, IV (1968), 98–109.

[3]See Robert Stevenson, "Some Portuguese sources for early Brazilian music history," *Yearbook*, Inter-American Institute for Musical Research, IV (1968), 33.

[4]Ibid., p. 35.

[5]This manuscript was uncovered by Régis Duprat in 1959.

as to the poet or the composer, but the piece has been attributed to Caetano de Mello Jesus on the grounds that Mello Jesus not only served in that year as Bahia cathedral chapelmaster "but was also acknowledged the premier composer and conductor of the area, and therefore entitled to treat as equals all the foremost musicians of both Portugal and Brazil."[6] Mello Jesus, a native of Bahia, was credited in José Mazza's biographical dictionary of Portuguese musicians (compiled in the 1790s) with "various works for four and more voices extant at Bahia and Pernambuco, also an *Arte de Canto de Orgão* in question-and-answer form, and a treatise on the modes." The first volume of the *Arte de Canto*, on polyphonic music, dates from 1759, the second from 1760. The *Recitativo e Aria* is dedicated to José Mascarenhas Pacheco Pereira de Mello, a magistrate of the "Casa da Suplicação," Portugal's supreme court of justice, and was composed on the occasion of Mascarenhas's recovery from a serious illness.[7] The work is written in the most typical Italian melodramatic style (for the recitative) and the galant style of the time (for the aria). The long recitative (thirty-eight lines of text) reveals a careful and expressive setting of the text and a good balance between the soloist and the string accompaniment. The aria, although originally labeled "Da Capo," follows an unusual formal scheme, of the type AA'BB. The heavily embellished vocal line with its contrasting dynamics is of a typical bel canto character (Example 3-1).[8]

Many other musicians (especially chapelmasters and organists) were active in the various churches and convents of the many orders established in Bahia, particularly the Benedictine monks of the Mosteiro de São Sebastião da Bahia (known as the Mosteiro de São Bento) and Nicolau de Miranda (flourished early eighteenth century), organist at the church of the Misericórdia and the Santa Casa da Misericórdia. Among the native musicians of the seventeenth century, several priests are praised in Barbosa Machado's *Bibliotheca Lusitana* (Lisbon, 1741), among them Eusébio da Soledade de Matos (1629–1692), brother of the poet Gregório de Matos. During the eighteenth century, church music in Bahia reached its apex. The St. Cecilia Brotherhood (Irmandade de Santa Cecília), the most important association in both Portugal and Brazil to function as a sort of musicians' union, was established in Bahia in 1785 and continued its activities into the next century. Native composers associated with it included Damião Barbosa de Araújo, José Pereira Rebouças, and others, some works of whom have been preserved.

---

[6]Stevenson, "Some Portuguese sources," p. 41.

[7]Mascarenhas was also known as a patron of the arts and letters, and while he was in Brazil his name was associated with the Academia Brasílica dos Renascidos ("of the Reborn"), a new academy of Bahia intelligentsia.

[8]For complete analysis and transcription, see Régis Duprat, "Recitativo e Ária para soprano, violinos e baixo," *Universitas* (Revista de Cultura da Universidade Federal da Bahia), nos. 8–9 (January–August 1971), 291ff.

EXAMPLE 3-1 Caetano de Mello Jesus (?), *Recitativo e Aria:* Aria, "Se o canto enfraquecido," mm. 22–35. Transcribed by Régis Duprat. Used by permission.

*Se o canto enfraquecido
não pode ser que cante
a gloria relevante
de nome tão subido
mayor vigor o affecto
gigante mostrará*

(*Translation*): *If the enfeebled song
cannot sing of the glory
of such an illustrious name
a greater vigor the gigantic
affection will show*

The first opera houses in Bahia appeared in the early eighteenth century, although previous theatrical representations with music are known to have taken place, such as one on the occasion of the wedding in 1662 of Charles II of England with the Portuguese infanta D. Catarina. The local theater repertory in the early eighteenth century reflected the same situation as that of Lisbon: it consisted essentially of Spanish plays presented in Spanish. Thus, we have specific references to the presentation in Bahia in 1717 and 1727 of several plays of Calderón de la Barca. The short-lived Teatro da Câmara Municipal (1729) was followed by the Casa da Opera da Praia (1760), established for the performance of "operas and other stage compositions." At the latter, three operas were produced in 1760 (*Alessandro nelle Indie, Artaserse,* and *Didone abbandonata,* perhaps by David Perez) on the request of the municipal council to honor the royal marriage of D. Pedro and D. Maria. Still during the colonial period, Bahia saw the establishment of the Casa da Opera (1798), the Teatro do Guadelupe, and the Teatro São João (with seating capacity for 800), which, however, was destroyed by fire in 1922.

As the major slave trade center of the South American Atlantic coast, Bahia was rapidly populated by Blacks and mulattoes. As in other areas of Brazil, numerous Black musicians flourished in Bahia. Documentary evidence points to formalized music instruction of Negro slaves as early as the 1600s.

Private orchestras and choruses made up of slave musicians were organized by professional maestros on the wealthiest sugar plantations and on the estates. Portuguese contacts with Black Africans even before the colony was established, and the resulting cultural subordination of persons of African descent in the colony, favored the formation of several colonial groups of mulatto composers and musicians. In addition, religious associations (*irmandades*) for Blacks were founded in Bahia, Pernambuco, and Minas Gerais, as will be seen below.

PERNAMBUCO

As in Bahia and Rio de Janeiro, a sizable historical documentation bears witness to a substantial colonial musical development in Pernambuco, particularly in Olinda (the seat of the diocese until 1833) and Vila do Recife. The earliest reference to music in Pernambuco mentions the chapelmaster Gomes Correia, who served at the church of Olinda from 1564. An impressive number of documents reveal some six hundred musicians (organ builders, instrumentalists, singers, and composers) working in the area during the seventeenth and eighteenth centuries.[9] One frequently praised musician of the seventeenth century is Father João de Lima, chapelmaster at the Bahia and Olinda cathedrals, whose works were considered even fifty years after his death "worthy of publication for the instruction of musical professors." Another musician considered both an excellent composer and performer in his own time was Father Inácio Ribeiro Noya (Nóia), born in Recife in 1688; none of his works, however, is extant. Similarly lost are the works of the mulatto Manoel de Almeida Botelho (b. 1721), "one of the most famous composers of the present age" (i.e., mid-eighteenth century); he was honored at the court in Lisbon, "not allowing his dusky color to diminish by an iota the deference due his gifts, virtues, and ingenuous deportment."[10] The same contemporary source mentions several of his works as being "eagerly seized by the best professionals in Portugal": they include a *Missa a 4* with two violins, a *Lauda Jerusalem*, three settings of *Tantum ergo, a 4* (one for double choir), and various sonatas and toccatas for keyboard and for guitar.

As a result of the discovery in 1967 of the music manuscript of a *Te Deum* by him, another mulatto (*pardo*) composer from Pernambuco claims our attention: Luiz Alvares Pinto (1719–1789). He studied in Lisbon under Henrique da Silva Negrão, the Lisbon cathedral organist and composer, well-

[9] Jaime C. Diniz, *Músicos pernambucanos do passado*, 2 vols. (Recife: Universidade Federal de Pernambuco, 1969, 1971).

[10] As quoted in Stevenson, "Some Portuguese sources," p. 13.

known for his thorough knowledge of counterpoint. Alvares Pinto himself wrote a treatise titled *Arte de Solfejar* (the manuscript is in the Lisbon National Library); completed in 1761, it is the earliest such work known to be written by a New World-born author. Upon the inauguration of the church of São Pedro dos Clérigos in Recife (1782), Alvares Pinto was appointed its first chapelmaster. His last achievement for the city's musical life was the founding of the Irmandade de Santa Cecília dos Músicos (ca. 1787). Several of his compositions are mentioned in contemporary documents; they include mostly liturgical works, of which only the *Te Deum* mentioned above and a *Salve Regina* are extant. Other works that might be attributed to Alvares Pinto on stylistic grounds include seven motets, a *Miserere*, a *Mandatum* without accompaniment, and a *Mandatum a 4 vozes* with instrumental accompaniment. The *Te Deum* (ca. 1760), for four mixed voices and orchestral accompaniment (of which only the continuo and horn parts remain), reveals good technical command of counterpoint and harmony and good melodic writing. The usual setting of the *Te Deum* treats the verses polyphonically in alternation with chant intonation, beginning traditionally with the second part of the first verse, "Te Dominum confitemur." The only exceptions found in Alvares Pinto's setting affect verses 5, 6, and 7 ("Sanctus"). In the "Judex crederis" section, Alvares Pinto adds verse 22 ("Te ergo quaesumus"), and from then to the end sets all the even-numbered verses. The text setting is predominantly syllabic, the composer generally following the natural accentuation of the Latin text. Example 3-2, from the beginning of "Te ergo quaesumus," illustrates his smooth and competent contrapuntal technique. A double fugue closes the setting.

EXAMPLE 3-2   Luiz Alvares Pinto, *Te Deum laudamus:* "Te ergo quaesumus," mm. 1–17. From Luiz Alvares Pinto, *Te Deum laudamus a 4 vozes,* ed. Jaime C. Diniz (Recife: Secretaria de Educação e Cultura de Pernambuco, 1968). Used by permission.

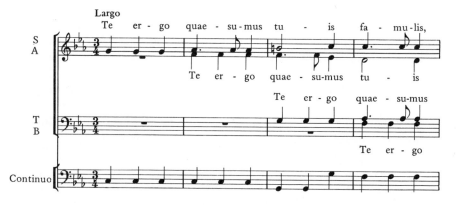

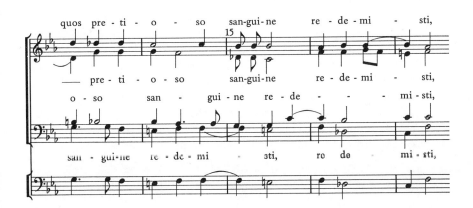

Alvares Pinto is also acknowledged as a playwright and poet. A three-act comedy of his, *Amor mal correspondido*, written in verses and containing a sung chorus, was produced at the Casa da Opera of Recife in 1780.

Agostinho Rodrigues Leite (1722–1786), also a native of Recife, was the main organ builder of eighteenth-century Brazil. Ample documentation concerning his activities indicates that he supplied organs not only for Olinda (before 1757), Recife (churches of S. Pedro Apóstolo, Igreja do Carmo), and Bahia (Mosteiro de S. Bento, Ordem Terceira do Carmo), but also for Rio de Janeiro (Mosteiro de S. Bento, 1773). According to contemporary accounts, his organs were excellent and of low price considering their high quality.

MINAS GERAIS

The formerly unsuspected importance of the colonial music life of Minas Gerais has been revealed only since the early 1940s.[11] The mining region of Minas Gerais, rich in gold and precious stones, was discovered in the late seventeenth century and exploited throughout the next century. Elevated to the rank of General Captaincy in 1720, Minas Gerais organized itself rapidly. Its society at first included Indians (both pure blood and mestizos), Portuguese and Brazilian colonizers, and Black slaves. By the middle of the eighteenth century, mulattoes and Blacks formed the majority of the population, despite migratory movement from Portugal and other areas of the colony. A large number of mulattoes who were free held important positions among the clergy and dedicated themselves to craftsmanship and art; the development of local Baroque architecture and sculpture and the practice of music were due in great part to mulatto artists. Substantial documentation attests to a unique musical development which reached its peak during the last quarter of the century. There were almost a thousand musicians active in Minas between about 1760 and 1800, especially in the cities of Vila Rica (present-day Ouro Preto), Sabará, Mariana, Arraial do Tejuco (present-day Diamantina), São João del Rei, and São José del Rei (present-day Tiradentes). Since most of these musicians were mulattoes, this phenomenon has been referred to as *mulatismo musical.*[12]

Following Portuguese precedents, musical life in the area was organized in and around various brotherhoods and not the Church. All practicing musicians belonged to one or another of the music brotherhoods, which

---

[11]Thanks to the prodigious efforts of Francisco Curt Lange.
[12]See Lange, "La música en Minas Gerais. Un informe preliminar," *Boletín Latino-Americano de Música*, VI (1946), 409–94.

included the Irmandade de Santa Cecília, Irmandade do Santíssimo Sacramento, Irmandade da Ordem Terceira do Carmo, Irmandade da Ordem Terceira de São Francisco, Irmandade de São José dos Homens Pardos ("of Black Men"), and many others. Thus brotherhoods supplied music and musicians for the Church or the municipality, which generally commissioned specific works (or simply performances) for religious festivities. The brotherhoods also established music archives.

In spite of the relative isolation of the main music centers in Minas, evidence indicates the existence of local organ builders (for example, Father Manuel de Almeida Silva), the use of harpsichord in the church, and the existence of manuscript copies and prints of contemporaneous European music (Haydn, Boccherini, Mozart, Pleyel, Beethoven), which further indicates the exposure of the area to the prevailing stylistic trends in Europe. Little is known about music instruction in Minas. Most likely, the first generations of musicians came from Bahia, Pernambuco, and Rio de Janeiro and were mostly secular priests. Monks, who had been the first music educators throughout Latin America, were never as much in evidence in Minas Gerais, since the building of convents or monasteries was forbidden, by royal decree, to prevent the smuggling of gold and precious stones. In all likelihood, composers received their training in the coastal cities of the colony, or their training was strictly empirical. In order to understand the particular style cultivated by these composers, one should remember that they assimilated the prevailing European styles of the time. Considering the results, their proficiency of imitation (at first) and assimilation (later) was admirable. Curiously enough, the Neapolitan style, which invaded the Iberian peninsula at the time, is not to be found in the repertory of sacred music of Minas Gerais. Almost all the composers whose works are extant seem to have cultivated a pre-Classic homophonic style. (Thus the term "Baroque," which was first applied to this music, is obviously inaccurate.) Compositions of the "Minas School" are, in general, liturgical works for four-part mixed chorus with an orchestral accompaniment of two violins, viola (or cello), bass, and two French horns. The use of basso continuo is not consistent. Double chorus appears, though infrequently, and counterpoint is eschewed, for the most part, in favor of homophony.

The most important composers active in the Captaincy were José Joaquim Emerico Lobo de Mesquita (ca. 1740s–1805), Marcos Coelho Netto (d. 1823), Francisco Gomes da Rocha (d. 1808), and Ignacio Parreiras Neves (ca. 1730–ca. 1793). The oldest music manuscripts hitherto discovered bear the date 1779, but the repertory was copied over as late as the 1880s for use in Minas Gerais and the neighboring provinces (especially São Paulo), and earlier manuscripts may have been discarded.

Lobo de Mesquita, a composer and organist, spent most of his life at Arraial do Tejuco and Vila Rica. He entered the brotherhood of Nossa

FIGURE 3-1 José Joaquim Emerico Lobo de Mesquita. *Regina Caeli laetare* "1779 Antiphona Com Violini, Corni, Viola obrigada Violoncello/Regina Caeli laetare. Autor: José Joaquim Emerico Lobo de Mesquita. Pertence a Antonio José Dias Ribeiro" (Archiepiscopal Palace. Mariana, Minas Gerais).

Senhora das Mercês dos Homens Crioulos (of Tejuco), which indicates that he was a mulatto. He was apparently the first organist of the Irmandade do Santíssimo Sacramento in Tejuco, working concurrently at the Irmandade da Ordem Terceira do Carmo. He moved to Vila Rica about 1795 and worked there for about a year and half as a composer, conductor, and organist for the Ordem Terceira brotherhood. For unknown reasons he then moved to Rio de Janeiro, where his professional activities have not yet been determined.[13] Judging by the number of his works hitherto uncovered, Lobo de Mesquita was the most prolific composer of the Captaincy. His earliest known works are the antiphons *Regina Caeli Laetare* and *Zelus Domus Tuae*, both of 1779. The first few measures of *Regina Caeli* illustrate the composer's Classic choral writing (Example 3-3). The beginning of the melodic line of

[13]Lange's assertion that he may have taught the Rio composer José Maurício Nunes Garcia is purely speculative. See Lange, "Os compositores na Capitania Geral das Minas Gerais," *Estudos Históricos*, nos. 3–4 (1965), 33–111.

EXAMPLE 3-3 José J. E. Lobo de Mesquita, *Regina Caeli*, mm. 1–7.

the soprano (soloist) constitutes the antecedent (a) of the phrase, followed by a consequent (b) of equal length (tutti). In this tutti, while the tenor part stays on the dominant (m. 2), altos and basses proceed by contrary motion. This procedure is maintained in measure 4 but the parts are inverted. The harmonic progressions and modulations in this passage are quite characteristic of the composer's sober style—namely, the use of simple chords with frequent tonic, dominant, and subdominant functions.

Other works by Lobo de Mesquita available in modern transcriptions (some of them published) include an *Antiphona de Nossa Senhora* (*Salve Regina*) (1787), a Mass in E-flat, a Mass in F, a *Te Deum*, several litanies, motets, and Offices for the Dead, among other works. The *Salve Regina* is perhaps the best example of the composer's homophonic concertante style. The tonal structure of this work reveals the typical symmetry along the circle of fifths of the early Classical period (e.g., C. P. E. Bach, Haydn). The vocal and instrumental parts tend to be independent from each other, with the concertante violins written in parallel thirds or sixths.

Lobo de Mesquita's *Missa* in E-flat, for mixed chorus and orchestral accompaniment of strings, two flutes, two oboes, and two horns, consists of the Kyrie and Gloria only, but is of very large proportions. It belongs to the concertante genre, with eight choral numbers, a duet, and three arias. While the Mass reveals an excessive use of homophony and of isometric rhythmic figures, it also provides some of the rare instances in Lobo de Mesquita's work of effective contrapuntal writing. Imitations, although not in a fugato style, appear in the Christe eleison, alternating with purely homophonic passages (Example 3-4). Instrumental parts double the vocal

EXAMPLE 3-4   José J. E. Lobo de Mesquita, *Missa* (E ♭ major): "Christe eleison," mm. 1–21. Instrumental parts omitted.

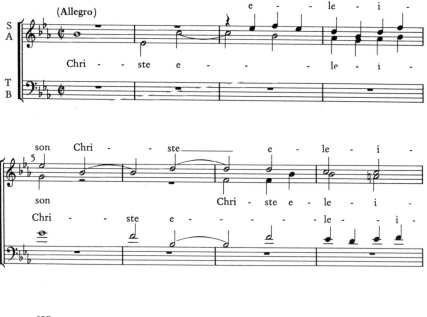

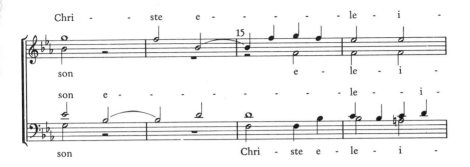

parts, a customary practice of European church music of the time. Lobo de Mesquita writes his arias in da capo form (e.g., the Quoniam, an aria for soprano) and even uses a short motivic development passage in the Domine Deus. All of these are stylistic components of European Classic practices.

Marcos Coelho Netto, probably a native of Vila Rica, was, like his father of the same name, a composer, conductor, and French horn player. Little biographical information has been gathered on either father or son. Evidence indicates that both were members of the Vila Rica Brotherhood of São José dos Homens Pardos, for St. Joseph's Church was connected especially with the many mulattoes in that city.[14] The son's activities in the brotherhood included primarily conducting at important festive occasions, from 1808 to 1815 according to extant documentation. A hymn, *Maria Mater Gratiae*, written in 1787, has been attributed to Coelho Netto the younger. This short work, for mixed chorus and an orchestral accompaniment of strings and French horns, effectively combines late Baroque and Classic stylistic traits. Other works attributed to Coelho Netto include a *Credo*, three *Ladainhas* (litanies), and three Masses.

Francisco Gomes da Rocha is mentioned as a contralto in a document of the Royal Senate of the city of Vila Rica of 1780. He succeeded Lobo de

[14]See Lange, "Os irmãos músicos da Irmandade de São José dos Homens Pardos, de Vila Rica," *Yearbook*, Inter-American Institute for Musical Research, IV (1968), 110–60.

Mesquita as the conductor for the Terceira Ordem do Carmo around 1800. In 1768 he had entered the "Black" brotherhood of São José dos Homens Pardos. The records of that association mention him as kettledrummer in the local regiment of the dragoons (which suggests the different sources of income sought by colonial musicians). Gomes da Rocha's extant works (*Novena de Nossa Senhora do Pilar a 4*, 1789; *Spiritus Domini a 8*, 1795; *Popule Meus a Quatro Vozes*; *Cum Descendentibus in Lacum para Sexta Feira da Paixão*) exhibit perhaps the most original assimilation of purely Classic stylistic traits in both choral treatment and instrumental accompaniment among the composers of the area. The *Spiritus Domini a 8* treats the responsory polyphonically in three parts, Andante, Allegro, Andante. The first Andante is an example of the composer's choral style. Set for the double chorus, this thirty-seven-measure passage reveals textural variety through antiphonal imitation. The second Andante exhibits a more dramatic character created by means of chromatic tension and dynamic indication (*piano* to *forte*, with *mezza voce* and *sforzando*).

The first indication of Ignacio Parreiras Neves's activities as a singer comes from the records of the Brotherhood of Nossa Senhora da Mercê. In 1752 he entered the Irmandade de São José dos Homens Pardos, in which he participated actively as a musician. Two works bearing his name are extant. A *Credo*, written between 1780 and 1785, for mixed chorus and orchestra, follows the pre-Classic homophonic style of the Minas school. In 1967 an incomplete *Oratoria ao Menino Deos para a Noite de Natal* (1789) came to light; its importance is enhanced by the fact that it is the only known secular choral work from Minas Gerais. The extant parts suggest that this Christmas oratorio, originally conceived for solo voices, chorus, and orchestra, was a work of large proportions.[15]

Theatrical activities in the Captaincy of Minas Gerais are well documented, but not a single work produced there is extant. The first Casa da Opera was built in Vila Rica in 1770; it consisted of a large room with scenery and appropriate ornamentation. The opera repertory, known through a report of expenses of the Vila Rica Municipality, included Portuguese operas (or at least operas coming from Portugal) but apparently also some locally composed. The writer Cláudio Manuel da Costa, from the group "Arcadia Ultramarina," wrote the play *O Parnaso obsequioso* (based on Molière's *Le bourgeois gentilhomme*) indicating it as an "opera to be narrated with music"; he probably had a composer available for this endeavor. In 1786, the Vila Rica Municipal Chamber commissioned three operas on the occasion of the festivities held to celebrate the engagement of the royal infants of Portugal and Spain; Marcos Coelho Netto is mentioned as the musical

---

[15]For a more detailed description see Béhague, "Música mineira colonial à luz de novos manuscritos," *Barroco*, 3 (July 1971), 25.

director, and a Francisco Furtado da Silveira as the "composer of the music."[16] Local opera troupes consisting of Blacks and mulattoes are reported not only in Bahia and Rio de Janeiro but in places as remote from the coast as Cuiabá, where in 1790 an opera probably by Jommelli, *Ezio in Roma*, was produced by an all-mulatto cast.

RIO DE JANEIRO

Little is known about the music culture of Rio de Janeiro in the seventeenth and eighteenth centuries. Several seventeenth-century monks associated with the Mosteiro de São Bento were musicians, among them the organists Frei Francisco da Cruz, Frei Plácido Barbosa, and Frei Plácido das Chagas. Two priests active as chapelmasters at the church (later cathedral) of S. Sebastião were Pe. Cosme Ramos de Moraes (appointed in 1645) and Pe. Manoel da Fonseca (appointed in 1653). The next known chapelmaster, Antonio Nunes de Siqueira (1692–1759), a native of São Paulo, also held the post of rector of the diocesan seminary founded in 1740. Barbosa Machado cites in his *Bibliotheca Lusitana* (1741) the musician João Seyxas da Fonseca, born in Rio in 1681, who studied at Bahia before going to Italy. He apparently had a book of his keyboard sonatas printed at Florence in 1732, under the title *Sonatas de Cravo compostas por Ludovico Justini de Pistoya*; this collection has been shown to be the same collection as one printed in 1732 under the title *Sonate Da Cimbalo di piano, e forte detto volgarmente di martelleti . . . Composte Da. D. Lodovico Giustini di Pistoia*, recognized as "the first known, dated music of any sort that specifies the use of the pianoforte."[17]

When it became the Brazilian capital in 1763, Rio de Janeiro acquired a new importance in the musical life of the country. But with the transfer of the royal family to Rio in 1808 it became overnight the main center of the huge Portuguese Empire. The career of the mulatto composer and priest José Maurício Nunes Garcia (1767–1830) is closely connected with the sojourn in Rio of D. João VI (to 1821) and with the reign of the Emperor Pedro I. Son of a poor lieutenant, José Maurício (as he is generally referred to in Brazil) may be considered the most distinguished Brazilian composer up to his time. Nothing definite is known about his musical training, which probably was quite empirical. There is no evidence that he studied music at

[16]See Lange, "La Opera y las Casas de Opera en el Brasil colonial," *Boletín Inter-americano de Música*, no. 44 (November 1964), 3 11.

[17]William S. Newman, *The Sonata in the Baroque Era* (Chapel Hill: University of North Carolina Press, 1966), pp. 194–95. See also the evidence of Stevenson in "Some Portuguese sources," pp. 3–6.

the Fazenda Santa Cruz established by the Jesuits in the surroundings of Rio de Janeiro, as has often been reported.[18] He apparently did have some training in solfège under a local teacher, Salvador José, and he received formal instruction in philosophy, languages, rhetoric, and theology. In 1784, he committed himself to participate in the foundation of the Brotherhood of St. Cecilia, one of the most important professional musical organizations of the time, and entered officially the Brotherhood São Pedro dos Clérigos in 1791. He was ordained a priest on 3 March 1792. (The priesthood was then the salvation of many musicians without fortune or noble birth, as well as being an ideal base for a musical career.) The fact that he was a mulatto does not seem to have been an obstacle to his ordination. Many of his contemporaries praised his intellectual and artistic as well as priestly qualities.

On 2 July 1798, José Maurício was appointed to the post of chapelmaster of the Rio de Janeiro cathedral; it was the most significant music position in the city. The chapelmaster fulfilled several functions: he had to be organist, conductor, composer, music teacher, and appointer of musicians. Even before that date, José Maurício had established a music course open to the public and free of charge; he maintained this activity for some twenty-eight years, teaching some of the best known individuals of the time, such as Francisco Manuel da Silva. By the time of the arrival of the Prince D. João and the Portuguese court, José Maurício's fame was well established in the colony, and he had composed several works, including graduals, hymns, antiphons, and Masses. Following the precedent of the Bragança royal family, D. João was a patron of music. José Maurício, whose talents were immediately recognized, took advantage of the patronage system operative at the court. In 1808 he was appointed chapelmaster of the Royal Chapel, for which he wrote thirty-nine works during the year 1809 alone. The prince's enthusiasm for the Brazilian composer was also signified by his bestowing upon him the Order of Christ. Soon the composer became fashionable and famous for his improvisational skill at the keyboard in the noble salons of the time; Sigismund Neukomm (1778–1858), the Austrian composer and former pupil of Haydn, who lived in Rio from 1816 to 1821, referred to José Maurício as "the foremost improviser in the world."

With the arrival in 1811 of Marcos Portugal (1762–1830), the most famous Portuguese composer of his time, José Maurício's power and production began to decline. His humility and benevolence forbade him to counteract Portugal's intrigues. His activities as composer and conductor concentrated thereafter on the city's brotherhoods, although his position at the Royal Chapel was nominally maintained. About 1816 his health began to fail, and his working capacity was reduced considerably. Yet he conducted

---

[18]Lange believes that the Santa Cruz conservatory is a legend. See Lange, "A Música Erudita no Regência e no Império," *História Geral da Civilização Brasileira*, II, 373.

on 19 December 1819 the première in Brazil of Mozart's Requiem, an event reported by Neukomm in the Viennese *Allgemeine Muzikalische Zeitung*. The return of D. João VI and part of the court to Portugal in 1821 had the effect of diminishing the importance of Rio's musical life. Although Emperor Pedro I was himself a musician, the years following independence (1822) were not favorable for artistic development. Financial difficulties and precarious health undermined José Maurício's last nine years. He died in extreme poverty.

According to Cleofe Person de Mattos, who compiled a thematic catalogue of José Maurício's output, some 237 works (sacred, secular, and instrumental) are extant. The oldest manuscript dates from 1783 (the antiphon *Tota Pulchra es*) and the last work (*Missa de Santa Cecilia*) from 1826. His most productive period ranges from about 1795 to about 1811. Some eleven works attributed to him are of doubtful authorship, mainly on stylistic grounds. At least 171 works known to have existed (through written references or catalogues compiled in the latter part of the nineteenth century) have not so far been rediscovered; among these is an opera, *Le Due Gemelle*, known to have been produced at the Teatro Régio in 1809 in observance of Queen Maria I's birthday.

José Maurício's total production, mostly sacred music, has been divided into two distinct periods, but there is little justification for such a division since one can hardly find a uniform stylistic development; side by side are major works of a well-defined stylistic tendency and lesser ones without concordance of style. The years 1810–1811 do, however, disclose a change in stylistic orientation, probably as a result of the new performance possibilities with the presence in Rio of the royal court, as well as of Marcos Portugal. The latter dictated the stylistic trend of Portuguese music, which continued at that time under the influence of the Neapolitan school. Italian operatic influences therefore permeate both the choral numbers and the arias of José Maurício's Mass-settings and other works after about 1810 (see an example in *StLACA*, pp. 173ff.). The *Missa de N. Sra. da Conceição* (1810) seems to be the clearest evidence of the transformation of style that affected the sacred repertory of the colony at that time. Rossinian bel canto style appears in the solo sections (in da capo form) of this Mass, as do concertante passages. The *Missa Pastoril para a Noite de Natal* (1811) recalls the Mass-settings of Cherubini; it calls for nine solo singers and a four-part (SATB) chorus, accompanied by an orchestra without violins. The elaboration of the viola parts indicates the presence in Rio of accomplished violists at that time. The rather low tessitura of the orchestral accompaniment reappears in subsequent works. The opening of the Gloria illustrates the impact of operatic models upon the composer's sacred music, not only through the three-measure instrumental introduction (clarinets) but in the initial unison choral phrase (Example 3-5). The arias are highly ornamented and virtuosic. The

EXAMPLE 3-5   José Maurício Nunes Garcia, *Missa Pastoril* (1811): Gloria, mm.
1–4. From Cleofe Person de Mattos, *Catálogo temático das obras do Padre José
Maurício Nunes Garcia* (Rio de Janeiro: Ministério da Educação e Cultura, 1970),
p. 159. Quoted by permission.

original manuscript indicates that the soprano parts were intended for
castrati, some of whom had been brought over with the royal court.

The choral treatment in José Maurício's early works is generally more
refined than in later ones and responds to a clear desire for devotional
expression. Almost all the early motets, graduals, and pieces for Holy Week,
among others, reveal varying degrees of this intention, as in an a cappella
Crux Fidelis (ca. 1805) whose expression is enhanced by chromaticism in a
prevailing homophonic texture (Example 3-6).

Most of the composer's sacred works are for four mixed voices with
orchestral accompaniment. Very few call for a cappella performance. Until
about 1800, José Maurício frequently used an orchestra of strings and a few
woodwinds (in general flutes and horns), but after about 1808 his orchestra
most typically included woodwinds in pairs, two trumpets, an occasional
trombone, and strings. A clarinet added to the ensemble around that time is
the woodwind most in evidence in his later works. Influences of the Viennese
Classic style are found together with a continuation of Baroque practices.
It is known that a splendid music library was at José Maurício's disposal,
with copies of the best classic European works of the time; it is not surprising, therefore, that he had a perfect knowledge of contemporaneous European
musical practices.

Masses form the backbone of José Maurício's output. Of some
thirty-two settings known to have been written, nineteen are extant, exclud-

ing the Masses for the Dead and for Holy Week services. Ten separate Credos listed in the thematic catalogue of his works may be evidence that he wrote even more Mass-settings. Only seven of the extant Masses include all five parts of the Ordinary; and seven are limited to the Kyrie and the Gloria. Although diverse in treatment, the Masses present the following general characteristics. The proportions of the various sections follow a more or less fixed pattern of a short Credo after monumental Kyrie and Gloria movements. José Maurício exhibits obvious preferences in the distribution of solo parts, in the character assigned to the various movements, and in the use of homophonic or imitative texture in specific sections. For example, the Christe eleison is often treated as a fugue or a fugato-like section. The Laudamus generally appears as a soprano solo or a duet. The Cum Sancto Spiritu is very often divided into two contrasting sections, a short and slow one followed by a fugal one on the same text or on "Amen." The settings postdating 1808 present fugato passages or real fugues more frequently than do the earlier ones. It has been pointed out, however,[19] that not all the elements of fugal procedure are present: a rather narrow modulatory scope marks the various expositions, and in the first exposition there is often

EXAMPLE 3-6 José Maurício Nunes Garcia, *Crux Fidelis*, mm. 1–8. From Cleofe Person de Mattos, *Catálogo temático das obras do Padre José Maurício Nunes Garcia* (Rio de Janeiro: Ministério da Educação e Cultura, 1970), p. 300. Quoted by permission.

[19]By Cleofe Person de Mattos, *Catálogo Temático das Obras do Padre José Maurício Nunes Garcia* (Rio de Janeiro: Ministério da Educação e Cultura, 1970), p. 357.

material in a contrapuntal voice that does not function as countersubject. Also, José Maurício rarely uses stretto and seldom follows the eighteenth-century practices of fugal writing.

Among the several settings for funeral services, the Requiem Mass of 1816 is considered the composer's work of highest artistic significance. Indeed, it is one of the most successful Masses ever written in the Americas. Apparently commissioned by D. João VI for the funeral rites of Queen Maria I, the Mass represents the noble and grandiose character of courtly funeral music of the time, although it is not devoid of religious eloquence. Written originally for four-part chorus and soloists, with strings, two clarinets, two horns, and "flutes, trumpets and kettledrums ad libitum" (as mentioned in the autograph), this work presents a great deal of thematic repetition in the various movements, suggesting that it was composed in a short period of time. The Dies Irae is quite elaborate, with unusual proportions. As a sample of the style of this Mass, the beginning measures of the Introit, the Kyrie, and the Dies Irae are reproduced in Examples 3-7a, 7b, and 7c.

FIGURE 3-2 José Maurício Nunes Garcia. *Missa dos Defuntos.* "Composta pelo Pe. José Mauricio Nunes Garcia, no anno 1816. com Flautas, clarins e Timballes ad Libitum" (Escola de Música da Universidade Federal do Rio de Janeiro Library).

EXAMPLE 3-7a José Maurício Nunes Garcia, *Missa dos Defuntos* (1816):
Requiem aeternam, mm. 1–5. From Cleofe Person de Mattos, *Catálogo temático das
obras do Padre José Maurício Nunes Garcia* (Rio de Janeiro: Ministério da Educação
e Cultura, 1970), p. 269. Quoted by permission.

EXAMPLE 3-7b José Maurício Nunes Garcia, *Missa dos Defuntos* (1816): Kyrie
eleison, mm. 1–5. From Cleofe Person de Mattos, *Catálogo temático das obras do
Padre José Maurício Nunes Garcia* (Rio de Janeiro: Ministério da Educação e
Cultura, 1970), p. 269. Quoted by permission.

EXAMPLE 3-7c José Maurício Nunes Garcia, *Missa dos Defuntos* (1816): Dies irae, mm. 1–7. From Cleofe Person de Mattos, *Catálogo temático das obras do Padre José Maurício Nunes Garcia* (Rio de Janeiro: Ministério da Educação e Cultura, 1970), p. 269. Quoted by permission.

The few extant examples of José Maurício's orchestral music include the overture *Zemira*, a *Sinfonia* in D, the *Sinfonia Fúnebre*, and the *Sinfonia Tempestade*; these follow mostly the form and character of Italian operatic overtures of the time. Of the secular vocal works, only a *Coro para o entremês*, choral numbers for the drama *O triunfo da América*, and *Ulissea, Drama Eroico*, remain. The only work that reached print (and, at that, seven years after his death) was the *modinha* "Beijo a mão que me condena."

The Brazilian *modinha*, a type of love song in many ways similar to the French vocal romance of the eighteenth century, probably originated in the colony. Thanks to the popularity of the Brazilian poet and priest Domingos Caldas Barbosa (1738–1800), the prevailing types of *modinha* in the late eighteenth-century salons of Lisbon (as of Rio de Janeiro) were those of Brazil. A manuscript collection of anonymous *Modinhas do Brazil* (MS 1596, Ajuda Library, Lisbon) contains perhaps the earliest specimens known, the texts of which can be attributed to Caldas Barbosa.[20] The thirty songs of the collection are mostly duets, with a prevailingly syllabic setting of the text and, on the whole, systematically syncopated vocal lines. In addition,

---

[20]A full description of the collection is given in Béhague, "Biblioteca da Ajuda (Lisbon) MSS 1595/1596: Two Eighteenth-Century Anonymous Collections of Modinhas," *Yearbook*, Inter-American Institute for Musical Research, IV (1968), 44ff. See also Mozart de Araújo, *A Modinha e o Lundu no século XVIII* (São Paulo: Ricordi Brasileira, 1963).

almost all are written in duple meter and show a constant parallel motion in thirds and/or sixths, which is also a feature of most printed *modinhas* "a duo," as found in the *Jornal de Modinhas*, published regularly at Lisbon from 1792 to 1795 by the Frenchmen Marchal and Milcent. The instrumental accompaniment of many printed *modinhas* is a complete harpsichord or piano part, but as a rule only a bass line (often with figures) is supplied; according to contemporary accounts, it was performed on a guitar. In Ajuda MS 1596, the character of the accompaniment (broken-chord figures, arpeggios, occasional figured bass) suggests the original guitar accompaniment rather than the more refined harpsichord part of the printed *modinhas*. In this respect Modinha No. 8 of the collection, "Quem ama para agravar," attracts one's attention by the following annotation in the manuscript: "Este acompanhamento devese tocar pela Bahia" ("This accompaniment must be played around Bahia"), because the style of this accompaniment is associated with Brazil. Indeed, the bass line exhibits in the first section the syncopated figure ♪♪ ♩ , recognized as a trait of New World Black musical tradition. In other pieces of the collection, the vocal line systematizes another rhythmic procedure very close to the Brazilian musical vernacular: a simple suspension (by ties over the barline) used at cadential points, producing a feminine ending for the phrase (see Example 3-8a). The same procedure, again involving ties over the barline, is heard in the first measures of Example 3-8b, in a subtle variation on the basic formula, which became a cliché a century later in most early composed sambas.

Related to the *modinha* was the *lundu*. Originally an Afro-Brazilian dance, it too became in the late eighteenth century a popular genre of dance and song cultivated in the aristocratic salons of Rio and Lisbon. By the 1830s the *lundu* song of the urban areas was very reminiscent of the sentimental character of the salon *modinha*.[21]

EXAMPLE 3-8a Anonymous *modinha:* "Os me deixas que tu das," mm. 1–3.

EXAMPLE 3-8b Anonymous *modinha:* "Eu nasi sem coração," mm. 1–5.

[21]See Mário de Andrade, *Modinhas Imperiais* (São Paulo: Casa Chiarato, 1930), and "Cândido Inácio da Silva e o lundu," *Revista Brasileira de Música*, X (1944), 17–39.

SÃO PAULO

Although the city of São Paulo was founded in 1554, its first documented musical references date only from 1611, when the cathedral was established. From that time it maintained a chapelmaster whose duties included musical composition and instruction. Manoel Pais Linhares, Manoel Vieira de Barros, and Manoel Lopes de Siqueira served the cathedral in the seventeenth century, and Angelo de Siqueira, Mathias Alvares Torres, Antonio Manso da Mota, and André da Silva Gomes in the eighteenth. Gomes (b. Lisbon 1752) occupied the post for almost fifty years (1774–1822) and dominated the musical life in the city during that period, which coincided with the installment of the third bishop, Dom Frei Manoel da Resurreição, who promoted brilliant religious feasts. Some eighty-seven works by Gomes are extant in the archive of the Metropolitan Curia and the São Paulo Conservatory library; additional works exist in smaller towns within the state of São Paulo. Gomes's fame is attested to by his collaboration with the Municipal Chamber on certain feasts, such as S. Sebastian and Corpus Christi, and with the flourishing brotherhoods of the Ordem Terceira do Carmo and the Santíssimo Sacramento. Although Gomes's creative period extended, according to present knowledge, from 1784 to 1823, most of his works maintain late Baroque stylistic practices, including the occasional use of a basso continuo. His *Missa a 8 Vozes e Instrumentos*, consisting of Kyrie and Gloria alone, displays a solid contrapuntal knowledge, including an imaginative eight-voice fugue in Kyrie II and another in the Cum Sancto Spiritu, well-balanced antiphonal writing (Gloria, Domine Deus), and a general harmonic richness.

BIBLIOGRAPHICAL NOTES

There are general histories of music in Brazil by Guilherme de Melo, *A Música no Brasil*, 2nd ed. (Rio de Janeiro: Imprensa Nacional, 1947), and Renato Almeida, *História da Música Brasileira*, 2nd ed. (Rio de Janeiro: F. Briguiet e Compania, 1942). More specific studies, besides those mentioned in footnotes, are Régis Duprat, "A Música na Bahia Colonial," *Revista de História*, no. 61 (1965), 93–116; and Hebe Machado Brasil, *A Música na Cidade do Salvador, 1549–1900* (Salvador: Prefeitura Municipal do Salvador, 1969). Historical references to music in the sixteenth and seventeenth centuries are gathered in Pe. Jaime Diniz, "Uma Notícia sobre a Música no Brasil dos séculos XVI e XVII," *Estudos Universitários* (Revista da Universidade

Federal de Pernambuco), no. 2 (April–June 1972), 41–57. A review of the activities of Bahian organists is provided in Diniz, "Velhos Organistas da Bahia, 1559–1745," *Universitas*, no. 10 (September–December 1971), 5–42. Régis Duprat gives a useful review of musicological research in Brazilian colonial music in his article "Metodologia da pesquisa histórico-musical no Brasil," *Anais de História* (Faculdade de Filosofia, Ciências e Letras de Assis, São Paulo), no. 4 (1972), 101–8. Francisco Curt Lange's studies of Minas Gerais's colonial music and musicians are numerous; particularly informative, besides the items mentioned in footnotes, are his articles "La Música en Villa Rica (Minas Gerais, siglo XVIII)," *Revista Musical Chilena*, nos. 102 and 103 (1967–68), 8–55 and 77–149, respectively; "A Música em Sabará," *Estudos Históricos*, no. 5 (December 1966), 97–198; and "As Danças Coletivas Públicas no Período Colonial Brasileiro e as Danças das Corporações de Ofícios em Minas Gerais," *Barroco*, no. 1 (1969), 15–62. Music at Rio de Janeiro in the late eighteenth and early nineteenth centuries is the subject of Lange's "Pesquisas Esporádicas de Musicologia no Rio de Janeiro," *Revista do Instituto de Estudos Brasileiros* (São Paulo), no. 4 (1968), 99–142. The composer André da Silva Gomes's activities in São Paulo are studied in Clovis de Oliveira, *André da Silva Gomes (1752–1844)* (São Paulo, 1954) and Régis Duprat, "Música na matriz e Sé de São Paulo Colonial," *Yearbook for Inter-American Musical Research*, xi (1975) [1977], 8–68. A complete bibliography and discography for José Maurício Nunes Garcia is given in the thematic catalogue of the composer's works compiled by Cleofe Person de Mattos (pp. 393–99).

No anthology of Brazilian colonial music is as yet available. Three works by composers from Minas Gerais are published in *Archivo de Música Religiosa de la 'Capitania Geral das Minas Gerais' (Siglo XVIII), Brasil*, ed. by Lange (Mendoza: Universidad Nacional de Cuyo, 1951). Also available is Damião Barbosa de Araújo, "Memento Baiano para côro e orquestra: estudo introdutório, restauração e revisão de Jaime C. Diniz," *Estudos Baianos*, no. 2 (1970), 1–30. José Maurício Nunes Garcia's *Opera Omnia* is being edited in Rio de Janeiro, under the direction of Cleofe Person de Mattos, but the first volume has not yet been published.

The few recordings of Brazilian colonial music are available for the most part only on Brazilian labels. Music of Minas Gerais appear on two records, *Mestres do Barroco Mineiro* (Festa LDR 5005, 5006). Alvares Pinto's *Te Deum* was recorded and released in 1968 (Rozenblit CLP 80.032). André da Silva Gomes's *Missa* is available on Festa IG 79.501. Other works of the colonial repertory appear in *Música Sul-Americana do Século XVIII* (Chantecler CMG 1030). Five albums make up the series *Música na Côrte Brasileira* (extending into post-colonial music period) (Angel 3 CBX-410–414). Finally, José Maurício's Requiem Mass is now available on U.S. Columbia M-33431, in the series titled *Black Composers Series.*

part two

The Rise of Nationalism

FOUR

NINETEENTH-CENTURY ANTECEDENTS
OF NATIONALISM

Throughout Latin America, the period between 1810 and 1830 marked the beginnings of national independence, which was to have considerable influence on the musical life of the emerging nations. These two decades were a time of gradual transition during which the sentiment of nationalism shaped fundamentally the sociopolitical organization of the new countries. Colonial institutions were maintained, however, well into the nineteenth century, if not in theory at least in practice. In the arts, the concept of nationalism developed only after the mid-century. During the first half of the century, most countries witnessed a conscious effort to develop artistic activity with the assistance and promotion of local artists. Organization musically took the form of the establishment of national music institutions and conservatories and the erection of theaters for opera performance (in which, however, foreign professionals and visiting virtuosi still dominated). A definable national musical style appeared only in the last decades of the century, under the influence of similar trends in Europe and the emergence of musical genres with folk and popular characteristics which could constitute an obvious source of national identity.

Opera and lighter musical theater, songs, and piano music dominated the cultivated musical life, which in general reflected that of Europe. With some notable exceptions, symphonic and chamber music became possible only during the latter part of the century, which also saw the rise of virtuosi, especially pianists.

MEXICO

As elsewhere in the hemisphere during the nineteenth century, Italian opera dominated the Mexican musical scene. This development in opera was unmatched by other genres, primarily because, until the end of the century, concert life was guided by persons lacking in a professional understanding of music. At first the cultivated genres were Spanish-derived (zarzuela, *tonadilla escénica, sainete*), but the Coliseo Nuevo theater, which had been presenting such works since 1735, went into bankruptcy during the revolutionary period. Only after independence (1821) were Mexican operas produced.

The composer most prominent during the revolutionary period was José Mariano Elízaga (1786–1842), who was also influential in the nascent field of music education in Mexico. A child prodigy, he was sent from his native city of Morelia to the capital for study at the choir school of the Mexico City Cathedral (Colegio de Infantes de Coro). He went back to Mexico City later for further study under the well-known teacher Soto Carrillo. At thirteen he became third organist of the Morelia cathedral. General Iturbide had him appointed imperial chapelmaster in the capital city in 1822. There he founded in 1825 a music conservatory (which, however, had only a brief existence) and wrote two influential theoretical treatises, *Elementos de música* (1823) and *Principios de la armonía y de la melodía* (1835), the latter an introduction to the study of four-part harmony. His efforts toward providing the new republic with solid foundations for music education have been compared to those of Lowell Mason in the United States, but during his lifetime, at least, they were in vain because of what he called the "disgracefully low level" of Mexican music at the time. More likely, however, Elízaga was insensitive to the real needs of his country in music education in the post-revolutionary period. After him, in 1866, the Sociedad Filarmónica Mexicana founded in Mexico City a conservatory that eventually developed into the government-subsidized Conservatorio Nacional de Música (1877). As a composer Elízaga wrote mostly sacred works which reveal his adherence to the Classical style.

Italian opera, sung in Italian, was popularized in Mexico by Manuel

García, whose company had been successful in introducing foreign-language opera to New York in 1825. In 1831 the Teatro Principal began to hold a regular annual season of Italian opera, and, by mid-century, local composers were embarking on careers as composers of Italian opera. Among the better known were Luis Baca (1826–1855), Cenobio Paniagua (1821–1882), and Melesio Morales (1838–1908); their operas, to Italian libretti, were generally adequate imitations of the original models. The opera *Guatimotzin* by Aniceto Ortega (1823–1875), premiered in 1871 with the Mexican soprano Angela Peralta, is generally considered to have been the first serious attempt to incorporate some native elements within the prevailing Italian format. The libretto, which romanticized an Aztec theme, appealed to the nationalist sentiment of the time.

A very large number of pianist-composers (works by over three hundred are in the library of the Conservatorio Nacional) cultivated salon-music genres and European-style Romantic piano music during the latter part of the century. The most popular salon-music composer was Juventino Rosas (1868–1894), an Otomí Indian and author of a set of waltzes in the tradition of French salon-music: *Sobre las olas*, which acquired a resounding fame throughout the world. European salon dances—polkas, mazurkas, schottisches, waltzes—constituted the musical vogue, reflecting the cultural dependence on Europe of the Mexican urban middle class of the time.

The piano virtuosi during the dictatorship of Porfirio Díaz (1877–1910) included Tomás León (1826–1893), Julio Ituarte (1845–1905), Ernesto Elorduy (1853–1912), and Felipe Villanueva (1862–1893). As the very concept of nationalism in the arts stemmed from European Romanticism, it is with these Romantic pianists that the first vernacular elements appeared in Mexican music. Piano arrangements of folk or popular dances and songs were common even before 1850. The *jarabe* particularly, which became the most popular national dance following independence, received the attention of many salon composers. José Antonio Gómez, active at Mexico City, wrote a series of virtuoso variations (actually a fantasy) using a *jarabe* as his theme (1841). Tomás León followed suit in his *Jarabe nacional* (ca. 1860), as did Ituarte in *Ecos de México* (ca. 1880), which is a stylized arrangement of popular materials and, according to Mayer-Serra, the first example of the integration of Mexican melodies within a "representative [i.e., characteristically Mexican] style."[1] The national airs contained in this piece include *El Palomo, El Perico, Los Enanos, El Butaquito, El Guajito,* and *Las Mañanitas,* and Ituarte attempted to preserve the character of each song. The refrain of *El Perico,* for example—"pica, pica, pica, perico" ("peck, peck, peck, para-

[1]Otto Mayer-Serra, *Panorama de la Música Mexicana* (México: El Colegio de México, 1941), p. 126.

keet")—is conveyed by means of rapid staccatos on a repeated tone, to a light accompaniment (Example 4-1a). Similarly, Ituarte captures the spirit of the burlesque text of *Los Enanos* by contrasting the somewhat grotesque melody

EXAMPLE 4-1a   Julio Ituarte, *Ecos de México:* "Allegretto," to the tune *El Perico*. From Otto Mayer-Serra, *Panorama de la Música Mexicana* (México: El Colegio de México, 1941), p. 128.

EXAMPLE 4-1b   Julio Ituarte, *Ecos de México:* "Allegretto," to the tune *Los Enanos*. From Otto Mayer-Serra, *Panorama de la Música Mexicana* (México: El Colegio de México, 1941), p. 129.

(in octaves in the bass) with a three-octave repetition of a single note in the high register (Example 4-1b). *Ecos de México* illustrates the sort of garb in which popular music had to be clothed to make it presentable to concert audiences. Ituarte also wrote a collection of one hundred *habanera* dances, entitled *Bouquet de flores*.

Elorduy and Villanueva cultivated the *danza* (or *contradanza*) *mexicana*, following the model of the Cuban *contradanzas* of Manuel Saumell and Ignacio Cervantes. The Cuban *contradanza*, which developed in the late eighteenth and early nineteenth centuries, was the source of many other Cuban popular dances (such as the *danza*, the *habanera*, and the *danzón*) that were extremely influential throughout Latin America. The *contradanza* emphasized for the first time such typical Afro-Cuban (as well as Dominican, Puerto Rican, and Haitian) syncopations as ♫ ♫♩♫♩♩ . The rhythmic figure ♩. ♩♫♩ (often called *habanera*) also appeared in the early nineteenth-century Cuban *contradanzas*; this conspicuous figure was also, however, the rhythmic foundation of the *tango andaluz* and had been present in Mexican dances of the colonial period. Whatever the historical priority may have been, with Villanueva's and Elorduy's piano pieces the *danza mexicana* emerged as a type of stylized popular music. Their pieces are in a two-part form, with evenly divided and contrasting sections (each eight measures long, and to be repeated). Four- or eight-measure phrase lengths are the norm. Example 4-2, from Villanueva's *Danzas humorísticas*, illustrates the rhythmic combinations (with syncopations and cross-meters) in two of these pieces, which feature a variant of the habanera rhythm (♪. ♪♫♩). The use of polymeter (2/4

EXAMPLE 4-2 Felipe Villanueva, *Danzas humorísticas:* (a) "Venus," mm. 9–15; (b) "Enredo," mm. 20–26. From Rubén M. Campos, *El folklore musical de las ciudades* (Mexico: Publicaciones de la Secretaría de Educación Pública, 1930), pp. 408 and 399.

versus 3/4) is significant, for it reveals the composer's awareness of the "national" quality of hemiola. Virtuosity per se tends to disappear in such works in favor of a more intimate salon style.

Ricardo Castro (1864–1907), the most successful of the Mexican piano virtuosi, had two of his works (the Piano Concerto and the opera *La Légende de Rudel*) published in Germany. In 1903 he went to Europe for study and succeeded immediately in having his Cello Concerto performed in Paris. A concert by him at the Salle Erard won the praise of *Le Figaro* and *Le Monde Musical*. His Piano Concerto, presented at Brussels in 1904, was termed by a local critic "a dashing and effective work." Indeed, Castro's works were effective because he had mastered the conventions of European music of the time. *La Légende de Rudel* (1906), with a libretto translated into Italian for its Mexican première, got an uneven reception, but Gustavo Campa (1863–1934), composer of the opera *Le Roi Poète* (1901) and of piano music, praised it as Castro's best work, full of feeling and technical competence. Campa was himself strongly influenced by Saint-Saëns and Massenet.

Most Mexicans have looked at this nineteenth-century musical production of operas and piano music as a barren imitation of Europe. Understandably, twentieth-century composers such as Chávez, Sandi, and others have repudiated this period of art music in Mexico because of its alienation from Mexican culture. Even a Mexican musicologist such as Otto Mayer-Serra shared this view, being willing to make exceptions only for Villanueva and Elorduy, since they opened the way with their *danzas* for Manuel M. Ponce, the father of Mexican musical nationalism.

CUBA AND PUERTO RICO

Music teaching and publishing began in Cuba during the first years of the nineteenth century. Music at the Havana cathedral seems to have reached its apogee around that time, although specific studies of the historical and music archives of the cathedral are lacking. The first *Academia de Música* was founded in 1814, followed by the *Academia de Música Santa Cecilia* in 1816. One of the first pieces of music published in Cuba was a *contradanza*, *San Pascual Bailón*; it was followed by works in other popular musical genres such as the *guaracha* and *bolero*. However, as in other regions of Latin America, salon music soon dominated sheet-music publishing, and Italian and French opera dominated the theaters (Teatro Principal, Teatro Tacón, Liceo Artístico y Literario) and concert halls of philharmonic associations. Numerous European and Cuban opera composers provided a large repertory until the beginning of the twentieth century. Among the most successful was Laureano Fuentes Matons (1825–1898), author of *La Hija de Jefté* (1875) and four zarzuelas but more successful in religious and symphonic music.[2] Gaspar Villate (1851–1912), who studied at the Paris Conservatoire under Bazin and Danhauser, had three of his operas premiered in Europe with considerable success (*Zilia*, Paris, 1877; *La Czarine*, The Hague, 1880; and *Baltazar*, Madrid, 1885). In addition, Villate cultivated salon-music genres, including many examples of the "criolla" *contradanza*, for which he is better remembered than for his operas.

Antonio Raffelín (1796–1882) and Nicolás Ruíz Espadero (1832–1890) are the two major Cuban figures representing Classic and Romantic styles, respectively. Raffelín cultivated symphonic and chamber music and, later in his life, sacred music with excellent technical achievement. Espadero, many of of whose works were performed in Europe by his good friend Louis Moreau Gottschalk, developed a typically Romantic piano style, including fashionable fantasies on operatic themes. On rare occasions he turned to the vernacular, as in his piece *Chant du Guagiro*, published in Paris with the subtitle "grande scène caractéristique cubaine." Cuban traits are conveyed in this piece through an interesting repetition of cross-rhythms, but they finally yield to the banal virtuosic figuration of so many of Espadero's other piano works.

It was with Manuel Saumell (1817–1870) and, later, Ignacio Cervantes (1847–1905) that the first decisive steps toward musical nationalism in Cuba were taken. As early as 1839 Saumell had the intention of writing a national opera that would stress certain aspects of Cuban folkways, but he never carried it out. He was at his best in the small piano piece of the Cuban *contradanza* type, and wrote more than fifty exquisite examples in which his "rhythmic and melodic invention . . . is prodigious."[3] In 2/4 or 6/8, these works reveal an extraordinary variety of rhythmic combinations. Their

---

[2]According to such critics as the Cuban writer Alejo Carpentier, who considers Fuentes's sacred music production his best contribution. See Carpentier, *La Música en Cuba* (México: Fondo de Cultura Económica, 1946), p. 257.
[3]Ibid, p. 260.

second sections generally present the most "national character," by means of rhythmic figuration. Certain rhythmic patterns later developed into dance formulas were firmly established by Saumell. For example, the Cuban *danzón*, as cultivated by urban popular composers (with the tango figure ♩. ♪♫♩ , over which are superimposed constant sixteenth-note pulsations: ♬♬ , appears in measures 5-8 of *La Tedezco* (Example 4-3). In many of Saumell's *contradanzas* in 6/8, the figure ♩ ♫♩ occurs frequently in the second sections; this was later to become the rhythmic foundation of such popular genres as the *clave*, *guajira*, and *criolla*. Called the "father of the *contradanza*," Saumell did indeed create a style, in which rhythmic interest prevailed, quite removed from the virtuosic and superficial salon style of his time.

EXAMPLE 4-3   Manuel Saumell, *La Tedezco* (Contradanza), mm. 5–8.

Ignacio Cervantes, the most important nineteenth-century Cuban composer from a technical as well as an aesthetic point of view, was a student of Espadero in Havana, then of Marmontel and Alkan at the Paris Conservatoire. His solid musical training prevented him from succumbing to the fashion of the time for virtuosity; he also became the first Cuban to handle the orchestra like a professional composer, although his orchestral works are not as significant as those for the piano. He had a successful career as a concert pianist in Cuba, in Europe, and in the United States. Among his many works, the twenty-one *Danzas Cubanas* for piano (1875–1895), many of which are real *contradanzas*, constitute his best achievement within the early nationalistic trend. He followed the pioneering efforts of Saumell, incorporating musical elements of both Afro-Cuban and Guajiro traditions into a Romantic piano style. Although they have a clear affinity with Chopinesque harmony, these pieces are undoubtedly the most original contribution to nineteenth-century Cuban art music. Cervantes maintains the two-part form (with sixteen-measure sections) of the *contradanza* and follows the rhythmic patterns associated with the tango and habanera. The rhythmic anticipations typical of the *son cubano* appear in many of his *danzas* (e.g., *Zigs-Zags*). Example 4-4 reveals some of the most characteristic national traits in Cervantes's danzas. The bass line of the first four measures is founded on the most conspicuous Afro-American type of syncopation, conveyed here with ties over the bar lines. Popular throughout the hemisphere, this figure is a variant of the Cuban *conga* rhythmic formula. Measures 25ff (Example 4-4b) provide a good illustration of the most characteristic figure of Cuban folk and popular music, the rhythm ♩ ♪♪♪♫ or ♩ ♫ ♫ , known as the *cinquillo*, which appears in a number of Afro-Caribbean dances and is the basis for much ritual drumming. Melodically, Cervantes has an obvious preference for feminine phrase endings and frequently uses melodic sequences at fairly widely spaced intervals.

Besides its intrinsic qualities, Cervantes's music foreshadowed a new awareness of Cuban folk and popular music by Cuban composers; this made possible the further development in the 1920s of a Cuban musical nationalism based on the deepest cultural roots of the country, specifically "Afrocubanismo."

In Puerto Rico, several composers of the second half of the nineteenth century turned their attention to the *danza puertorriqueña*, which began to

EXAMPLE 4-4   Ignacio Cervantes, *Danzas Cubanas* (a) mm. 4–8; (b) m. 25.

(a)

(b)

appear with this name in popular compositions of the 1830s. The actual origin of the *danza* has not been precisely determined. There is little doubt, however, that the Cuban *contradanza, habanera,* and *guaracha* and the Puerto Rican *seis* (the most widespread folk dance, with several sub-types according to choreographic traits) were influential in the characterization of the *danza.* From the Cuban popular forms, the *danza* may have inherited such typical rhythmic formulas as ♩. ♪♩ ♪♩ and ♪♩♩ ♩ ; from the *seis* and the *guaracha,* the prevailing triplet figures ♫♫ ♪♩ and ♪ ♫♫ ♪♩ , mixed with syncopated binary figures. Always in duple meter, the *danza* is in sectional forms, generally alternating several sections of eight or sixteen measures. Among the various composers who cultivated the *danza,* Juan Morel Campos (1857–1896) was the most creative and influential. Of some 550 works attributed to him, about half are *danzas* for the piano. These reveal a diversified treatment of the popular form, but the two dominant varieties are the stylized, highly Romantic *danza* and the popular *danza criolla.* The first type includes pieces with long phrases, three- or four-part varied harmonies, a few virtuoso passages, and a strongly sentimental character. The second type is simpler, with short, isometric phrases, incisive rhythmic patterns, and less emphasis on harmony. The generally vivacious and often witty character of this latter type brings it close to its popular counterpart. To this type belong such pieces as *No me toques, La Bulliciosa, La Majabaca, El Torbellino;* the Romantic type includes such pieces as *La Lila, Alma sublime, Felices dias, Vano empeño,* and *La Niña Bonita.*

ARGENTINA

Argentina's music activities were much more important during the nineteenth century than during the colonial era. During the revolutionary period, patriotic and theater music accompanied important national events. During the first half of the century, Argentine musical life was intensified with the creation of new musical associations, especially in the capital city of Buenos Aires. Music was concentrated primarily in the churches, opera houses, and, to a lesser degree, philharmonic societies. Salon music also flourished. Among the musicians associated with the Buenos Aires cathedral during this period, the chapelmaster José Antonio Picasarri (1769–1843) was a major influence on musical life of the capital city: he taught the first Argentine professional musicians, founded musical societies, and organized instrumental ensembles. He inaugurated the Escuela de Música y Canto in 1822, under the auspices of the minister (later president) Rivadavia. He also helped to found the Sociedad Filarmónica (1822), of which he became the director, and premiered important works such as Beethoven's *Missa Solemnis* (in 1836). His nephew, Juan Pedro Esnaola (1808–1878), an accomplished pianist and composer, cultivated the European Romantic idiom in his songs and symphonic and choral music (including an *Himno a Rosas*, referring to the Argentine dictator). Other well-known Romantic composers of the time, including Amancio Alcorta (1805–1862) and Juan Bautista Alberdi (1810–1884), wrote many salon pieces for piano, among them minuets, waltzes, polkas, and *contradanzas*. Alcorta's grandson, Alberto Williams, considered the precursor of Argentine musical nationalism, found Alcorta's works slightly nationalistic "in spite of their overwhelmingly Rossinian influence."[4]

Salon music developed in Argentina especially during the period 1830–1850. Among the types of salon music for piano, dances of European origin with some local adaptation, such as the *Minué Montonero* or *Nacional*, were particularly fashionable during this period, as were fantasias and variations on operatic arias. But at the same time the popular tradition of song and poetry of the *gauchos* (the *vaqueros* of the pampas) began to be explored in Argentina's urban areas. Sarmiento's *Facundo* (1845), the first major literary work to romanticize the *gaucho*, described the various dances and songs of the pampas—the *gato*, *vidalita*, *triste*, and others; these were the major sources to which the first nationalist composers were later to turn. Ever since the revolutionary period, the *gaucho* character had symbolized the national folk, but during the Rosas regime the *gaucho* came to epitomize Argentina herself. It was only natural that the music of the *payadores* and *gaucho* guitarists exerted a profound influence on art-music composers who had nationalistic concerns.

Opera in Buenos Aires had begun during the eighteenth century. The Teatro de Operas y Comedias (opened in 1757), followed by the Teatro de la Ranchería (1783), presented *tonadillas* and zarzuelas. Italian opera, however, began to appear regularly in the 1820s—as at the Teatro Coliseo (established 1824), for example, where Rossini's *Il Barbiere di Siviglia* was produced in 1825. The popularity of Italian and French opera and lighter genres was such that no fewer than ten theaters opened during the century. In 1854, perhaps as the result of rivalry between an Italian and a French opera troupe, thirty operas were produced in Buenos Aires, half by Italian composers (Rossini, Donizetti, Ricci, Mercadante, and Verdi), and half by French (Auber, Halévy, Hérold, Meyerbeer, Thomas, and others). The original Teatro Colón opened in 1857; it was followed by the establishment of the Teatro de la Opera (1872), the Teatro Politeama (1879), and the Teatro Nacional (1882). Thereafter, major European and local companies continuously ensured Buenos Aires's status as a major opera center of the world. (The new Teatro Colón, which would become internationally famed, was to open in 1908.)

[4]Alberto Williams, "Amancio Alcorta," *Antología de Compositores Argentinos* (Buenos Aires, 1941).

During the latter part of the nineteenth century, Argentine opera and piano music began to be extensively produced, mostly in Buenos Aires. Two composers representative of this period were Francisco A. Hargreaves (1849–1900) and Juan Gutiérrez (1840–1906). Hargreaves, an opera composer, was one of the first Argentine musicians to draw on folk-music sources. The grandson of an American established in Buenos Aires since 1819, he studied piano with local professional musicians, then with Maglioni at the Royal Musical Institute in Florence. His first published work was a "polka de concert" for piano (four hands), titled *El Pampero*. His lyric work *La Gatta Bianca*, premiered in Italy in 1875, was at the time considered the first truly Argentine opera. He received an honorific prize for his second opera, *El Vampiro* (1876). While he wrote numerous piano pieces in a virtuoso salon style (e.g., *Les Larmes du Coeur* and *Gouttes de Rosée*), he also paid attention to *música criolla* ("native music"). He is often considered in Argentina as a pioneer of national music because he stylized such typical folk songs and dances as the *gato*, *estilo*, *vidalita*, *décima*, and *cielito* in his *Aires Nacionales* (ca. 1880), for piano. Among these, one of the most popular was the caprice *El Gato*, "Baile Nacional del Gaucho Argentino," which was known in Europe, Peru, and Chile. The *gato* in its authentic setting is a dance accompanied by singing to a guitar or by instruments alone (guitar, harp, accordion). The prevailing meter is 6/8 and the major mode frequent, especially in the sung versions. Hargreaves's *El Gato*, even in all its Romantic stylization, tends to maintain some of the traits of the original model. His "danzas habaneras" *Chinita*, *Negrita*, and *Catita* were written in a pianistic style somewhat analogous to Gottschalk's.

The period after about 1880 was decisive in the professional musical life of Argentina. Some thirty important musical societies to promote symphonic, choral, chamber, and stage music were established in Buenos Aires alone during the second half of the century. This development encouraged the appearance of visiting virtuosi such as Thalberg, Napoleão, Gottschalk, Ritter, and Sarasate, among many others. In addition, a series of "National Concerts" organized in Buenos Aires between 1874 and 1882 introduced a large number of local professional musicians and gained them initial recognition. By the end of the century, several symphonic works with some national character had been produced and performed. The band director and composer Saturnino F. Berón (1847–1898), for example, included various national dances (such as the *pericón*) in his symphonic poem *La Pampa*, premiered at the old Teatro Colón with considerable success in 1878. Likewise, Arturo Berutti (1862–1938) composed a *Sinfonía Argentina* in 1890, having already composed several piano works tinged with national elements, such as the *Seis Danzas Americanas* (1887). Although he lived half of his life in the twentieth century, Berutti belonged esthetically and stylistically to the nineteenth, as did so many of his contemporaries. He also followed a Romantic nationalist trend in his operas, among which *Pampa* (1897) and *Yupanki* (1899) draw on actual folk themes from the *gaucho* and Andean Indian folk traditions. Although the truly "national" content of these works is limited, they reveal the nationalistic tendency of the time.

The real thrust toward musical nationalism in Argentina came, however, with Alberto Williams (1862–1952), venerated as the progenitor of Argentine national music. During his long and very productive life, Williams exerted a fundamental influence in the entire country. Born in Buenos Aires, he was (as mentioned earlier) the grandson of Amancio Alcorta. He received his training at the School of Music of the Province of Buenos Aires (inaugurated in 1875), where he studied piano and music theory. In 1882, the Provincial government awarded him a scholarship which took him to the Paris Conservatoire and to composition study with César Franck, under whose influence he wrote his first compositions. Two of his early piano works, *Souvenir d'Enfance*, Op. 2, and *Première Mazurka*, Op. 3, were published in Paris in 1887. Soon after his return to Buenos Aires (1889), he took a vacation trip in the Buenos Aires province, acquainting himself with the country folk and the tunes, rhythms, and forms of their music. Of this trip, he later remarked:

> I wanted to saturate myself in the music of my homeland, so that I would not feel a stranger in it. I wanted to write music with an Argentine atmosphere, not just transcriptions, but art music of the native atmosphere, color, and essence. For this I went to the ranches of the Province of Buenos Aires, to learn the songs and dances of our gauchos. I had the chance to meet Julián Andrade, the companion of Juan Moreira, the great (popular) improviser. There I got to know authentic *payadores* [gaucho singers], of *chiripá* [typical gaucho trousers] and boots, vibrant native interpreters of *hueyas*, *gatos*, *zambas*, *vidalitas*, *tristes*, and *décimas*. . . .[5]

The result of this trip was *El Rancho Abandonado* (1890), Williams's first work to be inspired by *gaucho* folk music; it was to achieve wide popularity. From that time on, he strove to find and develop what has been called "the union of accent between the country *payador* and the cultured musician; one, the natural voice, the other, the intellectualized voice of the same land."[6] Williams's piano works reveal the extent to which he was able to establish this synthesis of distinctive modes of expression. The first album of the *Aires de la Pampa* (*Tres Hueyas*) appeared in 1893, followed by many others, to a total of over fifty pieces, including *vidalitas*, *gatos*, *cielitos*, *marotes*, *zambas*, and an especially large number of *milongas*. Williams's most characteristic

[5] As quoted in Vicente Gesualdo, *Historia de la Música en la Argentina* (Buenos Aires: Editorial Beta S.R.L., 1961), I, 526.
[6] Ibid., p. 527.

milongas tend to follow the danced folk *milonga,* related to the habanera and the tango, with their dotted rhythm, ♩. ♪ ♩ ♪ , and typical syncopation, ♪♪ ♩ , previously mentioned. Examples 4-5a and 4-5b, from Williams's Opus 63, show some of these rhythmic figures. The other folk type of *milonga*—a solo secular folk song to guitar accompaniment in a picked style ("punteado"), with 6/8 meter in the accompaniment and duple meter (2/4 or 4/8) in the vocal line—is also used by Williams, but less often.

In the development of Argentine musical nationalism it is significant that Williams chose to center his attention on the music of the *gauchos,* for the nationalist trend in the other arts of Argentina emphasized the so-called "gauchesco" tradition. In this connection it is pertinent to recall the dictum of Ricardo Rojas concerning the essence of Argentine nationalism, or *argentinidad*—namely, that this "is constituted by a territory, by a people, by a state, by a language, and by an ideal that tends to define itself better every day." In Argentine literature this ideal came to be embodied in the "gauchesco" tradition, of which the masterpiece is the epic poem *Martín Fierro* (1872) by José Hernández. Rojas (1882–1957) himself wrote the bible of the gauchesco tradition in his *History of Argentine Literature* (1917–1922), particularly the two volumes titled *Los Gauchescos,* in which he pays much attention to the folk music and dances of the pampa, with numerous musical examples. Musical composition was the last of the arts to identify itself with this tradition; when it did so, literature often served as the connecting link. (Several examples are presented in Chapter 7.)

EXAMPLE 4-5 Alberto Williams, *Milongas:* (a) "Bailarina Sandunguera," mm. 1–4; (b) "Equilibrista sobre botellas," mm. 1–4. Copyright 1951 by La Quena. Casa de Música S.R.L. Buenos Aires. Used by permission.

Besides his *Aires de la Pampa*, Williams evoked the various types of folk songs and dances associated with the pampa in many other works, such as the *Primera Sonata Argentina*, Op. 74 (1917), whose scherzo movement, titled "Malambo," later inspired similar treatment of that folk dance among nationalist composers. His orchestral works include additional references to the pampas, and some descriptive tone-poems cover the entire Argentine territory, from the Iguazú falls to the Antarctic (e.g., *Poema de los Mares Australes* and *Poema del Iguazú*). His three *Suites Argentinas*, for strings, represent a further attempt at a systematic "musicalization" of the Argentine scene. Williams also composed many works without a particular "national" character, including nine symphonies, all programmatic, in which the cyclical thematic usage inherited from Franck appears frequently, as well as certain impressionistic traits such as whole-tone scales and pentatonicism.

Williams was also an educator; his activities as such included the founding of the Buenos Aires Conservatory of Music (1893), later named the Conservatorio Williams, and the writing of music theory texts (*Teoría de la Música* and *Teoría de la Armonía*).

In spite of Williams's industry (his works run to 110 opus numbers) and a smooth craft acquired in Paris, our present perspective allows us to say that he remained musically remote from the cultural tradition that he attempted to evoke, mostly because of his academic orientation. The fact, however, that he did espouse musical nationalism and advocate its spread in his country makes him an important forerunner of the trend.

A stronger empathy for native music is reflected in the music of Julián Aguirre (1868–1924), two of whose Argentine dances for piano, *Gato* and *Huella*, as orchestrated and performed by Ernest Ansermet (1930), entered the international repertory. Though born in Buenos Aires, Aguirre spent his early years in Madrid, where he studied at the National Conservatory with Emilio Arrieta. He became an accomplished pianist and wrote some sixty pieces for piano, mostly in Argentine popular style (*Aires Nacionales Argentinos*). Upon returning to Argentina in 1887 he lived for some years in the provinces, making a firsthand study of Argentine folk music, unlike many other nationalist composers. His *Rapsodia Argentina*, for violin and piano, represents a more extended development of folkloristic elements than his previous works. The essence of Aguirre's music is *criollismo*—the native blending of European and American elements. Many composers have attempted this mixture, but the secret of the right blend, in addition to special skill and knowledge, lies in empathy. Perhaps Aguirre's empathy for *criollismo* was nourished by his formative years in Europe, where nationalism was one of the major trends. Particularly in Aguirre's small-scale instrumental pieces and his numerous songs (*Canciones Argentinas, Caminito, Cueca, Vidalita*, and others) can the results of *criolla* inspiration be judged; they constitute the true fountainhead of musical nationalism in Argentina.

BRAZIL

Even after the Portuguese royal court left Rio and returned to Portugal in 1821, the most important center of Brazilian musical activity remained the city of Rio de Janeiro, where the Emperors Pedro I and Pedro II maintained their permanent residence. But in comparison with the previous decades the 1820s were a period of decline. Both José Maurício and Marcos Portugal were old and relatively inactive. The Imperial Chapel (formerly the Royal Chapel) experienced such a deterioration that its orchestra was dissolved in 1831, with D. Pedro I's abdication; by 1838 the chapel's music personnel was reduced to twenty-seven persons—two chapelmasters, two organists, three instrumentalists and twenty singers. It was only in 1843 that the orchestra was reinstated, mostly under the influence of the most active composer of the first half of the century, Francisco Manuel da Silva (1795–1865). By 1843, da Silva was master composer of both the Imperial Chamber and the Imperial Chapel. Remembered today primarily as the composer of the Brazilian national anthem (officially recognized as such in 1890), da Silva was instrumental in the organization of musical life in Rio de Janeiro during the major part of the Empire. In 1833 he founded the *Sociedade Beneficiencia Musical* to "promote the cultivation of art and to exercise mutual improvement among the associated artists." Many local talents were encouraged through the concerts organized by the society. Da Silva also collaborated in the development of the Philharmonic Society, founded in Rio in 1834 but dissolved in 1851 as a result of untenable competition with operatic activity. As an orchestra conductor, he was mostly associated with opera and ballet productions.

Da Silva's most significant project was the foundation of the Music Conservatory of Rio de Janeiro (1847). Official music instruction in the city had been practically nonexistent until that date, with the exception of some at the government-supported Colégio Pedro II. At first the conservatory's curriculum included instruction in music elements and solfège, voice for both males and females, string instruments, woodwind and brass, and harmony and composition. In 1855 the Government decided to administer the conservatory directly, annexing it to the newly created Academy of Fine Arts. The number of subjects offered was increased and a system of competitive examination for teachers established. The establishment of an annual fellowship for a year in Europe for the best students had important consequences, as several composers benefited from it later on. It was also at this time (1850s) that the government established the principle of free music instruction in Brazil. The founding of the conservatory represented the first significant attempt to create real music professionalism in the country. Da Silva directed the conservatory until his death.

As a composer, Francisco Manuel da Silva cultivated the fashionable genres without much distinction. Most of his works, intended for the church, display a theatrical and grandiloquent character. His secular works were mostly the result of commissions for special occasions; they include many salon pieces, romances, waltzes, and songs of the *modinha* type discussed in the previous chapter.

The Brazilian operatic scene during the nineteenth century can be seen as consisting of three main periods: that of the Royal and Imperial theater, 1808–1831 and 1844–1856; that of the National opera, 1857–1864; and that of Antônio Carlos Gomes, 1861–1890s.

The theatrical scene during the first period was dominated by the activities of Marcos Portugal and to a lesser extent, José Maurício. The first opera known to have been written by a Brazilian composer was *Le Due Gemelle* of José Maurício, written on the occasion of Queen D. Maria's birthday and first performed in 1809 at the Teatro Régio (not for the São João inauguration, as reported in most sources); the score is not extant. The most important theaters in Rio de Janeiro were the Teatro Régio and the Real Teatro de São João, the latter inaugurated in 1813, later rebuilt and renamed in 1826 São Pedro de Alcântara. The São João Theater was a replica of the São Carlos Theater of Lisbon, attesting once more to Prince D. João's determination to establish a new royal capital. The first seasons of the new theater included some operas by Portugal (e.g., *L'Oro non compra amore*, 1817) but emphasized mostly Italian operas by Salieri, Puccitta, Noccolini, Rossini, and others. Mozart's *Don Giovanni* was first produced at the São João in 1821.

The gap in theatrical performance between 1831 and 1844 was due to the discontinuance of regular operatic seasons after the abdication of Pedro I in 1831. Pedro II became emperor in 1840, but not until four years later were lyrical spectacles reinstated, when, in January 1844, the theater opened again with the first performance in Brazil of Bellini's *Norma*; it received some twenty performances during that year. This was the beginning of the prima donna personality cult and the first phase of the official protection of Italian opera, which extended to 1856. The period was characterized by the appearance of some of the' most famous Italian and French singers (Augusta Candiani, Clara Delmastro, Rosine Stoltz), performing the main works of the repertory, sometimes within only a few years after their European premieres.

In 1857, a movement toward the creation of a national lyric theater began. By that time the former Provisorio theater had been renamed Teatro Lírico Fluminense.[7] The work that appeared as a precursor of the movement

[7]For a discussion of the Provisorio theater, see Eric A. Gordon, "A New Opera House: An Investigation of Elite Values in Mid-Nineteenth-Century Rio de Janeiro,"

was a cantata on a native historical subject, *Véspera dos Guararapes* (1856), with a text by Manuel de Araújo Pôrto Alegre and music by Joaquim Giannini, an Italian professor at the Conservatory. Not only was the opera's subject matter quite novel (a war episode against the Dutch invasion in Pernambuco) but, more importantly, Araújo Pôrto Alegre's Portuguese text was left untranslated. Da Silva attempted at the same time to promote the use of the vernacular in the operatic repertory. In the presence of the Emperor he made a speech in 1857 lamenting that "the national language—sonorous and beautiful—still awaits the opportunity to be set in dramatic actions. It is impossible to think that what has been done with the French, English, German, and Spanish languages cannot be similarly accomplished in the sweet language of Camões, Basilio da Gama, and Caldas."[8] The Imperial Academy of Music and National Opera was founded in March 1857 under the auspices of the government, with the basic goal of promoting opera performances in the vernacular and of producing at least once a year a new opera by a Brazilian composer. The noble Spaniard, D. José Zapata y Amat, in Rio since 1848 and an active participant in the national operatic movement, was entrusted with the management of the new institution. After some fourteen months, he relinquished his duties as impresario and musical director of the Academy, but under his administration the Academy had sponsored the representation in the vernacular of some sixty-two spectacles, including numerous Spanish zarzuelas, Italian *opere buffe*, and Bellini's *Norma*.

In 1860, the Academy ceased to exist and a new organization called the Opera Lírica Nacional replaced it. This organization immediately produced at the theater of S. Pedro de Alcântara the first opera to deal with a local subject and to be written (both score and libretto) by Brazilians: Elias Alvares Lôbo's *A Noite de São João*, with a libretto based on poems by the Indianist writer José de Alencar. And during the next opera season (1861) the movement towards the establishment of a national lyric theater took on real significance with the presentation at the Teatro Lírico Fluminense of *A Noite do Castelo*, by Antônio Carlos Gomes, the most successful opera composer of the Americas in the nineteenth century.

A native of Campinas (São Paulo), Gomes (1836–1896) was the son of a modest provincial musician. He began composing at an early age and at eighteen wrote a Mass that was performed in a local church by the Gomes family ensemble. At twenty-three he left for Rio de Janeiro and entered the Imperial Conservatory of Music, where he studied composition under Joaquim Giannini. By that time opera was already the genre that appealed most to him, and his conservatory period reinforced this predilection. He soon became acquainted with the works of Rossini, Bellini, Donizetti, and Verdi; the last-named was to exert a particularly profound influence on him

---

Yearbook, Inter-American Institute for Musical Research, V (1969), 49–66.

[8] As quoted in Luiz Heitor [Corrêa de Azevedo], *150 anos de música no Brasil* (*1800–1950*) (Rio de Janeiro: Livraria José Olympio Editôra, 1956), pp. 64–65.

throughout his career. His first opera, *A Noite do Castelo* (mentioned above) had its inception when a copy of the already existing libretto (by Antônio José Fernandes dos Reis) was given him by José Amat; Gomes's setting was produced on 4 September 1861. Its clamorous success, and that of his next opera, *Joana de Flandres* (1863), gained Gomes a government scholarship to study in Italy, and in 1864 he began studies with the opera composer Lauro Rossi, director of the Milan Conservatory. Thereafter, most of his life was spent in Italy, and his compositional ideals became thoroughly Italianized.

Gomes's fame in Italy began with two musical comedies, *Se Sa Minga* (1867) and *Nella Luna* (1868), which give clear evidence of his ability to write in a bel-canto-like popular style. But it was the triumphal success of *Il Guarany* at the Teatro alla Scala on 19 March 1870 that brought him international fame. The opera was produced at Rio de Janeiro on the emperor's birthday (2 December 1870), as well as in almost all European capitals in the next few years. Verdi heard it in Ferrara in 1872 and referred to it in a letter as the work of a "truly musical genius." Gomes's next opera, *Fosca*, on a good libretto by Ghislanzoni, was produced on 16 February 1873 at La Scala, but it was a failure because of a quarrel between the defenders of Italian bel canto and the Wagnerian reformers; the latter supposedly comprised all foreigners (including Gomes). However, a new version of *Fosca* achieved a considerable success in 1878 when it was staged at La Scala. There followed *Salvator Rosa*—it too on a libretto by Ghislanzoni, written according to the prevailing taste of Italian operagoers and presented at Genoa on 21 March 1874—and *Maria Tudor* (Milan, 27 March 1879).

During a sojourn in Brazil in 1880, Gomes got from his writer friend the Viscount of Taunay a suggestion for the subject of his next opera, *Lo Schiavo*. At that time a movement for the abolition of slavery was gathering force in Brazil, and Taunay wrote a drama whose main characters were to represent Black slaves. The librettist, Paravicini, decided, however, to make fundamental changes in order to submit to the standard "scenic necessities" of Italian opera. Black slaves were replaced by Indians, and the action was transposed to the sixteenth century instead of the eighteenth, as had been planned by Taunay. Nevertheless, the premiere (Rio de Janeiro, 27 September 1889) was a success.

Gomes's last opera, *Condor* (Milan, 21 February 1891), reveals his late orientation towards *verismo*. In 1892, on Columbus Day, his last major work, the oratorio-like *Colombo*, was presented in Rio. By that time the new republican government had been established, and Gomes lost his official support. He accepted in 1896 an appointment to direct the local conservatory at Belém, Pará, but died a few months later.

Gomes possessed the main qualities of an opera composer. His works reveal a high dramatic sense, his melodic invention, a rich lyricism. Within the established molds of Italian opera of the second half of the nineteenth century he displayed uncontested mastery. While some of his works (*A Noite do Castelo, Salvator Rosa*) reflect direct influences from post-Rossinian Italian operas (Bellini, Donizetti, early Verdi), they also attest to his ability to be genuine and often original. The triumph of *Il Guarany*, which remains his most important work, was due to its effective melodic content, its dramatic construction, and not least the choice of its libretto. The opera is based on the celebrated novel of the same title by the Brazilian Indianist writer José de Alencar. The picturesque libretto, with its Indian heroes and its Romantic stylization of indigenous dances, undoubtedly made the work all the more appealing for European audiences of the time, and, within the limits of its style, the opera exhibits imaginative traits. The final version of the overture, written in 1871, has become virtually a second national anthem in Brazil. The first theme, which takes on an epic character in the context of the whole opera, functions as a leitmotif and presents a typically Romantic idealization of "indigenous" music (Example 4-6). The natural flow of arias and duets, the timing and sequence of scenes, and the striking contrasts in the staging reveal Gomes's technical competence in the genre. At the same time, he followed the necessary conventions of the time: the orchestration of the work, although quite effective, remains standard, and the opera does not depart from the stereotyped cabalettas, or the "religious" and "ballad" passages, of Italian mid-nineteenth-century opera.

Fosca, the most Italianate of Gomes's operas, is considered by Mário de Andrade, Brazil's foremost musicologist, as one of his best musical achievements. The work includes a number of leitmotifs elaborated somewhat in the Wagnerian fashion, but its melodic nature and its overall structure derive from Italian opera. *Lo Schiavo* is the most gratifying of the later operas, as it reveals a technically more mature writing—especially more inventive harmonic progressions, orchestral coloring, and structural balance. Both *Il Guarany* and *Lo Schiavo* treat Brazilian subjects, however transfigured they may appear in Romantic spectacle. These subjects maintain a symbolic value of social significance, in the form of national and racial ideas or of social vindication.

EXAMPLE 4-6 Antônio Carlos Gomes, *Il Guarany:* Sinfonia, mm. 1–4. Ricordi, 1955. All rights reserved. Used by permission.

While Gomes endeavored on several occasions to instill a Brazilian feeling in his works, his nativistic orientation has often been overstated. De Andrade has written that a native feeling pervades the early works "in some aspects, such as certain rhythmic traits, a certain abruptness of awkward melodic writing, and certain coincidences with our popular melody," but he has also observed that a nationalistic concern was in Gomes's time considered incompatible with the operatic repertory.[9] There are, however, reminiscences of *modinha* in some arias of *A Noite do Castelo* and *Joana de Flandres*, and some passages in *Il Guarany* and *Lo Schiavo* present rhythmic traits that were to become characteristic of urban popular dance music of the late nineteenth century. For example, the well-known "Dance of the Tamoios" from *Lo Schiavo* is based on a melodic motif whose rhythmic figuration has a clear popular flavor (Example 4-7a) and whose accompaniment reminds one of the habanera syncopation (Example 4-7b). Occasionally, Gomes introduces some reminiscence of Luso-Brazilian folk polyphony, mostly in parallel thirds and sixths, to authenticate his "indigenous" passages. This is, however, the extent of his reliance on native musical traits.

EXAMPLE 4-7   Antônio Carlos Gomes, *Lo Schiavo:* "Dança dos Tamoios": (a) main melodic motif; (b) accompaniment. Ricordi. All rights reserved. Used by permission.

(a)

(b)

Concurrently with opera, concert life began to emerge in Brazil, especially at Rio de Janeiro, during the last thirty years of the century. Newly founded concert societies and clubs stimulated the appearance in Brazil of some of the most celebrated performing artists of the time (Thalberg, Napoleão, Gottschalk). This period also saw the beginning of musical nationalism in Brazil. The year 1869 saw Gottschalk's triumphs in Rio de Janeiro and the provincial capitals of the Southern region. His example may have deeply impressed young composers, for the introduction of popular

[9]See Mário de Andrade, *Pequena História da Música* (São Paulo: Livraria Martins, 1942).

elements into art music was certainly not common at that time. The first Brazilian "nationalist" composition was published in 1869 by Brasílio Itiberê da Cunha (1846–1913), an amateur composer and a remarkable pianist; his piano piece *A Sertaneja* attempts to re-create in various ways the character of urban popular music of the time, even quoting a characteristic popular melody. *A Sertaneja* presents national elements derived from popular forms such as the *modinha*, the Brazilian tango, and the nascent maxixe. The popular melody quoted is from the song "Balaio, meu bem, balaio," associated with the Southern *fandango*, a social festive entertainment with dancing. The song exhibits the basic dotted figure and the striking syncopation of almost all Brazilian *fandango* dances, calling at the same time for repeated notes, a characteristic of Luso-Brazilian folk music. Although *A Sertaneja* had no influence on later developments of musical nationalism in Brazil, it nevertheless remains significant as a symptom of what was to come.

Joaquim Antônio da Silva Callado (1848–1880) was the composer responsible for popularizing the habanera rhythm. His most celebrated piece, *Querida por Todos* (labeled a "polka"), was in fact one of the earliest examples of an authentic maxixe. In it the composer very ingeniously transforms the figure   into   and   in the bass accompaniment, pointing the way to the rhythmic patterns of later urban popular forms (Example 4-8).

Romantic musical nationalism in Brazil in its early phase is best represented by the music of Alexandre Levy (1864–1892). Of French descent, he was born in the city of São Paulo, where he studied piano and composition with European professional immigrants. He went to Europe in 1887, staying first in Milan, then longer in Paris, where he took some lessons with Durand

EXAMPLE 4-8 Joaquim Antônio da Silva Callado, *Querida por todos* ("Polka para piano"), mm. 9–16.

at the Conservatory. Upon his return to São Paulo he attempted to organize a regular symphony orchestra but did not find much support. His approach to folk and popular music was strictly sentimental: his knowledge of folk music remained limited to widespread traditional songs, such as those he used in some of his nationalist works. Levy's awareness of urban popular music, especially of Callado's pieces, is readily seen in his most characteristic piano piece, *Tango Brasileiro* (1890). The popular appeal of this piece results primarily from its attempt to re-create the atmosphere of the tango. Around 1890 the tango was still very similar to the habanera; in fact, in Brazil "tango" was the name given to the habanera itself. What is difficult to determine with any accuracy is whether the habanera came from Spain (possibly via the West Indies) or through the tango from the River Plate region. According to Vicente Rossi, the habanera was also known as tango in Argentina and Uruguay around 1890.[10] The tango had the same basic rhythmic pattern as the habanera but was slightly faster and used variants of the syncopation that also defined the maxixe. The tango therefore underwent rhythmic transformations under the influence of the maxixe to such an extent as to make it impossible to differentiate musically between pieces called diversely "Brazilian tango" and "maxixe." These changes are exemplified in Levy's *Tango* by variations of the habanera formula ♩. ♪♫ into ♫♪♫ , ♫♪♫ , or ♩. ♪♫ , all of which are present in Callado's polkas. The introduction of Levy's piece (Example 4-9) has a close relationship to the maxixe, mainly because of the rhythmic drive of the melodic line.

Levy's *Tango Brasileiro* is historically important for being the first known Brazilian nationalist work written by a professional musician. His *Suite Brésilienne* for orchestra (1890), however, is much more significant and symptomatic of this early phase. The *Suite* is the forerunner of many Brazilian suites produced by later nationalist composers. Although conceived with some programmatic intention, it was also planned as a series of dances, as indicated by the titles of two of its four movements: *Prelúdio*, *Dança Rústica-Canção Triste*, *À Beira do Regato*, and *Samba*. Of these, only the *Prelude* and the *Samba* fall strictly within the scope of our survey of musical nationalism, the other two being of a general descriptive nature.

The *Prelude* is based on a popular tune, "Vem cá Bitu," which determines the main component of the thematic material but is never quoted in its entirety and undergoes such fundamental changes as to be sometimes barely expressed or merely suggested. The harmonic vocabulary and the orchestration are conventional for the period. Ninth chords are used mostly as transitory consonances, while numerous pedal points on the tonic and dominant, as well as the usual perfect, deceptive, and plagal cadences are

---

[10]Vicente Rossi, *Cosas de Negros; los orígenes del tango y otros aportes al folklore rioplatense* (Córdoba: Imprenta Argentina, 1926).

EXAMPLE 4-9   Alexandre Levy, *Tango Brasileiro*, mm. 1–4 (*Diario Popular*, 1890).

found throughout. Levy's orchestra is also representative of the early Romantic period; it includes strings, harp, kettledrums (tuned to tonic and dominant), two trombones, bass trombone, two trumpets, four horns, and woodwinds in pairs. Worthy of note is the use of the bass trombone, which most composers had replaced by a tuba since about 1830.

The last movement, *Samba*, can be considered as the first decisive step toward musical nationalism in Brazil. Although it remained unpublished, it was performed with great success in Rio de Janeiro in 1890 under the direction of the composer-conductor Leopoldo Miguéz and became during the early twentieth century one of the most acclaimed pieces of the symphonic repertoire in Brazil.

There is no doubt that a program was attached to this piece. The piano reduction (made by the composer's brother, Luiz Levy) includes a description of a dance which is assumed to be a rural samba, and gives its author's name, Julio Ribeiro. Julio Ribeiro's novel *A Carne* (*The Flesh*), from which the quotation was extracted, was first published in 1888, and immediately became the subject of extreme controversy. As a result of the ensuing scandal, everyone in Brazil was reading *A Carne*. There is thus a strong possibility that the passage mentioned, which in the original refers to a samba dance on a farm, made a deep impression on Levy. Out of context, however, this description does not specifically refer to the samba, and it is doubtful that the composer himself ever had the opportunity of observing a performance of a folk type of samba. Musically, Levy drew on quite different sources, for the samba in this movement is based on two traditional tunes well known in urban areas— "Balaio, meu bem, Balaio," already mentioned in connection with Itiberê da Cunha's *A Sertaneja*, and "Se eu te amei," a very popular tune in São Paulo, written by the composer José de Almeida Cabral, who was chapelmaster at the São Paulo Cathedral. Neither of these tunes corresponds to the melodic structure of the rural samba of São Paulo. Levy remains closer to the urban dances which developed around this time, and their influence can be easily traced in this piece. The formal aspect of the *Samba*, however, is determined by the extramusical material.

The decisive step toward the emergence of national music in Brazil was achieved in the 1890s and early 1900s. It was then that Brazilian art music began to display a characteristic national individuality. In this development the composer Alberto Nepomuceno (1864–1920) played a role of primary importance, through his own works and his stimulation of a genuine national music by others.

Nepomuceno was born in Fortaleza (Ceará), but he spent most of his adolescence in Recife. In 1885 he moved to Rio de Janeiro for further studies. As early as 1887 he showed an interest in popular music, for together with mazurkas, romances, and berceuses his early works included a *Dança de Negros*, the first "Negro dance" of the Brazilian repertoire. A trip to Europe took him to the most celebrated music schools there: Santa Cecilia in Rome, the Akademische Meister Schule and Stern'schen Konservatorium in Berlin, and finally the Paris Conservatory, where he studied organ with Guilmant. His friendship with Edvard Grieg may have had a profound influence on his resolution to embrace the nationalist trend.

When Nepomuceno returned to Brazil in 1895, he had already written some compositions of national character: the String Quartet no. 3 ("Brasileiro"), the piano piece *Galhofeira*, and a large number of songs in the vernacular. His activities in Rio de Janeiro in promoting the recognition of Brazilian music and composers are best exemplified by his campaign against the Italophile and Germanophile music critic Oscar Guanabarino; by his inclusion of works by Brazilian composers in the programs of the "Association of Popular Concerts," which he directed for ten years; by the edition of some works of José Maurício Nunes Garcia; and finally by the support he gave to popular composers such as Catulo da Paixão Cearense by having their music performed.

Nepomuceno's extensive production reveals his eclecticism. He wrote in practically all the traditional musical forms or genres: art songs with Portuguese, French, Italian, Swedish, or German texts; sacred music, including a *Mass* and a *Tantum ergo*; secular choral music, including *As Uyaras*, based on an "Amazonic legend," with text by the folklorist Mello Morais Filho; numerous piano and organ pieces; four string quartets and a trio; operas and lyrical comedies; a symphony; several tone poems; and three suites for orchestra. Of these, the *Série Brasileira* and the prelude O *Garatuja* (both for orchestra), the String Quartet No. 3, the piano pieces *Galhofeira* and *Brasileira*, and numerous art songs present folk or popular material.

The String Quartet in D minor, No. 3, carries the designation "Brasileiro," and the manuscript bears the place and date of composition (Berlin, 1891), as well as a dedication to the composer, Leopoldo Miguéz, then director of the Rio School of Music. In spite of its subtitle the work shows only slight national characteristics. Parts of the thematic material and some rhythmic traits draw from the local atmosphere. In such a traditional and classical genre as the string quartet, Nepomuceno must have experienced a sense of limitation, for three years later, when he wrote the piano piece *Galhofeira*, he revealed fully his knowledge of urban popular forms. *Galhofeira* is the last of a group of four pieces called *Quatro Peças Lyricas, Op. 13*. The other three pieces—*Anhelo, Valsa,* and *Diálogo*—are conventionally written within a strictly Romantic style. However, *Galhofeira* (jovial, merry, playful) derives from the maxixe and the *chôro* the essential elements for its descriptive intent. The entire piece is based on a syncopated accompaniment pattern found in most urban popular forms: . Above it are constant reiterations and variants of a descending broken-chord figure (Example 4-10) alternating with a characteristic melodic theme.

EXAMPLE 4-10 Alberto Nepomuceno, *Galhofeira*, mm. 5–6. Copyright 1910 by E. Bevilacqua & Cia.

In 1897 Nepomuceno presented in a concert at the National Institute of Music his most recent symphonic works, including the Symphony in G minor, *Suite Antique, As Uyaras, Epitalâmio,* and the *Série Brasileira.* The last named was the second suite, after Levy's, to become a standard item in the repertoire of contemporary Brazilian music. Going beyond the mere use or adaptation of popular melodies and rhythms, this work in four movements was the first attempt to depict some typical aspects of Brazilian life. In the first movement, *Alvorada na Serra,* Nepomuceno used a lullaby known throughout Brazil—"sapo-jururu" or "cururu," still found in almost all collections of children's songs; it originated in a popular *auto* (a folk dramatic representation with music and dance) of the Brazilian northeast called *Bumba-meu-boi.*

The second movement, *Intermezzo,* develops and extends the rhythmic and thematic material of the third movement of the String Quartet No. 3. The general atmosphere of this movement is more frankly popular than the previous one. The theme is more fully developed and the characteristic rhythms more systematically employed than in the corresponding movement of the quartet. The theme undergoes a rhythmic transformation that is typical of the maxixe in the restlessness of the melodic line.

The last movement, *Batuque,* divided into two sections, is an amplified version of Nepomuceno's early piano piece *Dança de Negros* (1887). This finale imitates Afro-Brazilian dance by exploiting exclusively its rhythmic elements. In fact, the entire movement stresses rhythmic elements. Heavy and strongly stressed syncopations at the beginning continue to serve as accompaniment throughout. Two syncopated melodic figures are employed as building material for the first section (Example 4-11a and b). The second of these motives simulates the responsorial practice of Afro-Brazilian singing as found in *batuques* and sambas, the solo part being represented by the woodwinds and the answering chorus by strings and brass. The first part of the movement constantly reiterates this motive, except for two statements of the second figure, and modulates between C major and E major in order to lessen the monotony of the repetitions. The second section (Doppio movimento) bears the following instruction: "This movement, which begins playfully [*en badinant*], becomes more and more savage toward the end." The description of the frenzy of the dance is the programmatic content of this section, which relies upon modulations, dynamics, and changes of tempo around a syncopated melodic figure incessantly repeated. Modulations alternate between F major and A♭ major. The "savage movement" of the initial indication is rendered by a gradual acceleration of tempo and a crescendo reaching a "furioso fortissimo," without, however, any alteration of the thematic figure. In this *Batuque* Nepomuceno made the most of the lack of melodic characterization. The piece is indeed symptomatic of the discovery of the rhythmic primacy of popular music, prefiguring similar accomplishments in subsequent twentieth-century compositions.

EXAMPLE 4-11   Alberto Nepomuceno, *Série Brasileira:* "Batuque" (a) mm. 5–8; (b) mm. 20–21. Propriedade dos Editores Sampaio Araujo e Cia. Casa Arthur Napoleão.

(a) (Allegro)

(b)

BIBLIOGRAPHICAL NOTES

Biographical information on all the composers mentioned in this chapter is readily available in Otto Mayer-Serra's two-volume dictionary, *Música y Músicos de Latinoamérica* (Mexico: Editorial Atlante, S. A., 1947). Chapter 4 of Robert Stevenson's *Music in Mexico* (New York: Thomas Y. Crowell Company, 1952) presents a fairly comprehensive overview of nineteenth-century Mexican music. José Mariano Elízaga's biography appears in Jesús C. Romero's *José Mariano Elízaga* (Mexico: Ediciones del Palacio de Bellas Artes, 1934). Salon music in Mexico is thoroughly documented in Rubén M. Campos's *El Folklore Musical de las Ciudades* (Mexico: Secretaría de Educación Pública, 1930), with reproductions of numerous pieces. Jesús C. Romero's *La Opera en Yucatán* (Mexico: Ediciones "Guión de América," 1947) is an overview of operatic activity in Mexico since the eighteenth century. The most informative study of the Mexican antecedents of musical nationalism is, however, Otto Mayer-Serra's *Panorama de la Música Mexicana*, cited in note 1. Cuban music and musicians of this period are studied in detail in Alejo Carpentier's *La Música en Cuba*, cited in note 2.

Argentine music of the nineteenth century is studied comprehensively by Vicente Gesualdo in the first two volumes of his *Historia de la Música en la Argentina* (Buenos Aires: Editorial Beta S.R.L., 1961). Biographical data and information on Argentine music institutions, folk song genres, and dances are provided in Rodolfo Arizaga, *Enciclopedia de la Música Argentina* (Buenos Aires: Fondo Nacional de las Artes, 1971).

A fairly comprehensive bibliography for the music of Brazil is Luiz Heitor Correia de Azevedo's *Bibliografia Musical Brasileira (1820–1950)* (Rio de Janeiro: Instituto Nacional do Livro, 1952). An excellent source, with ample documentation, for Rio de Janeiro's music institutions and activities during the period 1808–1865 is Ayres de Andrade's *Francisco Manuel da Silva e seu Tempo*, 2 vols. (Rio de Janeiro: Coleção Sala Cecília Meireles, 1967). A special issue of *Revista Brasileira de Música* dedicated to the life and works of A. Carlos Gomes appeared in 1936 (Vol. III). Also useful are *Relação das Operas de Autores Brasileiros* (Rio de Janeiro: Ministério da Educação e Saúde, 1938) and *Música e Músicos do Brasil* (Rio de Janeiro: Livraria Editôra da Casa do Estudante do Brasil, 1950), by Luiz Heitor Corrêa de Azevedo. Gomes's correspondence is available in *Antonio Carlos Gomes, carteggi italiani raccolti e commentati da Gaspare Nello Vetro* (Milano: Nuove Edizioni, 1976). I have written on the works of Itiberê da Cunha, Alexandre Levy, and Alberto Nepomuceno, in the short monograph *The Beginnings of Musical Nationalism in Brazil* (Detroit: Information Coordinators, Inc., 1971).

FIVE

THE TWENTIETH CENTURY:
MEXICO AND THE CARIBBEAN

In the first half of the twentieth century, the most significant single phenomenon in Latin America was the rapid growth of nationalism in the social and political development of the continent. Music, as one aspect of culture, did not escape this salient feature of contemporary life. While musical nationalism was largely abandoned in Europe after about 1930, it remained very much alive in Latin America until the 1950s. However, Latin American musical nationalism has never been defined to the satisfaction of all; in spite of some agreement as to its fundamental characteristics in Europe, its meaning and functions varied frequently according to the personality being affected. Socio-musical considerations very often explain the attitude of many Latin American composers towards musical nationalism. Examination of a given composer's social environment frequently reveals his deliberate avoidance of breaches between himself and the prevailing artistic conditions. A composer, for example, active in the 1960s in Cuzco, La Paz, or Belo Horizonte may have found it inappropriate, for socio-political reasons, to alienate himself deliberately from the local musical traditions. On the other hand, he may have been convinced that he could win international recognition only as a translator of his own culture and not as an imitator of Europe. Finally, as mentioned in Part 3 of the present survey, many young experimental composers from Latin America chose to flee to Europe or North America to find the desired response to and stimulation of their creative activity.

MEXICO

Manuel M. Ponce and His Contemporaries

The Mexican revolution, which began in 1910 and lasted for over ten years, had an extraordinary impact on the country's artistic life. As a result of their patriotic fervor, musicians tended towards a musical nationalism based on sources in either Indian or mestizo cultures. The composer Manuel M. Ponce (1882–1948), considered the pioneer of Romantic musical nationalism in Mexico, drew from all types of mestizo folk music (*corrido, jarabe, son, huapango*, etc.), which he studied very earnestly. He cultivated, however, a Romantic style, at times quite akin to nineteenth-century salon music. His celebrated song *Estrellita*, written in 1912 and first published in 1914, brought him international recognition. This song, considered by one of Ponce's biographers as "mexicanísima,"[1] has been successful throughout the Western world—probably, however, because it relates to the typical style of the European Romantic elegy (in which respect it belongs to the same tradition that earlier produced Juventino Rosas's *Sobre las Olas*).

Born in Zacatecas, Ponce was raised in Aguascalientes. After a year of studies at the Mexico City Conservatory, he returned to Aguascalientes to teach in the local music school. In 1905 he went to Italy, where he studied composition under Torchi at the Liceo Musicale in Bologna. A year later, he was in Berlin studying piano at the Stern Conservatory. He became a piano teacher at the Mexico City Conservatory in 1909. The year 1912 saw the première of his Piano Concerto and the beginning of the composition of his *Canciones Mexicanas* for piano; the former follows the standard Romantic style of solo concerto writing, but the latter are significant, if simple, arrangements of folk tunes (such as "La Cucaracha" and "Valentina") popular during the revolution. During these years Ponce began to advocate a native musical development, but his own examples remained rather constrained. From 1915 to 1917, he lived in Havana and was music critic for *La reforma social* and *El heraldo de Cuba*. Back in Mexico City, he resumed his teaching activity at

[1]David Lopez Alonso, *Manuel M. Ponce, Ensayo biográfico* (Mexico, 1950), p. 53.

the conservatory and for two years conducted the National Symphony Orchestra. Together with Rubén M. Campos, he edited the short-lived *Revista musical de México* (1919–1920).[2]

An important turning point in Ponce's career as a composer was his residence in Paris from 1925 to 1933. His studies there with Paul Dukas and his exposure to the various European currents of the time influenced considerably his own stylistic orientation. At that time his nationalistic concern was reflected in greater autonomy of popular elements within an overall neo-Romantic, Impressionist, and neo-Classic style. To this period belong the three symphonic sketches titled *Chapultepec* (1929, revised 1934), which reveal an assimilation of French Impressionist methods and a slight preoccupation with folk material itself. The "Mexican" flavor of such a work resides essentially in the thematic material, which at times has folk-tune characteristics. Only in the later tone poem *Ferial* (1940), more frankly nationalistic, did Ponce resort to actual folk-melodic material. In this work, the programmatic intent, relating to a village marketplace, led Ponce to borrow folk tunes and to orchestrate them "authentically" (employing, for example, a *chirimía* [oboe] with small drum accompaniment) to imitate a folk-music setting, including the ubiquitous village band. The harmonic language of this work, with its dissonances and occasional tonal instability, is also characteristic of the style of Ponce's later period. The *Cuatro Danzas Mexicanas* (1941), for piano, exemplify Ponce's awareness of the necessity for proper balance between the popular elements of his music (conveyed here mostly through melodic and rhythmic traits) and the modern tendencies of its harmonic vocabulary. Rhythmically, these pieces reveal an unmistakably Mexican character, through the use of cross-rhythms (especially hemiola) and an alternation of duple and triple groupings, and of figures associated with the nineteenth-century *contradanza* and habanera (Example 5-1a, b). Chromaticism and dissonances resulting from it give to the *Danzas* their "modern" sound.

In Ponce's works, Indianism remained inconsequential for his development as a nationalist composer. Perhaps as a result of the so-called Aztec Renaissance of the 1920s, he turned to Indianist subject matter on several occasions, as in his *Canto y Danza de los antiguos Mexicanos* (1933) and *Instantáneas Mexicanas* (1938; its second piece is titled *Música Yaqui*), but the Indianist material in such works is limited to a few quotations on which the composer elaborates. This essentially folkloristic approach to Indian music did not constitute, however, a firm foundation on which Ponce could build a nationalist esthetic.

Although Ponce's interest in folk music was further evidenced in the 1930s by his teaching folklore at the Universidad Nacional Autónoma, his later style stressed neo-Classic elements, with a more complex harmony, at

---

[2]He was also, later, editor in Paris of the Spanish-language *Gaceta Musical.*

EXAMPLE 5-1 Manuel M. Ponce, *Cuatro Danzas Mexicanas*, No. II. (a) mm. 13–19; (b) mm. 23–30. Editorial Cooperativa Interamericana de Compositores. Copyright Instituto Interamericano de Musicología, Montevideo, 1941. Used by permission.

times highly chromatic, with more obscure tonalities. His Violin Concerto (1943), the second movement of which makes use of the tune of *Estrellita*, reveals such neo-Classic traits, including profuse counterpoint.

As a result of his friendship with Andrés Segovia, Ponce developed an early interest in the guitar. He wrote a considerable number of guitar works, some of which became (thanks to Segovia's performances of them) standard items of the twentieth-century guitar repertory. Such works as the *Sonata No. 1* ("Mexicana"), the *Sonata Clásica* (*Homenaje a Fernando Sor*), and the *Concierto del Sur*, for guitar and orchestra, reveal a neo-Classic idiom within a virtuoso style characteristic of Spanish guitar performance-practice.

Ponce wrote a large number of songs, some twenty-six of which are arrangements of folk songs. His best known song cycles are *Tres Poemas de Mariano Brull, Cuatro Poemas de Francisco de Icaza* (posthumously published), and *Tres Poemas de Lermontow*. Quite diversified in style, these songs summarize the various styles cultivated by Ponce. He also composed some sixty-eight songs of popular character related to the salon-music tradition. This apparent contradiction is easily understood if one remembers that some of the best known tunes of Mexican popular music ("Cielito lindo," "Las Mañanitas," "La Valentina," "La Cucaracha," etc.) emerged as an extension of the popular Romantic style of the nineteenth century. In addition, the importance in Mexico of European waltzes, polkas, and mazurkas left a deep imprint on Mexican *jarabes, sones, sandungas*, and other folk-music genres.

Among the Mexican composers born in the 1880s who adhered to the early phase of musical nationalism as expressed by Ponce's orientation were José Rolón and Candelario Huízar.

Rolón (1883–1945) is remembered in Mexico mainly as a symphonic composer. He first studied in his hometown of Guzmán, Jalisco, then went to Paris (1904), where he studied under Moskowsky (piano) and Gédalge (composition) until 1911. In the late 1920s he returned to Paris, this time studying with Nadia Boulanger and Paul Dukas. As with Ponce, the French Impressionist style—not, surprisingly, the esthetics of "Les Six"—influenced Rolón deeply. The ballet *El Festín de los Enanos* (1925), for example, reveals Impressionist harmonies and techniques of orchestration mixed with nationalist rhythmic and melodic traits. Mestizo folk music from the state of Michoacán appears in a stylized manner in Rolón's *Baile Michoacano* (premiered in 1930), and his best known incursion into Indianism is the tone poem of 1929 in three movements, *Cuauhtémoc* (the last Aztec Emperor), in which the principal themes are pentatonic (reflecting, most likely, Carlos Chávez's preaching). Rolón's Piano Concerto (1935) exhibits a modernistic virtuoso style whose rhythmic intricacies result from the combination of folk or popular rhythms.

As a composition student of Gustavo Campa at the Mexico City conservatory, Candelario Huízar (1888–1970) fell under the influence of nineteenth-century Romantic music and French Impressionism. His first major symphonic work, *Imágenes* (premiered by Chávez with the Orquesta Sinfónica de México in 1929), whose program refers to a peasant wedding in a village, is written in a Romantic folkloristic style. *Pueblerinas* (1933), one of Huízar's most typical nationalist works, borrows from authentic folk music of his native state of Zacatecas (including a *jarabe* dance), which he incorporates into a personal and sensitive style from harmonic, contrapuntal, rhythmic, and orchestral standpoints. Indianist nationalism appears in his four symphonies (premiered in 1930, 1936, 1938, and 1942), either by the use of Indian or pseudo-Indian melodies (mostly pentatonic) or Indian instruments of pre-Columbian origin (*teponaztli, huehuetl*), or by resorting to Aztec and modern Indian subtitles, such as *Oxpaniztli* (Second Symphony) and *Cora* (Fourth Symphony).

Carlos Chávez

The post-revolutionary period 1920–1934, an era of reconstruction under Presidents Obregón and Calles, saw the emergence of the so-called Aztec Renaissance and a consequent Indianist movement in the arts of Mexico. In an attempted return to pre-Conquest Indian musical practices, the crucial factor was not so much authenticity in reviving those practices as it was a subjective evocation of the remote past, or of the character and physical setting of ancient (and, for that matter, contemporary) Indian culture. In October 1928 Carlos Chávez delivered a lecture at the Universidad Nacional in Mexico City praising the pre-Columbian virtues of Indian music as expressing "what is deepest in the Mexican soul." He also thought the musical life of the Indians "the most important stage in the history of Mexican music." He expressed his basic ideas concerning the melodic system of the Aztecs:

> The Aztecs showed a predilection for those intervals which we call the minor third and the perfect fifth; their use of other intervals was rare. . . .
>
> This type of interval preference, which must undoubtedly be taken to indicate a deep-seated and intuitive yearning for the minor, found appropriate expression in modal melodies which entirely lacked the semitone. Aztec melodies might begin or end on any degree of the five-note series. In discussing their music one might therefore appropriately speak of five different melodic modes, each of them founded on a different tonic in the pentatonic series.
>
> Since the fourth and seventh degrees of the major diatonic scale (as we know it) were completely absent from this music, all the harmonic implications of our all-important leading tone were banished from Aztec melody. If it should seem that their particular pentatonic system excluded any possibility of "modulating"—which some feel to be a psychological necessity even in monody—we reply that these aborigines avoided modulation (in our sense of the word) primarily because modulation was alien to the simple and straightforward spirit of the Indian. . . .
>
> For those whose ears have become conditioned by long familiarity with the European diatonic system, the "polymodality" of indigenous music inevitably sounds as if it were "polytonality." (Polytonality in music we might say is analogous to the absence of perspective which we encounter in aboriginal

painting. The paintings of the pre-Conquest codices show us what this absence
of perspective means.)[3]

Such ideas were soon to become authoritative for anyone following
the Indianist trend. Chávez (1899–1978), the most influential composer in
Mexican musical life from the 1920s to the 1950s, appeared as the theorist
and the most accomplished practitioner of the nationalist movement. This
is not to say that Chávez has been an exclusively nationalist composer; on
the contrary, about two-thirds of his total output has no direct relationship
with musical nationalism, as will be seen in Part 3 of this survey. And it is
inaccurate to refer to a "nationalistic period" in his career, for although we
find a Mexican tendency which begins with *El Fuego Nuevo* and attains its
peak in the 1930s, it appears only sporadically thereafter. Chávez has been
particularly successful in assimilating the essence of folk-music elements.
Whether in his works of Indianist character or in his most abstract compositions (such as the last three symphonies), his highly personal style and
Mexican sense are so intimately connected that his music has been characterized as "profoundly non-European." His individual conception of musical
nationalism has been the subject of much controversy. He has been tagged
as a "folklorist" and "Indianist" composer, but his attitude is much more
resourceful and sophisticated. As observed by the Argentine composer
Roberto García Morillo,[4] Chávez's basic concern has been to incorporate
the essence of previously assimilated folk elements through the use of
representative formulas, whether of a melodic, harmonic, rhythmic, or instrumental nature, that can confer on a piece a distinctly national flavor. His
purpose required a fairly methodical process of synthesis and elaboration of
the popular and folk musical elements at his disposal. Like some other nationalist composers, such as Villa-Lobos or Vaughan Williams, Chávez came to
believe that art must be national in character but universal in its groundwork
and must reach the majority of the people.[5] While the evocation of Indian
music—whether that of contemporary isolated tribes or remote pre-Columbian high cultures—constitutes a fundamental aspect of his nationalistic
purpose, he also gives a great deal of attention to the mestizo folk tradition
and to urban popular musical genres. Although he first repudiated the operatic nineteenth century in Mexico, he later redefined his views:

> Indian music is Mexican, but so is the art of Spanish origin. It is correct and
> plausible to consider even the native operas in the Italian style or the Mexican
> symphonies of German inspiration as Mexican. Obviously the condition of

---

[3] As translated in Robert Stevenson, *Music in Mexico* (New York: Thomas Y.
Crowell Company, 1952), pp. 6–7. Used by permission.
[4] Roberto García Morillo, *Carlos Chávez: vida y obra* (Mexico: Fondo de Cultura
Económica, 1960), p. 211ff.
[5] Cf. *ibid.*, p. 83. The author reproduces a letter from Chávez expressing such
thoughts.

being Mexican does not add anything to the esthetic quality of an artistic production. Only when Mexican music reaches artistic quality does it become national art.[6]

The "profoundly non-European" character of Chávez's music results from the evident exoticism of his Indianist works, as compared with contemporaneous Western European art music or, for that matter, with contemporaneous Latin American nationalist music. The Aztec ballets *El Fuego Nuevo* and *Los Cuatro Soles* or the later composition *Xochipilli-Macuilxóchitl*, for example, are not popular works, in the sense of appeal or in utilizing indigenous material for mere "local color." Most of such works combine modernistic and primitivistic elements in an austere but unique style. While Chávez studied carefully the archaeological exemplars of pre-Columbian musical instruments and the colonial documentation concerning Aztec music in the sixteenth century (the results of which he incorporated in his music evocative of Aztec culture), his attempts at reconstructing pre-Conquest Indian music constitute ultimately a pretext (in line, of course, with the prevailing nationalism of the time) for writing music of a specifically new character.

After the overtly Romantic tendency of his youthful compositions, Chávez switched with the ballet *El Fuego Nuevo* (1921) in a new direction toward Indianist, primitivistic style. "My purpose was not to arrange Indian melodies," he wrote. "Everything in the ballet was my own invention; I thought that the expression should come from the spirit of the music."[7] He had not yet studied the music of the Indians; as he explained, "My contact with Indian music was not the result of a pre-determined proposition, but of the circumstance of having been exposed to it in Tlaxcala from the time I was 5 or 6." Thus, the spirit of the 1921 ballet was simply a result of his remembrance of and affection for certain elements of Indian music. The ballet is based on a ritual ceremony of the ancient Mexicans: at the end of each Aztec century (fifty-two sun years), their fear that a total catastrophe might occur (such as the destruction of the sun by earthquake) prompted the Aztecs to invoke their gods ceremonially, to make sure that the new sun (the "new fire" of the ballet's title) would appear throughout the next century. Chávez's score, written for female chorus and orchestra (as revised definitively in 1927), calls for a considerable number of percussion instruments, including such Aztec instruments as the *teponaztli* (a two-tongued wooden slit-drum) and various types of rattles, in addition to a group of ocarinas, six kettledrums, four güiros, and others. Aside from this battery of percussion and wind instruments and the use of pentatonic melodies, the "Indian"

[6] Quoted ibid., p. 212.
[7] Quoted ibid., p. 22.

character of the ballet remains very subjective. One could certainly take issue with Chávez's theories on pre-Cortesian music on simple ethnomusicological terms. Such Mexican ethnomusicologists as Daniel Castañeda and Vicente Mendoza have argued that one cannot take any current Indian groups (Yaquis, Series, Huicholes, or others) as completely indigenous. Yet Chávez believed that

> the Indian music best preserving its purity is not what remains of Aztec culture, but that of more or less primitive or nomad tribes which never, properly speaking, achieved a culture. Such are the Yaquis, the Series, and the Huicholes.[8]

It seems extremely unlikely that the music of the Indians has remained static for such a long time, and it is even accurate to affirm that the Indian material used by Chávez is "imbued with massive European influences," since contemporary Indian music in Mexico also shows such influences. The source of the convincing nature of Chávez's "Indianist" music is in fact to be found ultimately in his deep identification with the emotions and character of the Indian as the essential Mexican. Commenting about the Indian music which inspired *Los Cuatro Soles*, he wrote:

> Our whole being is moved by this music. . . . In it we find ourselves. Its essence corresponds to our emotions. Its expressive qualities are related to our character and our unrest.[9]

Chávez's later writings emphasize aspects of primitive music in general. For example, his *Musical Thought* includes a long discussion of the origins in magic of music, the significance of repetition, the social and ritual uses of music, and other such matters. In *Toward a New Music*, he discusses the formation of scales and the use of polyphony in primitive music. He seems convinced that polyphony was indeed used, although his favorite missionary source, Juan de Torquemada's *Monarquía Indiana*, affirms positively that part-singing of the kind practiced in Spain was unknown in Mexico before the Conquest, and that during their dances the Indians always sang in unison with the *teponaztli* tune. Chávez bases his assumption on the presence of polyphony in contemporary Indian music, feeling also there must have been instrumental polyphony in ancient ensembles that included flutes.

Some generalizations can be made about Chávez's use of what he considers to be indigenous musical features, keeping in mind that many of

---

[8]Carlos Chávez, "Introduction," *Mexican Music*. Notes by H. Weinstock for concerts arranged by Carlos Chávez (New York: The Museum of Modern Art, May, 1940), p. 10.

[9]Quoted ibid., p. 27.

them can also be found in several of his non-Indianist works or even in some modern European music. Certainly he makes abundant use of modal melodies, both pentatonic and diatonic. Sometimes he quotes contemporary Indian melodies. Several rhythmic features may be related to his ideas about indigenous music, such as repetition (including much use of ostinato, and a consistent underlying rhythmic unit); irregular meters (Chávez comments on the rhythmic variety of indigenous music); frequently changing tempos (recalling Torquemada's observations on increasingly fast tempos). Cross-rhythm and syncopation (mestizo features) are used more than polyrhythm. Chávez seems to have a predilection for the triplet as a fast underlying rhythmic unit.

The predominant polyphonic texture of most of Chávez's compositions reflects his statements about polyphony in contemporary Indian music and the importance of melody and rhythm rather than harmony in primitive music, and his speculations concerning Aztec instrumental polyphony. Another textural feature has a more vague relation to Indians, namely the wide spacing and range and the frequent doublings in three or four octaves.

Timbre is sometimes an Indianist feature in Chávez's music, as when he calls for copies of ancient instruments (especially in *Xochipilli-Macuilxóchitl* and *Sinfonía India*) or many percussion instruments, or uses other instruments in a percussive way. Chávez comments on the wealth of instrumental sonorities in indigenous music, and he surely achieves this in his skillfully integrated timbral effects, based on a large variety of instruments with subtle color differences.

Harmonically, the most important contribution to an Indianist character in Chávez's music is his avoidance of Romantic chords, and the relative unimportance of harmony as such in his compositions. However, his particular ways of avoiding Romantic harmonies seem to be more related to contemporary European trends than to speculation about pre-Cortesian music, aside from his conviction that such music was "never romantic and never plaintive."[10] His own vocabulary includes parallelisms, a percussive use of dissonance, abundant octaves, sevenths, ninths, and non-triadic three-note chords, a favorite being

Acknowledging that we "will probably never arrive at a definite unchallengeable understanding" of forms used in indigenous music, Chávez has worked in forms that are quite traditional yet somehow do not seem forced upon the very individual musical substance of his work.

Examples of Chávez's compositions—from the *Seven Pieces for Piano* (1923–1930), the Sonatina for Piano (1924), and the ballet *Los Cuatro Soles* (1925) to the *Sinfonía India* (1935–1936), the Piano Concerto (1940), and

[10]Quoted in Stevenson, *Music in Mexico*, p. 242.

Xochipilli-Macuilxóchitl (1940)—can illustrate for us the different sense and extent of his Indianist style. Some later works, such as the Sinfonía No. 3 (1951–1954), also exhibit a Mexican quality, although less explicitly.

Seven Pieces for Piano was at first subtitled *Piezas Mexicanas*; however, most of the individual titles are abstract (e.g., *Poligonos, 36, Solo, Unidad*), and the music is in a complex, international avant-garde style. Yet it can also be related to Chávez's Indian ideals. *Poligonos*, for example, is a loud, percussive, rhythmically complex piece, with frequent changes of meter and tempo. There is a predominant repetition of very small motives; and a wide range, numerous sevenths, octaves, and ninths, and percussive dissonance prevail. The favored three-note chord mentioned earlier occurs frequently in the first *Vivo* section, and, although the piece is quite chromatic, modal scale passages are used in the middle section, recalling the composer's comments on the polymodality of Indian music. The piece titled *36* has the same character, with a relatively constant triplet figure, frequently changing meters, and irregular accents. Many melodic figures are diatonic, but the harmonies are chromatic. Its beginning measures (Example 5-2) reveal a conjunct, diatonic triplet figuration typical of Chávez's music.

The Sonatina for Piano was felt by Paul Rosenfeld, in the 1920s, to be "Amerindian in its rigidity and peculiar earthy coarseness." It is difficult to see why this piece should be considered "Amerindian," except perhaps for the fact that Chávez wrote it while saturated with Amerindian cultural idealism. The bass line takes on, in the middle section of the sonatina, the function of a steady percussive ostinato (a feature associated with "primitivism") as the section builds in intensity. The melodies are modal (mostly falling within the scale shown in Example 5-3a), as in the melodic line of Example 5-3b, the substance of which is used almost throughout. Other features that could be considered "primitivistic" are the repetition of melodic-rhythmic motives, the driving rhythmic impulse, and the crescendos to the end of each section (except the interlude at measure 31). However, the

EXAMPLE 5-2   Carlos Chávez, *Seven Pieces for Piano: 36*, mm. 1–2. New Music Edition. Copyright 1936 by Carlos Chávez. Used by permission.

EXAMPLE 5-3 Carlos Chávez, *Sonatina for Piano*. (a) Scale of the piece; (b) mm. 91–96. Copyright, 1930, by Cos Cob Press Inc. Used by permission of Boosey & Hawkes, Inc. Sole agents.

harmonies, especially the frequent augmented octaves and major sevenths, can be related to Ravel and neo-Classicism. Here, the qualities of the Indian and his environment seem to be already a part of Chávez and his individual style, so that we begin to associate his style with Indian culture or character, if not properly its music.

The *Sinfonía India*, composed in New York City about ten years later than the Sonatina, makes use of many more specific musical references to Indian music. However, the essential spirit of Indian music and its makers is absent, since the composer favors an exotic-primitivistic expression. Actual Indian elements in the symphony include authentic Indian melodies and native percussion instruments, such as Indian drum (Yaqui drum), clay rattle, water gourd, two *teponaztlis*, and *tlapanhuehuetl* (large *huehuetl*, an upright cylindrical drum). Although the Indian instruments are said, in the published score of the work, to be "not absolutely essential," comparison of the available recordings will easily convince a sensitive listener of the opposite. Exotic or primitive elements in the score are repetition of melodies and melodic fragments, rhythmic vitality and variety (generally with a constant underlying beat grouped into irregular meter within sections), and pentatonic and modal melody, along with the actual Indian melodies—which, ironically, are not pentatonic.

The introduction (*Vivo*) to the symphony uses fragments of a pentatonic melody, and a constant eighth-note rhythm in irregular meter. Just before the exposition of the first theme, the texture thins to present a "native" instrumental sound: Yaqui drum, *tenabari* (a string of butterfly cocoons), *grijutian* (a string of deer hoofs), and *tlapanhuehuetl*, along with E-flat clarinet. The first theme (Example 5-4) is a Cora melody obtained in 1905 by Konrad T. Preuss at Jesús Maria, Nayarit, and transcribed by Erich von Hornbostel.

EXAMPLE 5-4   Carlos Chávez, *Sinfonía India*; Cora Indian melody as it appears at mm. 42–47. Copyright 1950 by G. Schirmer, Inc. Used by permission.

It is a rhythmically simple tune in major mode, first presented by oboes and strings, accompanied by trumpets in fourths and light percussion stressing the first two beats of the melody. The Mexican instruments and dashes of piccolo give this section an Indian flavor.

Chávez himself has indicated that structurally the *Sinfonía* has all the elements of a symphony in a condensed form. The slow movement appears between the exposition and the recapitulation of the Allegro. The tonal relationship through the circle of fifths is maintained among the elements of the Allegro. According to the composer, the *Sinfonía* follows the structure given in Table 5-1.[11]

Rather than developmental techniques, Chávez resorts to repetitive patterns, with varying texture and orchestration. The second theme of the exposition (Example 5-5) is a Yaqui melody from Sonora, similar to the first Cora melody in its use of repeated notes and its major mode. The setting of its first statement is a simple two-part polyphony in the flutes, with light drum accompaniment—a clearly Indianist rendition, as Indian music of both Central and South America frequently calls for this type of instrumentation (woodwind for the melody, drum as accompaniment). With each repetition, the texture thickens. Thus the setting moves from an exotic to a more conventional one, easing the tune into its new symphonic atmosphere. The

[11]After García Morillo, *Carlos Chávez*, p. 94.

TABLE 5-1.

REHEARSAL NUMBERS	SECTIONS	KEY CENTERS
Beginning	Introduction	B ♭ Maj
9	Allegro. Exposition: Main theme and its development	B ♭ Maj
14	Bridge	B ♭ Maj to E ♭ Maj
27	Second theme and its development	E ♭ Maj
43	Slow movement (poco lento). Main theme and its development	
59	Allegro. Recapitulation: Main theme and its development	B ♭ Maj
64	Bridge	F Maj to B ♭ Maj
73	Second theme and its development	B ♭ Maj
81	Coda of the Allegro (elements of the Introduction)	B ♭ Maj
88	Finale	F Maj

EXAMPLE 5-5 Carlos Chávez, *Sinfonía India:* Yaqui Indian melody, mm. 128–35.
Copyright 1950 by G. Schirmer, Inc. Used by permission.

exotic elements of percussive rhythm, repetition, and crescendo carry this
exposition to a rather abrupt appearance of a third Indian melody in the slow
middle section (Example 5-6). This is a Sonora melody, accompanied by soft
brass, woodwinds, and harp in steady quarter-note chords constructed of
fourths and moving in parallel fashion. A conjunct, modal countermelody
is added in bassoon.

The grandiose finale, using a Seri melody and very repetitious in
nature, is the epitome of Indianist style; critics referred to it in the 1930s as
"powerful" and "barbaric." Here the strings lose their traditional melodic
function in favor of a percussive effect recalling Stravinsky's *Le Sacre du*

EXAMPLE 5-6   Carlos Chávez, *Sinfonía India:* Sonora Indian melody, mm. 183–88. Copyright 1950 by G. Schirmer, Inc. Used by permission.

printemps. The simultaneous use of different metric subdivisions of the basic

pulse (such as $\begin{smallmatrix}6\\8\end{smallmatrix}$ and $\begin{smallmatrix}6\\8\end{smallmatrix}$, the latter

the hemiola feature of mestizo rather than Indian music in Mexico) appears both polyphonically and in succession. Glissandos in the winds punctuate the melody, adding one more intensifying element to the climactic ending.

While the *Sinfonía India* is one of Chávez's more overtly Indianist compositions, it has a clear affinity with neo-Classical works by such composers as Stravinsky and Copland. Brilliant orchestral effects and occasional Impressionist techniques (parallelism, for example) more than counteract references to either pre-Columbian musical culture or contemporary Mexican Indian music. Yet it is a well-integrated work, expressing the exuberant musicality of its composer even if remote from the roots of its ideological pretext.

The Guggenheim Foundation commissioned Chávez to write a piano concerto in 1938, and it was premiered in 1942 by the New York Philharmonic under Dimitri Mitropoulos with the pianist Eugene List. A synthesis of Mexican folk-music elements was apparently the composer's intent in this work.[12] While a number of features can be considered as folk-derived, they are indeed blended into a personal style that is "international" as well as national.

Specific features related to Indian models in the Piano Concerto are those that have been mentioned earlier: diatonic and sometimes pentatonic melody, linear polyphonic texture, rhythmic drive through a constant flow of the basic rhythmic unit, repetition of melodic fragments and rhythmic

[12]Cf. Otto Mayer-Serra, *The Present State of Music in Mexico* (Washington D.C.: Pan American Union Music Series, 1946), pp. 40–41.

patterns, percussive treatment of the piano, and a very clear orchestration that displays an interaction of many sonorities. The harmonic vocabulary is similar to that of most of Chávez's other works of this period, with many fourths, tritones, sevenths, octaves, ninths, and open chords. The opening of the first movement (Example 5-7) illustrates the type of melody and parallel harmonization used often in the movement. Scale passages are numerous and serve to emphasize the diatonicism of the piece. The movement is very long and almost continuously agitated, with a frame of a slow introduction and a coda which brings back the introductory material. The coda relaxes the pace but not the intensity, which is maintained by steady repetition of the theme and related motives, with a crescendo to the final *fff* chord. The thematic material of this movement stresses pentatonicism and modality (Example 5-8).

The second movement relaxes the intensity as well as the pace and is reminiscent of Impressionism in its use of timbre. Yet some of its dissonances are harsher than those of Impressionism, and rhythmic vitality reasserts itself somewhat as the movement leads into several repetitions of the theme from the first movement.

EXAMPLE 5-7 Carlos Chávez, *Piano Concerto*, first movement, mm. 1–4. Copyright 1942 by G. Schirmer, Inc. Used by permission.

EXAMPLE 5-8 Carlos Chávez, *Piano Concerto*, first movement: mm. 81–84. Copyright 1942 by G. Schirmer, Inc. Used by permission.

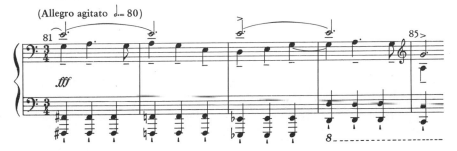

Some of the material of the relatively brief but brilliant concluding movement is related to the preceding movements, but in style this movement seems to be the least related to Indianist elements. It is more chromatic and relies more on major tonality in melodic fragments. The typical "cadence by repetition" at the end, however, could be construed as an Indianist trait; it is in any case a favorite device of Chávez.

The delightful composition, *Xochipilli-Macuilxóchitl,* named for the Aztec god of music, dance, flowers, and love, is subtitled "An Imagined Aztec Music." It was written for Chávez's Mexican Orchestra, consisting of copies of ancient instruments, with a trombone used to approximate the sound of a sea snail's shell. Chávez felt that our knowledge of these instruments, based on archaeological discoveries, was accurate enough to allow a sonorous reconstruction of Aztec music. In his notes for the Columbia recording *Mexico: Its Cultural Life in Music and Art,* he describes the instruments used, mentioning that the antique flutes preserved produce diatonic series of five, six, and seven tones almost perfectly, the pentatonic instruments being most numerous. Beyond the mere use of authentic-sounding instruments, however, much more is involved in imagining a lost music. Chávez shared some of his speculation on matters of polyphony, use of "themes," and musical style in his notes on this piece; they shed light not only upon *Xochipilli* but on Chávez's personal style in many other pieces. In delineating two main types of musical style—that used for large religious festivals and that used for lyrical, poetic expressions—Chávez says that the latter, being vocal, must have had "a loose melodic line, although based on the repetition of simple musical phrases." The religious festival music, on the other hand,

> must have been predominantly rhythmical and dynamic. . . . It must have been music of great power, implacable in its rhythm, strong and obstinate in general, although the chroniclers of that period tell us of certain contrasts of crescendos and diminuendos, accelerandos and rallentandos.

According to Chávez, *Xochipilli*'s melodies and rhythms "are more than anything else the result of my prolonged thoughts on topics of Mexican antiquity" (including study of the plastic arts).

The work is in three parts, the first and last suggesting the great sacred festivals, the middle part more lyrical. All the melodies are pentatonic and on several different planes overlapping one another. Several rhythmic patterns are superimposed, but most are combinations of eighths and quarters, and the pulse is steady. Various groups of instruments drop in and out, giving the piece a textural shape besides the overall three-part form. A low-pitched solo flute opens the slower, lyrical section with an almost continuous melody. Drums introduce the last section with faster, more complicated rhythms. The trombone appears only towards the end, with a group of flutes.

The type of polyphony that Chávez described is present almost throughout.

While the musical elements characterized by the composer as Indian can be isolated by an analyst of his scores, they are not necessarily the primary source of the Mexican Indian quality of Chávez's music. His convincing Indianism emanates from a subjective evocation of ancient and contemporary Indian culture, rather than from specific references to its musical style. Aaron Copland has expressed this in perceptive if extravagant terms:

> To me [Chávez's music] possesses an Indian quality that is at the same time curiously contemporary in spirit. Sometimes it strikes me as the most truly contemporary music I know, not in the superficial sense, but in the sense that it comes closest to expressing the fundamental reality of modern man after he has been stripped of the accumulations of centuries of aesthetic experience.[13]

Chávez has been very active in various capacities—as composer, teacher, government official, writer on music—but none has been as influential for the development of Mexican national music as that of director and permanent conductor of the *Orquesta Sinfónica de México* (OSM), founded in 1928. Before this, while residing in New York from 1926 to 1928, he developed a relationship with Copland, Varèse, and Cowell, with whom he was active in the International Composers' Guild and the Pan American Association of Composers, conducting various premieres of Latin American composers' works; and during the twenty-one years he directed the OSM, he conducted the Mexican premieres of some 155 works from the contemporary repertory, 82 of them from the Mexican symphonic production. The orchestra toured the Mexican provinces regularly, fulfilling a social function by reaching the majority of the people. In addition, Chávez invited some of the best known conductors and composers to Mexico, thus making Mexico City an important musical center of North America.

As an educator, Chávez provided in the 1930s a forward-looking orientation for Mexican music education. He held the post of director of the National Conservatory from 1928 to 1933 and during most of 1934. His basic reforms of the curriculum, his organization of concerts of choral, chamber, and orchestral music, and his founding of three research "academies" (for the study of folk and popular music, of history and bibliography, and of "new musical possibilities") had long-lasting repercussions. While in the United States in 1932, he studied electric sound reproduction, the first report on which was the basis of his book *Toward a New Music: Music and Electricity* (New York, 1937).

The year 1932 also saw the première at Philadelphia (under Stokowski) of Chávez's ballet *Caballos de vapor* (*H.P.*) (Horse Power), performed by

---

[13] Aaron Copland, *Music and Imagination* (Cambridge, Mass.: Harvard University Press, 1952), p. 91.

the Philadelphia Grand Opera Company with the Catherine Littlefield Ballet Company. Subtitled "sinfonía de baile," this work contains the largest gathering of folk elements in any score by Chávez. The ballet has a modern setting, with the warm, sensual life of the Latin American tropics being contrasted with the North American industrialized society. The message of Northern capitalistic exploitation of the Southern neighbors is expressed symbolically through choreographic, musical, and plastic means (the scenery was by Diego Rivera). The tropics are musically represented by two well-known folk dances of Mexico, the *huapango* and the *sandunga,* while some Mexican *sones* appear in the final scene ("Dance of Men and Machines"), in which tropical rhythms are set against those of modern machinery. The ballet is better known nowadays as a symphonic suite, shortened to three numbers (*Danza del Hombre, Barco hacia el Trópico,* and *El Trópico*) from the six of the original ballet. Chávez reveals himself as a master of orchestration in this work. The orchestra calls for a large variety of timbres (with piccolo, E-♭ clarinet, and two saxophones; also an enormous percussion section including a large marimba), which are blended in a uniquely virtuoso manner. Rhythmic drive and complexities and contrapuntal elaboration are the major qualities of *H.P.* In the second number of the suite, Chávez introduces an Argentine tango, suggesting, according to the ballet's synopsis, the seductiveness of tropical sirens; the character of nostalgia, sentimentality, and sensuality of the popular dance is cleverly conveyed through the orchestration (saxophones and percussion), the irregular rhythmic accents, and the sudden contrasts of dynamics (Example 5-9).

The folk dances of the last number of the suite represent a suitable pretext for a virtuosic orchestration. The successful exploitation of *huapango* rhythmic patterns (specifically the hemiola effect) and of the character of the *sandunga* (a waltz-like sentimental popular dance), imbues this movement with a most attractive nationalist expression.

EXAMPLE 5-9   Carlos Chávez, *Suite de Caballos de Vapor,* II: "Barco hacia el Trópico," tango section, mm. 314–17. Copyright 1959 by Hawkes & Son, Ltd. Used by permission of Boosey & Hawkes, Inc.

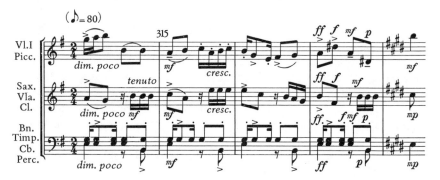

Besides this incursion into mestizo folk music, Chávez expressed his affinity with the post-revolutionary cultural ideology in somewhat populist works such as the "proletarian symphony" *Llamadas*, the "Mexican ballad" *El Sol* (both for chorus and orchestra), and the *Obertura republicana* (later retitled *Chapultepec*). The latter is an arrangement for band or orchestra of three tunes representing different types of popular music: the provincial military march, *Zacatecas*, a nineteenth-century salon waltz, *Club Verde*, and a revolutionary *canción*, *Adelita*.

The "Grupo de los Cuatro"

At the exhibition "Twenty Centuries of Mexican Art," held at the Museum of Modern Art in New York in May 1940, Chávez organized a series of concerts of Mexican music, presenting besides his own works several arrangements of Mexican songs and dances by other nationalist composers, among them Blas Galindo.

Blas Galindo (Dimas) (b. 1910), of Huichol Indian descent, studied at the Mexico City Conservatory under Chávez (composition), Rodríguez Viscarra (piano), and Candelario Huízar and José Rolón (theory). (The influence of Chávez is everywhere apparent in Galindo's early compositions.) He later studied at the Berkshire Music Center with Copland and gained a commission from the Koussevitzky Foundation. He was appointed director of the Mexico City Conservatory in 1947, a post he held until 1961.

During his early years as a composer, Galindo joined Daniel Ayala, José Pablo Moncayo, and Salvador Contreras to form what came to be called, after the Russian "Mighty Five" and the French "Les Six," the "Grupo de los Cuatro." This group was formed to promote the activities of its members, all focusing attention on Mexican nationalist music. Galindo's *Sones de Mariachi*, presented at the Museum of Modern Art concerts, soon became a standard piece of the modern Mexican symphonic repertory. Although advertised as an "arrangement," with the original version calling for an orchestra of Mexican instruments, the definitive version for symphony orchestra (published by Ediciones Mexicanas de Música) is a composition in its own right. This work reveals a most obvious use of mestizo elements. The three *sones* (i.e., folk tunes) are adapted from the original tunes "La Negra," "El Zopilote," and "Los Cuatro Reales." The instrumentation suggests an authentic mariachi band, with its violins, guitars, *jaranas* (small guitars), and *guitarrones* (and, in more recent and urbanized mariachis, brass instruments, especially trumpets as melodic and accompanying instruments). The original version of Galindo's work included vihuela and *guitarrón* added to the usual symphonic orchestra, but these are not included in the published symphonic score. Mestizo folk-music elements occur as follows: alternation and combination of 6/8 and 3/4 meters with various standard syncopations;

prolific use of parallel thirds and sixths, following Spanish-related mestizo folk polyphony; the same harmonic structure as in native *sones*, i.e., I, IV, V, V₇ of IV, V₇ of V. In addition, the usual mariachi reiteration of tonic-dominant chord structures as introductory material is utilized by Galindo in the twenty-eight-measure introduction, as well as a typical cadence formula consisting of a falling second with a syncopation on the tonic triad. Other stylistic traits include guitar-like effects in the violas and cellos, and interesting shifts of accents in the basses, pizzicato.

　　While Galindo tended to cultivate a neo-Classic style in his works of the 1940s and '50s, he did not altogether abandon the mestizo elements found in *Sones de Mariachi*. For example, the Five Preludes for Piano (1945), the Sonata for Violin and Piano (1945), the *Sinfonía breve*, for strings (1952), the Symphony No. 2 (1957), and the Flute Concerto (1960) all show a preference for combining 3/4 and 6/8 meters. The combination of triple and duple units to form five-beat units is common (as in no. IV of the Five Preludes and movements 1 and 3 of *Sinfonía breve*; and Prelude II, where 3 + 2 metric division of the melodic phrase occurs in 4/4 time). Since this is such a prominent feature of Mexican folk music and since Galindo uses it so extensively, a relationship can safely be assumed. Likewise, the extensive use of sequence in Galindo's melodies may derive from the sequential character of much mestizo music. The very nature of his melodies points to a striking folk-song likeness. Example 5-10, from the last section of *Sinfonía breve*, is characteristic: the diatonic character, the use of 3/4 meter and running quarter notes (with typical 6/8 pattern in supporting lines), the final cadences built on a falling third from dominant to mediant (with a feminine cadence, as in so many of the Mexican ballads known as *corridos*), and the repetition of the phrase which precedes the final cadence all show marked resemblances to mestizo folk-melodic practice.

　　José Pablo Moncayo (1912–1958), student of Chávez at the Mexico City Conservatory who was to become artistic director and conductor of the OSM, is remembered chiefly for his appealing *Huapango* (1941), an overtly nationalist piece, and the opera *La mulata de Córdoba*, premiered at Mexico City in 1948. *Huapango* is based on three authentic folk dances with their respective *sones* ("Siqui Siri," "Balajú," "El Gavilán"). The general stylistic

EXAMPLE 5-10　Blas Galindo, *Sinfonía Breve para Cuerdas*, III, mm. 72–82 (violin parts only). Copyright 1956 by Blas Galindo. Used by permission.

traits mentioned in connection with Galindo's *Sones de Mariachi* are also found in this score, the most conspicuous one being the hemiola rhythmic effect.

Silvestre Revueltas

Silvestre Revueltas (1899–1940), a nationalist composer of international reputation, drew mostly from the popular and folk music of contemporary Mexico and made it the source of his style. His spontaneous and good-humored temperament is clearly present in many works. He studied violin and composition at Mexico City, at St. Edward's College (Austin, Texas), and at the Chicago Musical College. After working as a performer in Texas and Alabama during the 1920s, he was appointed by Chávez assistant conductor of the OSM in 1929 and held the post until 1935. Concurrently he taught violin and chamber music at the Conservatory of Mexico City.

Most of Revueltas's works date from the last ten years of his life. His first orchestral piece, *Cuauhnahuac* (1930), which is titled with the earlier name for the town of Cuernavaca, defines the style that he cultivated in the whole of his small output. Romantic in inspiration, *Cuauhnahuac* employs a decidedly modern harmony, with a high level of chromaticism and violent dissonances, colorful and imaginative orchestration, a heavy percussion background, and vigorous rhythmic drive, with sudden shifts and irregular stresses. The much performed *Sensemayá* (1938), which is Revueltas at his best, reveals the unique rhythmic quality of his music. The verses of the Afro-Cuban poet Nicolás Guillén that inspired this work imitate onomatopoeically the sounds and rhythms of Afro-Cuban cult music (most likely the *Abakuá* cult, since the Congo-related words *mayombé, bombé, mayombé* appear as a sort of refrain in the poem). The work builds to a grandiose climax created gradually through the thickening of the texture (with the three main themes of the score combined contrapuntally) and the orchestration, and through increased activity of polyrhythms. Rhythmic ostinatos—irregular, heavy-accented rhythmic patterns combined with highly dissonant chord formations—and repetitive short melodic motifs are all reminiscent of Stravinsky's *Rite of Spring*.

In 1933, Revueltas wrote a chamber piece with the enigmatic title *8 x Radio* (*Ocho por radio*), variously interpreted as "8 minutes of radio music" or "8 musicians broadcasting." It is one of the composer's most alluring works and one which indicates his cynical humor. Commenting on this composition, Revueltas said "*8 x Radio* is an algebraic equation which cannot possibly be solved unless one possesses profound knowledge of mathematics. The composer has attempted to solve it by means of musical instruments."[14] These are violins I and II, cello, doublebass, clarinet, bassoon,

---

[14]As quoted in Nicolas Slonimsky, *Music of Latin America* (New York: Da Capo Press, 1972), p. 249.

trumpet, and Indian drum—that is, an octet. Characteristic traits include mestizo folk-like polyphony (parallel thirds and sixths), folk rhythmic figures ($\frac{6}{8}$ ♩ ♪♩ ♪ | ♫♩ ♩ ♪ , for example), frequent ostinatos, polytonal harmonies, and tripartite form. In addition, Revueltas's themes here follow the shape and the isometric rhythm of folk melodies. Another work of 1933, the symphonic poem *Janitzio*, portrays the resort island of Lake Patzcuaro; Revueltas called it his contribution to "national tourism." It typifies the composer's melodic style, one totally reflective of folk models. With such works as these, Revueltas has been viewed as the most obvious representative of "mestizo realism," i.e., the genuine expression of the popular culture of contemporary Mexico.[15]

Other Mexican Nationalists

The nationalist trend is also expressed in the works of Luis Sandi, Miguel Bernal Jiménez, and Salvador Contreras. Sandi (b. 1905) has been active especially as a choral composer and conductor. In 1929 he became head of choral activities at the Mexico City Conservatory, and in 1938 he founded the Coro de Madrigalistas, which became the best organization of its kind in Mexico. The May 1940 concerts of Mexican music at New York's Museum of Modern Art included his *Yaqui Music*, described as an "arrangement" of Indian music from Sonora. The same general characteristics described in Chávez's Indianist works can be seen here, especially in relation to melodic pentatonicism and instrumental coloring. Other significant works by Sandi on Mexican-related subjects are the opera *Carlota* (premiered in 1948) and *Bonampak* (premiered in 1951), a suite which has received numerous performances.

Bernal Jiménez (1910–1956), an organist and musicologist, shows as a composer a rather eclectic tendency. He wrote much sacred vocal music in a traditional style, but also several compositions of local color in a prevailingly neo-Romantic style, with Impressionist traits. A native of Morelia, he explored to a certain extent, in his symphonic *Suite Michoacana* (1940) and his *Noche en Morelia* (1941), folk-musical traits of the province of Michoacán. His opera *Tata Vasco* (premiered at Morelia in 1941; libretto by Manuel Muñoz written for the celebration of the fourth centenary of the arrival of the first Bishop of Michoacán, Vasco de Quiroga) is conceived within traditional forms. Called significantly a "symphonic drama" by the composer, its various episodes rely on major forms of Western music for characterization. For example, the first part (*Agonía y Redención*) is a prelude of large proportions; the second (*El Oidor*) includes a fantasy, fugue, and minuet; the last (*El Civilizador*) is written in the general form of a sym-

[15]Otto Mayer-Serra, *The Present State*, p. 12.

phony. The vocal and orchestral writing derives from Italian *verismo*, but Gregorian chant is used for characterizing the "theme of faith," a troubadour-like song for the "canción del franciscano" in Scene Two, and something like a typical sixteenth-century motet appears in Scene Three. Bernal also resorts to national sources such as popular religious songs (*alabado*), mestizo songs and rhythms, and even traditional instruments (*teponaztli, chirimía*, percussion).

Salvador Contreras (b. 1912), active as a violinist and a conductor, has not received the same support as several of his contemporaries: none of his works has been published or recorded commercially. Nevertheless, he made a reputation as a nationalist composer in the 1930s and 1940s, with works combining folk-like tunes (*corridos*) and dance rhythms with a modern neo-Classic contrapuntal and harmonic treatment. In the 1960s, however, he turned to atonality and serialism, as in his *Divertimiento para siete instrumentos* (1965) or his *Dos piezas para orquesta de cuerdas* (1970).

In the 1950s and 1960s musical nationalism declined in Mexico, perhaps as a result of the emergence of a dynamic group of avant-garde composers. They will be discussed in Part 3.

THE CARIBBEAN AREA

Cuba

Among the numerous Cuban composers active during the early twentieth century, Eduardo Sánchez de Fuentes (1874–1944) advocated an Indianist approach to musical nationalism. As an opera composer, he cultivated Italian *verismo* based on pseudo-Caribbean Indian music. The opera *Doreya* (1918), for example, on an Indianist libretto, presents an imagined *areito*, a ritual dance of the early Antillean Indians.[16]

The establishment in 1923, in Havana, of the "Grupo Minorista," which included young revolutionary poets, artists, and musicians, animated a renovation in Cuban music and inspired attempts at investigating and exploring the African traits of Cuban culture. The various studies of Fernando Ortiz, Cuba's foremost ethnomusicologist, were very influential in the rediscovery of Afro-Cuban culture (known as *afrocubanismo*) and its music. *Afrocubanismo* became the most suitable source of national expression for the outstanding representatives of musical nationalism in Cuba: Amadeo Roldán and Alejandro García Caturla.

Born in Paris, Roldán (1900–1939) studied at the Madrid Conserva-

---

[16]For historical data and synopsis of Sánchez de Fuentes's operas, see Edwin T. Tolón and Jorge A. González, *Operas cubanas y sus autores* (Havana, 1943), pp. 279–412.

tory, where he was awarded the Sarasate violin prize. After studying harmony
and composition with Conrado del Campo, he returned to Cuba (1919) and
later became concertmaster of the Philharmonic Orchestra of Havana, which
was founded in 1924 by the Spanish musician Pedro Sanjuán.[17] As the titular
conductor of the orchestra from 1932 to his death, Roldán was able to raise
its standards and make it one of the most distinguished organizations in
Latin America. He also presented much contemporary music and contributed
in various capacities to the substantial development of professional musical
life in Havana.

Roldán's *Obertura sobre temas cubanos*, premiered by the Havana
Philharmonic in 1925, was the first major symphonic work by a Cuban composer to reveal the new trend of nationalism based on Afro-Cuban sources,
the most obvious of which were actual Afro-Cuban musical instruments.
His next work, *Tres pequeños poemas* (*Oriental, Pregón, Fiesta negra*), written
in 1926, reveals the assimilation of folk-music elements into his own style.
The *Fiesta negra*, particularly, confirms the recognition of the prevailingly
rhythmic character of Afro-Cuban music. The same is found in the piano
piece *Preludio cubano*, in which the syncopated figure ♪♪♩ is used systematically against a rhythmic ostinato (Example 5-11), which gives to the piece
an unmistakably Cuban flavor. Cult music from groups such as the Lucumi
and the Abakuá inspired the Afro-Cuban ballet *La Rebambaramba*, Roldán's
most celebrated work. Based on a story by Alejo Carpentier, the ballet

EXAMPLE 5-11	Amadeo Roldán, *Preludio Cubano*, mm. 61–68. © copyright 1967
by Southern Music Publishing Co., Inc. Used by permission.

[17]Previously, the Havana Symphony Orchestra had been established under the
direction of Gonzalo Roig, the composer of the well-known zarzuela *Cecilia Valdés*.

attempts to evoke Havana's popular life on Kings' Day (January 6) in the 1830s. According to Carpentier, the characters of the ballet include such typical colonial types as Negro cooks, a Spanish soldier, *calash* drivers, and popular *comparsas* (processional groups). Local elements in the score include Cuban *contradanzas* and a somewhat personal rendition by the composer of the rhythmic complexities of Afro-Cuban music. A symphonic suite from the ballet, in five movements, retains the most obvious nationalist passages, such as the finale of the first tableau in which, in the words of Carpentier, "a 6/8 meter evocative of French contredanses gradually africanizes itself to carry [the listener] to the Black world of the Kings' fiesta."[18] The *comparsa Lucumí*, which forms the third movement of the suite, is represented by divided strings in heavy chordal stresses; voices (as part of the orchestra) sing the various stanzas of the *comparsa de la Culebra* (fourth section). Another story by Carpentier furnished Roldán with the argument for his second ballet, *El milagro de Anaquillé* ("African mystery"), composed in 1928–1929 but premiered as a ballet only in 1960. Here the composer resorts to both Guajiro (use of *décima* and *zapateo*, Cuban-Hispanic folk song and dance) and Afro-Cuban (Abakuá initiation ceremonial music) folk traditions. As in his other works, the folk themes are mixed with the most advanced harmony and orchestration.

The approximation to original folk sources of the works just mentioned tends to disappear with the series of *Rítmicas*, six chamber pieces, four of which are for wind quintet and piano, but the last two exclusively for typical Cuban percussion instruments. The folkloristic nationalism is sublimated here in a subjective re-creation of the spirit of Afro-Cuban music, within a refined neo-Classic harmony and tone-coloring. With the orchestral work *Tres toques* (*de marcha, de rito, de danza*), written in 1931, Roldán de-emphasizes the percussion instruments he had previously made so much of, but he treats the whole chamber orchestra percussively. In a highly personal manner, he achieves a full synthesis of the characteristic elements of Afro-Cuban and mestizo folk music. Among his vocal works, *Motivos de Son* (1934), eight songs for voice and a small instrumental ensemble, stands out as a very effective rendition of the expressiveness of Afro-Cuban singing. Composed to a set of Guillén's poems, the cycle reveals the composer's talent as a lyrical melodist and as an exquisite contemporary craftsman. The set abounds in rhythmic intricacies resulting from various treatments of syncopations particularly associated with Afro-Cuban dances, and in colorful orchestration in which typical Cuban instruments, such as *bongó, güiro,* and *claves,* fulfill an important role.

The work of Alejandro García Caturla (1906–1940) represents perhaps the most significant achievement in Cuban musical nationalism. A student

[18] Alejo Carpentier, *La música en Cuba* (Mexico: Fonda de Cultura Económica, 1946), p. 313.

of Pedro Sanjuán in Cuba and of Nadia Boulanger in Paris, he consistently showed a singular power of assimilation. His sojourn in Paris allowed him to discover European contemporary music, which had clear repercussions in the development of his own style. A judge by profession, he lived most of his life in the provincial town of Remedios; he was assassinated there by a suspect who was to be tried in his court.

García Caturla's first works were written in a popular vein (a *bolero*, a *canción*, and three *danzones*), revealing, according to Carpentier, a curious treatment of rhythmic elements from Creole folklore.[19] After a short period under the influence of Satie, Milhaud, Stravinsky, and others, he began feeling a profound empathy for Afro-Cuban culture. He married a Black woman despite the prejudices of his family. His approach to Cuban folk music, whether Afro-Cuban or Guajiro, was quite subjective in that he did not attempt to treat separately any given folk-music genre. Rather, he tended to create his own style with some important ingredients from many genres of folk music. One technique he used in works of the 1920s was to imitate— and successfully—the timbres of typical folk instruments with conventional European instruments; one example is the first song (*Mari-Sabel*) of the *Dos poemas afrocubanos* (1929), to a text by Alejo Carpentier, in the original version for voice with piano accompaniment: the piano imitates the accompaniment of a *tres* (a Caribbean guitar-like instrument), in spite of fairly dissonant harmony. The *Tres Danzas Cubanas* of 1927, for orchestra, reveal some of the most characteristic traits of Caturla's style. His Afro-Cuban suite *Bembé* and a symphonic movement on the poem *Liturgia* by Carpentier, *Yamba-O* (1928–1931), show a very advanced idiom, with bold harmonies and imaginative instrumental and rhythmic effects. Unusual scales also became part of his musical language. There is a marked tendency to a narrow range and an avoidance of the minor second in his melodic writing, partly because he often uses pentatonic melodies without semitones[20] (Example 5-12). Pentatonicism is persistent, through Caturla's assimilation of Afro-Cuban folk music; it creates at times the impression of primitivistic style. Salazar has compared Caturla's manner with that of the Cuban popular *son* itself, whose main traits consist of a "generally pentatonic melody, presented by an instrument of a distinct timbre, in a tonally indefinable sonorous atmosphere, sustained by the multiplicity of simultaneous rhythms played by typical instruments."[21] While polytonality and frequent polyrhythmic textures occur, the use of native instruments is limited to the simplest instruments (like a conga drum), avoiding those of characteristic timbre. Such is the case of the orchestral piece *La Rumba* (1933), which calls for "timbales

[19]Carpentier, *La música en Cuba*, p. 319.
[20]Adolfo Salazar, "La obra musical de Alejandro García Caturla," *Revista Cubana*, XI/31 (January 1938), 31.
[21]Ibid., p. 17.

EXAMPLE 5-12a   A. García Caturla, *Tres danzas cubanas:* first motif.

EXAMPLE 5-12b   A. García Caturla, *Bembé:* first theme.

cubanos" (literally "Cuban kettledrums," but probably conga drums were intended). Caturla handles Cuban rhythms just as effectively without percussion instruments, as in the *Primera Suite Cubana* (1931) for piano and eight wind instruments. This suite is certainly one of the most severe in style of Caturla's works, yet it still explores rhythmic and melodic elements of Cuban folk music.

Both Roldán and García Caturla have had a particular significance in Cuban twentieth-century music not only because they created works of high quality rooted in authentic national sources but also because they mastered in their own ways the prevailing, sometimes even avant-garde, European techniques of their time (see Chapter 8). In retrospect, the Afro-Cuban elements in their music are ultimately transcended to such a degree as to convince any historian of Cuban music that their contributions were highly original. In addition, both composers raised the level of musical professionalism in Cuba and opened the way to international music circles for the following generation of Cuban composers.

The Spanish-born composer José Ardévol (b. 1911) dominated the art-music scene in Cuba in the 1940s and 1950s, promoting and influencing young Cuban composers. He settled in Havana in 1930 and began exploring Cuban stylistic elements to a certain extent in his *Tres Ricercari* (1936) for string orchestra, his *Música de Cámara* (1936) for six instruments, and in his *Suite Cubana No. 1* (1947) and *No. 2* (1949), the last an orchestration of his *Seis piezas* for piano of the same year. Although he shared Roldán's and Caturla's esthetic ideals, he came to believe that the Afro-Cuban trend had been only a preliminary, if necessary, step and needed to be followed by another which would give Cuban music a greater international meaning. Thus, his major works were written in a neo-Classic style.

Two students of Ardévol who nevertheless preferred to follow the trend initiated by García Caturla and Roldán were Argeliers León and Hilario González. León (b. 1918) has been particularly interested in traditional Afro-Cuban music as a composer and an ethnomusicologist. Song types of the various Afro-Cuban cult groups have served him in his numerous works, including the two-voice *Four Inventions* for piano (1944) and the four *Escenas de ballet* (1944) for clarinet, trumpet, piano, and Afro-Cuban percussion (with authentic ritual drums in an outstanding role). The contrapuntal nature of much of León's music of the 1940s may have resulted from Ardévol's influence, but melody and rhythm are closely related to national sources. The beginning of the third invention (Example 5-13) is a pertinent illustration, with its pentatonic descending motive and its conspicuous syncopation. Another example of León's direct utilization of popular elements is found in *Danzón No. 2* (1945), for piano, in which the so-called Cuban *cinquillo* ($\frac{2}{4}$ ♩ ♪♩ ♪♩) appears throughout.

León consistently maintained his interest in and affinity for Afro-Cuban music even in the 1950s. Among his most nationalist works of that period we find *Yambú, Bolero y Guaguancó* (1956), and *Akorín* (1956), both for piano; *Cuatro Danzas Cubanas*, for string orchestra (1959); and, nationalist to a lesser extent, the *Canciones lentas*, for guitar (1959). *Akorín* is an interesting series of piano pieces adapted from transcriptions of Afro-Cuban ritual songs. The monodic character of cult music has been retained in most of these, as well as its rhythmic subtlety and its modal or pentatonic nature (Example 5-14).

Hilario González (b. 1920) appears to be the spiritual heir of García Caturla. His is not, however, a folkloric type of nationalism. He handles rhythmic elements of folk and popular music in a very personal manner. His style is dissonant and his expression restrained, but he does not share in general the austere character of the neo-Classic works of his contemporaries in Cuba. His most typical works of the 1940s include the *Tres Preludios en Conga* (1938) and the *Danzas Cubanas* (1938), both for piano (the latter orchestrated in 1945), two suites of *Canciones Cubanas* for voice and piano (1940 and 1945), a Piano Sonata (1942) which contains both national and

EXAMPLE 5-13   Argeliers León, *Invención No. 3*, mm. 1–7. Ediciones del Departamento de Música de la Biblioteca Nacional "José Martí." La Habana, 1964.

EXAMPLE 5-14   Argeliers León, *Akorín:* "Babalú-Ayé," mm. 1–10. Ediciones del Departamento de Música de la Biblioteca Nacional "José Martí." La Habana, 1962.

non-national traits, and a *Concertino* for oboe, bassoon, viola, and piano (1944). In subsequent works he turned to orchestral and choral media, writing a ballet, an opera, a cantata, a symphony, and an important cycle of songs, *Cantos de Amor y Lucha,* for voice and orchestra. The third *Preludio en Conga* provides an illustration of his early style. For the purpose of re-creating the popular dance (the conga), he utilizes its typical syncopation, but the parallelism of chords and their strikingly dissonant formation are effective personal means to convey the impression of a battery of drums.

Other Cuban composers of the same generation cultivated a sort of subliminal nationalism in conjunction with their adherence to neo-Classicism. Almost all were students of Ardévol and are mentioned in Chapter 9.

In Puerto Rico the most outstanding representative of musical nationalism is Héctor Campos-Parsi (b. 1922), who turned, however, to neo-Classicism in the 1950s and experimental techniques in the 1960s. After initial studies at the Universidad de Puerto Rico, he studied composition at the New England Conservatory, then at Tanglewood with Copland and Messiaen, and finally in France with Nadia Boulanger. Since 1955 he has been very active in Puerto Rican music education programs. His production includes three ballets, orchestral and chamber works, choral pieces and songs, and piano works. In some of them he re-creates some aspects of Puerto Rican folk music, such as those of the *plena* genre (a folk dance-song of Afro-Puerto Rican tradition).

Venezuela

As mentioned in the Preface, Venezuela is included within the Caribbean area not only for geographical but for musical reasons. The Afro-Antillean musical tradition is very much a part of Venezuelan folk music, which, in turn, has often served as source material for nationalist composers.

The "twentieth century" in Venezuelan art music began only around 1920, when musical professionalism became possible under a flourishing economy and political stability. A movement towards the updating and renovation of composition in Venezuela emerged under the stimulation and leadership of Vicente Emilio Sojo (1887–1974) and Juan Bautista Plaza (1898–1965), followed by Miguel Angel Calcaño and José Antonio Calcaño. They provided the city of Caracas with a renewed musical life and helped establish regular musical organizations. Sojo founded with Ascanio Negretti and Vicente Martucci the Orquesta Sinfónica Venezuela (1930), which he directed for almost twenty years. He also founded and directed the choral association Orfeón Lamas, for which he wrote numerous works and encouraged other composers to do the same. Sojo's influence as a teacher of composition and theory was paramount; at the Escuela Nacional de Música of Caracas, which he directed from 1936, he taught a large number of composers. Although not a folklorist, he collected and harmonized over four hundred Venezuelan folk songs and dances, the first albums of which, containing *canciones*, *joropos*, *guasas*, *golpes*, and other genres, were published in the early 1940s. As a composer, he cultivated a national style mixed with impressionistic stylistic traits.

Juan Bautista Plaza's position as a nationalist composer manifests itself in a number of ways. His career as a musician in Caracas and his sizable body of writings reveal his nationalistic tendencies; as a composer, his is the most significant achievement of his generation within the nationalist trend. Plaza was born in Caracas, and, with the exception of three years of study at the Institute of Sacred Music in Rome, he spent all of his life there. For twenty-five years he occupied the post of chapelmaster at the Caracas Cathedral. He also served as professor of music pedagogy of the Ministry of Education and professor of composition, history, and harmony at the Escuela Nacional de Música. At the same time he collaborated in the organization of the Venezuelan Association of Concerts and for some years served as that association's president. In 1948 he became the director of the Juan Manuel Olivares Music School, a position he retained until his retirement in 1962.

Plaza's writings include both historical and critical work. He studied the archives of Venezuelan colonial music and was responsible for editions of many colonial composers' works. As early as 1938 he advocated the need to collect, study, and classify Venezuelan folk music and suggested the establishment of a national archive as a source of study and information for future Venezuelan composers who might wish to work from authentic folk tradition.

Besides religious music, Plaza cultivated "música criolla." His arrangements of national tunes show a genuine interest in them; the best known of these are fifteen popular children's songs. His arrangement of the Venezuelan national anthem (which became the official version) further indicates his interest in the music of his country. He often utilized music of the *criolla* tradition of Venezuela, which includes songs and dances of partially European origin, such as the *joropo* (Venezuelan national folk dance), related in origin to the Spanish *fandango*.

The stylistic traits of folk-music extraction found in the works of Plaza are most easily defined by rhythmic and melodic patterns. Among the folk dances that influenced him most are the *vals* (𝄽), the *merengue* (𝄽 or 𝄽), and the *joropo*. The last-named genre, the prototype of Venezuelan mestizo music, includes, according to Ramón y Rivera, four different types.[22] Two of these, the *corrido* and the *galerón*, are sung to narrative texts and use non-measured melodies against a rhythmically organized bass. The *pasaje*, which is sung to a descriptive text, uses a measured melody, but it is entirely independent of the rhythm established by the bass. The fourth type is known either as *golpe* or *joropo*. This type adheres most closely to European practice, in that the melody is measured and is dependent on the basic rhythmic pattern; it also is characterized by a very regular phrase structure. The typical instrumentation for all forms of the *joropo* is harp, *cuatro* (small guitar), and maracas.

The *joropo* is a fairly rapid dance and often makes use of hemiola. It also consists of strongly accented rhythms, but unlike the other Venezuelan dances no single rhythmic pattern is associated with it. Some of the most commonly used patterns are:

It is important to note that each "rhythm" is defined not only by a certain sequence of durational values but by pattern of accents as well, which may or may not be consistent with the meter indicated.

Formally, the *joropo*, *vals*, and *merengue* are simple and repetitive. Repetition occurs on all levels: one-measure rhythmic patterns, melodic phrases, and entire sections. Overall thematic forms generally consist of an alternation of two distinct sections (ABAB).

The *Siete canciones venezolanas* of Plaza can serve as an illustration of his national style. They may have been inspired by de Falla's *Siete canciones españolas*, each of which draws on a different popular genre and is named accordingly. Plaza's songs are also clearly related to the popular tradition (that of Venezuela), even if they are not called "joropo" or "vals."

22Cf. Luis Felipe Ramón y Rivera, *El Joropo, baile nacional de Venezuela* (Caracas: Dirección de Cultura y Bellas Artes, 1953).

The texts, perhaps the most obvious national feature of Plaza's work, come from a book of poems, *La respuesta a las piedras*, written by Luis Barrios Cruz, himself a nationalist and a "poeta llanero," whose poetry describes the most intimate expressions of the plains. Five of the seven poems chosen by Plaza mention the Venezuelan "llano," and all of them describe landscapes associated with the plains. Beyond the texts, there are purely musical relationships to popular *criollo* traditions. However, though Plaza borrows certain characteristics of popular songs and dances, he does not strictly imitate any specific genre.

The seven songs present an alternation of quick, accented, dance-like pieces (Nos. 1, 3, 5, and 7) and slower, more lyrical, song-like compositions (Nos. 2, 4, and 6). Both types are formally similar and, in turn, similar to the formal structure of popular dances. Plaza consistently makes use of very regular four-bar phrasing; these short phrases are frequently repeated, resulting in an aa bb scheme. On a larger level, each of the songs falls into a sectional pattern of A B A, often with piano introductions and interludes between sections. The harmonies are quite simple. Modulations occur, but generally between very closely related keys (i.e., dominant, parallel major or minor, relative major or minor). In "La noche del llano abajo," for example, the A sections are in F major and the B section in D minor, while in "Cuando el caballo se para" the A sections are in D minor and the B section is in F major. "Por estos cuatro caminos" includes modulations to the dominant as well as the parallel minor. A syllabic setting of the text is characteristic throughout.

Joropo elements appear in two of the dance-type songs. "Yo me quedé triste y mudo," for example, uses hemiola throughout: the vocal line alternates between 6/8 and 3/4, while the accompanying lines are mostly in 6/8. In addition, the *joropo* rhythm ♩♪♪♪♪ (= ♩ ♪♪♪♪ , as shown above) is quite prominent in the accompaniment. The other two dance-type songs are more closely related to the *vals*. "Por estos cuatro caminos" makes use of a variant of the *vals* rhythmic pattern ♪♪♪♪ ♩ (variant of ♪♩ ⁊ ♪♩). The accenting of the first and third beats, which is very characteristic of the *vals*, is much in evidence in both the accompaniment and the vocal line. "Palma verde, garza blanca" uses a totally different rhythmic pattern, but heavy accents on the first and third beats are again quite prominent.

Among Plaza's orchestral works of national character is the *Fuga criolla* (1932), for string orchestra, based on the patterns of the *joropo*. The composer combines very effectively certain accompanimental figures of popular harpists (in a stylized fashion) with the normal contrapuntal nature of the fugue. Finally, his obvious inclination toward neo-Romanticism, in such works as his *Fuga romántica* (1950) and *Elegía* (1953), has often been related to the Venezuelan popular sentimental *canción* of the nineteenth century.

Musical nationalism based on descriptive or actual folk elements has had numerous followers in subsequent generations of Venezuelan composers, among them Evencio Castellanos (*Suite Avileña*), Inocente Carreño (*Margariteña*), Gonzalo Castellanos (*Suite caraqueña*), and Antonio Estévez (*Cantata criolla*).

BIBLIOGRAPHICAL NOTES

Gilbert Chase's *Introducción a la Música Americana Contemporánea* (Buenos Aires: Editorial Nova, 1958) provides general information on musical nationalism in Latin America in the twentieth century. Extremely useful (in spite of many factual errors and the lack of updating of the material) is the series *Composers of the Americas*, published by the Pan American Union, which provides biographical data and catalogues of the works of composers from all countries of the Western Hemisphere. The series includes eighteen volumes published between 1955 and 1972. The last volume contains a list of the composers' names, by volume and by country, appearing in all previous issues.

Special studies of the life and works of Manuel Ponce are Jesús C. Romero's "Efemérides de Manuel M(aría) Ponce," *Nuestra Música*, no. 18 (2nd trimester, 1950), 164–202, which includes a list of the composer's works and writings; Gerónimo Baqueiro Foster's "Manuel M. Ponce, el Compositor Romántico de México," *Boletín de Xela*, no. 477 (April 1961); and David López Alonso's *Manuel M. Ponce* (Mexico: Ediciones Botas, 1971), an updating of Alonso's earlier biographical essay. A discussion of Ponce's pioneering work in the study of folk music and a series of interviews about his compositions are presented by Carmen Sordo Sodi in *Manuel M. Ponce: Iniciador de la Etnomúsica en México* (Oaxaca: Ediciones de la Universidad Autónoma Benito Juárez, 1973). Carlos Chávez's life and works have been the subject of numerous studies. García Morillo's book (cited in note 4) is undoubtedly the best analytical study; it includes a catalogue of Chávez's works, a bibliography, and a discography. Still informative are Herbert Weinstock's "Carlos Chávez," *Musical Quarterly*, XXII (1936), 435ff, and Aaron Copland's "Composer from Mexico," in his *The New Music: 1900–1960* (New York: McGraw-Hill, 1968). A catalogue of Chávez's compositions was compiled by Rodolfo Halffter and others in *Carlos Chávez. Complete Catalogue of his Works* (Mexico: Sociedad de Autores y Compositores de Música, 1971). Chávez himself has written on "Blas Galindo," in *Nuestra Música*, no. 1 (1946), 7–13, and on "Luis Sandi," in *Nuestra Música*, no. 15 (1949), 175–79. Moncayo and other nationalist composers are reviewed by Pablo Castellanos in "Aspectos del Nacionalismo Musical Mexicano," *Heterofonía*, nos. 1–2 and 4 (1968 and 1969). Revueltas's music is studied in the several general studies of Mexican music already mentioned. Otto Mayer-Serra's "Silvestre Revueltas and Musical Nationalism in Mexico," *Musical Quarterly*, XXVII (1941), 123–45, is still valuable. For English-speaking readers, Dan Malmström's *Introduction to Twentieth-Century Mexican Music* (Ph.D. dissertation, Uppsala University, 1974) contains good general information, although the musical analyses leave a great deal to be desired.

Cuban nationalism and the study of *afrocubanismo* are best treated in Alejo Carpentier's *La Música en Cuba*, cited in note 18. Roldán's article, "The Artistic Position of the American Composer," in Henry Cowell (ed.), *American Composers on American Music* (Stanford, Calif.: Stanford University Press, 1933), pp. 175–77, is a pertinent statement of his own position. Cowell himself wrote on " 'Motivos de Son,' A Series of Eight Songs for Soprano, with a Small Orchestra," *Musical Quarterly*, XXXVI (1950), 270ff. García Caturla wrote on "The Development of Cuban Music," in Cowell's *American Composers on American Music*, pp. 173–74. Nicolas Slonimsky's "Caturla of Cuba," in *Modern Music*, XVII/2 (January 1940), 76–80, provides some analytical comments. Alejo Carpentier has also written on "Music in Cuba," in *Musical Quarterly*, XXXIII (1947), 365ff.

A general survey of Venezuelan music up to the 1950s in José Antonio Calcaño's *La Ciudad y su Música* (Caracas: Conservatorio "Teresa Carreño," 1958).

SIX

THE TWENTIETH CENTURY:
THE ANDEAN AREA

It is possible to refer to a cultural homogeneity among nationalist composers of the Andes, despite obvious regional differences. Highland Indian music reveals general common traits, whether in Ecuador, Peru, or Bolivia, and Indian musical instruments throughout the area show a remarkable sameness not only in types but in functions as well. Pre-Columbian instruments included vertical flutes, clay and reed panpipes, trumpets (conch or clay), and drums of various sizes among the Quechua and the Aymará. These instruments have been maintained in modern-day folk music of the area. The post-Conquest period in the Andean countries also saw the emergence of a mestizo folk-music tradition; this does exhibit considerable diversity in the various countries, as a result of ethnic and historical circumstances. While Colombia, for example, is undoubtedly an Andean country, its Pacific and Atlantic coastal areas stem musically from predominantly Black and Caribbean cultural spheres. At the same time mestizo folk music of the whole Colombia area is largely Spanish in origin, whether in the actual ingredients of folk-song and dance genres or in the adoption of instruments (especially strings).

The nationalistic production of art-music composers of the Andes naturally reflects in varying degrees the traits of the vernacular music. It is not surprising to see the major creative personalities of twentieth-century Chile embracing European contemporary trends rather than musical nationalism, for Chilean folk music is certainly less "indigenous" and consequently less susceptible as a source of "nationalizing" than that of the other Andean republics. In addition, in spite of the mestizo nature of its population, Chile tends to identify itself, from an art-music viewpoint, with its markedly European ancestry. Even in Chile, however, a few composers adhered to the nationalist trend.

COLOMBIA

The groundwork for the development of musical nationalism in Colombia was laid during the republican period, which opened a new phase in nineteenth-century Colombian music, mostly through the cultivation of European operatic and symphonic repertories and styles. Active during the century were Juan Antonio de Velasco (d. 1859), Nicolás Quevedo Rachadell (1803–1874), and Henry or Enrique Price (1819–1863). Velasco dedicated himself mainly to opera arrangements for piano and military band, and organized a series of concerts in Bogotá to promote the Viennese classicists. Quevedo, of Venezuelan birth, attempted to establish a regular concert life in the capital city of Bogotá. Price, born and educated in London, settled in Colombia in 1840. Together with Quevedo and others, he founded the Sociedad Filarmónica (1847), and attached a music school to it; this was the first step toward the establishment of the Academia Nacional de Música in 1882 by his son Jorge W. Price (1853–1953). In 1909 the Academia became the Conservatorio Nacional, from which many twentieth-century composers graduated. As a composer, Henry Price left many solo songs and overtures, and numerous piano pieces, among which is a *Vals al estilo del país* (1843)—a stylized *pasillo*, one of Colombia's most widespread folk dances.

José María Ponce de León (1846–1882), the author of the only two operas produced in Bogotá in the nineteenth century (*Ester*, 1874, and *Florinda*, 1880), appears as the immediate forerunner of Colombian nationalism. A student of Gounod and Thomas at the Paris Conservatoire, he followed closely European models of the time in his operas and works of sacred music. But some of his works, such as *La Hermosa Sabana* and *Sinfonía sobre temas colombianos* (1881), denote an early concern for national music within a predominantly Romantic vocabulary. Several compositions are based on typical Colombian folk dances like the *bambuco*, *pasillo*, and *torbellino*. But

Ponce de León's music was considered incomprehensible in his own country, which indicates that even standard European styles of the nineteenth century had not penetrated effectively Colombia's musical life. (During the early twentieth century this was compensated for and remedied by a dynamic preoccupation with music education.)

Composers associated with the Conservatorio Nacional included Andrés Martínez Montoya (1869–1933), Santos Cifuentes (1870–1932), and especially Guillermo Uribe-Holguín (1880–1971), director of the conservatory for twenty-five years (1910–1935) and the most influential composer of his generation. Trained at the Schola Cantorum under Vincent d'Indy, he acquired real skill in compositional techniques and writing in the larger forms. His autobiography, *Vida de un músico colombiano*, retraces in detail his activities as the organizer and conductor of the concerts of the Sociedad de Conciertos Sinfónicos del Conservatorio.[1] Very prolific, Uribe-Holguín wrote numerous academic pieces but also many works incorporating national elements within Impressionist technique. The national elements can be inferred from the melodies and rhythms of some of his works, especially his three hundred piano pieces known as *Trozos en el sentimiento popular*, written over a period of many years. (They begin with Op. 22 and end with Op. 71). Although these pieces are not based on specific folk or popular themes, they derive their melodic, rhythmic, and formal traits from folk dances, especially the *pasillo* and (less frequently) the *bambuco*. Particularly frequent in these pieces is the alternation of 3/4 and 6/8 (or simply ternary and duple meters) (Example 6-1).

EXAMPLE 6-1a Guillermo Uribe-Holguín, *Trozos en el sentimiento popular*, no. 34, mm. 1–4.

EXAMPLE 6-1b Guillermo Uribe-Holguín, *Trozos en el sentimiento popular*, no. 54, mm. 1–4.

[1]A list of the works of the classical and modern symphonic repertory performed by the Sociedad is presented in *Vida de un músico colombiano* (Bogotá: Editorial Librería Voluntad, S.A., 1941), pp. 271–79.

Uribe-Holguín's symphonic output contains clear nationalistic works, such as the *Tres danzas* (*Joropo, Pasillo, Bambuco*), Op. 21; the *Suite típica*, Op. 43; and the Second Symphony, Op. 15, subtitled "del terruño." Of some eleven symphonies, the Second is the only one which is programmatic and borrows directly from folk music. The first movement describes a "Journey to the village of the miraculous Virgin" by a pilgrim; it is cast, however, in the classical structure of a sonata-allegro movement. The second movement, "El pueblo en fiesta," follows the form and character of a scherzo, with a trio section evoking the spirit of a village band playing a *bambuco*. The slow movement, "La tarde en los alrededores," includes a section derived from the music of popular strolling musicians with their guitars and *tiples* (small guitars). "Baile popular," the last movement, is an effective symphonic stylization of Colombian folk dances, reminiscent of numerous final dance movements of symphonic suites of the Latin American nationalist repertory. Occasionally, Uribe-Holguín resorted to Indianist subject matter, either musically or simply as an evocation, as in the lyric tragedy *Furatena*, Op. 76, and the orchestral work *Ceremonia indígena*, Op. 88.

Among the many composers of the nationalist trend, Jesús Bermúdez Silva, Daniel Zamudio, José Rozo Contreras, and Antonio Maria Valencia should be mentioned. Of these, Zamudio and Valencia are especially noteworthy.

Zamudio (1885–1952), a noted folklorist and author of *El Folklore musical de Colombia* (1944), wrote several instrumental pieces and songs in the popular vein. José Rozo Contreras (b. 1894), whose training was largely obtained in Rome and Vienna, allies a solid technical craft with a good knowledge of Colombian folk music. He has cultivated a picturesque folkloristic style, with a direct incorporation of folk-music material in the Afro-Colombian-tradition of the Chocó area. His most representative works are the orchestral suite *Tierra colombiana* (1930) and the *Obertura No. 2* (1932), both on national themes. As a band director and teacher, Rozo Contreras has contribued a sizable repertory of transcriptions for band.

Antonio María Valencia (1902–1952), born in Cali, studied piano at the Conservatory of Bogotá before going to Paris, where he became a student of Vincent d'Indy in composition and Gabriel Pierné in chamber music; he also studied with Manuel de Falla. He then returned to his native city and founded there a Conservatory and School of Fine Arts (1933). Moreover, he distinguished himself as a concert pianist, introducing European modern piano literature to Colombia. His first compositions follow a "criollo" style indicative of his early concern for national music. Under the influence of his Parisian friends and teachers, he later aimed at a more European musical style, concentrating his efforts on religious choral works in which he revealed a solid and imaginative technique of choral writing. His handling of counterpoint is particularly remarkable in his Requiem Mass (1943).

Toward the latter part of his life, Valencia tended to go back to his earlier interests in national music. Some of his secular choral works (e.g., *Coplas populares colombianas*, *Cinco canciones indígenas*, and *Canción del boga ausente*) are effective evocations of the rich popular "cancionero" of his country. For the piano he wrote both Impressionist and nationalist pieces, the latter based on stylizations of the *bambuco* and the *pasillo*. In his *Chirimía y bambuco sotareño* (1930), orchestrated in 1942, he defines the basic rhythm of the *bambuco* as a combination of binary and ternary divisions (3 + 2), but 6/8 meter prevails, and there is often a change in meter from 5/8 to 6/8 at the cadences.

Among Valencia's chamber music pieces, the trio *Emociones caucanas* (1938), for violin, piano, and cello, is generally considered the most emphatic expression of his nationalist style. Each of its four movements expresses a different mood. The first, "Amanecer en la sierra" (Vallecaucano landscape), is a delightful piece with a remarkable economy of means and some descriptive intents, such as the opening five-octave-range reiteration of the same pitch by the piano, each time with a different phrasing (most likely associated with the profile of the mountain chain). In three sections, this movement relies also on Impressionist techniques of composition. "Pasillo," the second movement, presents an imaginative stylization of the basic rhythm of the popular dance, with an appealing isometric design to the first thematic motif. The final movement ("Fiesta campestre") has the spontaneous character of mush peasant dance music of Colombia, whether the *bambuco*, the *bunde*, or the *cumbia*. However, the composer does not borrow overtly from any specific folk dance genre, although the figure $\overset{>}{}$ 𝄽 can be related to several folk dances of the Andean nations.

To the same generation of Valencia belongs Guillermo Espinosa (b. 1905), who had a decisive influence in his country as a conductor and, subsequently, as chief of the music division of the Pan American Union. The National Symphony Orchestra, established in Bogotá in 1936, was at first under his direction. During his tenure of office in the Pan American Union he organized the Inter-American Music Festivals in Washington, promoting and exposing new works by Latin-American composers.

Although younger composers in Colombia have preferred to cultivate other stylistic currents, several of them, such as Luis Antonio Escobar (b. 1925) and Blas Emilio Atehortúa (b. 1933), have maintained concurrently a vivid interest in national music. Escobar, for example, has resorted to national sources in his ballet *Avirama* (1955), the piano preludes *Bambuquerías* (1954–1958), and the choral pieces *Cánticas colombianas* (1960). Atehortúa's individualistic style is frequently based on nationalist content, together with a use of the most advanced techniques of composition. His works of some nationalist persuasion include *Cantata sobre poemas colombianos*, a *Pieza concierto sobre formas folklóricas colombianas*, and an

Intermezzo sobre motivos colombianos. His more original works of the 1960s, however, do not follow the same trend.

ECUADOR

Not until the latter part of the nineteenth century were efforts made in Ecuador to establish a professional musical life. Under the stimulation of the educational policy of the García Moreno regime, the Conservatorio Nacional de Música was founded (1870) and put under the direction of Antonio Neumann (1818–1871), of German descent, who was author of the national anthem and founder of the Philharmonic Society in Guayaquil.

Early in the present century, the Italian Domenico Brescia came from Santiago de Chile to direct the conservatory in Quito. During his eight years as director (1903–1911) he helped develop music education in Ecuador on sounder bases than had been possible previously. He opened the path to musical nationalism in the country with such works as his *Sinfonía ecuatoria-na* and the *Ocho variaciones* on an indigenous sacred song. Several of his students adhered to the nationalist trend. Among them, Segundo Luis Moreno (1882–1972), a well-known folklorist and ethnomusicologist, wrote many works with a marked Indianist tendency (*3 Suites Ecuatorianas,* for orchestra) and popular dance pieces such as *pasillos, sanjuanitos,* and *ron-deñas.* Luis H. Salgado (b. 1903), considered the leading musician of his generation, has been the most successful nationalist composer of Ecuador. His symphonic suite *Atahualpa o El Ocaso de un imperio* (1933), *Suite coreográfica* (1946), and the ballets *El Amaño* (1947) and *El Dios Tumbal* (1952), among many other works, reveal a strong nationalistic style, based either on native themes or scales (pentatonic) or on simple allusions to national history. His opera *Cumandá* (1940, revised 1954) has an Indianist libretto adapted by the composer from a novel by Juan León Mera; the action takes place in the Oriente provinces of Ecuador (Amazon).

Pedro Pablo Traversari (1874–1956), a very prolific composer and musicologist, combined a neo-Romantic style with native musical charac-teristics. After training at the Santiago, Chile, conservatory he studied in Rome, Basel, and Paris for two years. His teaching activities in the major Ecuadorian institutions, including the Universidad Central, were quite influential. He wrote twenty-two dances in a "highland indigenous style," several hymns (e.g., the *Pentatonic hymn of the Indian race*), the tone poem *Glorias andinas,* and melodramas such as *Cumandá, La profecía de Huira-cocha,* and *Los hijos del Sol,* all based on native legends. He left an important collection of native and world instruments which make up the Instrument Museum of the Casa de la Cultura Ecuatoriana in Quito.

PERU

The splendor of colonial musical life in Peru as surveyed in our Part 1 had no counterpart in the period of independence, during which operas and salon music genres predominated. Church music continued to be written in a secularized Romantic style, as seen in some of the works of José Bernardo Alzedo (Alcedo), the author of the Peruvian national anthem.

It was only by the end of the nineteenth century that Peruvian composers began to acquire professional competence. At the same time, most of them turned their attention to Peruvian folk music. Immigrant musicians were actually the first to treat Peruvian subject matter, although in works written within the Romantic tradition. For these composers, musical nationalism consisted mainly in collecting folk songs, harmonizing them, and rewriting them in an art-music framework. This was true, for instance, of the Italian Carlo Enrique Pasta (1855–1898), who wrote the first opera on a Peruvian story, *Atahualpa* (premiered in Lima in 1877). Another Italian, Claudio Rebagliati (1847–1909), wrote a Peruvian rhapsody, *Un 28 de julio*, performed by the Lima Philharmonic Society in 1868, and a piano album of folk dances and songs entitled *Album Sud Americano* (1870). The great aim of many such composers was to include authentic or "pure" Indian melodic material in their works.

Nationalist Romanticism was also expressed by José María Valle Riestra (1858–1925), the first competent professional Peruvian composer, who was educated in London, Paris, and Berlin. His opera *Ollanta* (1901), based on a well-known, half historical and half legendary story, acquired resounding fame as being the first major work written by a Peruvian composer. In addition, Valle Riestra's solid technical competence in handling the larger forms made a formidable impression on his Peruvian contemporaries. *Ollanta* was in fact an ambitious attempt to create a national opera. Perhaps ineffective because so closely imitative of Italian operatic models, it nevertheless stood at the time as a symbol of truly Peruvian art music, which meant essentially music made in Peru, with Peruvian motifs. Valle Riestra's numerous orchestral works, piano pieces, solo songs (*Canción de Heine*), and religious choral music display a refined harmonic chromaticism.

Less ambitious but in certain ways a more impressive composer, Luis Duncker Lavalle (1874–1922) wrote attractive piano pieces in a semipopular style inspired by mestizo folk-music genres. His *Quenas, vals característico indígena*, and *Vals cholito* re-create the most typical *criolla* musical expression of the urban areas.

By the beginning of the twentieth century, a search for national

identity among Peruvian composers was much in evidence, and the first
systematic collecting and study of Peruvian folk music was undertaken.
Music of the Quechua-speaking Indians of the highlands, with its ubiquitous
pentatonicism and characteristic rhythmic formulas, became the main source
of that identity. The Indianist trend is found in varying degrees in the works
of several folklorist-composers of the time. Among them Daniel Alomía
Robles (1871–1942), although largely self-taught, acquired a substantial
understanding of the various folk and popular traditions of Peru. For more
than twenty years, he collected folk-music material in the most remote areas
of the highlands and the coastal area. This material included what he called
Incaic motives (800 tunes) classified by regions, 300 colonial folk tunes, and
170 mestizo songs of more recent origin. As a composer, Robles tended to
re-create rather than simply imitate Indian music. His numerous piano pieces
and songs present typical traits related to such folk genres as the *huayno*,
triste, or *yaraví*. (The *yaraví* is a love-song type of Indian origin.) The piece
Despedida (Example 6-2), subtitled "Yaraví colonial," is a clever stylization

EXAMPLE 6-2   Daniel Alomía Robles, *Despedida*, mm. 1–12. Copyright 1952 by
Ricordi Americana S.A.E.C. Used by permission.

of a duet of *quenas* (Peruvian end-notched vertical flutes), as played typically in unison or at the octave, or in parallel thirds or sixths.

Three other composers of the same orientation—José Castro (1872–1945), Luis Pacheco de Céspedes (b. 1895), and Federico Gerdes (1873–1953)—contributed to the Indianist current in substantial ways while cultivating at the same time a Romantic piano style. Castro was one of the first, before the French d'Harcourts, to preach the much disputed pentatonic thesis of pre-Columbian Andean Indian music. Pacheco de Céspedes studied in Paris under Gabriel Fauré and Reynaldo Hahn; a ballet and an opera by him were premiered in France. Several of his works are evocations of Inca music, such as his symphonic *Danzas sobre un tema Inca* or the piano piece *Danza India*. The latter exhibits duple and triple divisions (in alternation) within a 2/4 meter, as well as the anhemitonic (i.e., without semitones) pentatonic motif that is typical of indigenous melody (Example 6-3). Gerdes evoked Indian legends in his numerous piano pieces, but did so in a rather superficial manner. His style is perhaps the most Europeanized of the composers of his generation.

An abundant production of piano music in which Romantic traits are combined with southern Peruvian folk music flowed from Manuel Aguirre (1863–1951), of Arequipa. Several of his works were published in Europe, the best known of which are the *Siete Piezas* (1937) and the two albums *De mis montañas*. Within a well-established Romantic idiom, he was able to write with a certain originality, through a frequently effective utilization of folk-music traits, such as, for example, sequential reiterations and the characteristic cadences on E-flat major and C minor (Example 6-4).

EXAMPLE 6-3 Luis Pacheco de Céspedes, *Danza India*, mm. 7–10. Copyright 1952 by Ricordi Americana S.A.E.C. Used by permission.

EXAMPLE 6-4 Manuel Aguirre, *Siete Piezas:* "Humoreska," mm. 37–40. Copyright 1937 by Schott Frères, Brussels. Used by permission.

Among the many nationalist composers born around the turn of the twentieth century, the most representative were Teodoro Valcárcel (1902–1942), Carlos Sánchez Málaga (b. 1904), Monseñor Pablo Chávez Aguilar (1898–1950), and Roberto Carpio Valdés (b. 1900). Valcárcel, of Indian descent and a native of Puno, was the most prolific and creative artist of his generation. After studying with Duncker Lavalle in Arequipa, he went to Italy but returned to Peru with the outbreak of World War I. His early works of the 1920s were literal imitations of Debussy's style, even in their suggestive French titles, but he soon became interested in treating indigenous folk music in a modern style. He produced a fairly large number of piano and orchestral works. Lacking proficiency in orchestration, he had to resort to Rodolfo Holzmann for orchestrating such works as the ballet *Suray-Surita* and the tone poem *En las ruinas del templo del Sol.* A concert of his works in 1928 in the presidential palace brought him special recognition, and he was designated as the Peruvian representative to the Barcelona Festival of Ibero-American Music in 1929. His *Suite Incaica* was premiered on that occasion. In four movements (*Danza imperial, Bacanal indígena, Danza del cortejo nupcial,* and *Feria en el ayllu de Kalassaya*), this work took the public and the music critics by surprise because of its clearly displayed exoticism and its original and dynamic rhythmic writing. Valcárcel received a resounding acclaim at the Sevilla fair when his early ballet *Saccsahuamán* (1928) was performed (with the new title *Chori Kancha*) in the presence of the Spanish royal family. A concert of his music at the Salle Pleyel in Paris (1930) presented, according to the *Guide Musical,* a "program of rare enjoyment and total novelty. Peruvian folk music is of extreme richness and its pentatonic structure sounds to our ears with a freshness of renovation."

Valcárcel had in fact a natural musical talent enhanced by a genuine understanding of traditional Indian ritual songs and dances and mestizo musical genres. He was thus able to achieve an imaginative stylization of Indian material. His thirty *Cantos de alma vernacular* and his *Cuatro canciones incaicas* (published in Paris, 1930) are the best examples of his style. The song *Suray-Surita* from the *Cuatro Canciones,* with text in the Quechua language, reveals two of the most typical features of Andean Indian music, namely, pentatonic melody and an omnipresent falling third at the cadences (Example 6-5), which Valcárcel harmonizes with a progression from the tonic major triad (here A♭) to the relative minor tonic triad (F minor). At the same time, the elegiac quality of the melody can be considered as a most adequate translation of Indian expressiveness.

Valcárcel's piano works include *12 Estampas peruanas,* from the ballet *Suray-Surita*; two symphonic suites of 1939 consist of orchestrated versions of several of these "estampas," subtitled "Aires y danzas sobre motivos del folklore de los Incas del Perú." They offer the best evidence in support of the opinion, generally held in Peru, that Valcárcel is indeed the precursor of a genuinely Peruvian art music. Here, the composer not only refers to traits of

Indian music but also to mestizo features, as may be heard in the rhythmic features of the piece *Bailan los Llameros*, which calls for 6/8 and 3/4 simultaneously.

 Carlos Sánchez Málaga, a choral conductor, music teacher, and composer, followed the same Indianist trend as Valcárcel, though with somewhat less emphasis on pre-Conquest or Inca musical evocations; perhaps because

EXAMPLE 6-5 Teodoro Valcárcel, *Suray-Surita*, mm. 6–10.

he was a native of Arequipa, where mestizo art expressions are most conspicuous, he paid more attention to modern-day Peruvian folk music. His
production as a composer was limited to piano and vocal pieces. *Caima* and
Yanahuara, for piano (both of 1928), reveal the early elements of the Indianist
style, i.e., pentatonicism, harmonic parallelism, and some touches of virtuosity. In his songs, Sánchez Málaga avails himself of mestizo folk genres such
as the *huayno* and the *marinera*. The song *Huayno* exhibits some of the
rhythmic figures associated with that dance, especially the syncopated figure
♪ ♩ ♪ .

Pablo Chávez Aguilar's *Ocho Variaciones sobre un tema incaico*
(1926), for piano, illustrates the extent of his involvement in national music.
The theme is authentically "Inca" in its descending pentatonic motive (D-C-
A-G-F) and in its metric arrangement of 5/4, underlining the anacrusis. The
harmonization, however, combines mestizo folk-like progressions (parallel
sixths) and Romantic harmonies (diminished seventh chords and predominance of leading tone at cadences) (Example 6-6). Significantly, the eight
variations appear as a scholastic exercise, along the lines of harmonizing a
given soprano part, making use of the easiest type of variation technique,
the melodic-harmonic ornamentation. All of the figurations in the variations
rely on the most common type of nineteenth-century piano writing.

Most of the composers thus far mentioned who cultivated the nationalist trend suffered from inadequate academic training in music. This also
explains in part the reasons for the very limited Peruvian orchestral repertory
of their time. With the settling in Lima during the 1920s and 1930s of several

EXAMPLE 6-6   Pablo Chávez Aguilar, *Ocho Variaciones sobre un tema incaico:*
Theme.

TEMA

European-born musicians, the situation changed substantially for the following generations of composers. The Italians Enrique Fava Ninci and Vicente Stea and the Austrian Theo Buchwald were influential music teachers. Ninci (1883–1949) taught music theory at the Academia Nacional de Música and at the Conservatory, which he directed from 1931. Stea (1884–1943), a voice teacher, opera producer, and orchestra conductor, helped develop orchestral activities in Peru. As the first conductor of the Orquesta Sinfónica Nacional, founded in 1938, Buchwald actively promoted Peruvian composers.

The most effective European teachers and composers, however, were Andrés Sas and Rodolfo Holzmann. Sas (1900–1967), of Belgian-French origin, developed into an influential musicologist, teacher, and composer. Although born in Paris, he was raised in Belgium, where he acquired his first musical training (studying chemical engineering at the same time). The Peruvian government engaged him in 1924 to teach violin and chamber music at the Academia Nacional, where he also taught music history courses. With his wife Lily Rosay, a pianist, he founded the Sas-Rosay Academy of Music in 1930, which became famous among Peruvian pianists and composers. He later directed the Lima Conservatory for a short time and continued to teach theory and composition until 1966. He founded the music review *Antara*, and co-edited other journals (*Anacrusa*, *Música*) in the 1950s. He was also active as conductor, lecturer, and folklorist, and participated in international music organizations.

As both a musicologist and a composer, Sas disclosed throughout his life a special interest in Peru's indigenous music. He understandably felt a need to incorporate himself into the culture of his adopted country, an attitude shared by many foreign-born professionals. Important writings by him in the 1930s on Inca and Nazca music resulted from scientific studies of pre-Columbian instruments. He was the first serious student in Peru of colonial cathedral music, especially the music of Torrejón y Velasco. His various writings on the subject culminated in the monumental *La música en la catedral de Lima*, published posthumously (1970–1972).

Sas's compositions are largely cast in the folkloristic nationalist style. In such works as *Rapsodia peruana*, for violin and orchestra (1928), *Tres Estampas del Perú* (1936), *Poema Indio* (1941) for orchestra, and the triptych *Ollantai* for a cappella mixed chorus, he attempted a synthesis of Impressionist techniques with pseudo-indigenous thematic material. The Sonata for piano and the *Seis Cantos Indios del Perú* (1946) are good examples of his style. Pentatonic modes predominate in his melodic writing; his concise harmonic practice often relies on Debussyan patterns of parallel altered chords; and the rhythmic structure gravitates around persistent figures in a given passage, as can be seen in the first movement of the Sonata.

Clear stylizations of Peruvian folk-music types abound in Sas's works. The "Huayno" section of *El Pajonal* from the *Seis Cantos* maintains a close association with the original models in its dotted and syncopated rhythms, the 3 + 2 divisions of the theme (hence the 5/4 meter), and pentatonic motives with characteristic falling-third cadences (Example 6-7). The "Kcashwa" (Kashua) dance is cleverly imitated in the *Suite Peruana*, for piano, not only by means of the ostinato figures of the accompaniment but also through the melorhythmic design of the theme, with its alternating regular eighths, dotted figures, and triplets (Example 6-8).[2]

Rodolfo (Rudolph) Holzmann (b. 1910), together with Sas, was very influential in shaping the development of Peruvian musical life in the 1940s and 1950s. He studied in Berlin under Vogel (1931), in Strasbourg under Scherchen (1933), in Paris under Rathaus (1934), then again under Vogel. He moved to Lima in 1938, as an oboe teacher at the Alcedo Academy and as a violinist in the newly established National Symphonic Orchestra. In 1945 he was appointed professor of composition at the National Conserva-

EXAMPLE 6-7 Andrés Sas, *Seis cantos indios del Perú:* "El Pajonal," mm. 17–21. Copyright 1957 by Ricordi Americana S.A.E.C. Used by permission.

[2]See also Sas's *Himno y Danza* in *Latin American Art Music for the Piano*, ed. Francisco Curt Lange (New York: G. Schirmer, 1942), pp. 40–43.

EXAMPLE 6-8 Andrés Sas, *Suite Peruana:* "Kcashwa," mm. 1–8. Copyright 1935 by Andrés Sas. Used by permission of the Sas family.

tory of Music, where he played a most significant role. His numerous students, who included Iturriaga, Pinilla, and Garrido-Lecca, were first exposed by him to current European trends, especially atonality and the music of the Viennese serialists. Holzmann did extensive work in style analysis and theoretical matters, published catalogues of works by nine-teenth- and twentieth-century Peruvian composers, and promoted the study of archives of colonial music. His ethnomusicological activities over the years included extensive collecting of Peruvian folk and primitive music, some of which appears transcribed in his *Panorama de la música tradicional del Perú* (Lima, 1966). As the head of the Musicological Service of the National School of Folk Music and Dance, he accomplished a great deal with serious publications of folk music.

As a composer, Holzmann seems to have felt from around 1940 a need for self-integration into the culture of his new country, for he wrote many works related to some aspects of Peruvian folk-music traditions. He cannot be considered, however, a typical nationalist composer, since he has

cultivated several contemporary European trends, including a fairly orthodox serialism in his later works. In his article "Aporte para la emancipación
de la música peruana,"[3] Holzmann discusses the question of whether or not
it is possible (and adequate) to use the pentatonic scale to create a music of
distinctively Peruvian character. His answer is affirmative, but he advocates
the need for some transformation, since in his judgment this primitive scale
in itself does not afford enough harmonic variety. There should be, he says, a
way of treating the scale according to contemporary compositional techniques, without which the scale itself seems useless to him. One possible
solution he proposes is a procedure of building chords and themes on successive fourths, by ordering the pentatonic scale on a basis of fourths, in a
manner similar to chord-formation by superimposed thirds from the diatonic
scale (Example 6-9a). Example 6-9b is also illustrative of this. Holzmann

EXAMPLE 6-9a   Holzmann's explanation of chord-building on successive fourths.

EXAMPLE 6-9b   Holzmann's ordering of the pentatonic scale.

concludes that with such a procedure "it is then possible to create a contemporary musical language totally unsuspected within the framework of
the pentatonic scale." But he may be naïvely optimistic when he asserts that
"it has been demonstrated that ample possibilities for developing an authentic
manner of composition in Peru do exist. . . . With a study in depth, above all
of the problem of form (i.e., how to fill it with a content adequate to our
time), . . . we will have something with which to fill in the prevailing vacuum."

An application of these and others of his theories was undertaken by
Holzmann in his *Suite sobre motivos peruanos* (also known as *Cuarta pequeña
suite*), for piano, and his *Suite arequipeña* (1945), for orchestra, among other
works. The first section, "Preludio pastoral," of the *Cuarta pequeña suite*,
based on the pentatonic scale of Example 6-9b, reveals the fairly systematic
use of the fourth and its inversion in the harmonic writing (Example 6-10a).
According to the composer, monotony is avoided in this piece by a frequent
transfer of the melody to various registers of the piano. The contrapuntal
writing in the prelude culminates with a stretto in the final measures (Example
6-10b). The second number of the suite, "Bailan las muchachas," is based on

[3] *Revista de Estudios Musicales*, I/1 (August 1949), 61–80. An earlier, shorter version
was published in 1944 in *Nuestro Tiempo*.

EXAMPLE 6-10 Rodolfo Holzmann, *Cuarta pequeña suite:* "Preludio pastoral," (a) mm. 9–10; (b) mm. 22–25. Copyright Instituto Interamericano de Musicología, Montevideo, 1944. Used by permission.

another pentatonic scale, with two added tones that create a scale similar to the Aeolian or "natural" minor scale (Example 6-11). Holzmann adheres fairly strictly to this scale, as can be seen in Example 6-12, the harmonic accompaniment of which derives from the basic scale. Holzmann points out in the last section of the suite ("Danza final") his use of a bitonal chord (B♭ major ⁶₄ chord together with E♭ major ⁶₄ chord), which he says is no more than a ninth chord on the dominant, determined however by a different procedure than that of traditional tonal harmony.

EXAMPLE 6-11 Holzmann's building of the "natural" minor scale from a pentatonic scale.

EXAMPLE 6-12 Rodolfo Holzmann, *Cuarta pequeña suite:* "Bailan las muchachas," mm. 3–4. Copyright Instituto Interamericano de Musicología, Montevideo, 1944. Used by permission.

In his *Suite Arequipeña*, Holzmann dealt with mestizo folk music of Peru, especially the essential character of the *yaraví*; the theme of the *yaraví* used is given in Example 6-13. The C♯ and C♮ of the second measure provide the composer with another chord formation of bitonal impiications (C major and A major chords), and his use of this structure on various degrees of the chromatic scale confers on this passage of the suite a certain degree of harmonic unity. Likewise, melodic motives in this section are built from the same chromatic semitone of the original theme. The author points to the end of the "Yaraví" section of the Suite as an illustration of this principle of composition.

EXAMPLE 6-13   Rodolfo Holzmann, "Yaraví" theme from *Suite Arequipeña*.

It is quite apparent that Holzmann did not embrace musical nationalism in the same fashion as did most of his Peruvian contemporaries. He never advocated for himself the Indianist current, and his few incursions into indigenous material (approached from a rather convoluted outlook) appear to have resulted from the prevailing taste of the 1940s. Indeed, his production of the 1950s and 1960s shows no association with any local musical element.

With the younger generations of Peruvian composers, several new questions of a philosophical and functional nature have arisen. Translated into stylistic terms, such questions involve the difficulty of attempting to integrate native roots with European contemporary models and still achieve results that are relevant to the contemporary national culture. The most typical development of such composers is sketched out in Part 3 of this study. Suffice it to say here that the beginning of this development reveals in general a subjective national orientation that has produced works of a non-nationalistic nature—at least, works without deliberate intent to be "national."

BOLIVIA

Culturally and ethnically, Bolivia is recognized as one of the most "Indian" countries of South America. Unlike other South American countries, therefore, the simple utilization or imitation of Indian and mestizo folk music by Bolivian nationalist composers should not a priori result in mere exotic display. Most of these composers, however, cultivated during the first half of the twentieth century a national style which restricted itself to a Romantic stylization of folk elements.

La Paz, the effective capital of the country (Sucre is the nominal one), began organizing its musical life around the mid-nineteenth century, but not until the early twentieth were musical organizations established with any degree of continuity. The foundation of the Military School of Music (Escuela militar de música) (1904), the National Conservatory (Conservatorio Nacional) (1908), the Circle of Fine Arts (Círculo de Bellas Artes) (1910), and several other such institutions contributed to the city's musical life. The National Symphony Orchestra was established in 1944 but suffered, until recently, a lack of sufficient support to enable it to recruit good performers and conductors.

The first Bolivian composers of national orientation were those belonging to the generation of the last quarter of the nineteenth century. Among others, the following names should be mentioned: Eduardo Caba (1890–1953), Simeón Roncal (1870–1953), Teófilo Vargas Candia (1886–1961), Humberto Viscarra Monje (b. 1898), and José María Velasco Maidana (b. 1900).

Caba and Roncal appear as the two pioneers of twentieth-century Bolivian art music. Both were strongly nationalistic. Caba, a native of Potosí, studied in Buenos Aires under Felipe Boero and in Spain under Turina and Pérez Casas. His output included a ballet *Kollana*, a tone poem, *Quena*, for flute and orchestra, and eighteen piano pieces entitled *Aires Indios*. The piano pieces reveal a modal and pentatonic idiom, ABA forms, and rhythmic figures associated with folk dances of the Bolivian plateau. Harmonically, they imitate the polyphonic singing and playing, in parallel octaves and fourths, that are frequent in Aymara music.

Roncal, born in Sucre (or Chuquisaca), dedicated most of his career as a composer to the stylization of Bolivia's national dance, the *cueca*. An album of twenty *cuecas* for piano constitutes his major contribution to Bolivian music; it still enjoys great popularity among Bolivian pianists. The pieces show a clear awareness of the folk *criolla* tradition, and in the process of stylization a transfer of this tradition to the salon milieu and the concert hall. Highly virtuosic, they follow a standard tripartite design in which a short rhythmic formula related to the *cueca* ($\frac{6}{8}$ ♩ ♪♪ ♩ ♪♪ ♪♪♪) recurs throughout, together with a rather dense texture and a typically Romantic, Chopinesque harmony. The first and last parts of each piece are generally monothematic, in contrast to a varied middle section.

Viscarra Monje and Velasco Maidana developed a nativistic attitude combined with a Romantic and academic orientation. Viscarra Monje, a pianist-composer trained in Europe, became quite influential as director of the National Conservatory in La Paz. He also founded and directed for a time the Academia Man Césped in Cochabamba. His best known works, all for piano, include *Andante, Rondino, Impresiones de Altiplano*, and *Canciones collas*, all of which reveal the most characteristic Romantic nationalism. The *Rondino* still enjoys a wide popularity in Bolivia.

Velasco Maidana, considered the leading Bolivian nationalist composer, contributed greatly in the 1930s to the improvement of professional competence in Bolivia. He helped found the National Orchestra and wrote many orchestral works, among them the ballet *Amerindia*, which was premiered in Berlin in 1938. His tone poems of the 1930s (*Cuento brujo, Los Khusillos, Vida de cóndores*) and his more recent chamber works—*Pensamientos indios* (1964) for woodwind trio, *Paisaje andino* (1963) for string quartet, and *Suite andina* (1956) for woodwind quintet—are all descriptions or evocations of Aymara-Quechua music. Like his tone poems, Velasco Maidana's opera *Churayna* (1964) is based on Indian mythological subjects.

CHILE

The influential Chilean composer Domingo Santa Cruz expressed in 1957 the following views in connection with the national music of Chile:

> ... Our music will end up being Chilean, different from that of a Frenchman or a German, to the extent that we are different from them, although our techniques are similar. . . . Our music will be Chilean in the same manner as our language is Spanish, without being confused with a Spaniard or other nations of the American continent. . . . Likewise our music, which resembles that of European countries, will be recognized from the outside when compared with any other, not through its exoticism, which would be false in Chile, but because it reflects our manner of existence, our sense of humor, our mountain nostalgia, our tolerance—in short, our personal traits through which we Chileans resemble and join each other without distinction of origins or social classes. . . .[4]

Such an idealistic attitude and explanation resulted from Santa Cruz's own disdain for musical nationalism; they also betray, however, his awareness of the significance of the trend in Latin America. But Indianism and nationalism have had in general few followers in Chile, most likely because cultivated Chilean musicians have felt little affinity with local folk and popular musical traditions, as these reflect only a small portion of Chilean modern national culture. The essence of that culture in the twentieth century arises basically from an urban situation with international aspirations. Thus indigenous music—which provides a truer cultural expression (though exotic, at times) in most Andean countries—has been viewed by most Chilean composers as artificial and limiting rather than potential.

In spite of this prevailing attitude, there have been several Chilean

[4]*Buenos Aires Musical*, XII, no. 197 (1 October 1957), 7.

composers who cultivated musical nationalism, by invoking mestizo folk music or Indian traditional music in literary or, less frequently, in actual musical terms. Pedro Humberto Allende (1885–1959) was the pioneer of such musical nationalism in Chile. He studied at the National Conservatory of Music in Santiago, which had been established in 1849. Later he taught harmony and composition there, exerting a considerable influence on many Chilean composers of subsequent generations. After a trip to Europe (1910–1911), he was elected to the Chilean Folklore Society, for he had already shown a deep interest in folk and traditional music of his country. He conducted extensive research, collecting *in situ* the first samples of Mapuche music (Araucanian Indian songs and dances). His many activities in favor of music education and as a composer were formally recognized in 1945, when the prestigious *Premio Nacional de Arte* was awarded to him; it was the first time this prize had gone to a musician.

Allende cultivated a national style based on mestizo folk-musical references, in a context of French Impressionist techniques. In 1913–1914, he wrote the symphonic suite *Escenas campesinas chilenas*, which appeared at the time as the first Chilean nationalist symphonic work with modernistic overtones in both harmonic and orchestral idioms. Urban popular music furnished the national contents of the tone poem *La Voz de las calles* (1919–1920), which is based on typical street cries of Santiago hawkers; melodic fragments of such cries serve as a basis for the thematic material. Overt folkloristic elements run through the twelve *Tonadas de carácter popular chileno* for piano (1918–1922), six of which were orchestrated in 1925 and 1936. (Several of these pieces were premiered in France in the 1920s by Ricardo Viñes.) A *tonada* is a simple folk tune of a lyrical quality, generally in 6/8 or 3/4 meter; Allende harmonized such tunes in a sober Impressionist-like manner while maintaining the free-flowing rhythm of the original melodies, as can be seen in *Tonada No. 5*, for example.

Musical Indianism in Chile was pursued most notably by Carlos Lavín (1883–1962) and Carlos Isamitt (1885–1974), both composers and ethnomusicologists. Lavín, although self-taught, had the opportunity to study later in Paris and at the University of Berlin with von Hornbostel. During his European residence (1922–1934) he visited archives of folk music from Spain to Romania. His own fieldwork in Chile began around 1910, especially among the Araucanian Indians. As a member of the Institute of Folk Music Research at the University of Chile, he directed the university's music archive for many years. He wrote essays on indigenous music and contributed articles to the better known European journals and to many encyclopedias. As a composer, Lavín tried to incorporate in his works his knowledge of and experience with Indian music. Several ballets have Indianist subjects, and other works such as the *Lamentaciones huilliches* (1928), for contralto and orchestra, or the *Mitos araucanos*, four pieces for piano

(1926), resort to actual Araucanian songs and Mapuche texts. The symphonic "impression" *Fiesta araucana* (1926) and the *Suite Andina* (1929) for piano, among other works, reveal a neo-Romantic and Impressionist harmonic vocabulary. Lavín's melodic writing, on the other hand, tends towards short and sober motives and is quite repetitive, probably as a result of his stylization of Indian melodic traits.

Although Isamitt also studied and collected Araucanian Indian music extensively, his compositional style reveals two diametrically opposed tendencies, one related to musical nationalism, the other to abstract expressionism and dodecaphony. His national interest as a composer did not limit itself to indigenous music but extended to mestizo folk music as well. In his article "El folklore en la creación artística de los compositores chilenos," he refers to some of his works in which "criolla" Araucanian and Huilliche musical manifestations are integrated in various manners. He also states:

> With Allende's and Lavín's works, which evidence an understandably high esteem of folk sources, Chilean music literature raised its artistic significance, abandoned the limitation to classic and Romantic procedures, extended the range of its spiritual contents and its technical resources (formal, harmonic, rhythmic, of instrumental coloration), and ended by acquiring certain characteristics of national significance.[5]

Thus, musical nationalism appeared to Isamitt as a liberating current, while for most twentieth-century Chilean composers it has represented a true limitation. Isamitt's works of most obvious Indianist or folkloristic topics and traits include the ballet *El Pozo de oro* (1942), *Friso Araucano* (1931) for voices and orchestra, the *Suite sinfónica* (1932), *Cinco cantos huilliches* (1945), *Mitos araucanos* (1935), and numerous piano works such as the *Sonata "Evocación araucana"* (1932) and *Tres arabescos característicos* (1946). In these, he recreates the essential aspects of the folk or primitive music of Chile, with few direct quotations. However, the overall style relates to post-Romantic Impressionism.

Sporadic attention has been paid to national musical sources by many Chilean composers who have not adhered to nationalism as such. Such neo-Romantic or Impressionist composers as Enrique Soro (1884–1954), Próspero Bisquertt (1881–1959), and Alfonso Letelier (b. 1912) have often referred to local sources. Soro's *Aires chilenos* (1942) for orchestra, Bisquertt's *Taberna al Amanecer* (1922), *Procesión del Cristo de Mayo* (1930), and *Aires chilenos* (1947), and Letelier's early work *La vida del campo* (1937) are all pertinent examples. And many other Chilean composers who later associated themselves with other esthetics and methods of composition wrote some of their first works under the influence of musical nationalism.

---

[5]In *Revista Musical Chilena*, XI, no. 55 (October–November 1957), 30.

BIBLIOGRAPHICAL NOTES

The art music of the Andean area has not been studied as much as that of other South American areas. Colombian music history of the twentieth century is comprehensively surveyed in José Ignacio Perdomo Escobar, *Historia de la Música en Colombia*, 3rd ed. (Bogotá: Editorial A.B.C., 1963), and Andrés Pardo Tovar, *La Cultura Musical en Colombia* (Bogotá: Ediciones Lerner, 1966). A special study on Uribe Holguín was undertaken by Guillermo Rendón G. and published as "Maestros de la Música: Guillermo Uribe Holguín (1880–1971)," in *Boletín de Música* (Casa de las Américas, Havana, Cuba), no. 50 (January–February 1975), 3–16; no. 51 (March-April 1975), 2–21. On Valencia, consult Andrés Pardo Tovar, *Antonio María Valencia, Artista Integral* (Cali: Biblioteca Vallecaucana, Extensión Cultural, 1958). Ecuadorian music history has been studied very sparsely. One general survey is Segundo Luis Moreno, "La Música en el Ecuador," in J. Gonzalo Orellana (ed.), *El Ecuador en Cien Años de Independencia*, II (Quito: Imprenta de la Escuela de Artes y Oficios, 1930), 187–276.

A general historical survey of music in Peru is Carlos Raygada, "Panorama Musical del Perú," *Boletín Latino-Americano de Música*, II (1936), 169–214. Also useful is Rodolfo Barbacci's "Apuntes para un Diccionario Biográfico Musical Peruano," *Fénix*, no. 6 (1949), 414–510; it is complemented by Carlos Raygada's "Guia Musical del Perú," *Fénix*, no. 12 (1956–1957), 3ff; no. 13 (1963), 1ff; and no. 14 (1964), 3ff. Rodolfo Holzmann's article, "Ensayo Analítico de la Obra Musical del Compositor Peruano Theodoro Valcárcel," *Eco Musical*, II/6 (March 1943), 23–33, provides an informative analysis of that composer's production. Enrique Pinilla's "La Música Contemporánea en el Perú," *Fanal* (Lima), no. 79 (1966), 17–23, is an overview of Peruvian composers active since the beginning of the twentieth century. Bolivian music is surveyed in Atiliano Auza León, *Dinámica Musical en Bolivia* (La Paz: Cooperativa de Artes Gráficas E. Burillo Ltda., 1967).

Chilean music of the twentieth century has been studied fairly comprehensively. Numerous articles on Chilean music institutions, composers, and compositions have been published in the *Revista Musical Chilena*, a general index of which appears in no. 98 (October–December 1966) and nos. 129–30 (January–June 1975). A general survey of Chilean music since 1900 is Vicente Salas Viu, *La Creación Musical en Chile, 1900–1951* (Santiago: Editorial Universitaria, S.A., 1952). A fairly comprehensive catalogue of Chilean compositions is given by Roberto Escobar and Renato Yrarrazaval in *Música Compuesta en Chile, 1900–1968* (Santiago: Ediciones de la Biblioteca Nacional-Chile, 1969).

SEVEN

THE TWENTIETH CENTURY:
BRAZIL AND THE RIVER PLATE AREA

The early phase in the development of musical nationalism in Brazil and Argentina was examined in Chapter 4. In the present chapter we shall discuss the maturation of this trend in both countries, and in Uruguay, from about 1920 to the 1940s. This was the period during which Brazilian, Argentinian, and Uruguayan composers began to produce works of both nationalist content and international significance. Three factors contributed to this golden period of nationalism. First, a dynamic and varied popular and folk culture allowed a wide range of national expressions. Second, there existed during this period talented art-music composers who not only had an obvious empathy for the popular and folk music of their respective countries but frequently had had firsthand exposure to it. Third, the establishment of institutions and organizations such as concert associations, orchestras, and ballet groups, and support from governmental agencies, made it possible for these composers to be promoted nationally, sometimes internationally. Even the historical conditions of the time favored the doctrine of political nationalism, especially with the dictatorships of Vargas (1930–1945) in Brazil and Perón (from 1943) in Argentina.

The international significance of some of the works produced during the period emerges out of the attempt to create a unique style, incorporating modern European compositional techniques and reinterpreted elements of national music. Lacking a usable tradition in their own immediate past, many of the composers mentioned in this chapter had to face the twentieth century head on rather than follow a gradual and slow development. In the most successful works, composers did not merely imitate new European styles but attempted to assimilate them. In the process of assimilation, a natural qualitative selection took place, followed by a re-creation and transformation of the original models according to individual conditions and needs.

BRAZIL

There is no doubt that the major composers of Brazilian art music during the period under consideration adhered to musical nationalism. Few of them, however, were able to transcend the folkloristic aspect of the nationalist current; many have thus remained of only local significance. However, as opposed to the earlier attempts of Levy and Nepomuceno, they resorted to more authentic folk-music expressions and did not neglect the urban popular scene.

Heitor Villa-Lobos

Once referred to as the "Rabelais of modern music," Villa-Lobos (1887–1959) was the most creative Latin-American composer of his generation. Extremely prolific and imaginative, he wrote about a thousand works (if various arrangements of many pieces are included) in all media and genres. In many ways, his personality, his career, and his production reflect typical Brazilian traits such as grandeur, flamboyance, restlessness, lack of organic unity, disparity, and gaudiness, along with others such as individuality, spontaneity, allurement, and sophistication. He often said that musical composition constituted for him a biological necessity. This not only explains his gargantuan production but also his instinctive approach to music. Throughout his career he avoided conformity, in his life as well as his musical style. His nonconformity helped him in achieving strength, originality, and success.

A nationalistic phase of a folkloric sort represents the most original aspect of Villa-Lobos's output, but it also reveals artistic universality through the creation of formal elements suggested by various popular musical traditions. He once stated, "I am folklore; my melodies are just as authentic as those which originate from the souls of the people." Feeling such a close association with Brazilian popular culture, it is not surprising that he considered nationalism an inescapable course. In his opinion, the musical idioms of his people were "indispensable for a vital and genuine art."

Indianism in the works of Villa-Lobos has often been overstated. It is doubtful that he had a primary knowledge of Indian music, although he traveled to Mato Grosso and utilized some Indian melodies collected in old chronicles (e.g., Jean de Léry's sixteenth-century account of a trip to Brazil) and in modern scientific works, such as *Rondônia* of Roquette Pinto. Probably Villa-Lobos sensed the inappropriateness of Amerindian music as an expression of national music, for it remained outside the mainstream of Brazilian music. He resorted to Indian music mainly to evoke a total vision of Brazil and as an element of the exoticism that was so much in vogue in the 1920s.

A native of Rio de Janeiro, Villa-Lobos joined at an early age the popular musicians known in Rio at the turn of the century as *chorões*. This experience (he played guitar) afforded him a practical knowledge of urban popular music, which was characterized at that time by improvisations and variations on simple, sentimental melodies associated with Afro-Brazilian rhythms. Villa-Lobos learned from his father Raul, a good amateur musician and a functionary of the National Library, how to play the cello, which he studied seriously under Niederberger at the Instituto Nacional de Música and which remained his principal instrument; together with the guitar, the cello receives very special attention in some of his mature works. His musical education remained unorthodox, as he avoided then and in his later life the routine of academic instruction. Rather than limiting himself to an academic environment, he undertook a series of trips all over Brazil which lasted almost eight years and brought him firsthand acquaintance with the rich musical heritage of the rural areas, which was to be so strongly reflected in his works. Several of his apologists have seen in these trips Villa-Lobos's discovery of the music of Brazil through the collecting and study of folk music of the various traditions. But while he may have collected themes, his interest and training were certainly not scientifically oriented, as were Pedrell's or Bartók's; as in his approaches to other matters, his approach to folk-music materials was intuitive.

By the time he settled down in Rio in 1913, Villa-Lobos had written some fifty-five compositions, among which the *Suite dos cânticos sertanejos* (1910) seems to be the first instance of his elaboration of thematic material derived from folk-music sources. This and other early works, such as the march *Pro Pax* for band, the *Suite populaire brésilienne* for guitar, and the operas *Aglaia-Izaht* and *Elisa* (both of which were recast into *Izaht*), show the composer's eclecticism. In November 1915 several compositions of his were presented in a public concert, including some piano pieces, the Piano Trio No. 1, the Sonata No. 2 for violin and piano, and several songs. Other such concerts followed. His music soon became controversial; some critics praised it highly while others despised it openly. Thanks to the presence of Darius Milhaud in Rio during the World War I years, Villa-Lobos acquainted himself with the music of Debussy and the French "Six." Although still unaware of Stravinsky's early style, he had developed by then a rather anti-Romantic esthetic attitude, from which (and from his works' tendency to tonal instability) originated the controversial reaction to his works.

In February 1922, a "Week of Modern Art" took place in São Paulo, with the participation of such notable artists and intellectuals as Mário de Andrade, Oswald de Andrade, Ronald de Carvalho, and Villa-Lobos. This event culminated in the establishment of *modernismo*, a movement seeking a national artistic renovation based on the principle of adoption of avant-garde European techniques in the arts mixed with an enthusiastic promotion of Brazilian folk topics. Such a principle had been put into practice already for some time, as Villa-Lobos's own works bear witness: he had already begun to use typical native subjects in his tone poems and ballets (*Uirapurú, Saci-Pererê*, and *Amazonas*, all of 1917) and had systematically introduced harmonic and rhythmic elements of popular music as well as tunes of children's songs in his piano pieces, such as the first series of *A Prole do Bebê* (1918) and *Lenda do caboclo* (1920), and in his String Quartets nos. 3 and 4 (1916–1917).

Villa-Lobos went to Europe in 1923 but before that wrote one of his most characteristic nationalistic works, the *Nonetto*—subtitled "Impressão rápida de todo o Brasil" ("Rapid impression of all Brazil")—for flute, oboe, clarinet, saxophone, bassoon, harp, piano, mixed chorus, and percussion. Besides celesta, kettle drums, triangle, and other conventional instruments, the percussion section calls for typical Brazilian instruments such as *chocalhos* (wooden or metal rattles), *prato de louça* (dinner plate), *reco-reco* (güiro), *côco* (a pair of dry coconut shells), and *cuíca* or *puíta* (friction drum). Referred to by Villa-Lobos himself as a "new form of composition which expresses Brazil's sonorous atmosphere and most original rhythms," the *Nonetto* reveals an obvious influence of urban popular music of the time, especially in its rhythmic character and color blendings involving the woodwind. The clearly contrapuntal writing as well as the various imitations of fragmented rhythmic motives in the woodwinds could be construed as a subtle stylization of the improvisatory nature of the *chôro* (see p. 193).

Some recurring rhythmic figures of the *Nonetto* that are related to popular music are given in Figure I. Example 7-1 illustrates the syncopation obtained exclusively through melodic means in the tango *Arreliado* by the popular composer Ernesto Nazareth; the same device is seen in the harp part of Villa-Lobos's *Nonetto* (Figure I [7]), although there the pattern occurs entirely on the weak parts of the beats. Particularly noticeable in the re-creation of Brazilian "original" rhythms are all the variants involving the basic dotted figure, the syncopation of the ♪♪ ♩ figure, and the various cross-rhythmic combinations. This rhythmic predominance also charac-terizes the melodic material, as the opening saxophone motif shows (Example 7-2). Throughout the work the technique of melodic fragmentation prevails, enabling the composer to stress rhythmic elements and sonorous effects. The voices are used as an added timbre in the ensemble, in a rather typical Impressionist manner (including *bocca chiusa*, glissandos, and graduated dynamics). Actually, the *Nonetto* is one of the earliest examples of Villa-Lobos's daring experiments with timbres and medium and is at times remi-niscent of Debussy and early Stravinsky. The harmonies are very Impressionistic also, with altered chords, formations by fourths and fifths, frequent pedal points, and parallelism; the use of tone clusters, however, reveals Villa-Lobos's search for new sonorous combinations.

While Villa-Lobos's early works had aroused resentment in Brazil for their bold unconventionality, they were quite well received in Paris around 1925, mostly in avant-garde circles, and he soon became one of the composers most in evidence. Concerts of his works in 1924 and 1927 won enormous recognition. Henry Prunières, Florent Schmitt, and the music critic Clarendon all proclaimed, if in different terms, the uniqueness of the composer's style. Most likely the spontaneous, improvisatory character of some of his works, and their saturation with national elements, seemed in partial conformity with the "commonplace" esthetics of the Parisian musicians of the 1920s. Moreover, some critics seem to have been overwhelmed by the prodigality of Villa-Lobos's artistic personality; Schmitt referred to him as "three-fourths god with burning eyes and crocodilian teeth!"

The 1920s were a period of intense creative output for Villa-Lobos.

EXAMPLE 7-1   Ernesto Nazareth, Tango *Arreliado* (unpublished), mm. 1–2.

EXAMPLE 7-2   Heitor Villa-Lobos, *Nonetto:* opening motif, mm. 1–2. Copyright by Editions Max Eschig, Paris. Assigned to Associated Music Publishers, Inc. Used by permission.

Moderato (♩ = 56)
Saxophone

He wrote then some of his most celebrated piano pieces, plus the series of *Choros* and the songs of *Serestas*. Although he was a cellist and guitarist, his pianistic writing is very idiomatic and quite varied in style. His piano works include the three series of *A Prole do Bebê* (The Baby's Family; the manuscript of the third set is lost), the *Carnaval das crianças brasileiras*, the *Cirandas*, and *Rudepoema*, all considered outstanding achievements in twentieth-century piano literature. As opposed to the piano works of the 1910s, in which the influence of Impressionist style is clear, those of the 1920s are unpredictable stylistically. Although relying on such Impressionist traits as glissandos, parallel harmonies, modality, and pentatonicism, they are more complex, incorporating increasingly dissonant chord formations and rhythmic intricacies, and a wider use of the coloristic possibilities of the instrument together with tremendously virtuosic technical demands. The pianist Artur Rubinstein, who visited Brazil in the early 1920s, premiered the first set of the *Prole do Bebê* in 1922 and later included many of the composer's works in his repertory, thus calling the world's attention to his music. Written in 1918, the first series contains eight "doll" pieces, each based on a children's folk tune; each ethnic type of doll (white, brunette, *cabocla* [Brazilian mestizo], mulatto, and black) is represented. The best known piece of the series, *0 Polichinelo*, is an early example of the *Petrushka*-like "bitonal" effect (use of white versus black keys) typical of the composer's later piano music (Example 7-3). *A Prole do Bebê No. 2* (1921) deals with toy

EXAMPLE 7-3   Heitor Villa-Lobos, *O Polichinelo*, mm. 1–2. Copyright by Editions Max Eschig. Used by permission.

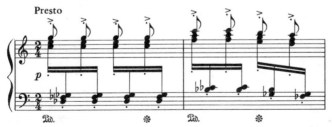

animals, is technically more challenging than the first set, and much less under the earlier French influences. The nine pieces of the set are nationalistic, but in very subtle ways. The pieces *A baratinha de papel* ("The little paper bug") and *O boisinho de chumbo* ("The little tin ox") may serve as illustrations. An ostinato in the first measures of the former piece reveals an ingenious invention of the composer (which he often used subsequently): an asymmetrical figuration between the white and black keys of the piano (Example 7-4). Each four-note pattern stresses a different use of the white and black keys. In the first pattern the first, third, and fourth notes correspond

EXAMPLE 7-4   Heitor Villa-Lobos, *A Prole do Bebê No. 2:* "A baratinha de papel," mm. 1–12. Copyright 1927 by Max Eschig & Cie, Editeurs. Used by permission.

to the white keys, the second note to a black key. In the second pattern, the placement is different: white keys for the second and third notes, black keys for the first and fourth. While this asymmetry is not extended to intervallic relationships, it affects the rhythm almost throughout the piece. The cunning cross-accentuation of such patterns highlights the popular character of the piece. If we notate the accentuation ♪. ♪ ♪ , we realize the connection immediately, for the resulting figure is typical of the rhythmic accompaniment of many Brazilian popular dances, such as the Brazilian polka, the maxixe, and the *chôro*. Local flavor pervades the main theme (below the ostinato) as well, not only because of its syncopated rhythmic structure but because of its contour, which is characterized by an initial chromatic motif and by repeated notes. Attention should be called to the repetition of a figure, in progressive diminution, in measures 10 to 12 of Example 7-4, because of its recurrence in so many other works.

From a pianistic viewpoint, *O boisinho de chumbo* demands an experienced performer in both technical command and interpretation. There are many instances of fast scale passages in varying intervals, glissando effects, large intervallic skips in octaves, and use of the extreme ranges of the keyboard, as well as rhythmic intricacies and meticulous dynamic indications. The composer creates a Brazilian atmosphere in the piece through rhythmic ostinatos with characteristic syncopated figures and a descending chromatic motif with a rhythmic flexibility reminiscent of popular-music performance practice. The programmatic evocation of the ox is achieved by an overall massively sonorous quality in the piece, deriving from dense chord formations, heavy figurations (glissandos, embellishments), and an unusually expansive use of the piano's range, as the "grandiose" final section of the work clearly reveals (Example 7-5).

Many of the techniques and traits present in *A Prole do Bebê No. 2* are vastly amplified in *Rudepoema* (1921–1926), undoubtedly one of the most complex works, both technically and esthetically, of the twentieth-century piano literature. Dedicated to Artur Rubinstein and proposed as a portrait of the pianist, this long work creates at times a primitivistic atmosphere through its lengthy, dissonant, and loud ostinatos. But the overall complexity of the work arises from the phenomenal variety of moods—

EXAMPLE 7-5 Heitor Villa-Lobos, *A Prole do Bebê No. 2:* "O boisinho de chumbo," mm. 63–68. Copyright 1927 by Max Eschig & Cie, Editeurs. Used by permission.

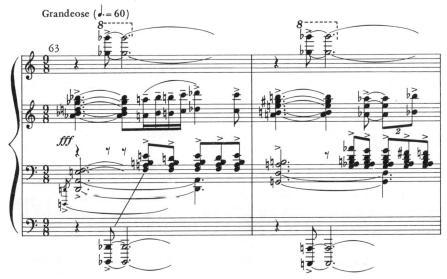

probably the result of the intended portrayal of Rubinstein, "the true author of this work." The sonorous magnificence is such that *Rudepoema* may be said to have been "orchestrated" for the piano. Villa-Lobos's daring experiments with timbres find one of their happiest examples here. A rather dense texture, including combinations of melodic motives, virtuosic figuration, repeated fourth-based chords, and numerous pedal points, contributes to the coloristic character of the work. Special coloristic effects include glissandos applied to any interval and complex chordal structures (with two- or three-octave jumps), grace notes, and harmonics. Examples 7-6a and b illustrate the use of harmonics: the unstruck sustained tone (D♯) vibrates sympathetically when the lower fifth (G♯) is struck. The tone clusters in dynamic crescendo together with the harmonics create a unique timbre.

Despite its heterogeneity of moods, *Rudepoema* relies on thematic and rhythmic relationships for unification. Several themes appear through-

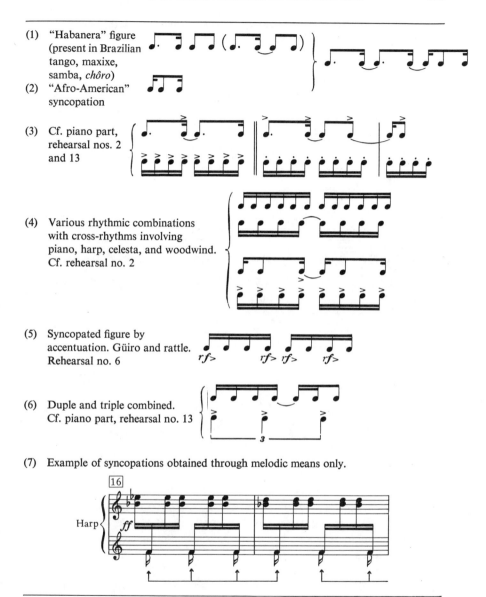

FIGURE 7-1 Some of the rhythmic figures related to popular music in Villa-Lobos's *Nonetto*

out the seven sections of the work, each theme serving as a unifying element. The melodic material does not have the lyrical quality commonly associated with Villa-Lobos's works; rather, narrow-range, often chromatic, and short motives prevail. They tend to be characterized by their rhythmic figuration, and some are reminiscent of popular or folk tunes. Villa-Lobos's imagination

EXAMPLE 7-6   Heitor Villa-Lobos, *Rudepoema:* (a) mm. 269–74; (b) mm. 279–86.
Copyright 1928 by Editions Max Eschig. Used by permission.

(a)

*) ♯♪ Baissez la touche sans articuler

(b)

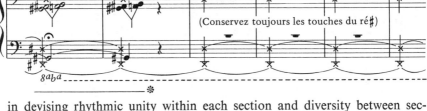

in devising rhythmic unity within each section and diversity between sections is praiseworthy. One could consider rhythm as the main structural factor of *Rudepoema*. Various rhythmic patterns appear as structural units in the seven main sections. In addition, some interrelated rhythmic figures recur in various passages.

If the local flavor of *Rudepoema* is minimal, the sixteen piano pieces *Cirandas* (1926) are overtly nationalistic. Each piece is built on a traditional children's folk tune whose treatment varies from simple reproduction (as in "Xô, xô, passarinho") or slight alteration (as in "Therezinha de Jesus" or "Passa, passa gavião") to substantial modification (as in "À procura de uma agulha"). Very idiomatic, rich in tone color, and "spontaneously Brazilian,"[1] this cycle is considered by many in Brazil to be Villa-Lobos's

---

[1]Vasco Mariz, *Heitor Villa-Lobos, Brazilian Composer* (Gainesville: University of Florida Press, 1963), p. 54.

piano masterpiece. The appeal of the *Cirandas* rests not only on the alluring treatment of the children's rounds but also on the composer's original rhythmic and harmonic procedures. "Therezinha de Jesus," for example, has a uniformly syncopated accompaniment throughout, quite engaging in its popular flavor (Example 7-7). "Xô, xô, passarinho" stresses percussive effects and graceful Impressionist harmonization, enhanced by indolent double-dotted figures which accent the appoggiatura chords.

His monumental series of sixteen *choros* (counting *Introducão aos choros* and *Choros bis*) is undoubtedly Villa-Lobos's most valuable contribution to musical nationalism in Brazil. The term *chôro* has various meanings in Brazilian popular music. Generically, it denotes ensemble music performance in an urban context, with a marked preference for a soloist set off against the rest of the ensemble. Specifically, it refers to the ensembles of musician serenaders (*chorões*) that developed during the latter quarter of the nineteenth century. At that time the instrumental ensemble generally included flute, clarinet, ophicleide, trombone, *cavaquinho* (a ukulele-like instrument), guitar, and a few percussion instruments (in particular, tambourine). The repertory of such ensembles consisted mostly of dances of European origin, and they performed at popular festivities. For serenades, the function of the band was to accompany sentimental songs, of the *modinha* type, performed by a soloist. In the twentieth century, the *chôro* or *chorinho* became a composed, popular musical form and dance closely connected with typical urban dances, such as the maxixe and the samba. Such dances all present the same rhythmic patterns (syncopated binary figures) but are distinguished from each other by tempo. The real originality of the *chôro* of the 1920s and 1930s (those of Pixinguinha and Lacerda, for example) resides in the performers' virtuoso improvisation of instrumental variations and the imaginative resulting counterpoint.

Inspired by the native background of the *chôro*, Villa-Lobos wrote his series from 1920 to 1929, during a period of experimentation resulting from his exposure to new European stylistic currents. Intended for the most varied media, from solo guitar (*Choros No. 1*) to large orchestra and mixed chorus (*Choros No. 10*) or orchestra, band, and chorus (*Choros No. 14*), the

EXAMPLE 7-7 Heitor Villa-Lobos, *Cirandas:* "Therezinha de Jesus," mm. 1–4. Copyright Casa Arthur Napoleão.

works in the series display little stylistic unity; their only common traits involve musical manifestations of various popular and primitive cultural traditions, and these materials, moreover, are variously treated. In a mimeographed study of the series, Villa-Lobos wrote the following comments:

> The *Choros* were written according to a new special technique based on the musical manifestations of Brazilian natives, as well as on the psychological impressions brought about by certain popular characters, extremely original and quite remarkable. *Choros No. 1* was deliberately written as if it were an instinctive product of the ingenuous imagination of these popular musical characters, to serve simply as a point of departure and broaden itself gradually later, in its form, technique, structure, and genre.[2]

While this "new technique" was never explained by Villa-Lobos, his esthetic intention entailed the glorification of his country, through a subjective recreation of the musics of Brazil. His own programmatic descriptions are for the most part abstractions or simply circumstantial comments on the tropical and exotic nature of the music of Brazil for the benefit of uninformed foreign listeners of the 1920s.

Numbers 1, 2, 4, 5, and 7 of the *Choros* reveal some aspects of popular musical ensembles of the turn of the twentieth century, while numbers 3 (*Pica-pau*, "Woodpecker"), 6, 8, and 10 resort partially to primitive indigenous music or mestizo ("caboclo") folk music. Numbers 5 and 10 may serve to illustrate the different styles cultivated by the composer in the series.

Choros No. 5, subtitled "Alma brasileira" ("Brazilian soul"), for solo piano, provides the best characterization of the familiar serenading music of the popular *chôro*. The lyrical and expressive quality of this piece comes from its basis in the *modinha*, that sentimental song genre cultivated, as we have seen, in the eighteenth and nineteenth centuries by Portuguese and Brazilian composers. During the second empire in Brazil, the *modinha* acquired the character of an Italian opera aria, and some of its aspects came to be identified as "national" by popular composers, e.g., embellishments of the vocal line and frequent use of melodic sequence. Although in the first printed collections of *modinhas*, dating from the 1790s, a harpsichord is indicated as the accompanying instrument, the guitar came to be the most typical instrument of the serenaders. Villa-Lobos made the most of this association, as in the accompanimental figure of section A, with its guitar-like parallelism in sixth chords and the swaying quality of its rhythm (Example 7-8). The accompaniment figure symbolizes sorrow ("dolência"), according to the indication in the score, and the main theme should be "vague" in its rhythmic rendition but well separated from the accompaniment. "What is

---

[2]Reproduced in *Villa-Lobos, sua obra*, 2nd ed. (Rio de Janeiro: Museu Villa-Lobos, 1972), p. 198.

EXAMPLE 7-8 Heitor Villa-Lobos. *Choros No. 5:* "Alma brasileira," mm. 1–4.

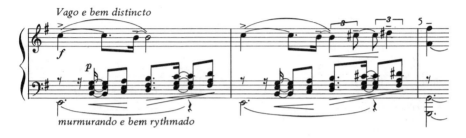

most interesting in this *Choros*," said the composer, "are the rhythmic and melodic cadences, irregular within a quadruple meter, giving the disguised impression of rubato, or of a delayed melodic execution, which is precisely the most interesting characteristic of the serenaders."[3] The contrasting middle section of *Choros No. 5* typifies the dance-like repertory of the *chorões*, with characteristic popular rhythmic patterns of the same nature as those in the *Nonetto*.

Choros No. 10 (1926), subtitled "Rasga o coração" ("Rend my heart"), provides a good indication of the composer's mature nationalist style. Written for large orchestra (including an imposing percussion section with typical Brazilian instruments) and mixed chorus, this work represents Villa-Lobos's most successful integration of local musical elements with contemporary progressive techniques. In his program notes for the work, Villa-Lobos wrote, "The variety of birds—rich in number and species—which exists in the whole of Brazil ... served for some motives of *Choros No. 10*." He identified the opening flute motif as a cell of the song of the bird known as "Azulão da mata." The entire first section suggests a series of descriptive impressions of the vastness, majesty, and richness of the Brazilian land. Pentatonic and other "primitive" (i.e., narrow-range) motives supported by rich, dissonant, and parallel harmonies with long pedal points (both as sustained tones and repeated ones) and varied timbres give to the section an unmistakably exotic Impressionistic character. The principal motif, which reappears in the last section of the work (Example 7-9a), is described by the

[3]Ibid., p. 200.

composer as "a compound of primitive melody and pentatonic song of Brazilian Indians." Likewise the chromatic motif that is repeated throughout the last section (Example 7-9b) is identified as imitating the resting songs of the Parecís Indians of Mato Grosso.

EXAMPLE 7-9   Heitor Villa-Lobos, *Choros No. 10:* "Rasga o coração" (a) princi-pal motif, mm. 62–63; (b) chromatic motif, mm. 89–90. Copyright 1928 by Editions Max Eschig. Used by permission.

The last section of *Choros No. 10*, which calls for mixed chorus, is conceived as a huge crescendo with clear primitivistic intensity. The motives previously mentioned serve as melodic ostinatos of such insistence and extreme rhythmic vigor that they soon reach a level of hypnotic obsession. The use of voices uttering a text consisting of syllables and vocalization without literary meaning but strong onomatopoeic effect ("Ja-ka-ta ka-ma-ra-ja" and "Ta-ya-po ka-ma-ra-jo," shifting to different vowel sounds and creating an amazingly complex counterpoint) enhances the frenzied rhythmic character of the section. For Villa-Lobos the onomatopoeia serves to echo the phonetic atmosphere of the "language of the aborigines." In contrast to the "savage" hammering of the vocal ostinatos, a lyrical and sentimental melody borrowed from the popular modinha *Rasga o coração* (by Anacleto de Medeiros, with text by Catulo da Paixão Cearense, one of Brazil's foremost popular poets) is introduced.[4] Thus the synthesis of Brazilian popular musical traditions which the composer alluded to as one of the goals of the *Choros* is well achieved here. In harmonic complexity, *Choros No. 10* is not comparable to No. 11, mainly because of frequent pedal points. Polytonality and tone clusters are prominent, however, and the rhythmic element predominates, with intricate multiple syncopations and cross-rhythmic groupings creating polyrhythmic passages. Villa-Lobos's orchestration in this work is fairly typical of other works by him as well: voices used as a coloristic instrument (more in evidence here than in the *Nonetto* and *Choros No. 3*)

[4]In his book *A Glória escandalosa de Heitor Villa-Lôbos* (Rio de Janeiro: Livraria Império Editora, 1960), the reactionary writer Carlos Maul claimed plagiarism because the name of the popular composer was not acknowledged by Villa-Lobos in the score (thereby revealing ignorance of centuries-old practices of parody, paraphrase, and cantus firmus).

and fulfilling an essential rhythmic function; fragmentary thematic material imitated in extreme instrumental ranges; instrumental doublings in several octaves; special effects such as glissandos in harmonics in divided strings and systematic double stops; and division of harmonies between different instrumental families, often producing dissonant or polytonal impact.

The title "Bachianas Brasileiras" (always in the plural) is applied to a series of nine works written between 1930 and 1945. Villa-Lobos referred to this set as a "genre of musical composition in homage to the great genius of Johann Sebastian Bach." Conceived as suites (in the Baroque sense of a sequence of dance movements), they were inspired by Bach, whom Villa-Lobos considered a universal source of music and the "intermediary between all cultures." They were not intended as a stylization of Bach's music but rather an adaptation to Brazilian folk and popular music (with undeniable liberty) of certain Baroque contrapuntal procedures. They should not be interpreted, however, as reflecting a back-to-Bach trend or a neo-Classic position of formalism and objectivity. In fact, as the Chilean composer Juan Orrego-Salas rightly observes, the overall stylistic difference between the *Bachianas* and the *Choros* is slight. Orrego-Salas points out that

> the similarities are abundant. These might be summed up in the following way: often in the *Bachianas*, as in the *Choros*, the vernacular element intervenes with much force; in the total cycle of both expressions, we see the same variety of means applied—ranging from those compositions written for soloistic instruments to those for a combination of orchestra and voices; and, the admixture of both European and Brazilian (folklore) aesthetics.[5]

The individual pieces call for the following performing media: No. 1 (1930) for eight cellos; No. 2 (1930) for orchestra; No. 3 (1938) for piano and orchestra; No. 4 (1930–1940) for piano (orchestral version, 1941); No. 5 (1938–1945) for voice and orchestra of cellos; No. 6 (1938) for flute and bassoon; No. 7 (1942) for orchestra; No. 8 (1944) for orchestra; and No. 9 (1945) for string orchestra or voices. While a similar variety of means is indeed present in the *Choros*, the *Bachianas* reveal certain stylistic devices absent from any previous major work by their composer. In them, Villa-Lobos seems to aim at the universality of Bach's music through an assimilation of its vitality. Such an aim might seem presumptuous or incongruous, but in fact the composer felt there existed clear affinities between certain of Bach's contrapuntal and rhythmic procedures and those of Brazilian folk and popular music. While this may appear farfetched, Villa-Lobos's intuition was not unfounded: Brazilian popular instrumental music in its improvisatory character exhibits a considerable melodic independence, with themes often made up of repeated notes and broken-chord figurations, and a strong

---

[5] Juan A. Orrego-Salas, "Heitor Villa-Lobos 'Man, Work, Style'," *Inter-American Music Bulletin*, no. 52 (March 1966), 27.

functional harmonic basis. In addition, and most importantly, many Afro-Brazilian dance genres share the typical rhythmic feeling of Bach's fast movements, especially those of his instrumental works that are founded on a constant pulsation (of the sixteenth-note type). To give but one example, the flute part of the "Badinerie" movement of Bach's Overture No. 2 in B minor (BWV 1067) presents a melodic contour (descending direction, repeated tones), a pulsating rhythm, and even a displacement of the phrasing in the last measures of the passage that are commonly found in Brazilian popular music. In any case, Villa-Lobos won international acclaim with the *Bachianas*, not only for the curiosity aroused by their evocation of Bach but also for their thoroughly captivating melodic and harmonic materials and their exciting rhythmic qualities.

The suites are in two (Nos. 5, 6, and 9), three (No. 1), or four movements (Nos. 2, 3, 4, 7, and 8). With a few exceptions, each movement bears a double denomination, one formalistic (such as "prelude," "introduction," "aria," "fantasia," "fuga"), the other clearly nationalistic (such as "embolada," "modinha," "chôro," and "the little train of the *caipira*"). Each movement tends to be cast in ABA form, with the first section (A) generally more elaborated than B. Some episodes are added to the A or B section for variety's sake, but without altering basically the tripartite form.[6] The harmony is rather Classic and strongly tonal, with added sevenths, sixths, or fourths and frequent use of passing tones and anticipations. Dissonances occur, but not as frequently as in the *Choros*. Irregular rhythmic patterns in the fast and moderate movements tend to highlight the national character of the *Bachianas*. Coloristic experiments are notable in the series (as in the *Choros*), particularly special string and vocal effects and programmatic orchestral associations (e.g., "the little train of the *caipira*" of *Bachianas No. 2*).

Bachianas Nos. 1, 2, and 5 are the best known of the cycle. Number 1, for an orchestra of cellos or a minimum of eight cellos, exemplifies the unique stylistic blend. The first measures of the Introduction (also titled "Embolada") reveal the national side of the style, through lively repeated rhythmic patterns with particular emphasis on the off-beats: ♩ ♫ 𝄾 ♬ . These patterns are related to those of the *embolada* (a popular dance form and a dual type of song), but interrupted by the rests. Added tones and alterations modernize the harmonies. The main theme (Example 7-10) reveals one of Villa-Lobos's favorite melodic types, an extensive and dynamic line in which a "chordal" beginning of the phrase gives way to a "scalar" ending. The range of the ninth in the first motive is as Bach-like as it is bel-canto-like. Particularly significant are the second and third phrases of the theme, because of their limitation to the range of an octave (thus

---

[6]Cf. Adhemar Nóbrega, *As Bachianas Brasileiras de Villa-Lobos* (Rio de Janeiro: MEC, Museu Villa-Lobos, 1971), p. 19.

EXAMPLE 7-10 Heitor Villa-Lobos, *Bachianas Brasileiras No. 1:* "Introduction (Embolada)," mm. 7–21. Copyright 1948 by Associated Music Publishers, Inc. Used by permission.

avoiding a literal repetition of the first phrase), the smooth overlap between the second and third phrases (on A♭), and the characteristic sequence in large intervals, to which is applied one of those nonchalant and hesitant rhythmic figures cited above in connection with *Choros No. 5.* Notable is the improvisatory character of this theme, produced entirely by such rhythmic means as the unpredictable placement of the triplets and the delayed cadences. In his study of the composer's style, Orrego-Salas mentions the essentially vocal quality of most of Villa-Lobos's melodies, which tend to develop independently from the accompanying rhythmic structures. "The latter," he writes, "are the varying elements while the melodic line is extended to different tonal planes, although almost always joined together by progressions whose harmonic formulas are sufficiently known and traditional."[7] The second movement of *Bachianas No. 1*, "Preludio (Modinha)," has another such lyrical melody progressing in descending sequences, like many in Vivaldi's slow movements (which influenced Bach's arias and adagios). It is no coincidence that this movement is entitled "Modinha," for, as we have seen, the lyrical character of the *modinha* was often derived from Italian opera aria.

The romantic lyricism that pervades the *Bachianas* and many later works by Villa-Lobos (especially those for guitar, and the solo songs) stemmed perhaps from the composer's deep interest in the *modinha*. Examples of cantabile melodies abound in his works, but none as powerfully expressive as the soprano line of the "Aria (Cantilena)" of *Bachianas No. 5* (Example 7-11). This melody has deservedly won international popularity. The improvisatory character of the long, wide phrase is created primarily by an impression of almost free meter, by the stressed irregular musical punctuation, and by unpredictable cadences. In addition, the sequential patterns of the second and third periods are disguised by the diversity of the syncopated rhythms used in each.[8] The sense of improvisation (recalling the *chorões* or serenaders) is also enhanced by the avoidance of full resolutions and emphasized by a deliberate harmonic vagueness. The expressive quality of the "Aria" is no

EXAMPLE 7-11   Heitor Villa-Lobos, *Bachianas Brasileiras No. 5:* "Aria (Cantilena)," Soprano line, mm. 3–8. Copyright 1947 by Associated Music Publishers, Inc. Used by permission.

7Juan A. Orrego-Salas, "Heitor Villa-Lobos," p. 16.
8Ibid., p. 21.

less attributable to its accompaniment by a cello ensemble. The pizzicatos in contrary motion of cellos II and IV in the first two measures and the descending progression of the bass line (cello III) suggest an amplified version of the picked style of guitar playing known in Portuguese as "ponteio." The doubling of the soprano line by cello I an octave below the voice adds substantial volume and coloristic depth.

Some have interpreted the *Bachianas* as representing a neo-Classic trend rather than strict nationalism, but this interpretation is only a matter of selective emphasis. Neo-Classic elements are most evident in the texture. In every measure of *Bachianas No. 1*, consonant chordal structures predominate. Doubling of the melodic lines in consonant intervals appears frequently. In general the texture is open and uncluttered, but this is probably related to the preponderance of consonances. The use of fugue or fugato sections as a formal principle might be construed as a neo-Classic device, but imitation is also characteristic of several popular Brazilian music genres, as are frequent ostinato figures and long pedal tones, both of which appear in the *Bachianas*. There are, nevertheless, instances in which both texture and form seem to overshadow the more purely rhythmic-nationalistic elements. The Fugue ("Conversa") of *Bachianas No. 1* is a case in point: the subject (Example 7-12), in repeated notes and syncopations, has a clear local flavor—according to the composer, it is in the manner of the *chorão* Sátiro Bilhar (1861–1929)—but its nationalistic effect is minimized by the polyphonic texture. Neo-Classicism presupposes abstract music, but Villa-Lobos could not abandon a programmatic concept.[9] Even in the "fugue" just mentioned, he had in mind, as the title indicates, a conversation between four *chorões* competing for the thematic advantage in successive questions and answers. Thus, ultimately, a national character, however subtle, predominates in the *Bachianas Brasileiras*.

The seventeen string quartets composed by Villa-Lobos cover an extensive period of his productive life and represent many facets of his style. The first two date from 1915, the last one from 1957. None was written during the 1920s; that decade was one of chamber music works principally for woodwinds, such as the *Trio* (1921) for oboe, clarinet, and bassoon, the *Quatuor* (1921) for flute, saxophone, harp, celesta, and female chorus, the *Quinteto em forma de choros* (1928) for woodwinds, and others. Some of the most typical procedures of Villa-Lobos's composition appear in the Quartets Nos. 5 and 6, of 1931 and 1938, respectively. Both are overtly nationalistic works, especially in comparison with the remaining eleven, which manifest a greater concern for absolute music. Although imitative techniques occur frequently, especially successive thematic presentation by the four

---

[9]Extra-musical associations actually prevail in the majority of the composer's works.

EXAMPLE 7-12   Heitor Villa-Lobos, *Bachianas Brasileiras No. 1:* "Fugue (Conversa)," mm. 1–6. Copyright 1948 by Associated Music Publishers, Inc. Used by permission.

instruments, sonata form is practically neglected. Developmental processes did not entice Villa-Lobos; as a substitute, he availed himself of the procedures of variation.

Quartet No. 6, one of the composer's better known chamber works, is one of the "popular" quartets, that is, in the "Brazilian" style. As opposed to the Fifth Quartet, which has an even more direct national flavor (with quotations of children's tunes), the Sixth presents subtle stylizations of typical mestizo folk and popular music. Relationships to that music include the use of varied rhythmic patterns, the improvisatory nature and lyrical mood associated with the *chôro* (the latter especially in the Andante movement), and special string effects frequently recalling the guitar and *cavaquinho* parts of popular ensembles. The dance-like character of the first theme of the first movement, with its rhythmic drive in short note-values and its popularesque syncopation, is fairly typical of Villa-Lobos's writing of the late 1930s. The contrapuntal designs and the sequential treatment of the fragmented theme throughout the movement show some affinity with the *Bachianas* of the same period: the rhythmic pattern of the transitional passage of the middle section 𝅘𝅥 𝄾 𝅘𝅥𝅮𝅘𝅥𝅮 𝅘𝅥 𝄾 had appeared in 1930 in the first theme of *Bachianas No. 1.*

The two central movements abound with that serenade-like lyricism which the composer was to cultivate extensively in the last twenty years of his life. The opening of the Andante, particularly, borrows Impressionist imagery, suggesting "music in the air" on a quiet tropical warm evening by means of muted strings and harmonics and the static shape of the theme supported by chromatic harmonies. Villa-Lobos attributed to this movement an "almost tragic sadness." He also referred in his notes to the "restless polyrhythms" of the finale, in which cross-rhythms, however, rather than polyrhythms emerge from the combination of the thematic figuration (in 9/8 meter) and the alternating eighth-note pizzicatos of the accompanying viola and cello (Example 7-13). The "picked-guitar" style is quite evident in the staccato descending phrase of the theme.

Villa-Lobos wrote many vocal works, both solo art songs (over one hundred) and secular and sacred choral compositions. Many choral works were for educational purposes, among them the well-known *Guia prático* ("Practical Guide"), consisting of a large number of harmonizations of Brazilian children's folk songs scored for children's chorus. The 1930s saw his involvement in a gigantic music education program sponsored by the Getúlio Vargas regime.[10] The patriotic fervor of the time made it possible for Villa-Lobos to implement his plan of using "Orpheonic" singing to provide a general music education in public schools and factories and to develop an interest in national music. For this he obtained the government's support and established and directed the SEMA (Superintendência de Educação Musical e Artística), through which he was able to organize immense singing rallies of up to thirty thousand or forty thousand voices, reminiscent at times of the concurrent European fascist manifestations of nationalism.

The solo songs by Villa-Lobos are of rather uneven quality. It is generally in his re-creation of Brazilian folk and popular songs that he proves most successful. The *Chansons Typiques Brésiliennes*, written as a series of thirteen compositions between 1919 and 1935, cover almost every folk-song aspect of the country—Indian, Afro-Brazilian, and mestizo. The songs *Xangô*

EXAMPLE 7-13 Heitor Villa-Lobos, *String Quartet No. 6*, fourth movement, mm. 1–3. Copyright 1948 by Associated Music Publishers, Inc. Used by permission.

[10]Cf. Heitor Villa-Lobos, *A música nacionalista no govêrno Getulio Vargas* (Rio de Janeiro: Departamento de imprensa e propaganda, 1940).

and *Estrêla é lua nova,* fourth and fifth of the set, are recollections of Afro-Brazilian religious songs of the *macumba* and *candomblé* types. Villa-Lobos achieves a good characterization of these popular genres—in *Xangô,* through the use of a repeated pentatonic motif and a hemiola rhythmic effect between the vocal line and the piano, which imitates a drum accompaniment; in *Estrêla é lua nova,* by means of repeated tones, syncopation, descending direction and range of a seventh of the vocal line, as well as a constant drum-like pattern in the accompaniment.

Two other collections of art songs, *Serestas* ("Serenades")—a set of fourteen songs—and *Modinhas e Canções,* written during a period of about twenty years, represent the composer's most nationalistic compositions in the genre. They range from simple harmonizations of popular tunes to original works imbued with elements of the most varied types of Brazilian folk music.

Villa-Lobos's most dynamic and lasting contribution stemmed from his deep empathy for the folk and popular music of Brazil. He was able to create a highly individual style which synthesizes in an intuitive manner the plurality of Brazilian music and some processes of the European art-music tradition. Musical nationalism in Latin America found in Villa-Lobos its strongest supporter and one of its most original creators.

Oscar Lorenzo Fernândez and Luciano Gallet

Among the Brazilian composers who came to maturity in the 1920s and 1930s, Oscar Lorenzo Fernândez (1897–1948) and Luciano Gallet (1893–1931) worked with different means towards the same goal: writing in a distinctively Brazilian style, however it might be defined.

Fernândez's first works, dating from 1918 to 1922, include mostly piano pieces and solo songs and reveal his early orientation towards Romanticism and Impressionism. With such works as the *Trio Brasileiro* (1924) and the *Canção Sertaneja* (1924), a trend towards musical nationalism utilizing contemporary techniques becomes evident. The period 1922–1938 was Fernândez's most productive and creative one. His most characteristic works of the period include the *Suite Sinfônica Sobre 3 Temas Populares Brasileiros* (1925), for orchestra; *Imbapara* (1929), an Amerindian tone poem; *Reisado do Pastoreio* (1930); and the opera *Malazarte,* written in 1933 but not produced until 1941. In these works the composer turned to different traditions of Brazil's folk and traditional music. The *Trio Brasileiro,* for piano, violin, and cello, exhibits original thematic ideas of a clear mestizo folk character, treated cyclically. The thematic material of the *Suite Sinfônica* originates in two folk songs from Bahia and a lullaby known throughout the country. *Imbapara,* on the other hand, utilizes authentic Indian melodies and percussion instruments; the orchestral sonorities result in exotic originality. With

Reisado do Pastoreio (1930), Fernândez turned to "Caboclo" and Afro-Brazilian folk traditions. While there is no direct quotation (with the exception of the first motive), the melodic and rhythmic traits of this piece are related to those traditions. The final movement, *Batuque*, has become a classical nationalistic piece of the Brazilian symphonic repertory.

Malazarte, on a libretto based on Graça Aranha's drama, can be considered the first successful Brazilian opera written in a nationalistic style. Each of the principal characters tends to be associated with a given folk or popular musical genre—Amerindian, Afro-Brazilian, Luso-Brazilian, and urban popular. All of the choral numbers of the opera are based on folk songs. An orchestral suite derived from *Malazarte* was written in 1941; the last section of the suite, another *Batuque*, won wide popularity.

Fernândez's solo art songs are often considered his most original contributions. A native inspiration pervades most of them. Among the best known are *Toada prá você*, on a text by Mário de Andrade, the previously mentioned *Canção Sertaneja*, the "modinha" *Meu Coração, Berceuse da Onda* (on a poem by the famous poetess Cecilia Meireles), *Noturno*, and *Essa Negra Fulô*, the last on a very popular poem by Jorge de Lima. Towards the end of his life Fernândez paid more attention to orchestral and chamber music, notably in a Violin Concerto (1941), two symphonies (1945–1947), and the *Variações Sinfônicas* (1948).

Together with Mário de Andrade, Luciano Gallet pioneered the study of folk music in Brazil. He was particularly concerned with defining the exact nature of Brazilian folk and popular music and of devising an adequate manner for utilizing their characteristics in his compositions. He began by harmonizing several folk songs, which resulted in the publication of *Canções Populares Brasileiras* in 1924. Among his piano works in a nationalist vein the suite *Nhô Chico* (1927), in three parts, is considered the most successful. He also wrote a series of *Exercicios Brasileiros*, for piano (four hands), based on the most typical melodic and rhythmic traits of folk-music genres. The *Suite sobre temas negro-brasileiros* (1929), for flute, oboe, clarinet, bassoon, and piano, gives evidence of Gallet's intimate knowledge of Afro-Brazilian musical characteristics. His *Estudos de Folclore*, which includes two important monographs on folk songs and dances collected in the field by the composer, was published posthumously by Mário de Andrade.

Camargo Guarnieri and Francisco Mignone

Within the Brazilian nationalist trend, the positions of Camargo Guarnieri (b. 1907) and Francisco Mignone (b. 1897) have been paramount. To be national composers and recognized as such remained one of their major concerns, together with a conscious endeavor for technical refinement. Guarnieri's impressive production—the result of numerous commissions—

covers several decades of intense activity. His first work to win uncontested success, the Piano Sonatina (1928), has been praised as the work of an imaginative lyricist.[11] Mário de Andrade's acknowledgment of Guarnieri's talent was probably motivated by his early recognition of a genuinely militant nationalist composer who opposed the prevailing European academicism. The Sonatina reveals a more subjective nationalism than Guarnieri's previous works such as the *Canção Sertaneja* or the *Dansa Brasileira* of 1928; in it, he combined a neo-Classically clear contrapuntal texture with an obvious native inspiration in the second movement (subtitled "Modinha"), in its reconstruction of the popular ostinato guitar accompaniment; and in the last movement, in a rhythmic vitality reminiscent of certain folk and popular dances. The *Dansa Brasileira*, for piano (later orchestrated), reveals stylistic processes related to urban popular dances, such as repeated tones and descending movement of the melody and rhythmic ostinato.

In the 1930s Guarnieri wrote mainly chamber works, including a string trio, a string quartet, a woodwind quintet, two violin sonatas, and a cello sonata, and he began a series of works inspired by the popular *chôro*. *Curucá* (1930), for orchestra, and *Flor do Tremembé* (1937), for fifteen solo instruments and percussion, reveal an imaginative timbral blending; in the latter work, this results from an effective use of typical Brazilian percussion instruments such as the *cavaquinho*, *cuíca* (friction drum), *agogô* (cowbell), and others. The first theme of *Chôro Torturado* (1930), for piano, is quite typical of the *chôro* models in its irregular accentuation. Later *choros* were for violin and orchestra (1951), for clarinet and orchestra (1956), and for piano and orchestra (1956).

Guarnieri's association with Mário de Andrade resulted in 1932 in a one-act comic opera (for which Andrade wrote the libretto), *Pedro Malazarte*, produced with great success at Rio de Janeiro in 1952. It was, however, in many solo songs written during the 1930s that Guarnieri excelled. In all the songs—from *Impossível Carinho* (1930) to the thirteen *Canções de Amor* (1936–1937) and *Vai, Azulão* (1939)—we find a basic lyrical quality quite typical of the composer. His large song output (over one hundred items) also reveals attempts at using Afro-Brazilian and Amerindian folk-song characteristics, e.g., *Sai Aruê* (1932) and *Acuti-parú* (1934). *Sai Aruê* is in many ways reminiscent of Villa-Lobos's *Xangô*: a *macumba* song (in an African language, but taken from Andrade's novel *Macunaíma*), it has the same dramatic effect, enhanced by a wide-ranging vocal line, glissando effects, and repeated drum-like patterns in the accompaniment. Important works by Guarnieri for voice and orchestra include the tragic cantata *A Morte do Aviador* (1932), *A Serra do Rola-Moça* (1947), *Três Poemas Afro-Brasileiros* (1955), and *Sêca* (1957).

[11]Mário de Andrade, *Música, doce música* (São Paulo: L. G. Miranda, 1963), p. 184.

Guarnieri turned more willingly to the orchestra after his first European sojourn (1938–1939). His *Abertura concertante* (1942) was followed by two symphonies in 1944; these are considered among his best works, and, together with a third one written in 1952, they typify his unique style, still in accord with the nationalist esthetic but definitely anti-exotic through a substantial stylization of national elements, and with a clear concern for further refinement of techniques of composition. He also wrote orchestral suites in which several Brazilian folk or popular dance-types were incorporated: *Brasiliana* (1950), *Suite IV Centenário* (1954, on the occasion of the fourth centenary of the foundation of the city of São Paulo), and the *Suite Vila Rica* (1958). Neo-Classic stylistic traits predominate in his piano concertos, the last one (No. 5, 1970) combining thematic material of the character of urban popular dances (samba, *chôro*) with twelve-tone techniques. A clear contrapuntal texture also prevails in the violin concertos.

The numerous piano pieces written by Guarnieri throughout his career have had an immediate appeal for most Brazilian pianists. Besides sonatinas and characteristic "national" pieces (*Toada, Lundu*, etc.), he wrote a series of piano etudes and waltzes, and fifty pieces in five albums entitled *Ponteios* (1931–1959), the title suggesting linear writing, since "ponteio" implies the melodic plucking of a string instrument. These pieces also exhibit the lyricism observed in the composer's early works.

During the 1960s Guarnieri interrupted his activities as a composer to reflect on his past activity. After overcoming doubts about his previous works, he decided to continue in the same esthetic orientation. The works of this period (such as *Homenagem a Villa-Lobos*, 1966) show a more direct involvement with national sources.

The extremely prolific Francisco Mignone's output covers almost all known musical genres in traditional media. Three major periods can be distinguished in his long creative life. The first (approximately 1917–1928) resulted from the phase of his musical training in Italy, with works structurally and harmonically akin to European Romanticism, such as the *Suite Campestre* (1918), the *Paráfrase sobre o Hino dos Cavalheiros da Kirial* (1919), and the tone poems *Festa dionisíaca* (1923), *Momus* (1925), and *No Sertão* (1925) (the last a fantasy inspired by the work of the writer Euclides da Cunha). At the same time, Mignone's interest in national idioms was revealed in such works as *Maxixe* (1925) and *Congada* for orchestra (1922), in which he dealt with Brazilian popular rhythms.

Strongly attracted to the ideals of musical nationalism as eloquently put forth by Mário de Andrade, Mignone began a new period of intense creativity around 1929. It was characterized by an imaginative exploration of all Brazilian folk and popular musical traditions. Concurrently, he further cultivated post-Romantic and neo-Classic styles. This second period extended to about 1959–1960. Quite typical of his nationalistic style are the ballets

Maracatu de Chico Rei (1933), on a topic by Andrade, *Batucajé* (1936), *Babaloxá* (1936), and *Leilão*, and the four *Fantasias Brasileiras*, for piano and orchestra (1929–1936). The ballets rely on Afro-Brazilian subjects and utilize almost exclusively actual Afro-Brazilian themes or themes akin to them in rhythmic characteristics and melodic contour. Almost all the collective dance numbers of *Maracatu de Chico Rei* are stylized folk and popular dances. Orchestral timbres are originally handled, with a stress on typical popular percussion instruments. The four *Fantasias* epitomize Mignone's style better than any other work of the period. As indicated by the title, these are rhapsodic pieces in character and structure, with piano parts reminiscent of the captivating, spontaneous, virtuoso manner of popular pianist-composers such as Ernesto Nazareth. Mário de Andrade has referred to the third *Fantasia*, along with *Babaloxá* and *Maracatu*, as "monumental landmarks," undoubtedly as a result of their national meaning in the context of Brazilian art music of the period.[12] The symphonic "impressions" *Festa das Igrejas* (1940), which were given worldwide exposure in a 1944 NBC Symphony concert under Toscanini, derive some of their thematic material from mestizo folk music.

Mignone's solo songs and piano pieces constitute some of the most successful works in the Brazilian repertory of the 1930s and 1940s. His first nationalist song, *Quando na roça anoitece* (1939), presents a typical melodic inflection and a guitar-like accompaniment. The *Seis Líricas* (1932), *Dentro da noite* and *Dona Janaína* from the cycle *Quatro Líricas* (1938), to texts by Manuel Bandeira, and *Pousa a mão na minha testa* (1942) are considered his best contributions to the song medium. Among his large piano output the pieces most obviously related to national expression include the collection of nine pieces titled *Lendas Sertanejas* (1923–1940) along with *Quatro Peças Brasileiras* (1930), *Cucumbizinho* (1931), *Cateretê* (1931), *Dança do Botocudo* (1940), and *Quase Modinha* (1940). Lyric melodies—some borrowed from folk songs—with a prevailingly tonal harmonic language and frequent syncopated rhythms (such as *Nazareth*, in the *Quatro Peças*) point to a heavy dependence on urban popular music characteristics. An easy assimilation of these elements is evidenced in the piece *Cucumbizinho*, particularly its imitation of the strumming of the *cavaquinho*. Two sets of waltzes, *Valsas de Esquina* (1938–1943) and *Valsas Choros* (1946–1955), extremely Romantic in inspiration and technique, attempt to re-create the atmosphere of the popular improvised waltzes of strolling serenaders of the early twentieth century, of popular piano pieces written by such composers as Nazareth, and, in their melodic content, of popular *modinhas*. The First Piano Sonata (1941) transcends somewhat the constant references to national music of Mignone's other piano works of the period. In his *Autocrítica de Um Cinqüen-*

12Ibid., p. 311.

tenário (1947) the composer's profession of faith goes as follows: "My music will have to be gradually more refined technically, but [be] clear, honest, and easily understandable to the majority." It is not surprising, therefore, to notice that the Piano Concerto of 1958 was written in the European Romantic manner, with colorful orchestration and brilliant bravura solo passages.

The late 1950s were active years in Mignone's chamber and symphonic music production. Such works as the Octet for strings (1956), the String Quartets nos. 1 and 2 (1957), and the *Sinfonia Tropical* (1958) indicate a turning point in the composer's career, as he tended to forsake his previously direct preoccupation with national sources and entered a third period in which he became quite eclectic. Any system or technique of composition could be followed as long as it was thought hospitable to the total freedom of expression that he sought. To this period belong a series of sacred works including seven Masses (1962–1968) and the *Pequeno Oratório de Santa Clara* (1961), a violin concerto (1961), three piano sonatas, a double concerto for violin and piano, and many other compositions. Their stylistic characteristics are difficult to generalize about, as heterogeneity prevails; however, a definite orientation towards polytonality (with use of tone clusters), atonality, and serialism can be detected.

In the past few years, Mignone has stated his interest in experimenting with new-music techniques. On a commission from the São Paulo Philharmonic he wrote the *Variações em busca de um tema* (1972) ("Variations in search of a theme") for orchestra, in which he attempted to use "all present-day compositional processes," including aleatory ones. He has also written a *Sinfonia Transamazônica* (1972), to welcome the Amazon highway undertaking.

Younger Composers

Among the Brazilian nationalist composers born in the early part of the twentieth century, José Siqueira (b. 1907), Radamés Gnatalli (b. 1906), and Luiz Cosme (1908–1965) should be mentioned. Siqueira turned to musical nationalism in the early 1940s and has since been one of Brazil's foremost promoters of the trend, even studying *in situ* Northeastern folk music, especially Afro-Brazilian music of the Bahia area. His production reveals a predilection for programmatic symphonic music. Works such as *4 poemas indígenas* (1944), *5 Danças brasileiras* (1944), and *Canto do Tabajara* (1946) reveal the most direct folkloristic nationalism. During the 1950s, however, Siqueira developed a more sophisticated style based on specific traits of the folk and popular music of his native state of Paraíba. He devised theoretical methods that he called "Brazilian tri-modal" and "Brazilian penta-modal" systems, which consist essentially in the adoption of specific modes of Northeastern folk music (such as pentatonic scales or a major scale with sharp fourth and flat seventh degrees) as well as its harmonic and rhythmic characteristics. Both the Cello Concerto (1952) and the Violin Concerto (1957) were written within such systems. Siqueira's abundant output during this period includes three symphonies, orchestral suites, and several works inspired by Afro-Brazilian ritual music, such as the Black cantata *Xangô*, the *Cavalo dos Deuses*, *Encantamento da Magia Negra*, and *Candomblé*, a "fetishistic oratorio" in thirteen parts. The work *Carnaval no Recife*, for orchestra, while maintaining a frankly popular atmosphere, exhibits an imaginative tone coloring by blending various percussion instruments associated with such carnival dances and festivities as the *frevo* and *maracatu*. An intensive period of chamber music writing followed in the 1960s, with *3 Trípticos*, a woodwind quintet, string quartets, *Adoração aos orixás*, and *3 Cantigas para Iemanjá*, for cello. The Second Quintet (1963), for string quartet and soprano, borrows its thematic material from religious songs of Afro-Bahian cults.

A native of Rio Grande do Sul, Radamés Gnatalli studied composition on his own and began his professional activities as a pianist and then a viola player in the Quartet Henrique Oswald. After settling permanently in Rio, he became the official conductor of the Radio Nacional orchestra. His wide popularity and success as a composer of music for soap operas and other radio genres of the time, his skillful arrangements and orchestrations of fashionable popular tunes and dance rhythms, and his general involvement with the popular musical scene of Rio de Janeiro have often been held against him and his concurrent career as an art-music composer. But, rather than harming it, his activities in the popular field have served very well his quest for a nationalist expression. His firsthand experience with popular music, however commercialized, afforded him a knowledge of it that few nationalist Brazilian composers could claim. This is particularly evident in the first period of his production (1931–1940), which is characterized by a clear national style in such works as *Rapsódia Brasileira* (1931) and a *Trio* for strings (1933), within a post-Romantic idiom. In addition, some jazz inflections, especially harmonic formulas and instrumentation, appear occasionally in his works of the 1930s.

Gnatalli's second period, which began about 1945 when he was elected a founding member of the Academia Brasileira de Música, can be characterized as one of a subjective nationalism expressed with more reserved and simpler means. He continued, however, to cultivate a musical style of easy and immediate comprehension. The series of *Brasilianas*, comprising ten pieces written between 1944 and 1962, illustrates the composer's varied approaches to nationalist composition. *Brasiliana No. 2* (1948), for example, is a clever stylization of different types of samba: *samba de morro*, *samba-canção*, and *samba de batucada*. Others, such as *Brasiliana No. 6* (1954) for piano and orchestra, or No. 8 for tenor saxophone and piano, reveal very imaginative timbral blendings as well as a more subdued involvement with national sources.

During the 1950s Gnatalli attempted deliberately to remove himself from musical nationalism. He turned to neo-Romantic and neo-Classic models, while maintaining the unmistakably light style often associated with symphonic jazz, in such works as the *Concêrto Romântico*, three guitar concertos, the *Sinfonia Popular*, and a concerto for mouth harmonica and orchestra. The works of the 1960s, however, reveal a further assimilation of folk and popular musical traditions. The *Concertos Cariocas*, the *Sonatina Coreográfica*, and the *Quarteto Popular*, among others, are delightful in their popular inspiration, while the Second Violin Concerto (1962) exhibits effective experiments with bossa-nova rhythmic patterns.

Luiz Cosme's activities as a composer were limited to twenty years of his life (1930–1950), and his production was very small. He first wrote miniature piano pieces, solo songs, and chamber music works. A quintet for piano and strings, *Vamo, Manuca*, and the string quartet, *Sambalelê*, of 1931 were later withdrawn by the composer on the ground that they represented a direct folkloristic nationalism incompatible with his later wish for independence from any given trend.

Cosme's first important work, the String Quartet No. 1 (1933), is devoid of national implications but is clearly Impressionistic in its timbral effects. Yet his regionalist tendencies are skillfully incorporated in certain contemporary compositional techniques in his most significant orchestral work, the ballet *Salamanca do Jaráu* (1935). Based on the Southern legend of the same name (one of Spanish origin), the ballet enhances the local color by using throughout a motive from the most popular song of the state of Rio Grande do Sul, *Boi Barroso*. The thematic material of the ballet derives from the song, although it is never quoted in its entirety. The work reveals an elaboration of popular melodic elements within a modern harmonic structure. Its rhythmic vitality is often reminiscent of Stravinsky's early ballets. Several passages of *Salamanca* show Cosme's kinship with French Impressionism, through long harmonic pedal points, chordal parallelism, and pentatonicism, but its national character nevertheless remains quite clear.

Many Brazilian composers born in the 1910s and 1920s have at times in their careers turned to national sources, although some of them remained rather eclectic. Cláudio Santoro (b. 1919), one of Brazil's most creative personalities in the 1950s and 1960s, began as a serial composer but gradually evolved towards first a subjective, then an overt, nationalist style, which however he abandoned altogether in the 1960s. His significant nationalistic works include the seven piano pieces entitled *Paulistanas* (1953), the String Quartet No. 3 (1953), *Ponteio* (1953) for string orchestra, and especially the Symphonies No. 5 (1955) and No. 7 ("Brasilia") (1959–1969). Santoro is essentially an experimentalist, however; his activities are therefore surveyed further in Part 3 of this study. César Guerra Peixe (b. 1914) followed at first a direction similar to Santoro's, but he does not seem to have fully realized his potential as a nationalist composer. Oswaldo Lacerda (b. 1927), a student of Camargo Guarnieri, incorporates a subtle national idiom in a modern harmonic context. His intimate knowledge of Brazilian folk music is best revealed in the seven *Ponteios* for piano (1955–1971) and the six suites grouped under the title *Brasiliana* (1965–1971). Lacerda's best known orchestral piece is the clearly nationalist suite *Piratininga*, for which he won first prize in the National Composition Contest of 1962.

ARGENTINA

The background of Argentine musical nationalism in the twentieth century was reviewed in Chapter 4, where we saw that a nationalist trend in the arts evolved from the so-called "gauchesco" tradition, upon which most Argentine composers of the first half of the century centered their attention. Two other sources were the Andean culture of the western provinces and, to a lesser extent, the urban culture ("porteño") of Buenos Aires. Following the lead of Williams and Aguirre, the subsequent generations of Argentine composers kept alive the nationalist current in opera, ballet, symphonic, and chamber music.

Nationalism has appeared conspicuously in Argentine operas. The foundation of the new Teatro Colón of Buenos Aires, inaugurated in 1908, was a strong incentive for the continuation of opera production. Opera composers found in Italian *verismo* a suitable model for their nationalist tendencies. Composers such as Pascual de Rogatis (b. 1881), a student of Williams; Enrique M. Casella (1891–1948), active mainly in Tucumán; Arnaldo D'Espósito (1907–1945); Constantino Gaito (1878–1945); and Felipe Boero (1884–1958) wrote numerous operas based on folk legends from Argentina or other Latin American countries and on actual folk or popular musical themes. De Rogatis's *Huemac*, on an Aztec myth, was premiered at the Colón in 1916, while Boero's *El Matrero*, based on the folkways of the pampas, premiered in 1929, won wide popularity in Argentina.

Carlos López Buchardo (1881–1948), Gilardo Gilardi (1889–1963), and Athos Palma (1891–1951), among others, reveal varying degrees of national concern. López Buchardo's symphonic poem *Escenas Argentinas* (premiered in 1922), a programmatic suite in three sections (*Día de fiesta, El arroyo, Campera*), utilizes folkloristic elements justified by the detailed program. A *gaucho* dance—the *gato*, based on the typical figure $\frac{6}{8}$ ♪ ♩ ♩ ♪ and including a frequent superimposition of 6/8 and 3/4 meters, as in the Argentine *zamba*—with simulation of the *rasgueo* (strumming) accompanying guitar serves as the main basis of the first section. Motives of a *vidalita* (a folk-song genre) appear in the *Arroyo* ("Brook") movement to accent the phrases of a "love dialogue," according to the program. *Campera*, a melancholy movement, is built on the melody of a popular *triste* (a sentimental folk-song genre) from the pampa. Within this direct folkloristic approach the harmonic and orchestral idioms are strongly Romantic. López Buchardo is remembered chiefly for his fine contribution to Argentine art song and his musical comedies. His two song albums, referred to as "canciones argentinas," also draw on *música criolla*. The same applies to Gilardi, whose numerous choral pieces, solo songs, and chamber works are largely skilled stylizations of folk melodies and rhythms. His *Serie argentina* (1929) and the humorous symphonic piece *El Gaucho con botas nuevas* (1934) include respectively a *chacarera*—a Northern folk dance musically similar to the *gato* and the *zamba*—and a *malambo*, the vigorous competitive dance of the gauchos. The first measures of Gilardi's *Chacarera*, from the *Serie* reveal some of the characteristics of the folk dance: an alternation or simultaneity of 6/8 and 3/4 meters, often creating cross-rhythmic effects, and the pattern $\frac{6}{8}$ ♪ ♩ ♩ ♪ , typical of the rhythmic structure of the *chacarera* as of the *gato*.[13]

As opposed to this direct utilization of folk sources, other composers advocated a greater cosmopolitan expression through the adoption of some contemporary European composition techniques while maintaining a subjective Argentine character. Such an attitude was held by Floro M. Ugarte (b. 1884); the brothers Juan José Castro (1895–1968), José María Castro (1892–1964), and Washington Castro (b. 1909); Luis Gianneo (1897–1968); Honorio M. Siccardi (b. 1897); and others. Ugarte's first tone poem, *De mi tierra* (1923), based on verses by Estanislao del Campo, and Siccardi's *Tres Poemas sobre Martín Fierro* (1925) are indicative of the reliance of nationalist composers of the period on the literary classics of the *gauchesco* tradition: Estanislao del Campo's *Fausto* and José Hernández's *Martín Fierro*, the nationalist popular poem par excellence, are the two major works of the gauchesco literature. Many subsequent nationalist compositions alluded to these literary works, thus building a musical trend on a well-established literary tradition. This trend reached its culmination in the 1940s in such works as Juan José Castro's *Martín Fierro* (1944), a cantata for baritone, chorus, and orchestra on texts from Hernández's poem, and Alberto Ginastera's *Obertura para el "Fausto" criollo* (1943), inspired by del Campo's work.

Juan José Castro and Luis Gianneo

Juan José Castro appeared as the leading figure in the Argentine nationalist movement in the 1930s, especially with his *Sinfonía argentina* (1934) in three movements ("Arrabal," "Llanuras," "Ritmos y Danzas"), the

---

[13]Cf. Isabel Aretz, *El folklore musical argentino* (Buenos Aires: Ricordi Americana, 1952), pp. 204–6.

first of which explores elements of the tango, and his *Sinfonía de los Campos* (1939). The latter, an Argentine "pastoral" symphony, is descriptive and subjectively evocative of the pampa folk traditions, and in harmonic language quite Impressionistic. Consisting of a sequence of six movements, it resembles formally more a suite than a symphony.

Rarely does Castro resort to direct quotations of folk materials. The national flavor of some of his works results from a synthetic reworking of rhythmic patterns of typical folk dances. The last movement of his String Quartet (1942), for example, draws on typical rhythmic figures in triple meter of the *pericón*, one of the most popular dances of the pampas since the late nineteenth century. Characteristic tango syncopations also appear in his *Tangos* (1941) for piano, which capture very effectively the somewhat dramatic character of the popular dance. Some of Castro's most skillful references to various Argentine national music genres are found in the *Corales criollos* nos. 1 and 2 (1947), for piano, the *Sonatina campestre* (1948) for *bandoneón* (a diatonic accordion, the instrument par excellence of popular tango ensembles), and the *Corales criollos No. 3* (1953), for orchestra. The latter work, for which Castro received first prize at the Caracas Latin American Music Festival (1954), reveals a sublimation of national traits.

Musical nationalism was not an exclusive interest of Castro; his formative training in Paris under Vincent d'Indy was a strong influence on his quest for a more international style. He felt particularly attracted by Spanish subject matters and Spanish music. Two of his operas are on texts by García Lorca: *La Zapatera prodigiosa* (1943) and *Bodas de sangre* (1953). He also set several of Lorca's poems to music, including *Verde que te quiero verde* and *La Casada infiel*. Works such as *Elegía a la muerte de García Lorca* (1945), for soprano, chorus, and orchestra, *De tierra gallega* (1946), for chorus and orchestra, and the *Sonatina española* (1953), for piano, attest to his empathy for Spanish music. In later life, however, he turned to expressionist aesthetics and to serialist techniques of composition.

Castro's career as an orchestra conductor of international renown deserves some attention. He began in that capacity in 1928 with the Orquesta de Cámara Renacimiento of Buenos Aires, then conducted for several years the orchestra of the Teatro Colón. His many activities as a conductor included the direction of the Orquesta Filarmónica of Havana, Cuba (1947–1948), the SODRE Orchestra in Montevideo (1949–1951), the Victorian Symphony Orchestra in Melbourne (1951–1953), and the Orquesta Sinfónica Nacional Argentina (1956–1960). He was responsible for introducing in many Latin American cities the major works of the twentieth-century European and Latin American orchestral repertories.

Castro's contemporary, Luis Gianneo, cultivated a nationalist style over a longer period and with more regional variety, including Indian elements (for example, *Cuatro cantos incaicos*, for string quartet). The two symphonic poems *Turay Turay* and *El Tarco en Flor* (respectively, 1928 and 1930), which remain his most popular works, draw on folk music and folklore of the Tucumán area. The *música criolla* tradition is represented in *Canción y Danza* (1932) and *Pericón* (1948), both for orchestra; in two string quartets (*Cuartetos criollos* nos. 1 and 2, 1936 and 1944); in *Cinco piezas* for violin and piano (1942) and other chamber works; in numerous piano pieces, including *Preludios criollos* (1927) and *Tres danzas argentinas* (1939); and in a number of songs, especially the *Pampeanas* (1924, anticipating a generic title to be used later by Ginastera) and the twelve *Coplas* (subtitled *Poesías populares argentinas*), in two sets (1929–1930). In addition, Gianneo wrote a major work of Amerindian character, with borrowing of actual Indian melodies, the *Concierto Aymará* for violin and orchestra (1942), and he also wrote one of the major works in which the tango—Argentina's most typical genre of urban popular music—is given prominence.[14] This is his *Variaciones sobre tema de tango* (1953) for orchestra, consisting of a prelude, a theme, and six variations. The theme is an original one in tango rhythm which is varied by means of contrasting mood and character, including a nostalgic allusion in the third variation ("1900") to the *milonga*, the precursor of the tango. In sum, for consistency, variety, and comprehensiveness over a period of thirty years, Gianneo's contribution to Argentine musical nationalism is unsurpassed by any of his contemporaries. Of the next generation, only Ginastera has approached this impressive record.

Alberto Ginastera

The stylistic development of Alberto Ginastera (b. 1916) has been truly exceptional. Recognized as one of the leading creative personalities in twentieth-century Latin American music, he came of age during the high tide of Argentine musical nationalism. In 1937, a year before graduating from the National Conservatory in Buenos Aires, he wrote the two works that established his reputation as a "national" composer: the *Danzas Argentinas* for piano ("Danza del viejo boyero," "Danza de la moza donosa," and "Danza del gaucho matrero") and the ballet *Panambí*, from which an orchestral suite was performed with notable success in the year of its composition. The ballet was produced at the Colón in 1940, and Ginastera received at that time the national prize for music. As a result of a commission from the American Ballet Caravan to write another ballet on an Argentine subject,

---

[14]The relative neglect of the tango by Argentine composers of art music can probably be explained by the overwhelming impact of the rural tradition on Argentine national music—by the pampa, the gaucho, the repertory of *criollo* songs and dances, and the supremacy of the guitar as the most typical instrument of the folk. One exception is Astor Piazzolla (b. 1921), a former student of Nadia Boulanger in Paris, who cultivated concurrently popular and art music; his sophisticated approach to the composition of tangos stimulated a new interest in the old dance form well into the 1960s.

he produced *Estancia* (1941), "on scenes of Argentine rural life." With this work "Ginastera definitely established himself as a leader of the national movement in Argentine music."[15] Since the Ballet Caravan was dissolved in 1942, the ballet was not staged until ten years later, but a concert performance of the dances from *Estancia* took place in 1943. Further works by Ginastera in the national vein appeared in the 1940s, consolidating his position of leadership, especially the *Obertura para el "Fausto" Criollo* (1943), the songs *Cinco canciones populares argentinas* and *Las horas de una estancia* (both 1943), and the *Suite de danzas criollas* (1946) for piano. Ginastera himself has called this a period of "objective nationalism" (1937–1947)[16] in which the *gauchesco* tradition (literary sources) prevailed, with strong local color and a conscious treatment of indigenous themes, though with rare direct borrowing of folk materials. During this period he cultivated a clearly tonal idiom, including, however, extremely dissonant passages.

Estancia appears as the most overtly nationalist of the larger works of Ginastera's "objective" phase. The inclusion of sung and recited excerpts from *Martín Fierro* connects the work instantly with the pampas. In addition, the climactic final section of the work, titled "Malambo," derives from the vigorous dance (of the same name) that has long been identified with the gauchos, especially in the kind of competition called *justa* ("joust"). Now extinct in the folk tradition, the *malambo* was characterized by a fast tempo and constant eighth-note motion in a 6/8 meter. Example 7-14 illustrates

EXAMPLE 7-14   Rhythmic variants of the *malambo*. From Gilbert Chase, "Alberto Ginastera: Argentine Composer," *Musical Quarterly*, XLIII/4 (October 1957), 455. Copyright 1957 by G. Schirmer, Inc. Used by permission.

[15]Gilbert Chase, "Alberto Ginastera: Argentine Composer," *Musical Quarterly*, XLIII/4 (October 1957), 441.

[16]See Pola Súarez Urtubey, *Alberto Ginastera* (Buenos Aires: Ediciones Cultural Argentinas, 1967), pp. 68–72, for the composer's own comments on the "three periods" of his music.

some of its more common rhythmic variants. Among these, the dotted quarter notes "often serve as points of repose, marking the end of a period and punctuating the impetuous motion generated by the repeated eighth notes."[17] This provided the composer with a model for other music, especially rhythmic, toccata-like final movements: even in the early *Panambí* and the *Danzas Argentinas*, the final sections utilize *malambo* rhythmic elements. The last number of the *Danzas* ("Danza del gaucho matrero") provides, in addition, an interesting example of what has been called a "braking" effect resulting from successive eighths, quarters, and dotted quarters (Example 7-15). The use of polytonality, both melodically and harmonically, may also be noticed in such an early piece.

EXAMPLE 7-15 Alberto Ginastera, *Danzas Argentinas:* "Danza del gaucho matrero," mm. 93–103. Copyright 1939 by Durand & Cie. Paris.

The *malambo* may be regarded as the rural, primitivistic antipode of the pastoral, cantabile vein that is also present in much of Ginastera's music of this period. This lyrical quality is frequently associated with the *criollo* folk song, especially the *copla* or octosyllabic quatrain used to sing *vidalitas*, *villancicos*, and others

In the *Obertura para el "Fausto" criollo*, Ginastera drew on the

---

[17]Gilbert Chase, "Alberto Ginastera," p. 455.

humorous *Fausto* by Estanislao del Campo. The poem is subtitled "Impressions of the gaucho Anastasio el Pollo at the representation of this opera." On a visit to Buenos Aires, Anastasio decides to see the "show" at the old Teatro Colón and finds himself confronted with Gounod's *Faust*. On his return home he describes to a friend, in the typical lingo of the gaucho, his deep impressions of Doctor Faustus's story. The score indicates that "the composer uses some fragments of Gounod's opera as thematic material and employs rhythmic and melodic elements of Argentine folklore." But, while the opening section refers to the introduction to the opera and several passages allude to Marguerite's theme, the Soldiers' Chorus, and the Kermesse, it is by no means a *pastiche*. The folk elements include above all the rhythmic figure $\begin{smallmatrix}6\\8\end{smallmatrix}$ ♩♩♩ ♪ ♩ associated with the *zamba*; it serves as an ostinato in the two *allegro vivace* sections. In this and other works of the period Ginastera's use of folk elements is highly personal. He does not exploit or develop specific folk-song "tunes" in the manner of nationalist composers such as Vaughan Williams or Copland. Rather, he assimilates various types of folk music for their symbolic and expressive value in relation to his own stylistic needs. He does not seek to evoke a reaction by association, which explains his opposition to folkloristic nationalism.

The series of *Pampeanas* which were begun in 1947 illustrates Ginastera's transition from an objective to a subjective treatment of vernacular elements. The transitional work *Pampeana No. 1* (1947), for violin and piano, leads into Ginastera's second phase, one of "subjective nationalism" or, as Chase has appropriately termed it, a "subjective sublimation" of musical nationalism. This period began with the First String Quartet (1948) and lasted until about 1954. Ginastera has maintained that the quartet contains "rhythms and melodic motives of the music of the pampas," but they are not distinctly stated. The same applies to the Piano Sonata (1952), in which, in Ginastera's words, "the composer does not employ any folkloric material, but instead introduces in the thematic texture rhythmic and melodic motives whose expressive tension has a pronounced Argentine accent." Finally, regarding the *Variaciones Concertantes* (1953), Ginastera expressed himself as follows: "These variations have a subjective Argentine character. Instead of using folkloristic material the composer achieves an Argentine atmosphere through the employment of original thematic and rhythmic elements." Thus the perception of national elements becomes evidently subjective. Yet it is still possible to identify a number of allusions to folk music in the works of this period. One specific trait found in both first and second periods is the conspicuous use of the "natural" chord of the guitar, with the open strings (E-A-D-G-B-E) often presented in chromatically altered form.[18] The "Impressionistic" character of this chord, if interpreted as a seventh chord

[18]Ibid., p. 448.

with an added fourth, and the wide association of the instrument with Spain had previously justified the presence of the chord in Manuel de Falla's works. In Argentina, the supremacy of the guitar as a folk instrument is yet another extension of the *criollo* tradition. Most of Ginastera's works from the late 1930s to the mid-1950s refer to this "symbolic chord."[19] Frequently the chord generates the main harmonies of a given passage, thus fulfilling a harmonic function as well.

The "symphonic pastoral" *Pampeana No. 3* (1954), for orchestra, marks the end of Ginastera's second period. Some features of this work can still be related to Argentine folk music, but the compositional techniques rely on non-national elements such as tone rows. The first and third movements are based on the harmonic and melodic series given in Example 7-16. Both series are treated freely, and a tonal feeling is still in evidence. A polytonal chord interpreted by Chase as an alteration of

EXAMPLE 7-16 Alberto Ginastera, *Pampeana No. 3:* Harmonic and melodic series of (a) first movement, and (b) third movement. Copyright 1954, 1964 by Barry & Cia. Used by permission of Boosey & Hawkes, Inc. Sole agents.

[19]Cf. ibid., p. 450.

the "symbolic" chord constitutes the fundamental structural element of the scherzo-like middle movement; national rhythmic patterns (including hemiola) are applied to this chord in the *Intermezzo quasi Trio* section of the movement.

The last creative period of the composer—one of neo-expressionism—began with his Quartet No. 2 (1958). Since polytonal and serial techniques prevail in the works of this period, they are examined in Part 3.

URUGUAY

Musical nationalism appeared in Uruguay at the beginning of the twentieth century in the works of Alfonso Broqua (1876–1946), Luis Cluzeau Mortet (1889–1957), Eduardo Fabini (1882–1950)—the best known composer of his generation—and Vicente Ascone (b. 1897). Broqua, who studied under d'Indy and Franck, attempted a national style with the lyrical poem *Tabaré* (premiered at the Teatro Solís in 1910) and the opera *La Cruz del Sud* (ca. 1920, never produced), both on Amerindian subjects, and the last movement of his Quintet in G minor is subtitled "Variations on regional themes." His most typically national works, however, are the *Evocaciones criollas*, for guitar, including a *vidala, chacarera, zamba,* and other folk music genres; the *Preludios Pampeanos*, for piano; and the *Tres cantos uruguayos*. Although not exclusively a nationalist composer, Cluzeau Mortet cultivated the *gauchesco* tradition intensively. The piano piece *Pericón* (1918), popularized by Rubinstein, was his first major nationalist composition. His symphonic and chamber music works of clearly native character include *Llanuras* (1932), *Rancherío* (1940), and *Tres movimientos criollos* (1955), all for orchestra, and the *Cuatro ritmos criollos* (1936), for string quartet, and the *Bagatelas criollas* (1945), for a quartet of flutes.

A decided champion of musical nationalism, Fabini wrote what is generally considered the culminating national work in Uruguay: the tone poem *Campo*, premiered in 1922. This was followed by another tone poem first conceived as an overture, *La Isla de los Ceibos* (1924–1926), and a series of *Tristes*, variously for orchestra, piano (original versions for guitar), or voice and piano. In these works Fabini re-creates some of the elements of "Rioplatense" folk music, in a thorough assimilation. His is not, however, a folkloristic type of nationalism.[20] The *triste*, which appears as an important source of evocation in Fabini's works, exhibits in its Uruguayan version a

---

[20]Cf. Roberto Lagarmilla, *Eduardo Fabini, Músico Nacional Uruguayo* (Montevideo: Organización Medina, 1953), pp. 234ff.

special feature of a descending half-tone in the cadences; this characteristic is evident in the first theme of *Campo*.[21] Moreover, the Andean *yaraví* from which the *triste* originated is effectively stylized in the fourth *Triste*, for voice and piano, by the modal flavor of the vocal line, which maintains at the same time a *criollo* character through the syncopated bass line of the accompaniment, with its 6/8 meter feeling set against the 3/4 division of the vocal line.

The Italian-born Vicente Ascone also adhered to musical nationalism in his works of the 1930s to the 1950s. Raised and educated in Montevideo, he developed a career as a performer (trumpet player), composer, and teacher. His opera *Paraná Guazú* (1930) is an evocation of the major periods of the history of the River Plate region. This evocation is effected musically by resorting to stylization of Indian, Spanish, and mestizo elements, such as the use of pentatonic motives in the overture, and of the melodic and rhythmic traits of the folk genres *estilo*, *vidalita*, *zamba*, and *pericón*.

BIBLIOGRAPHICAL NOTES

A great deal of attention has been given in Brazil to musical nationalism in the country in the twentieth century. Luiz Heitor Corrêa de Azevedo studied carefully the period 1900–1950 in his book *150 Anos de Música no Brasil (1800–1950)* (Rio de Janeiro: Livraria José Olympio Editôra, 1956). Mário de Andrade provided excellent insight into the question of national music in his epoch-making *Ensaio sôbre a Música Brasileira* (São Paulo: I. Chiarato e Cia., 1928).

The life and works of Heitor Villa-Lobos have been the subject of various books and monographs. The most up-to-date catalogue of his works in found in *Villa-Lobos, Sua Obra*, 2nd ed. (Rio de Janeiro: MEC, Museu Villa-Lobos, 1972). Reliable biographies are Andrade Muricy, *Villa-Lobos, Uma Interpretação* (Rio de Janeiro: Serviço de Documentação do MEC, 1961); Vasco Mariz, *Heitor Villa-Lobos: Life and Work of the Brazilian Composer*, 2nd ed. (Washington: Brazilian American Cultural Institute, 1970) (the 5th edition of this book, much enlarged, appeared in 1977 in Rio); and Lisa M. Peppercorn, *Heitor Villa-Lobos: Leben und Werk des brasilianischen Komponisten* (Zürich: Atlantis, 1972). Analytical studies are very few; those dealing with some aspects of Villa-Lobos's works include Souza Lima, *Comentários sôbre a Obra Pianística de Villa-Lobos* (Rio de Janeiro: MEC, Museu Villa-Lobos, 1969); Arnaldo Estrella, *Os Quartetos de Cordas de Villa-Lobos* (Rio de Janeiro: MEC, Museu Villa-Lobos, 1970); and Turibio Santos, *Heitor Villa-*

[21] As observed by Francisco Curt Lange (ed.), *Latin American Art Music for the Piano* (New York: G. Schirmer, 1942), pp. xi–xii.

Lobos e o Violão (Rio de Janeiro: MEC, Museu Villa-Lobos, 1975). A good appreciation of Villa-Lobos's activities in music education is given by Francisco Curt Lange, "Villa-Lobos, un Pedagogo Creador," *Boletín Latino-Americano de Música*, I (April 1935), 189–96, and David E. Vassberg, "Villa-Lobos: Music as a Tool of Nationalism," *Luso-Brazilian Review*, VI/2 (December 1969), 55–65. Discussion of Villa-Lobos's harmonic practice is found in Oscar Lorenzo Fernândez, "A Contribuição Harmônica de Villa-Lobos para a Música Brasileira," *Boletín Latino-Americano de Música*, VI (April 1946), 283–300. Besides his study of the Bachianas mentioned in note 6, Adhemar Nóbrega has also written *Os choros de Villa-Lobos* (Rio de Janeiro: MEC, Museu Villa-Lobos, 1975).

Albert T. Luper assessed the works of Lorenzo Fernândez and Camargo Guarnieri in "Lorenzo Fernândez and Camargo Guarnieri: Notes toward a Mid-Century Appraisal," in *Proceedings. Conference on Latin American Fine Arts, June 14–17, 1951* (Austin, Texas: University of Texas, Institute of Latin American Studies, 1952), pp. 98–114. A good assessment of Luciano Gallet's works is Mário de Andrade's short article, "Luciano Gallet e sua Obra," in *Weco*, no. 1 (October 1929), 3ff. Andrade has also written on Camargo Guarnieri's works; see particularly "Uma Sonata de Camargo Guarnieri," *Revista Brasileira de Música*, II (1935), 135ff. Francisco Mignone's auto-biography (*A Parte do Anjo: Autocrítica de um Cinqüentenário*, São Paulo, 1947) is essential for an understanding of the composer's works. Sister Marion Verhaalen has offered an analytical survey of Mignone's piano music in "Francisco Mignone: His Music for Piano," *Inter-American Music Bulletin*, no. 79 (November 1970–February 1971), 1–36.

Other Brazilian composers mentioned in this chapter are treated at some length in Vasco Mariz, *Figuras da Música Brasileira Contemporânea* (Brasília: Universidade de Brasília, 1970). I have written on Luiz Cosme's esthetic position in "Luiz Cosme (1908–1965): Impulso Creador versus Conciencia Formal," *Yearbook*, Inter-American Institute for Musical Research, V (1969), 67–89. The song repertory of all Brazilian composers mentioned here is studied in Vasco Mariz, *A Canção Brasileira* (Rio de Janeiro: Ministério da Educação e Cultura, 1959, 2nd ed., 1977).

A general overview of Argentine musical life during the late nineteenth and early twentieth centuries is given in Mario García Acevedo, *La Música Argentina Durante el Período de la Organización Nacional* (Buenos Aires: Ministerio de Educación y Justicia, 1961). The same author provided a general coverage of music after 1910 in his book *La Música Argentina Contemporánea* (Buenos Aires: Ministerio de Educación y Justicia, 1963). Opera in Buenos Aires is the subject of Roberto Caamaño (ed.), *La Historia del Teatro Colón* (Buenos Aires: Cinetea, 1969). A specific study of a nationalist opera is Malena Kuss, "*Huemac*, by Pascual de Rogatis: Native Identity in the Argentine Lyric Theatre," *Yearbook for Inter-American Musical Research* (University of Texas, Austin), X (1974) [published 1976], 68–87.

A series of individual biographies of Argentine composers was begun in the early 1960s by the Ministerio de Educación y Justicia: Series Ediciones Culturales Argentinas. It includes biographies on Carlos López Buchardo by Abraham Jurafsky (1966), Gilardo Gilardi by Jorge Oscar Pickenhayn (1966), Juan José Castro by Rodolfo Arizaga (1963), Jacobo Ficher by Boris Zipman (1966), and Alberto Ginastera by Pola Suárez Urtubey (1967). On Ginastera, see the doctoral dissertation by David Wallace, *Alberto Ginastera: an Analysis of his Style and Technique of Composition* (Northwestern University, 1964). Paul Hume, "Alberto Ginastera," *Inter-American Music Bulletin*, no. 48 (1965), 1ff, is a simple introduction to the composer's works.

Musical nationalism in Uruguay is thoroughly treated in Susana Salgado, *Breve Historia de la Música Culta en el Uruguay* (Montevideo: Aemus, 1971). This source includes comprehensive catalogues of Uruguayan composers' works.

part three

Countercurrents in the Twentieth Century

EIGHT

THE 1910S AND 1920S

Although musical nationalism dominated the art-music scene in Latin America during the first half of the twentieth century, currents opposed to it appeared from the outset of the century. At first these arose from an emulation of late nineteenth-century European Romantic music that bespoke an attitude of indifference to nationalism. Soon, however, several composers in the various countries began to voice their frank *opposition* to nationalism by adhering to the most advanced techniques and esthetic of their period. This attitude often resulted from a conviction that musical nationalism was producing works of dubious quality and that it demeaned Latin American music by resorting to a facile exotic regionalism. Some composers' inclination towards non-nationalist means can be construed as a deliberate endeavor to gain recognition through the intrinsic quality of their works rather than through external means: they strove to win approval by the international community of composers without concession to nationalism. Concurrently, many composers who had followed the nationalist trend at one time in their career now cultivated varying styles in works which combined national and non-national stylistic elements. Only a few such composers will be considered here.

It would be impossible to point out specific countercurrents cultivated systematically during any given period of the twentieth century, because, in general, eclecticism has prevailed among most composers. The main trends, however, have been post-Romantic, neo-Romantic, Impressionist, neo-Classic, expressionist, serialist, and heterogeneously experimental, with the first three particularly evident during the decades of the 1910s and 1920s.

MEXICO AND THE CARIBBEAN

The year 1910 saw the outbreak of the Mexican Revolution and the beginning of a period of profound transformation in the cultural and artistic life of the country. While the revolution favored the development of musical nationalism, as outlined in Chapter 5, two important figures who came to prominence during the 1910s and 1920s, Julián Carrillo and Manuel M. Ponce, gave little or no attention to national music. (Ponce's more definite interest in Mexican folk music and his more frankly nationalistic works came later.)

With the works of Julián Carrillo (1875–1965), a clearly expressed independence from the prevailing nationalist trend of the period appeared in Mexican music. Born in Ahualulco, San Luis Potosí, Carrillo studied at the Mexico City Conservatory from 1895. His teacher of composition there was Melesio Morales; he also studied acoustics under Francisco Ortega y Fonseca, who stimulated in him a lifelong interest in music theory. As an accomplished violinist, he was granted a scholarship from the Mexican government to study in Europe. His European sojourn lasted for about five years, first at the Leipzig Royal Conservatory (1899–1903), where he studied composition with Jadassohn, theory with Reinecke, violin with Hans Becker, and conducting with Nikisch and Hans Sitt, and later (1903–1904) at the Ghent Conservatory, where he continued his violin studies under Zimmer. At Leipzig he came under the influence of late German Romantic music, the style of which permeates his first major works. His Symphony No. 1 in D major (1902), performed by the Leipzig Conservatory Orchestra under his direction, is an example of a work modeled on Brahms but also somewhat determined by what he called "unidad ideológica y variedad tonal" (ideological unity and tonal variety).[1] "Ideological unity" has its application in

[1]In 1911 Carrillo was invited to the International Music Congress in Rome as the official Mexican representative. He presented there his ideas on "Unidad ideológica y variedad tonal," which, according to his account, were well received. See Julián Carrillo, *Pláticas Musicales*, 3rd ed. (Mexico, 1930), pp. 63–70.

the development sections of the symphony through a certain thematic recurrence, since most thematic material (especially that of subordinate themes) is derived from the introduction to the first movement.[2] "Tonal variety" is achieved by means of numerous passing modulations which do not, however, obscure the formal structures, since Carrillo felt a need for an increased emphasis on simple structures. Admittedly, these technical devices did not differ markedly from those in current use in German post-Romantic style. As part of Carrillo's cultivation of this style, he favored in some of his early works a complex harmonic vocabulary, including at times extreme chromaticism, and an intricate contrapuntal technique. The String Quartet in E♭, written in 1904 before his return to Mexico, illustrates his skillful harmonic and instrumental writing.

Carrillo's appointment to the National Conservatory as a professor of composition (1906) was followed by his nomination as Inspector General of Music in Mexico City (1908) and, during the first years of the revolution, by his first tenure as director of the Conservatory (beginning 1913). For many political reasons, not the least being his previous recognition by the Díaz government and his declared affinity with foreign cultures, he was unable to operate effectively as director of the Conservatory and left for New York in 1915. There he founded an orchestra named the Symphony Orchestra of America which, although poorly organized, nevertheless obtained considerable attention. Upon his return to Mexico in 1918 the revolutionary government asked him to direct the National Symphony Orchestra. (During the earlier years of the revolution he had founded the short-lived *Orquesta Beethoven*.) Between 1920 and 1924 Carrillo headed the National Conservatory for a second time. His activities as an educator went beyond the mere organization of music instruction: he felt the need for educational reforms, especially an updating of teaching methods and a broadening of musicians' educational exposure, and he advocated, for example, a general liberal arts education for all musicians.

By the 1920s Carrillo had developed and refined his theories of microtones, which he called *Sonido 13* ("Thirteenth Sound") and for which he achieved international recognition. Ever since his student years at the Conservatory he had manifested a keen interest in acoustical problems, and he states in his autobiography that he began to conceive of his microtonal theories in 1895. Sonido 13 was the term he invented to define the division of the octave into units smaller than semitones—microtones, of various sizes down to sixteenths of a whole tone. The traditional twelve semitones of the tempered octave, he felt, had reduced music to a very limited number of tones; the number 13 was for him a symbolic representation of smaller divisions of the octave. He limited his smallest microtones to sixteenth-tones

[2]Cf. Gerald R. Benjamin, "Julián Carrillo and 'Sonido Trece'," *Yearbook*, Inter-American Institute for Musical Research, III (1967), p. 39.

because of his conviction that this interval represents the limit of clear perception by the human ear. He called his discovery a "revolution," and "revolutionary" his devising of a new notation and new tunings for instruments suited to the microtonal system. His system obviously allowed a much greater number of tones (780 as against the 12 of the chromatic octave)[3] and also a greater variety, since theoretically Carrillo did not intend to limit his music's range to the traditional eight octaves of "classical" music. With customary grandiloquence, he declared:

> The historical primacy of the revolution of Sonido 13 can be summed up in one single sentence which has been pronounced by foremost personalities of both [Old and New] worlds: it initiates a new musical era, with elements undreamed of, with new intervals, new melodies, new scales, new rhythms. . . .[4]

While in theory the number of microtones possible (by using thirds, fourths, fifths, etc., down to sixteenths) is considerable, in his works written within the system of Sonido 13 Carrillo limited himself largely to third, quarter, eighth, and sixteenth tones. One of his first microtonal works, *Preludio a Colón* (1922)—it has remained his best known—is written for soprano, flute, guitar, and violin, all in quarter-tones; octavina (a string instrument designed by the composer) in eighth-tones; and harp in sixteenth-tones. Later versions call for different instrumentations: version III, for example, includes first and second violins, viola, and cello (in quarter- and eighth-tones) and omits the octavina. The *Preludio* is very successful in creating a wailing, incantatory atmosphere which appeared quite futuristic for its time. The first section presents a simple descending line, tightly microtonal, covering a range of two octaves, repeated by the violin and the voice. Short ostinatos appear throughout the work. Glissandi, harmonics, vocal portamentos, and mutes add a great deal to the new sonorities by enhancing the microtonal effects. Passages in unison often result in rather neutral timbres, which also contribute to the eerie character of the work.

Carrillo devised a special method of notation for these new sounds. This method was advertised as "something unique in the entire world! No more special paper to write music! No more staffs! No more clefs, notes, names of notes, sharps, flats, naturals, etc."[5] For all of the conventional signs he substituted a simple combination of a fixed line plus two other

---

[3] Carrillo arrived at this figure by calculating the number of divisions in each microtonal cycle; since there are six whole tones per octave cycle, he multiplied by 6 the number of divisions of the whole tone: 6×2 for semitones, 6×3 for third-tones, and so forth, to 6×16 for sixteenth tones. The total number of divisions is 780.

[4] Cf. Julián Carrillo, *"Sonido 13." Fundamento Cientifico e Histórico* (Mexico, 1948), p. 67.

[5] As expressed on the back cover of Carrillo's Six Preludes for Piano published by "the 13th Sound" in New York, 1928.

"ledger" lines, one above the fixed line, the other below, and twelve numbers (0 to 11). Any pitch of the chromatic scale (0 to 11) can be represented in the eight cycles or octaves in general use (Example 8-1). Carrillo recognized the long-standing practice of using numbers to write music; what seemed new to him was

> the logical order of their use, and the ideological reform of removing any idea of relationship between tones of the chromatic and diatonic scales, and the idea itself of the chromatic scale, as one takes the needed numbers according to the different tones existing in a given scale.[6]

EXAMPLE 8-1   Julián Carrillo's system of notation.

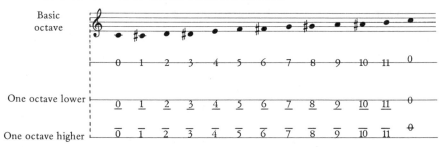

etc.

He developed a consistent method of notation that could be applied to several microtonal systems. For example, in sixteenth-tones, the ninety-six numbers represent the intervallic divisions of the octave (Example 8-2a); some of these can also be used for writing eighth-tones (Example 8-2b); and so forth for any other microtonal units. For "chordal" writing, the same principle applies, with the exception that the uppermost figure represents an absolute pitch while the lower numbers are relative to that pitch. Carrillo devised further notational conventions, such as specially placed numbers to indicate the displacement by one or two octaves of a given note of a chord, and special signs for note-values maintaining conventional shapes for all but half- and whole-notes (Example 8-3).

It goes without saying that such a method of notation, while very ingenious, was hardly practical for actual performance because of the complex numerical memorization required and the probability of visual confusion resulting from combinations of varying but intervallically compatible microtonal systems (e.g., quarter-tones, eighth-tones, and sixteenth-tones) in the same composition. Example 8-4 illustrates a passage from *Preludio a Colón* as published by *New Music*, with the numerical notation. The fact that the

---

[6]Julián Carrillo, *Teoria Lógica de la Música*, 2nd ed. (Mexico, 1954), p. 50.

EXAMPLE 8-2a   Notation for sixteenth-tones, according to Carrillo.

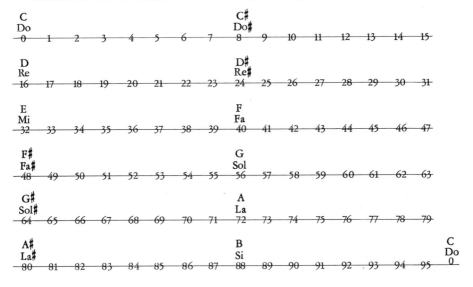

EXAMPLE 8-2b   Notation for eighth-tones, according to Carrillo.

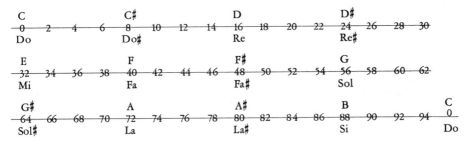

EXAMPLE 8-3   Carrillo's notation of note-values.

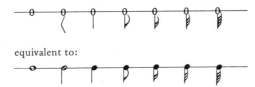

equivalent to:

composer felt the need to use conventional notation in a later version suggests that he recognized the impracticality of his original notation.

Another problem Carrillo faced was that a clear distinction between eighth- and sixteenth-tones cannot be made on most traditional instruments. Hence he had instruments constructed to microtonal specifications, especially pianos, in which the Czech Alois Hába and the Russian Ivan Vischnegradsky,

EXAMPLE 8-4 Julián Carrillo, *Preludio a Colón*, last eight measures: original notation.

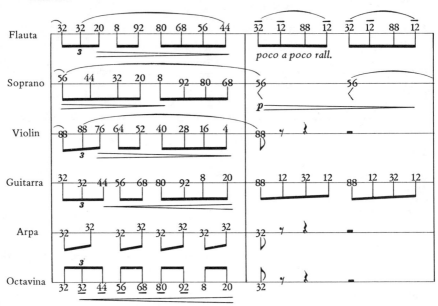

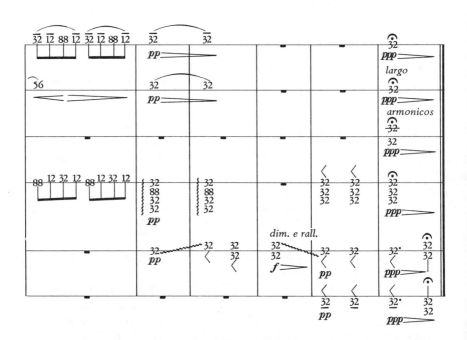

both early proponents of microtonal music, expressed a keen interest. During the 1930s Carrillo conceived the idea of fifteen microtonal pianos, one tuned in whole-tones, another in third-tones, etc., down to sixteenth-tones. He had to wait until the late 1950s, however, to realize his dream, when a German firm undertook the construction of such pianos, which were exhibited at the Brussels World's Fair of 1958, in performance of Carrillo's own music.

From 1926 Carrillo began to win recognition abroad. In that year his *Sonata Casi Fantasía* for violin, horn, guitar, octavina, cello, and harp (in quarter-, eighth-, and sixteenth-tones) was performed in a concert of the League of Composers at New York's Town Hall, with resounding success. Leopold Stokowski took an immediate interest in Sonido 13 and helped build Carrillo's reputation. As conductor of the Philadelphia Orchestra, Stokowski prompted him to write a work for it. This resulted (1927) in the *Concertino* for violin, guitar, and cello (in quarter-tones), octavina (in eighth-tones), and harp (in sixteenth-tones), with an accompaniment of large orchestra (in semitones). For this work Carrillo put into practice his theories of "musical metamorphosis." Written in New York in 1927, his *Leyes de Metamorfosis Musicales* reveal very ingenious ideas about certain types of melodic, harmonic, and rhythmic transformations. One type of metamorphosis consists in amplifying or reducing uniformly all intervals of a given work or passage. The expression metamorphosis "al duplo" (to the double), for example, "means that where there is an interval of a whole tone [in the original], one would write two whole tones [in the metamorphosis]."[7] The chromatic scale would become, in such a transformation, a whole-tone scale and would extend to two octaves. The same rule applies to transformation of chords. The metamorphosis "to the half" ("al medio") has a direct relationship to the microtonal system, since a semitone becomes reduced to a quarter-tone (or to a sixth-tone in the metamorphosis "to the third," and so forth to the eighth). A second type of metamorphosis consists in inverting the direction of intervals "in such a manner that the lower notes [i.e., the bass part] are situated in the superior part, and the higher notes in the bass part."[8] This exchange of location of melodic and harmonic elements, together with contrary direction, displacement of beats, retrogrades, modulations, and other devices produces at least fifteen different kinds of metamorphoses. In considering the various fractions of tone, the possibilities of permutations reach incredible proportions.

While the novelty and the consistency of these theories of metamorphosis are remarkable, Carrillo appears indeed as the "precursor of all ultrachromatic composers" (as stated by Vischnegradsky):[9] there is little

---

[7]Julián Carrillo, *Leyes de Metamorfosis Musicales* (Mexico, 1949), p. 13.
[8]Ibid., p. 40.
[9]"A Letter from Vischnegradsky," *Nouvelles du Mexique*, nos. 43–44 (October 1965–March 1966), 4.

doubt that in such later works as *Horizontes*, the Cello Concerto, the Piano Concerto, *Balbuceos*, and the Mass for Pope John XXIII, it is their micro-tonality that lends them their primary interest. The composer himself continues to be viewed essentially as a figure of paramount importance in the field of sound experiments in the early part of the century.

The ideas of Carrillo in the 1910s and 1920s were unique, for most Mexican composers at that time either cultivated a strictly Romantic style or were discovering Debussy's Impressionist style. This was certainly true of the other major figure to be considered here, Manuel Ponce. Ponce appeared in the 1910s essentially as a neo-Romantic composer, as his Piano Concerto (1912) and his piano *Trio Romántico* (1911) clearly reveal. At the same time, he introduced Debussy's piano music to Mexican audiences for the first time. As we observed in Chapter 5, he gradually submitted to the influence of Impressionist harmony in some of his orchestral works of the 1920s, such as the *Estampas Nocturnas* (1923). As a result of his seven-year residence in Paris, from 1925, however, Ponce developed a much more complex style which included by the 1930s an increased use of dissonant harmony and counterpoint, although his orchestrational techniques reveal an Impressionist method of tone-color blending and a general textural transparency. Other composers followed analogous practices.

As we noted in Chapter 5, Carlos Chávez was not an exclusively nationalist composer. While he appeared in the period under consideration as the theorist of the nationalist movement in Mexico, his style at the time was also imbued with modernistic elements unrelated to any type of folk or popular music. A concern with keeping up to date with European contemporary idioms is evidenced in his works of the middle 1920s. In 1925 he organized a series of concerts of "new music" at the National University, introducing Mexican audiences to the music of Debussy, Satie, Schoenberg, de Falla, Stravinsky, Bartók, Varèse, Milhaud, Poulenc, Auric, and others. Chávez's *Seven Pieces for Piano* (1923–1930), published in Henry Cowell's *New Music* in 1936, are written in a very complex, international avant-garde style. This style is marked by highly chromatic and dissonant harmonies that result frequently in an ambiguous tonal feeling which is reinforced by the simultaneous use of extreme registers (as in Example 8-5), polyrhythmic texture, and metric irregularity. His Piano Sonata No. 3 (1928) reveals in addition a percussive treatment of the instrument and has a deliberately austere and abstract character, conveyed through angular phrases, harsh counterpoint and harmony (often the result of cross-relations), very concise movements including a four-part fugue with rather thick texture, and intricate rhythmic combinations. The first movement of the sonata anticipates some of the stylistic traits of the *Ten Preludes for Piano* of 1937. We are indeed far from the dominant Impressionist style associated with several of Chávez's contemporaries.

EXAMPLE 8-5 Carlos Chávez, *36*, mm. 7–9.

In Cuba, the composers Roldán and García Caturla, whose nationalist styles have been discussed in Chapter 5, assimilated several traits of various contemporary European idioms of the 1910s and 1920s. Roldán's ballets *La Rebambaramba* and *El milagro de Anaquillé* combine authentic Cuban folk elements with harmonic and rhythmic complexities often reminiscent of Stravinsky's *Rite of Spring*, together with some clearly Impressionist effects of orchestration. A characteristic example of Roldán's harmonic style at this time is found in the accompaniment of the song *Sigue* (Example 8-6). The very ambiguous tonality of the passage results from the extreme dissonance in the bass, the progression of which is unpredictable. This dissonance includes frequent minor and major seconds, cross-relations, and tone clusters.

García Caturla's style of the 1920s was both modernistic and national. His harmonic practices, particularly, exhibit some affinity with Impressionism and with the neo-Classicism of the period. He often resorted to seconds, fourths, and fifths as main intervals for chord formations; tertian harmony turns up only on rare occasions. These traits appear profusely in the *Trois Danses Cubaines* for orchestra (1927), particularly in the first movement, "Danza del Tambor," which reveals a predominance of intervals of the fourth and fifth both horizontally and vertically (and even as an ostinato), harmonic parallelism, and chordal alterations. While García Caturla's melodies are frequently pentatonic or modal, his contrapuntal or harmonic accompaniments tend to have a different tonal or modal meaning, thus creating dissonant superimpositions. The piano piece *Comparsa* (1930) goes one step further in this direction and includes polytonal passages. The two-measure

EXAMPLE 8-6 Amadeo Roldán, "Sigue" from *Motivos de Son*, mm. 35–39 (piano reduction). Copyright 1935 by Amadeo Roldán.

pentatonic melody undergoes little transformation, but the accompaniment develops considerable harmonic complexity, being made up of independent transposed parallel figures and a great many alterations (Example 8-7). García Caturla's neo-Classic orientation in the 1920s is well illustrated in his *Preludio Corto* No. 1 and his *Sonata Corta*, both of 1927. The former, dedicated to "the eminent memory of Erik Satie," is without key or time signature (and even without barlines) and consists of a chain of parallel open fifths, with effective harmonic support of more open fifths, sevenths, and ninths. The character is nonchalant and the overall style quite sparing ("dépouillé"). The *Sonata Corta* is a two-part invention, with clear and straightforward counterpoint.

In Venezuela, Juan Bautista Plaza was quite productive in the 1920s as a composer of church music, for that period coincided with the beginning of his tenure as the Caracas cathedral chapelmaster (1923). His first four Masses date from the mid-1920s. In addition, he wrote several tone poems, among them *Vigilia* (1928) and *Campanas de Páscua* (1930), and the choral work with orchestra *Las Horas* (1930). The stylistic traits of his music of this period reveal the influences of his years of study in Rome, specifically the Romanticism of Puccini with its extreme lyricism, but at the same time also a search for harmonic originality.

EXAMPLE 8-7 Alejandro García Caturla, *Comparsa:* (a) main theme; (b) harmonization of theme (mm. 19–20); (c) increased complexity of harmonic accompaniment (mm. 78–82).

(a)

(b)

(c)

THE ANDEAN AREA

The Colombian composer most in evidence during the 1910s and 1920s was Guillermo Uribe-Holguín, the nationalistic aspects of whose style we mentioned briefly in Chapter 6. Residence in New York and Paris in the early years of the century exposed him to different European styles, such as post-Romanticism, Impressionism, and that of the cosmopolitan tradition of the French Schola Cantorum. From his teacher, Vincent d'Indy, he developed a strong attachment to the European "great tradition." His early works, which include many solo songs, piano pieces, chamber music (particularly the violin sonatas Op. 7 and Op. 16, and the String Quartet, Op. 12), and several orchestral works (such as *Carnavalesca*, Op. 34, and *Villanesca*, Op. 37), reveal some influence of d'Indy, such as thematic unity through cyclic treatment, pronouncedly classical formal designs, restrained lyricism, and complex harmonic and contrapuntal elaboration within a firmly established tonal idiom. Impressionist stylistic influences are most prevalent in the subtle and transparent orchestration of his tone poems of the period. His orchestra is still a large one, including a complete brass section (but only a few percussion, such as triangle, celesta, and small cymbals). He favored pure timbre over blending. In some of his later works, however, such influences extended to the harmony.

In Peru, neo-Romantic music associated with the beginnings of musical nationalism predominated during the 1910s and 1920s. Numerous salon pieces, both vocal and instrumental, were written by Daniel Alomía Robles, Luis Duncker Lavalle, José María Valle Riestra, Alfonso de Silva, Federico Gerdes, and others. Gerdes's song "Tu eras el huracán" (Op. 37, No. 3) provides a good illustration of the style cultivated by these composers. Although utilizing simple means, the song has a grandiloquent character, conveyed through a wide-ranging vocal line and a heavy harmonic accompaniment. The sentimental dramatizing of the text ("You were the hurricane and I the high tower which challenges its power") is translated musically by such means as the stormy accompaniment of sixteenth-note triplets, the restless rhythm of the vocal line, and the word-painting technique of stressing key words by setting them at high pitches for descriptive or dramatic effects, as in the accented word "alta" (high).

In Chile, musical life underwent a profound transformation during the 1920s. At the beginning of the twentieth century, Santiago was one of the least developed cities in South America from an art-music viewpoint. Regular concert performances did not take place there until the 1910s; not until 1913 were Beethoven's nine symphonies performed. During the second half of the nineteenth century, several musical institutions had been founded—e.g., the

Sociedad de Música Clásica (founded 1879) and the Sociedad del Cuarteto (1886)—but none lasted very long. The National Conservatory (1849) had had a good start but had become stagnant by the turn of the twentieth century. During the 1910s there appeared new musical associations—the Sociedad de Música de Cámara, the Orfeo Catalá, and the Sociedad Orquestal—but none had as much impact on future musical development in Chile as did another, the Sociedad Bach. Founded in 1917, this society was at first merely a small university choir under the leadership of Domingo Santa Cruz, but he reorganized it in 1923 and made it the basis for innovative changes in Chilean musical life. By 1925 the Bach Society had succeeded in bringing together for occasional performances a symphony orchestra and a large choir which presented ambitious programs, such as one of J. S. Bach's *Christmas Oratorio.* Supporting audiences for such activities materialized with the development of an urban middle class made up of numerous German, Italian, and Polish immigrants. The society obtained subsidies from the government for aiding Chilean music students abroad, and was primarily responsible for having music instruction introduced into the public schools. Such positive results generated conflicts with the National Conservatory, which had no alternative but to undertake in 1928 a plan for renovation of its own music instruction, thereby making a substantial contribution towards the improvement of music education in Chile. A solid foundation for the establishment of stable musical institutions was laid in 1929 with the creation of the Facultad de Bellas Artes within the University of Chile. This "Faculty" (= College) had jurisdiction over the Conservatory and the various schools of fine and applied arts. The next decades saw the success of such a system of musical instruction under the control of the university. Thus the Sociedad Bach turned out to have been a catalytic agent that made possible the very existence of numerous professional musicians who subsequently brought Chilean music to a high level of achievement. This groundwork had resulted from the efforts of Domingo Santa Cruz.

Santa Cruz (b. 1899) was the leader of the innovating movement in Chilean musical life from the 1920s to the 1960s and was very influential as a composer, a teacher, and an administrator. He studied law and political science at the University of Chile, graduating as a lawyer in 1921. He began his studies of theory and composition with Enrique Soro and continued them in Madrid under Conrado del Campo while in the Chilean diplomatic corps (1921–1924). Besides his active participation in the Bach Society, his most significant position in later years was that of Dean of the Faculty of Fine Arts at the National Conservatory (1932–1948), which was reorganized as the Faculty of Musical Arts and Sciences (which he served as Dean until 1951, and again from 1962 to 1965). Although his most important works were written from the 1930s to the 1950s, his first works (dating from 1918 to 1930) reveal some stylistic traits that were to be fully developed in subsequent years. The characteristic works of the early period include several songs, particularly the *Cuatro Poemas*, Op. 9 (1927), and the *Cantos de Soledad*, Op. 10 (1928); the *Viñetas* for piano (1925–1927); and the First String Quartet (1930). They show to a large extent Santa Cruz's orientation towards both Impressionist and atonal stylistic elements. The highly chromatic harmony and motif of the first and third songs (*Arbol muerto* and *Tres Arboles*) of the *Cuatro Poemas* indicate his atonal tendency. On the other hand, the piano pieces *Viñetas* exhibit certain harmonic and rhythmic elements associated with French Impressionist piano style, especially that of Ravel: appoggiatura chords, with predominant major sevenths and major seconds, and flexible rhythmic figures combining isometric designs with asymmetric formulas requiring numerous changes of time signatures. The First String Quartet inclines towards a rich and complex contrapuntal style comprising technical and formal elements close to Classic-era practice.[10] But to an essentially linear writing the composer adds a chromatically prominent tonality, which tends to show a stylistic resemblance to the style of Hindemith (Example 8-8). Yet Santa Cruz's themes sometimes reveal a strongly Hispanic flavor, resulting from the type of ornamentation associated with Andalusian folk singing, with short and fast conjunct motives, repeated notes or groups of notes, and cadences in which the characteristic interval is the augmented second. These elements constituted the bases upon which Santa Cruz developed his musical language in subsequent works.

Romantic, post-Romantic, and Impressionist styles were cultivated by several Chilean composers born in the late 1800s, particularly Enrique

EXAMPLE 8-8   Domingo Santa Cruz, *String Quartet No. 1*, second movement, mm. 271–72. Copyright 1956 by Peer International Corporation. Used by permission.

[10]For a comprehensive analysis of the quartets see Juan Orrego-Salas, "Los Cuartetos de Cuerda de Santa Cruz," *Revista Musical Chilena*, XLII (December 1951), 62–89.

Soro (1884–1954) and Alfonso Leng (1894–1974). Soro acquired his musical training in piano and composition at the Milan Conservatory. From 1907 to 1928 he was active at the Chilean National Conservatory, first as associate director and professor of composition, then as director. Within a rather academic post-Romantic language, his numerous works of the 1910s and 1920s exhibit the technical competence of a fine craftsman. In spite of his exposure to Italian music of the turn of the century, he paid no attention to opera; his works belong to symphonic, chamber-music, and solo piano genres, and he also cultivated the art song. Soro's *Sinfonía Romántica* (1920)—the first symphony written by a Chilean composer—typifies his attachment to the classical molds of composition, through its strong tonal language, lyrical melodies, developmental techniques such as sequence and fragmentation, and orchestral coloring reminiscent of Tchaikovsky's symphonies.

Leng produced his most characteristic works during the 1910s and 1920s. His experience at the Santiago Conservatory was so disappointing that he left it after having been enrolled for less than a year (1905). He developed a style in the 1910s akin to late German post-Romanticism, in such works as the *Cinco "Doloras"* (1901–1914) for piano, the *Preludios Orquestales* (1912), and several art songs. The symphonic poem *La Muerte de Alsino* (1920) is considered his most significant work; in the words of Domingo Santa Cruz, it seemed a revelation at the time of its premiere (1922) because with it "Chilean music abandoned the Italian fashion and acquired an international character which distinguished us henceforth."[11] Such a character was recognized in Chilean circles as post-Wagnerian Romantic style, especially that of Richard Strauss. Indeed, analysis of *La Muerte de Alsino* reveals traits in common with Strauss's tone poems, particularly in the formal structures (with their free treatment of Classic forms), the cyclical treatment of leit-motifs, the harmonies (combining highly dissonant chromatic or polytonal passages with diatonic tonal ones), and the predominance of a polyphonic orchestra. Leng also reminds one of Strauss in his harmonic vocabulary: its complexity creates a harmonic vagueness at times approaching atonality.

Acario Cotapos (1889–1969), although belonging to the generation of Soro and Leng, cannot properly be classified as belonging to any particular trend. He lived in New York from 1917 to 1927 and was one of the founders of the International Composers Guild; thus he was associated with the avant-garde of the time represented by Varèse, Cowell, and Milhaud. The Guild sponsored the presentation of his *Phillipe l'Arabe* (1925) for baritone and instrumental ensemble. Earlier, his *Le Détachement Vivant* (1918), for soprano and eighteen instruments, had been premiered (also in New York) by Eva Gauthier at a concert in homage to Debussy. These works possess

---

[11]Domingo Santa Cruz, "Alfonso Leng," *Revista Musical Chilena*, XI/54 (August–September 1957), 16.

some elements revealing the composer's imagination and independence from any pre-established stylistic current. The *Cuatro Preludios Sinfónicos*, premiered in Paris in 1930, received laudatory comments from local music critics. Later works, such as the operas *Voces de gesta* (unfinished) and *El Pájaro Burlón*, reveal a complex, highly dramatic style, with vivid orchestration and thick textures.

ARGENTINA AND URUGUAY

Until about 1930, nationalism predominated in Argentine music, with a Romantic academicism running it a close second; only occasionally did contemporary styles appear in Argentine works during the 1910s and 1920s. However, a few composers began to move away from folkloric nationalism to a more abstract style, assimilating some European contemporary techniques. These included Juan José Castro (1895–1968), his brother José María Castro (1892–1964), Floro M. Ugarte (b. 1884), Jacobo Ficher (b. 1896), and others. This period also saw a new development of symphonic and chamber music, which had been somewhat neglected during the nineteenth century as a result of the hegemony of opera. (Opera, however, continued to be preferred by many Argentine composers.) Concert activities expanded in Buenos Aires, thanks to the availability of professional orchestras such as the Orquesta Filarmónica de la Asociación del Profesorado Orquestal (APO) and of several magnificent concert halls. The new Teatro Colón, which opened in 1908, established its own orchestra in 1924, winning in a few years an excellent reputation, thanks in great measure to one of its conductors, Juan José Castro.

Castro's youthful orchestral works of the 1920s reveal his allegiance to his teacher in Paris, Vincent d'Indy (as in the tone poem *A una madre*, 1925). A more personal language appears, however, in the *Suite breve* (1929), with its polytonal harmonies and structural freedom. A further illustration of Castro's quest for a more international style is provided by his *Allegro, Lento e Vivace* (1930) for orchestra, for which he won a prize awarded by the International Society for Contemporary Music. In this work Stravinskian and Impressionist influences abound. Together with Juan Carlos Paz and his own brother José María, Castro founded the *Grupo Renovación* (1929), which advocated a deep involvement of Argentine composers with European modern trends. José María Castro himself cultivated a neo-Classic style in his most significant works written during the 1940s and 1950s.

Although Floro M. Ugarte appears primarily as a nationalist composer, his training at the Paris Conservatoire left undeniable traits on some of his works of the 1910s and 1920s. These are conceived within a post-

Romantic style of either strict tonal character or Impressionist harmonies. The Sonata for violin and piano (1928) is a very good example of this style.

Of Russian origin, Jacobo Ficher settled in Buenos Aires in 1923 and was to contribute substantially to the country's musical life. He was one of the founding members of the *Grupo Renovación*. His production of the 1920s includes a few orchestral works (*Poema heroico, Sulamita, Obertura patética*) and some chamber music (String Quartet No. 1, Violin Sonata) which reveal a composer still attached to the post-Romantic Russian composers, particularly Scriabin. In his subsequent works, however, he found a greater affinity with neo-Classicism.

While espousing musical nationalism, Uruguayan composers active during the period under consideration relied much on some of the techniques of the European post-Romantic style. Figures like Eduardo Fabini, Alfonso Broqua, and Luis Cluzeau Mortet leaned towards Romanticism and Impressionism in their early works but turned to Romantic nationalism in their mature works. Among the few non-nationalist composers were César Cortinas (1890–1918) and Carmen Barradas (1888–1963). Cortinas, who studied in Berlin with Max Bruch, wrote in an eclectic style combining Romantic elements of the nineteenth century (especially in his piano works) with a Pucciniesque lyric intensity (in his songs and his opera *La última gavota*, 1915). Barradas, whose works are primarily for the piano, was exceptional for her interest in experimenting with revolutionary music notation.[12]

BRAZIL

There existed in Brazil during the first quarter of the twentieth century a Europeanized school of composition represented mainly by such composers as Francisco Braga (1868–1945), Glauco Velasquez (1884–1914), Henrique Oswald (1852–1931), and Alberto Nepomuceno (1864–1920), the last-named being also an important figure in the beginnings of musical nationalism in the country (see Chapter 4). An even earlier Brazilian "classicist" was Leopoldo Miguéz (1850–1902), whose symphonic music (*Prometeu, Parisina*) relies on Liszt's principle of thematic transformation. During the last fifteen years of the nineteenth century, Miguéz became the chief spokesman for Wagner in Brazil. His opera *Os Saldunes* (1901) was conceived in the most orthodox Wagnerian mode of music drama.

Francisco Braga studied in Paris under Massenet and lived in Ger-

---

[12]Cf. Susana Salgado, *Breve historia de la música culta en el Uruguay* (Montevideo: Aemus, 1971), p. 149.

many from 1896 to 1900. As a professor of composition at the Rio de Janeiro Instituto Nacional de Música (1902–1938), he exerted considerable influence. For nearly twenty years he conducted the orchestra of the Sociedade de Concertos Sinfônicos of Rio de Janeiro (founded 1912). As a composer, he had great empathy for Wagner's techniques and aesthetics but drew on post-Romantic models, especially in the orchestral works which form the main substance of his production. Although academically oriented, his works exhibit good craftsmanship within the framework of the Romantic tradition. Some of his works (e.g., the tone poem *Marabá* and the incidental music for *O Contratador de Diamantes*) are based on Brazilian subject matter but with little or no reference to local musical sources.

    Breaking away from the prevailing German Romanticism of his time, Glauco Velasquez found a natural attachment in his later works (ca. 1906–1914) to the French school of Franck, d'Indy, and Debussy. His works, which include mainly chamber music, piano pieces, and solo songs, reflect these influences through their clarity of form, their harmonic coloring, and their restrained expressiveness. Of Swiss and Italian descent, Oswald studied in Florence and lived in Italy and France for some thirty years; he considered himself an adopted European even after permanently settling in Rio de Janeiro (1911). His extensive musical production shows a post-Romantic eclecticism. Style elements associated with the German post-Romantics, with the French of the Schola Cantorum, and with Debussy, as well as with Italian *verismo*, are present in Oswald's oeuvre. Qualities of craftsmanship and refinement appear in his numerous piano pieces (e.g., *Il Neige*), orchestral works (*Suite d'orchestre*; *Sinfonia*, Op. 43; Piano Concerto), and operas (*La Croce d'Oro, Le Fate*).

    Despite the fundamental contribution of Alberto Nepomuceno to the cause of musical nationalism, many of his works are written in a non-nationalist style. His *Sinfonia* in G minor, the six *Valsas humorísticas* for piano and orchestra, the choral works, and numerous songs and piano pieces are all of post-Romantic inspiration and technique. His mastering of these techniques is perhaps best revealed in his string Trio in F minor (1916), which possesses harmonic originality and clever formal treatment.

    There is little doubt that Villa-Lobos's works of the period 1910 to 1930 represent the boldest Brazilian achievement in the assimilation of contemporary techniques of composition. Although he became acquainted with Debussy's music only after he met Darius Milhaud in 1917, and although Stravinsky's music remained unknown to him until 1923, several of his works of the 1910s disclose technical procedures akin to contemporary European new styles. By 1915, Villa-Lobos professed an anti-Romantic attitude, which he conveyed especially through his treatment of tonality, made deliberately unstable by means of harsh unresolved dissonances. His harmonic language at that time included systematically altered or incomplete chords, parallelism, and tone clusters resulting from the use of bitonality and polytonality. Pentatonic and whole-tone scales lend an Impressionist flavor. But the irregular rhythmic patterns affecting short melodic motives, the polyrhythmic textures set against rhythmic pedals, and the unusual orchestral effects (especially percussive treatment of strings and use of extreme ranges of woodwinds and brass) all suggest a clear association with Stravinsky's development. The Fourth and Fifth Symphonies (respectively subtitled "Victory" and "Peace"), written in 1919 and 1920, provide perhaps the best examples of this eclectic but strongly intuitive style. The 1920s saw the development of the second important phase of Villa-Lobos's creative output. As we have seen in Chapter 7, the monumental series of *Choros* dominated this phase; they represent his most successful attempt at integrating national musical elements with contemporary techniques, which include primarily polytonality, polyrhythm, numerous ostinatos, dissonant polyphonic textures, narrow-range brief chromatic motives, and experimental tonal coloring.

In summary, the decades of the 1910s and 1920s denote a period of transition in Latin American music between nineteenth- and twentieth-century styles. With the exceptions noted, composers tended to adhere to the European "great tradition" and to acquaint themselves with the French Impressionist style, which stood out as the "modern" style par excellence in Latin America. Stravinsky's pre-World War I works appeared as the foremost examples of modernity and continued to exert a considerable influence during the subsequent decades.

BIBLIOGRAPHICAL NOTES

Julián Carillo's autobiography, entitled *Julián Carrillo: su vida y su obra* (Mexico: Edición del "Grupo 13 Metropolitano," 1945) contains useful if at times quite subjective information. Some of his theoretical writings on Sonido 13 are available in English translation in the unpublished dissertation by Laurette Bellamy, "The sonido trece theoretical works of Julián Carrillo: a translation with commentary" (Indiana University, 1972), and in *"The Thirteenth Sound*[:] Scientific and Historical Basis," trans. Patricia Ann Smith, *Soundings*, no. 5 (January 1973), 63–125. The items indicated in the bibliographical notes for Chapter 5 for Manuel Ponce, Carlos Chávez, Amadeo Roldán, and Alejandro García Caturla also contain relevant discussions of the non-nationalist aspects of their works. García Caturla's songs are analyzed by Edgardo Martín in "Las canciones de Caturla," *Música* (Casa de las Américas, Havana), no. 57 (March–April 1976), 9–25. Martín's book *Panorama histórico de la música en Cuba* (Havana: Universidad de la Habana, 1971) is quite informative but noticeably biased in its assessment of twentieth-century Cuban composers.

Guillermo Uribe-Holguín's life and works are discussed by Guillermo Rendón G. in "Maestros de la música: Guillermo Uribe Holguín (1880–1971)," *Música* (Casa de las Américas, Havana), no. 50 (January–February 1975), 2–16, and no. 51 (March–April 1975), 2–21. Chilean musical life of the period is reviewed by Samuel Claro and Jorge Urrutia in their book *Historia de la música en Chile* (Santiago: Editorial Orbe, 1973). A special issue of *Revista Musical Chilena* (no. 42, December 1951) is dedicated to the works of Domingo Santa Cruz. For Alfonso Leng and Acario Cotapos, see the special issues (respectively no. 54, 1957, and no. 76, 1961) of the same journal. The Chilean composer Roberto Escobar attempts to categorize Chilean twentieth-century composers in his rather controversial *Músicos sin pasado* (Santiago: Editorial Pomaire, 1971). The activity of Juan José Castro, both as conductor and composer, is the subject of a special issue of *Revista Ars* (1969). Non-nationalist Brazilian composers discussed in this chapter retain the attention of Luiz Heitor Corrêa de Azevedo in his book *150 Anos de Música no Brasil (1800–1950)*, (Rio de Janeiro: Livraria José Olympio Editôra, 1956).

NINE

THE 1930S AND 1940S

The 1930s and 1940s in Latin American music were the beginning of a new era, an era of awareness of some of the progressive trends in twentieth-century European composition and of conscious effort to follow or assimilate these trends. Properly speaking, then, the "twentieth century" in Latin American music seems to begin in the early 1930s. This period witnessed the creation of groups or associations advocating the modernization of Latin American composition in order to synchronize its development with that of Europe. The Argentine Grupo Renovación and Agrupación Nueva Música, the Cuban Grupo de Renovación Musical, the Chilean Asociación de Composi- tores and Instituto de Extensión Musical, the Brazilian Música Viva, and to a lesser extent the Mexican Conciertos de los Lunes and Instituto Nacional de Bellas Artes were organizations variously dedicated to the updating of art music in their respective countries. This period also saw the emergence of the first outspoken critics of musical nationalism. Perhaps the most severe censor was the Argentine composer Juan Carlos Paz, who considered that all nationalist composers worked with "dead" material and had thus caused the stagnation of Latin American music. Moreover, he attributed the "useless" production of such composers to their considerable delay in familiarizing themselves with the renovating techniques already developed elsewhere in the twentieth century.[1]

When Latin American composers did so familiarize themselves, they most often employed characteristic Stravinskian techniques as found in *Le Sacre du printemps*, or the predominant international style—neo-Classicism and neo-tonality as cultivated in France and Germany during the 1930s and 1940s. Twelve-tone music, generally introduced by European immigrants, also found some followers in Latin America. Paradoxically, even some nationalist composers attempted to use the twelve-tone method, although they often misunderstood its stylistic implications, adopting it freely with a simplified technique and applying it to works of national inspiration if not style.

MEXICO AND THE CARIBBEAN

The development of Mexican music during the 1930s and 1940s includes the culmination and decline of nationalism and the beginning of a cultivation, in a systematic manner, of styles and techniques such as neo-Classicism and polytonality. We have seen (in Chapter 5) to what extent nationalist compositions incorporated European styles such as Impressionist, post-Romantic, and neo-Classic, but during the 1940s there began to be an emphasis on such styles per se. Carlos Chávez wrote several non-nationalist works which rely wholly or partially on contemporary European techniques. The *Sinfonía de Antígona* (1933), the *Diez preludios para piano* (1937), the *Toccata* for percussion instruments (1942), and the Violin Concerto (1948–1950) are significant examples.

The *Sinfonía de Antígona*, based on the incidental music previously written by the composer for Jean Cocteau's adaptation of Sophocles' tragedy, is unquestionably one of Chávez's orchestral masterpieces. Its archaic modal flavor, sobriety, austere character, thematic polyphony, and wind-dominated orchestration remind one of Stravinsky's neo-Classic style (as elaborated, for instance, in *Oedipus Rex*). Nevertheless, it is one of Chávez's most characteristic works of this period. Less a symphony than a symphonic poem (from a structural viewpoint), it consists of a single movement divided into several sections. If there is, however, any programmatic intention at all, it is limited

[1]Juan Carlos Paz, *Introducción a la música de nuestro tiempo* (Buenos Aires: Editorial Nueva Vision, 1955), p. 363.

EXAMPLE 9-1a Carlos Chávez, *Sinfonía de Antígona:* motif *a*, mm. 2–3. Copyright 1948 by G. Schirmer, Inc. Used by permission.

EXAMPLE 9-1b Carlos Chávez, *Sinfonía de Antígona:* motif *b*, mm. 8–12. Copyright 1948 by G. Schirmer, Inc. Used by permission.

to a rather abstract psychological portrayal of Antigone: any extended interpretation of specific elements of the work as being descriptive of her conflicting feelings would be farfetched. The remarkably controlled tragic and tense expressiveness of the work, on the other hand, is very likely suggested by the tragedy itself. The Greek Dorian and Hypodorian modes (suggested by the constant use of both F♮ and F♯) establish the archaism of the work. Clear and simple melodic lines maintain this modal color. The motifs derive from one another. Chromaticism appears only occasionally. The first thematic motif, *a* (Example 9-1a), introduced by the first bassoon, is made up of three chromatic tones. The second motif, *b* (Example 9-1b), introduced by English horn and viola in unison, is diatonic. Both themes are presented in counterpoint by the violins in their extreme upper register, effectively creating tension. The work can be divided into seven sections and a short introduction; Figure 9-1 outlines the structure. The work is based harmonically on four tetrachords (Example 9-2),[2] and the transparent polyphonic texture stresses the modality suggested by them. The harmony is made up of chords built of a fifth and an octave; tertian harmony is virtually nonexistent. Although diatonicism prevails, the harmonies result in frequent harsh dissonances. The orchestration also contributes to the sober character of the symphony. Wind and brass dominate in very frequent short thematic passages accompanied by unusual timbral combinations. The absence of trombones is largely compensated for by eight horns and bass tuba. The woodwind family is fairly comprehensive, with piccolo, flute, alto flute, oboe, heckelphone, English horn, small clarinet in E♭, two B♭ clarinets, bass clarinet, and three bassoons.

[2]Cf. Jesús Bal y Gay, "La 'Sinfonía de Antígona' de Carlos Chávez," *Nuestra Música*, no. 17 (1950), 14.

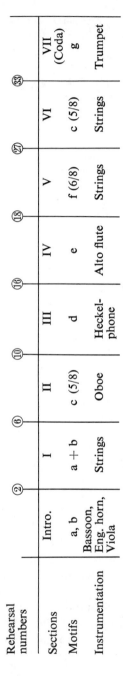

FIGURE 9-1. Outline of Chávez's *Sinfonía de Antígona*.

Rehearsal numbers	②	⑥	⑩	⑯	⑱	㉗	㉝
Sections	Intro.	I	II	III	IV	V	VI	VII (Coda)
Motifs	a, b	a + b	c (5/8)	d	e	f (6/8)	c (5/8)	g
Instrumentation	Bassoon, Eng. horn, Viola	Strings	Oboe	Heckel-phone	Alto flute	Strings	Strings	Trumpet

248

EXAMPLE 9-2 The four tetrachords of Carlos Chávez's *Sinfonía de Antígona*.
Copyright 1948 by G. Schirmer, Inc. Used by permission.

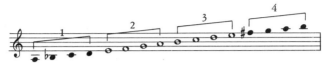

However, with the exception of section V, which represents the climax of the
work, orchestral tutti rarely appear. Typical traits of the orchestration are
the doublings at the unison or octave, creating somewhat hazy timbres, and
unique color mixtures, such as doublebass, first and second violins, bass
tuba, three bassoons, heckelphone, and alto flute, all assigned the same
melodic motive at rehearsal number 17.

While modal or pentatonic melodies have been regarded as elements
of Chávez's Indianism, the systematic diatonicism and linearity of the *Ten
Preludes* for piano could also be construed as examples of the pandiatonicism
associated with the neo-Classical movement of the 1920s and 1930s. The
preludes are predominantly in two-voice polyphonic texture and less complex
rhythmically than the earlier *Seven Pieces for Piano*, yet they present a great
variety of moods with such limited means. A consistent diatonicism appears
throughout. Preludes 1 through 6 use white keys only; a few sharps crop up
in Prelude 7 for dissonant percussive effect; Prelude 8 has a few B♭s and both
F♯ and F♮; Prelude 9 uses both C♯ and C♮ throughout; Prelude 10 is unique
in having a three-sharp key signature and in being very long and chromatic.
Prelude 1 may exemplify the style of this work. It is in the Phrygian mode and
essentially in an ABACA' form, with the inner sections intensifying melodic
ideas from the opening portion by adding repeated and parallel chords of
fourths, and by increasing the volume and dissonance. The most prominent
intervals used are fourths and sevenths, which, together with parallelism,
static harmony, and irregular meter, confer on the piece its neo-Classic
sound.

Chávez's *Toccata* for percussion instruments was written at the suggestion of John Cage, whose Chicago percussion ensemble was dispersed,
however, before it could perform the piece. The character of the *Toccata* is
abstract but not experimental (as one might expect of a percussion piece of
the period). In three movements, the *Toccata* appears as a study in rhythm
and timbre. The first movement calls for drums, the third for drums and
glockenspiel, while the middle movement establishes a contrast with metal
instruments and the xylophone. Rather simple rhythmic motives constitute
the basic material which is developed in the outer movements (Chávez refers
to "sonata form"). The rhythmic organization is predominantly contrapuntal.

The ballet *La Hija de Cólquide* ("Daughter of Colchis"), based on the
Greek theme of Medea and written for Martha Graham, is another charac-

teristic work of this period by Chávez. Originally composed in eight sections for a double quartet of strings and winds, it was recast in 1947 as a symphonic suite in five movements—*Preludio, Encantamiento, Zarabanda, Peán, Postludio*. As with *Antígona*, Chávez resorts to a prevailingly diatonic, linear, polyphonic style that confers on the work a neo-Classically austere and quiescent character. Thematic unity is achieved by means of thematic repetition in several sections. For example, the Prelude presents various motives, some of which reappear in the next section and are reintroduced in a retrograde fashion in the Postlude. Likewise, the *Zarabanda* derives its motives from those of the previous *Encantamiento*. The latter has a special rhythmic interest in its combination of an irregularly accented staccato clarinet motive and a constant pulsation of fourths in the cellos.

The Violin Concerto provides some of the best examples of Chávez's mature compositional processes. His attachment to classical techniques of composition is much in evidence in this essentially melodic work. Melodic inversions, variations, retrograde formal organization, and virtuosic writing for the solo instrument are the most conspicuous elements. In one long continuous movement, the work has the following sections: Andante, Allegro, Largo, Scherzo, Cadenza, Scherzo, Largo, Allegro, Andante.[3] The central Cadenza forms a keystone or pivot point of the work, and the sections which follow (in retrograde repetition of the beginning) include considerable modification of the elements presented in the first portion, the most obvious being inversion of the motives and different orchestration. The Cadenza is well known among violinists for its extreme difficulty of execution. Divided into four sections (about seven minutes in performance), it makes great demands on the solo instrument—sudden changes of registers, precise intonation despite wide intervallic leaps, consistent double and triple stops on intervals such as sevenths and ninths, suddenly contrasting dynamics, oscillating tempo, irregular rhythmic accents, difficult bowings and positions, and others (see Example 9-3). Although the concerto is a grand virtuoso work, the orchestra maintains an accompanimental function. Full tutti passages are rare. Unusual color effects appear, as in the last section of the first Scherzo (mm. 493–98), in which muted trumpets, trombones, and tuba are set against the solo violin or the second Largo, which offers a very interesting effect of resonance (mm. 933–40) resulting from the combination of the low register of the solo instrument (playing the main theme, *forte*) with the high register of muted first and second violins (playing the theme in inversion, *piano*).

---

[3]The orchestral score published by Mills Music, Inc. (1964), bears different tempo indications from these. The Andante section is marked Largo and a Scherzo indication does not appear after the Cadenza. The Andante/Largo difference most likely results from relabeling by Chávez himself, but the absence of the second Scherzo is an omission. The indications given above in the text are correct.

EXAMPLE 9-3 Carlos Chávez, *Violin Concerto*: Cadenza, mm. 514–22; 538–45; 695–703. Copyright 1964 by Mills Music, Inc. Used by permission.

The other major Mexican nationalist composer who also cultivated a neo-Classic style during the period under discussion was Silvestre Revueltas. His *Homenaje a García Lorca* (1936) in three parts—"Baile," "Duelo," "Son"—is perhaps one of his most significant works, because without losing its authentically Mexican character (it is decidedly but uniquely popular in character) it reveals a superb assimilation of the neo-Classic sound of the works of the early 1920s by Stravinsky. Calling for an orchestra of first and second violins, doublebass, piano, tam-tam, xylophone, tuba, trombone, trumpets, E♭ clarinet, and piccolo, the *Homenaje* displays effective timbral combinations such as strings and piano for rhythmic and harmonic support, or piccolo and tuba set against each other in duet passages (rehearsal nos. 14 to 18 of *Baile*). The middle part ("Mourning for García Lorca") is very static and contemplative in character. A dissonant ostinato presented by muted strings and piano prevails almost throughout, accompanying a laconic but deeply expressive theme given by the muted trumpet (Example 9-4).

In 1939 the Spanish-born composer Rodolfo Halffter (b. 1900) settled in Mexico; he adopted Mexican citizenship in 1940. As a professor of composition at the National Conservatory of Music, editor of the journal *Nuestra Música* (from 1946), and manager of the *Ediciones Mexicanas de Música*, among other activities, he exerted considerable influence. He was self-taught in composition but received some informal training from Manuel de Falla, whose neo-Classicism of the 1920s left a deep mark on his style. The most successful works that he wrote before his arrival in Mexico include the Suite for Orchestra (1924–1928), *Dos Sonatas de El Escorial* (1928), and the ballet *Don Lindo de Almería* (1935), the last providing a good example of the austerity and the highly expressive restraint of his style. His most significant works of the 1940s are the Violin Concerto, Op. 11 (1939–1940), the ballet *La Madrugada del Panadero* (1940), *Homenaje a Antonio Machado* (1944) for piano, and the *Epitafios* (1947–1953) for a cappella chorus. Great economy of means, both tonal and polytonal feelings, complex rhythmic patterns related to Spanish folk music, predominant linearity and contrapuntal elaboration, refined diatonic and dissonant harmony, and insight into tone-coloring characterize Halffter's language. The Violin Concerto, in three movements, is a virtuoso work and follows the classical models of the genre, yet it does

EXAMPLE 9-4 Silvestre Revueltas, *Homenaje a Federico García Lorca*, second movement ("Duelo"): (a) accompanimental ostinato; (b) trumpet theme, mm. 3–16. Copyright 1958 by Southern Music Publishing Company, Inc. Used by permission.

(a)

(b)

not display virtuosity per se and has none of the grandiloquence generally associated with solo concertos. The first movement exposes and recapitulates two themes, but the middle section of the movement does not resort to classical developmental techniques; instead one finds a series of contrapuntal variations on the first theme, using Baroque devices such as canon, augmentation and diminution, retrograde, and rich ornamentation.[4] The solo violin intervenes throughout and includes passages of very difficult execution. The opening recitative (Example 9-5) typically stresses intervals of fifths and fourths, while the short cadenza of the first movement (Example 9-6) harmo-

[4]Cf. Jesús Bal y Gay, "Rodolfo Halffter," *Nuestra Música*, no. 3 (July 1946), 145.

EXAMPLE 9-5 Rodolfo Halffter, *Violin Concerto*, first movement, mm. 1–6. Copyright 1953 by Ediciones Mexicanas de Música. Used by permission.

EXAMPLE 9-6 Rodolfo Halffter, *Violin Concerto*, first movement, mm. 200–13. Copyright 1953 by Ediciones Mexicanas de Música. Used by permission.

nizes and embellishes the first theme of the movement. The middle movement (*Andante cantabile*), a series of melodic variations, has an improvisatory character akin to the late Baroque concerto, partly conveyed by varying rhythmic figurations in each variation.

The argument of Halffter's ballet *La Madrugada del Panadero* ("The Awakening of the Baker") is reminiscent of Lope de Vega's comedies. The action revolves around the naive wife of a village baker and several of her admirers whom she invites to the bakery during her husband's absence. Upon the return of the latter, she hides her guests in flour sacks. Their attempt to escape during the night awakens the baker, who takes the flour-covered gentlemen for ghosts. Forced to spend the night in the oven, they emerge the next morning slightly toasted, to the surprise and laughter of the first bakery customers. The music of the ballet suite, which includes seven numbers, has a lively and descriptive character quite appropriate for these humorous episodes. The typically Spanish melodic ornamentation, the use of Spanish popular music (stylized *paso doble*), and the overall tonal language are all reminiscent of the zarzuela.

Homenaje a Antonio Machado and *Tres Epitafios* are further illustrations of Halffter's reserved neo-Classic style of the 1940s. The *Homenaje*, in four sections, reveals the deep influence of Domenico Scarlatti on the Mexican composer. Two-part and three-part forms, generally two-voice counterpoint, and a strong tonal basis predominate in this work. Despite the relative complexity of some of the chord formations, the presence of key centers and tonal functions is quite clear (Example 9-7). A Scarlatti-like style is provided, in the third section of the work, by the binary form, the counterpoint, and the melodic phrasing and ornamentation. In the *Epitafios* (respectively, for Don Quijote, Dulcinea, and Sancho Panza) on texts by Cervantes, the combinations of modal, diatonic, and conjunct contrapuntal lines create a modern flavor (through the resulting harmonies) and archaic flavor (through modality and counterpoint) at the same time. Occasional Spanish accents also appear in this work, as in the rhythms (6/8 and 3/4 metric divisions), ornamentation, and cadences (descending minor thirds) of the second piece "Para Dulcinea."

Without abandoning altogether the nationalist character of his early works, Blas Galindo cultivated in the 1940s and early 1950s a style akin to neo-Classicism. The mestizo folk music elements that were mentioned in Chapter 5 continued to pervade his later works. His harmonic vocabulary, however, became quite cosmopolitan: perhaps under the influence of Chávez, he tended to base his harmonies on the intervals of the fourth and fifth, with frequent parallelism in seconds, fifths, and sevenths, and an overall pandiatonicism. While 6/8 and 3/4 meters with typical rhythmic patterns continue to appear, combinations of triple and duple units (requiring changes of meters) become more frequent. Isometric figures and conjunct diatonic or modal melodies (intervallic skips of fourths and fifths primarily, for disjunct

EXAMPLE 9-7   Rodolfo Halffter, *Homenaje a Antonio Machado*, I, mm. 1–10.
Copyright 1944 by Rodolfo Halffter. Used by permission.

motion) predominate. These style characteristics are shown in a passage from
the Violin Sonata (1945) and another from the first of the *Siete Piezas para
Piano* (1952) (Example 9-8).

The Spanish-born composer José Ardévol, who settled in Havana in
1930, is considered the leader of modern Cuban composition. His influence
was felt especially after the deaths of Roldán and García Caturla. Ardévol
taught composition privately and at the Municipal Conservatory (later
renamed Roldán Conservatory) and founded the Chamber Orchestra of

EXAMPLE 9-8 Blas Galindo: (a) Violin Sonata, mm. 21–29. Copyright 1950 by Ediciones Mexicanas de Música; (b) *Siete Piezas para Piano*, first piece, mm. 1–4. Copyright 1955 by Ediciones Mexicanas de Música. Used by permission.

Havana (1934), which he directed for eighteen years. In 1942, together with some of his best students, he founded the Grupo de Renovación Musical with the purpose of creating a Cuban school of composers "which could reach the same degree of universality obtained by other countries." The group included, among others, Harold Gramatges, Edgardo Martín, Julián Orbón, Hilario González, Argeliers León, Serafín Pro, and Gisela Hernández. The philosophy of the group was not dogmatic, but craftsmanship and competence in the knowledge and treatment of musical composition were emphasized. In spite of the great diversity of personalities involved, the group expressed (through Ardévol, as its spokesman and leader) its profession of faith in freedom from any one trend. While none of its members pretended to write Impressionist, expressionist, atonal, polytonal, or nationalistic music, in their zeal for placing themselves in the orbit of contemporary music, they identified at first the neo-Classic movement as one of the most adequate trends for their purposes. Moreover, neo-Classicism also allowed them to put into practice their thorough training in theory and traditional techniques of composition. "Our neo-Classicism," wrote Ardévol, "had also somewhat the character of a training workshop."[5]

Ardévol has been a prolific composer. His output comprises over ninety works in all genres except opera. His works prior to about 1930 (chamber and piano music) show diverse influences, from Scarlatti to Debussy and Stravinsky. From 1930 to approximately 1936, he revealed himself as a radical experimentalist in a few works, writing in an atonal style or with the twelve-tone method. He himself sees 1936 as marking the beginning of a self-imposed stylistic simplicity in which Spanish and Cuban elements play a certain role. His *Música de Cámara* for six instruments (flute, clarinet, bassoon, trumpet, violin, and cello), in five short movements, illustrates this style. The title of the first movement—"Ricercar"—is symptomatic of the composer's empathy for older forms and techniques. His is an imitative type of ricercar which displays a well-balanced counterpoint. The large intervallic skips (sevenths and ninths) of the first part of the theme and the five imitative entries at different pitches create a dissonant, rich, and rhythmically novel counterpoint. Cuban and Spanish elements appear, particularly in the last three movements. The third movement, "Quasi Habanera," is a stylized habanera rhythmically (with figures like ♩. ♪♫ and ♫ ♩), but its counterpoint and harmony disclose a neo-Classic sound. Spanish traits appear mostly in the form of some typical rhythmic patterns of the fourth movement ("Fanfarria") and the hemiola effect of the "Finale."

Ardévol's full adherence to neo-Classicism in the 1930s and the 1940s is best seen in such works as the piano Sonatina (1934), the first five of the six *Sonatas a tres* (1937–1946), the two Concerti Grossi (1937), the ballet *Forma* (1942), and the Concerto for Piano, Winds, and Percussion (1944). The beginning eight measures (ritornello) of the Sonatina (Example 9-9), with its four-part "Bach counterpoint" based on clear overall tonal impression (see the bass part) in spite of its dissonances, prominently augur Ardévol's stylistic development of the next fifteen years. The *Sonata a tres No. 1*, for oboe, clarinet, and cello, is treated as a Baroque trio sonata as to instrumentation

[5] José Ardévol, *Introducción a Cuba: la música* (Havana: Instituto del Libro, 1969), p. 92.

EXAMPLE 9-9 José Ardévol, *Sonatina*, first movement, mm. 1–8. © 1955, Elkan-Vogel, Inc. Used by permission.

(two melody instruments and an accompanying low instrument), and form (beginning with a slow movement; prevailing two-part forms). The cello does not have, however, an accompanimental function; rather, it participates fully in the constant and systematic imitations and contrapuntal elaboration that occur throughout the work. Other neo-Classic components of Ardévol's style in these sonatas are their dissonant linearity, ostinatos, and static tone-coloring. In the ballet *Forma* for four-, five-, and six-part choruses and orchestra, the voices intervene in the manner of ancient Greek drama, commenting upon the action in a non-participatory way. The harmonic staticity of the choral numbers also belongs to neo-Classic techniques (as in Stravinsky's *Symphony of Psalms*).

Among the numerous students of Ardévol associated with the Grupo de Renovación Musical, Gramatges, Martín, León, González, and Orbón may be mentioned briefly. While nearly all of them cultivated a neo-Classic style, often combined with a neo-nationalism early in their career (the 1940s), they followed quite different paths during the subsequent decades (see Chapter 10).

Harold Gramatges (b. 1918) studied with Roldán and Ardévol at the Havana Municipal Conservatory. In 1942 he took the Berkshire summer course taught by Aaron Copland. Even in his first works, written in 1940, there appears his essential concern for mastery of compositional techniques. After a very austere, almost ascetic neo-Classicism, he turned to a substantially elaborated and refined nationalism.

Edgardo Martín (b. 1915), whose first significant works were written after 1950, manifested his early interest in a Cuban expression within a contemporary style. In his four *Fugas* for string orchestra (1947) he combines a tonal, contrapuntal style with rhythmic patterns associated with Cuban folk and popular music. These not only include dotted rhythms, syncopations set against regular sixteenth-note pulsation, but also the so-called Cuban *tresillo* ($\frac{2}{4}$ ♩. ♩. ♩ = ♩. ♩♩ ♩). Admittedly, Martín's are not very elaborate fugues. The four-voice *Fuga IV*, for example, has a full exposition and a short central episode but lacks other fugal devices such as countersubject and stretto and does not elaborate its harmony very much. Another characteristic work of this period, the *Seis Preludios* for piano (1949), resorts to different techniques but maintains the local, if transformed, flavor; these techniques include, above all, a vagueness of tonality created by increasingly complex dissonances and even by bitonality.

Argeliers León (b. 1918), although a student of Ardévol, was strongly influenced during the 1930s and 1940s by the national music of García Caturla and Roldán (see Chapter 5). During the 1960s he turned to serial composition, although without abandoning his strong nationalist feelings. To a lesser extent Hilario González (b. 1920) also shared these feelings. As early as 1938 he wrote his *Tres Preludios en Conga* and *Danzas Cubanas*, the latter orchestrated in 1945. The preludes utilize Cuban folk and popular rhythms in a strikingly dissonant harmony (see Chapter 5). His Piano Sonata (1942) shows a greater concern for linear writing.

The youngest and most independent member of the group, Julian Orbón (b. 1925), was also the first to withdraw from it. Of Spanish birth, he moved to Havana in 1940 and studied composition with Ardévol. An accomplished pianist, he gave frequent recitals in Havana. He also studied advanced composition under Copland at the Berkshire Music Center in the summer of 1945. His association with the Grupo de Renovación Musical lasted from 1942 to 1949. Essentially the "Cuban heir of the Spanish tradition,"[6] Orbón's international outlook has made him (together with Aurelio de la Vega) the most outstanding Cuban composer of his generation. His earlier works (mid-1940s) reveal his inclination towards Spanish neo-Classic style as developed by de Falla and the Halffter brothers (especially Ernesto). Rather classical technical procedures, a straightforward but intense expression, and a rhythmic forcefulness characterize that style. The *Tocata* (sic) of 1943, in three sections ("Preludio," "Cantares," "Sonata"), is not the virtuoso piece generally associated with the genre; it is, rather, written in the spirit of Frescobaldi, with expressive melodic contents, contrasting sections, and, at times, tense dissonances. Orbón's involvement with the Spanish neo-Classic movement is also conveyed by such works as the Piano Sonata of 1942 ("Homage to Soler"), the *Suite de Canciones de Juan del Encina* for a cappella choir (1947), and the *Homenaje a la Tonadilla*, a *divertimento* for orchestra. With his works

---

[6]Alejo Carpentier, *La Música en Cuba* (Mexico: Fondo de Cultura Económica, 1946), p. 341.

written after 1950, however, the Spanish traditions become gradually less evident. He seems to have been searching at that time for a more personal idiom, harmonically more tense and less committed to tonality. Examples of such a drive are found in his *Tres versiones sinfónicas* (1953) and other works up to his *Cantigas del Rey* (1960).

A particularly important figure whose first works appeared in the 1940s is the Panamanian composer, conductor, and teacher Roque Cordero (b. 1917). His advanced musical studies were undertaken in the United States (1943–1950): composition under Ernest Krenek and conducting under Mitropoulos, Chapple, and Barzin. Upon his return to Panama in 1950, Cordero became professor of composition at the National Institute of Music. During the next fifteen years he contributed substantially to the organization of professional musical life in Panama. While he followed the nationalist trend in several of his earlier works (such as *Capricho Interiorano*, 1939; *Sonatina Rítmica*, 1943; *Obertura Panameña No. 2*, 1944; *Ocho Miniaturas*, 1948; *Rapsodia Campesina*, 1953), he did so by combining national elements with modern compositional techniques. He does not consider his music deliberately nationalistic nor does he classify it in any other trend. His independent attitude is expressed in the following terms:

> If a composer is sincere towards himself and his fellow men . . . his music (by being his) will present more or less clear national characteristics—rhythmic figures, melodic contours, etc.—without resulting necessarily in local product. In such a case, the author . . . will create a work with strongly native character but with a spiritual message which communicates to the universe, obtaining thus a national art but not nationalistic in the narrow sense of the term.[7]

The national characteristics of Cordero's early works are expressed through rhythmic elements, especially those of such typical Panamanian dances as the *mejorana* or the *tamborito*. His, however, is not an overt, folkloristic national style but a uniquely modern Panamanian idiom. The *Sonatina Rítmica*, in three movements, illustrates this. The writing is tonal, although at times the tonality darkens, primarily through key fluctuations, frequent altered chords, and chromatic aggregates in melodic motives. Modulations occur at times in very distant keys in the circle of fifths (Example 9-10: B minor to B♭ minor as a result of the melodic sequence). Typical accompanimental rhythmic patterns of the *mejorana*, such as [musical notation], or melodic rhythmic figures such as [musical notation], recur especially in the first and third movements. Formal designs are traditional: sonata-allegro, song form, and rondo for the three movements, respectively. In spite of the individuality of such a style, Cordero's international recognition, which came during the 1950s and 1960s, was due primarily to his later style, which was based on a free utilization of twelve-tone methods.

[7]Statement in *Clave, Revista Musical Venezolana*, no. 5 (April 1957), 13.

EXAMPLE 9-10   Roque Cordero, *Sonatina Rítmica*, first movement, mm. 26–33.
Copyright 1954 by Roque Cordero. Used by permission.

THE ANDEAN AREA

Among the Andean nations which saw the production of significant non-nationalist compositions during the 1930s and 1940s, Chile occupies a leading position. The other countries—Colombia, Ecuador, Peru, and Bolivia—paid at the time closer attention to musical nationalism, yet concurrently several composers in those countries drew on other stylistic trends. In Colombia, for example, Carlos Posada-Amador (b. 1908) cultivated in the 1930s an Impressionist style; Roberto Pineda Duque (b. 1910) wrote many religious choral and organ works in the 1940s that exhibited a conservative style (he appeared, however, in later decades as an advocate of twelve-tone techniques); and Santiago Velasco Llanos (b. 1915), who studied in Chile under Santa Cruz, wrote in a neo-Classic manner. (The most significant works of all three, however, were written later.)

In Peru, Rodolfo Holzmann, even more than Andrés Sas, initiated a countercurrent to nationalism by exposing his many students to various contemporary European styles. Although Holzmann cultivated some aspects of Peruvian Indianist style (see Chapter 6), his early works of the 1930s and also those of the 1940s and 1950s exhibit quite different stylistic characteristics. Of European training and temperament, he was influenced by Hindemith's stress on craftsmanship in the composer's profession and by Hindemith's new tonal system. Some of Holzmann's most revealing works of the 1940s include *Divertimento Concertante* (1941) for piano and ten woodwinds, the *Cantigas de la Edad de Oro* (1944) for small orchestra, the *Tres Madrigales* (1944) for voice and piano, the First Symphony (1946), and the *Concierto para la Ciudad Blanca* (1949) for piano and orchestra. The *Divertimento*, in three movements, treats the piano in a soloistic manner and blends it effectively with the woodwinds. Holzmann's attachment to tradition is expressed through the work's formal designs (ternary form), compositional processes (developmental techniques, canon, variations, polyphony), and general adherence to the tonal system. The *Cantigas* are a suite of pieces by Renaissance Spanish polyphonists, orchestrated in a modern vein. The *Tres Madrigales*, settings of Pablo Neruda's poem, have strongly tonal and expressive vocal melodies accompanied by contrapuntal lines which are made more distinct through rhythmic differentiation. Pentatonicism appears quite frequently, an indication of the composer's continued interest in Peruvian national music.

The 1930s and 1940s saw a continued development of Chilean musical life as the result of the solid groundwork laid during the 1920s (see Chapter 8). After the achievements of the Sociedad Bach under the leadership of Domingo Santa Cruz, yet another institution contributed significantly to the organization of music professionalism in Chile: the Instituto de Extensión Musical at the University of Chile, created in 1940. Primarily a promotional institution dedicated to furthering musical activities in the country, the Institute's major achievements included the creation of a symphony orchestra, a choir, a ballet ensemble and chamber music groups, and the stimulation of musical composition through the establishment of annual composition contests. As early as 1941, an orchestra which came to be known as the Orquesta Sinfónica de Chile was founded; a string quartet and a school of dance were established in the same year. In the late 1940s, under the auspices of the Institute, annual prizes for composition and biennial festivals of Chilean music were also established. The first artistic director of the orchestra was the remarkable conductor Armando Carvajal, who was succeeded by Victor Tevah; both were enthusiastic promoters of Chilean music. In 1945, the Institute began publication of the important *Revista Musical Chilena*; its longevity (it is still being issued in the 1970s) is an unprecedented achievement in Latin American music periodical publication. In addition, the Institute became one of the most solid institutions of music learning in South America. Not only did it help to raise the standards of music performance in Santiago but it contributed greatly in establishing at the University of Chile one of the rare centers of music research in Latin America, the Institute of Musical Research, which was founded in 1946. The composer and teacher Domingo Santa Cruz exerted a decisive influence in all these endeavors as the first director of the Institute, coincident with his being Dean of the Faculty of Fine Arts (1932 1951).[8]

[8]For a detailed account of Santa Cruz's activities as an administrator and promoter of Chilean music and musicians, see Robert Stevenson, "Chilean Music in the Santa Cruz Epoch," *Inter-American Music Bulletin*, no. 68 (1968), 1–18.

Santa Cruz's most significant and characteristic works were written during the period under consideration and also the decade of the 1950s. Some of the elements that had figured in his style of the 1920s (see Chapter 8) were brought to full maturity during the period 1930–1950, as may be suggested by discussion of a few works in different media and of various genres. The Five Pieces for String Orchestra, Op. 14 (1937), rigorously elaborate some of the traits mentioned in connection with Santa Cruz's First String Quartet, especially a rich and contrapuntal style with technical and formal elements close to Baroque and Classic practices. The essentially horizontal writing with imitations, fugatos, and canons generates at times a polytonal harmony. The composer alternates thinly textured and densely webbed passages, with five or more voices, and polyphonic and homophonic sections. Added and chromatic tones also create dissonant chord formations. With the exception of the last movement, melodies are predominantly modal and fairly broad. They are often accompanied by ostinato motives, as in the second piece, "Inquieto y Doloroso," in the cello part. The fast and joyous last movement, in sonata form, contrasts with the previous ones in its rhythmic vitality. The characteristic rhythmic motives (in fast triple time, with figures such as

♩· ♪♪♪ and ♪♪♪ ♪♪♪) of that movement have been compared with the Spanish (Aragonese) folk dance known as *jota*.[9] Such Spanish traits are also evident in many other works of the period by Santa Cruz.

The *Sinfonía Concertante*, Op. 22 (1945), and the *Preludios Dramáticos*, Op. 23 (1946), both for orchestra, further illustrate Santa Cruz's consistent adherence to the Western art-music heritage. The first work calls for a solo flute and other concertante winds (oboe, two clarinets, bassoon, two French horns, and a trumpet) and, in a concerto grosso fashion, a ripieno orchestra including strings and piano. Structurally, however, the work appears as a symphony in the mid-eighteenth-century style, i.e., a three-movement sequence with a great deal of contrapuntal texture. The first movement is in sonata form, with a development of the first theme in the exposition before the presentation of the second theme. The thematic material is characteristic in its extended chromaticism and, in the first theme, its Spanish rhythmic flavor (Example 9-11). The second movement is in ABA form. The third follows a rondo form, which allows the composer to treat the movement almost like a concerto grosso, for it facilitates the presentation of an orchestral ritornello, contrasting in both melodic material and tone coloring with the alternating episode sections. The Baroque character of the movement is reinforced by systematic contrapuntal treatment of the thematic material.

With the *Preludios Dramáticos* ("Presentimientos," "Desolación," "Preludio Trágico"), Santa Cruz revealed his qualities as orchestrator while returning to the highly chromatic, Wagnerian harmony of some of his earlier

---

[9]Cf. Vicente Salas Viu, "Las obras para orquesta," *Revista Musical Chilena*, no. 42 (December 1951), 23.

EXAMPLE 9-11 Domingo Santa Cruz, *Sinfonia Concertante*, first movement: (a) theme I; (b) theme II.

(a) Muy alegre y movido

(b) Un poco menos movido

works. The Wagnerian atmosphere of the second Prelude especially is exceptional in Santa Cruz's works of the 1940s; it is conveyed through chromatic and wide-ranging melodies, outstretched or unresolved non-harmonic tones, and extensive changes in timbres, with woodwind and brass playing an important role in the presentation of thematic or motivic material. The systematic chromaticism and the highly dissonant harmonies of the last Prelude result at times in a lack of clearly evident tonal centers, reminding one of Schoenberg's pantonal style of the early part of the century.

Two significant works of the late 1940s by Santa Cruz—the Second Symphony for String Orchestra, Op. 25 (1948), and *Egloga*, for soprano, mixed chorus, and orchestra, Op. 26 (1949)—summarize his style up to that time, above all his preference for neo-Baroque contrapuntal writing, for textural density, for a new tonal language made up of modal, dissonant, and at times pantonal syntax, for traditional forms, and for generally expressive melodies. The relative lack of attention to instrumental color or to virtuoso writing for instruments reflects the greater concern of the composer for other technical elements such as counterpoint and form. From an aesthetic viewpoint, Santa Cruz's music exhibits a dramatic but reserved character expressed in purely musical terms. A Latin (Hispanic) subtle quality also often pervades his works, whether instrumental or vocal.

Finally, Santa Cruz's choral works of the 1940s should be singled out as a special expression of his aesthetic attitude. Besides the *Cantata de los Ríos de Chile*, Op. 19, and *Egloga*, Op. 26, already mentioned, he wrote *Cinco Canciones*, Op. 16, for mixed chorus or soloists; *Tres Madrigales*, Op. 17, for mixed chorus; *Tres Canciones*, Op. 18, for male chorus; and, for mixed chorus, *Cantares de la Pascua*, Op. 27, and *Seis Canciones de Primavera*, Op. 28. The *Tres Madrigales* draw to a great extent on Monteverdi's madrigals for their form and expression.[10] Highly dramatic, these settings (with texts by the composer) combine an expressively harmonic counterpoint with monodic, recitative-like designs (Example 9-12). Opus 28 (1950), which includes *canciones*, madrigals, and a villancico, is written in a more diatonic, simpler, and clearer style. This simplicity, however, does not diminish the intense expressions of love, sorrow, death, and nature conveyed by the text (which is by the composer).

Other composers of Santa Cruz's generation contributed to Chile's musical development. Jorge Urrutia Blondel (b. 1905) was certainly the most active promoter of Chilean musical institutions after Santa Cruz. A lawyer by profession, he studied music under Pedro Humberto Allende and Santa Cruz. In the 1920s he was an active member of the Sociedad Bach. For three years he lived in Europe (1928–1931), studying composition in Paris with Charles Koechlin, Paul Dukas, and Nadia Boulanger, and in Berlin with Hindemith and Hans Mersmann. He became a professor of composition at the Santiago National Conservatory upon his return in 1931. He has also been closely associated with the Instituto de Extensión Musical and the Facultad de Ciencias y Artes Musicales, both at the University of Chile. Although he paid some attention to musical nationalism, he appears in general as a post-Impressionist composer. His most significant non-nationalist compositions include the ballet *La Guitarra del Diablo* (1941), *Pastoral de Alhué* (1942)—a homage to Maurice Ravel—and the Suite No. 3 for orchestra (1948). While the ballet and the *Pastoral* abound in Impressionist musical techniques, the Suite reveals a tendency towards neo-Classicism.

Alfonso Letelier (b. 1912) was quite prolific during the period under

---

[10]Cf. Alfonso Letelier, "Las composiciones corales de Santa Cruz," *Revista Musical Chilena*, no. 42 (December 1951), 50–51.

EXAMPLE 9-12 Domingo Santa Cruz, *Tres Madrigales*, Op. 17: (a) "La Mala Nueva," mm. 1–9; (b) "Barcos Quietos," mm. 1–3. Copyright 1960 by Domingo Santa Cruz. Used by permission.

(b) ♩=69
p(como recitando)

El   hu - mo se   a - so - ma blan - co   el   hu - mo se

discussion. He studied composition under Allende at the National Conservatory. In 1940 he founded and directed the Escuela de Música Moderna and created the Madrigal Ensemble in that school. He belongs to that generation of Chilean composers sometimes classified as "formalists"[11] because of their adherence to the stylistically objective aims of neo-Classicism. Among Letelier's numerous works of the 1930s and 1940s, the *Sonetos de la Muerte* (1942–1948), for soprano and orchestra, and the piano *Variaciones* (1948) summarize the most typical elements of his style. Setting the well-known, deeply spiritual, desolate but utterly expressive sonnets by Gabriela Mistral (Chilean poetess, winner of the Nobel prize for literature in 1945), Letelier succeeds in depicting the dramatic substance of the poems. For this he resorts to a solo soprano voice and a huge orchestra treated as an equal partner of the voice, answering it or reacting to it.[12] The first two sonnets follow a free sonata-form design, while the last combines the main thematic material of the previous ones. The vocal line is treated as a free recitative with considerable sensitivity to the expressive tension of the text; it often has the character of "endless melody." Dramatic expression is also conveyed through dissonant and dense harmonies, frequent use of polytonality, contrasting dynamic levels, ostinatos, irregular rhythmic patterning, and special instrumental effects.

A more frankly neo-Baroque style, akin to that of Hindemith, pervades the Piano Variations in F major. Consisting of a theme, ten variations, and a finale, the work resorts to a certain extent to elements of the Baroque suite, since several of the variations are stylized Baroque dance forms (gigue, allemande, minuet, gavotte). Homophonic and contrapuntal textures are combined, and two-part form (but often disposed in *aab* bar form) predominates. Example 9-13 reproduces the theme, whose bar form, tonal and bitonal harmonization, modal first part (mm. 1-8), and tonal second part (mm. 8-14) are all worthy of note. The variations make use of various techniques, especially ornamental figuration, contrapuntal and harmonic development, and some rhythmic variation.[13]

[11]Cf. Roberto Escobar, *Músicos sin pasado* (Santiago: Editorial Pomaire, 1971), pp. 141–44.

[12]Cf. Jorge Urrutia Blondel, "Los 'Sonetos de la Muerte' y otras obras sinfónicas de Alfonso Letelier," *Revista Musical Chilena*, no. 109 (October–December 1969), 16ff.

[13]A complete and careful analysis is provided in María Ester Grebe, "Las variaciones en Fa para piano de Alfonso Letelier," *Revista Musical Chilena*, no. 109 (October–December 1969), 33–46.

EXAMPLE 9-13 Alfonso Letelier, *Variaciones en Fa:* theme, mm. 1–14. Copyright by Barry & Cia. Used by permission of Boosey & Hawkes, Inc. Sole agents.

The Chilean composer who has won the widest reputation outside his country is undoubtedly Juan Orrego-Salas (b. 1919), director of the Latin American Music Center at Indiana University since 1961. He graduated from the National Conservatory in Santiago, with studies in composition under Allende and Santa Cruz. After several years of activity as conductor of the Santiago Catholic University Choir and lecturer in music history at the Conservatory, he pursued graduate study under Rockefeller and Guggenheim fellowships in the United States (1944–1946). Randall Thompson and Aaron Copland were his teachers of composition, Paul Henry Lang and George Herzog, of musicology. In 1947, he became a professor of composition at the

University of Chile, serving at the same time as the editor of the *Revista Musical Chilena* (1949) and subsequently as the director of the Instituto de Extensión Musical. Orrego-Salas's large creative output, beginning in the 1940s,[14] includes over seventy-five works in all major genres (excluding grand opera) and media. Some of his most characteristic works of the period from 1940 to about 1952 are the Sonata for Violin and Piano (1945), the *Cantata de Navidad* (1945), *Canciones Castellanas* (1948), the Suites No. 1 and No. 2 for piano (1945 and 1951), the *Obertura Festiva* (1947), the First Symphony (1949), the Piano Concerto (1950), and *Rústica* for piano (1952). The first piano suite illustrates well Orrego-Salas's early neo-Classic style, one rooted to a large extent in the fugal style of Bach; it consists of prelude, interlude, fantasia, interlude, and fugue, and reveals at once the composer's concern for and command of traditional compositional techniques, which are treated, however, freely and quite individually. The three-voice fugue, for example, has a regular exposition (Example 9-14a) but its tonal structure (with unexpected modulations) is very free; particularly characteristic is the last harmonization (Example 9-14b) with its archaic sound resulting from the systematic use of open, parallel fifths.

A more archaistic neo-Classic style animates Orrego-Salas's *Canciones Castellanas*, Op. 20, for soprano and a chamber ensemble (flute, clarinet, English horn, trumpet, viola, cello, harp, and percussion). The five songs are settings of early Luso-Spanish Renaissance poetry (Gil Vicente, Marquis of Santillana, and Juan del Encina). Modal and linear writing prevails. A rhythmic intensity typical of Orrego-Salas, including polyrhythmic passages in the third song, "El Ganadico," is present. Two of the songs follow the structure of the Spanish villancico (*coplas* and *estribillo*). The instrumental ensemble, well chosen for the re-creation of Renaissance sonorities, tends to be treated in a concertante style. The melody instruments provide, most of the time, a subtle counterpoint to the vocal line. Timbral combinations are skillful and original. Some influence of Manuel de Falla can be seen in the smooth, lyrical melodies of certain passages. As with Santa Cruz, occasional Spanish traits appear in this and other works of this period by Orrego-Salas, such as arabesque-like figurations and rhythmic patterns alternating between 3/4 and 6/8 meters.

Orrego-Salas turned to the orchestral medium more often during the 1950s and 1960s; his first major orchestral works, however, were written in the late 1940s. The *Obertura Festiva*, Op. 21 (1948), and the Symphony No. 1 (1949) reveal his mastery of orchestration. As opposed to Santa Cruz, his is a very colorful, virtuoso orchestral writing, as his subsequent works, in which he experimented with orchestration, reveal.

[14]His first five works actually date from 1936–1938, but have been withdrawn by the composer.

EXAMPLE 9-14 Juan Orrego-Salas, *Suite No. 1*, for piano, Op. 14: "Fuga": (a) mm. 1–10; (b) mm. 42–44. Copyright 1953 Barry & Cia. Used by permission of Boosey & Hawkes, Inc. Sole agents.

(a) Andante (♩ = 72)

(b)

ARGENTINA AND URUGUAY

While neo-Classicism was followed by most non-nationalist composers in Argentina and Uruguay during the period under discussion, twelve-tone music, considered in the 1930s the most radical trend in musical composition, found its first Latin American supporter in the Argentine composer Juan Carlos Paz. As mentioned in Chapter 8, Paz participated in the foundation of the Grupo Renovación, whose members' basic purposes were to promote one another's music through mutual critical assessment, concert performance, and publication, and to renovate and update the art music of their country. Divergent ideas on the best method to achieve such goals splintered the group. Paz withdrew from it, founded the Conciertos de Nueva Música (1937), and eventually created his own group known as Agrupación Nueva Música (1944). Younger composers such as Esteban Eitler, Julio Perceval, and Daniel Devoto joined him. While the Grupo Renovación favored especially the promotion of neo-Classic composers such as Stravinsky, Milhaud, Hindemith, Copland, and de Falla, the Agrupación Nueva Música went further in the direction of the avant-garde, feeling particular affinity for the serial composers Schoenberg and Webern and for experimentalists such as Varèse, Cowell, and, by the late 1940s, Cage and Messiaen.

Juan Carlos Paz (1901–1972), the most radical composer of his generation, studied piano and composition in Buenos Aires and Paris (under Vincent d'Indy), but he was largely self-taught. Although he remained to a great extent an independent and isolated figure and never projected the patriarchal image of the Cuban Ardévol, his attitudes and unrestrained enthusiasm for new musical ideas exerted a beneficial influence on such significant later composers as Mauricio Kagel. Paz's opposition to programmatic musical concepts, his militant promotion of Schoenberg's serial techniques, and his consistent campaign against musical nationalism made him a unique pioneer of the avant-garde in Latin America. Until the middle 1930s he cultivated an essentially neo-Classic style, characterized in its more mature phase (ca. 1927–1934) by profusely contrapuntal writing and polytonal and at times atonal harmony (*Three Pieces for Orchestra*, 1930; *Octet for Wind Instruments*, 1930). The piano pieces *Tres Invenciones a dos voces* (1932), *Tres Movimientos de "Jazz"* (1932), and *Tercera Sonatina* illustrate this neo-Classic tendency. Besides the linear writing, which resorts to various contrapuntal devices such as invertible, double, and so-called "reckless" or *rücksichtsloser* counterpoint (disregarding harmonic considerations), these pieces reveal a melodic and harmonic language leading towards Paz's dodecaphonic idiom of subsequent years. Basically this is effected by an almost total chromaticism applied to both melody and harmony. The melodic organization is primarily motivic. In extreme cases the motives present an angular, chromatic configuration, often spaced in the most extreme ranges, thus creating melodic discontinuity, as, for example, in the second movement, "Spleen," of the *Tres Movimientos de "Jazz."* The harmonic structures imply tonal centers only minimally, as the result of widely spaced chromatic chords (Example 9-15); harmonic stabilization in such cases is assured through the recurrence of significant interval structures (seconds and fourths in Example 9-15), or through ostinatos.

A second phase in Paz's stylistic development may be discerned in compositions written by him after about 1934. Twelve-tone methods used in a free, personal way constitute the basis of this phase, which extended to about 1955. His first works based on those methods were *Primera Composición en los 12 Tonos*, for flute, English horn, and cello (1934); *Segunda Composición*, for flute and piano (1934–1935); *Diez Piezas sobre una serie de los 12 Tonos* (1935), for piano; *Passacaglia*, for orchestra (1936); *Tercera Composición en*

EXAMPLE 9-15 Juan Carlos Paz, *Tres Movimientos de "Jazz"*: "Paseo por el bosque," mm. 20–28. Grupo Renovación, 1934.

los 12 Tonos, for clarinet and piano (1937); and *Cuarta Composición en los 12 Tonos*, for solo violin (1938).

Paz has often been referred to as a follower of Schoenberg from both a technical and esthetic point of view. However, although he was quite knowledgeable about Schoenberg's work (as his books readily bear witness), his concept of tonality and twelve-tone techniques was markedly different. His tendency to construct tone rows on tonal patterns (major and minor triads, major and minor seventh and ninth chords, and, at times, more complex chords) and to establish, if only momentarily, references to tonal centers made him more akin to Alban Berg. He followed, however, Schoenberg's advocation of an "emancipation of the dissonance." The ways Paz uses the row in a composition differ radically from Schoenberg's manipulations. Paz tends to limit himself to the original or "prime" (P) and retrograde (R) forms of the row. Inversion (I) and retrograde inversion (RI) forms never appear in his early twelve-tone works; likewise, transposition of the row practically never occurs. The "Balada No. 2" of *Canciones y Baladas*, for piano (1936–1937), for example, is entirely based on the repetition with minor variants of P_0 (prime form, at the untransposed, "zero" level), used both horizontally and vertically.

A good illustration of Paz's treatment of twelve-tone techniques can be seen in the *Tercera Composición en los 12 Tonos*, for clarinet and piano, dedicated to Henry Cowell, who published it in the New Music Edition. All four sections of the work—"Toccata," "Tema con variaciones," "Canción," and "Tempo de Giga"—are based on the same row (Example 9-16). The P_0 and R_0 forms of the series (the row, or set) are used exclusively throughout the work; no inversions or transpositions of it appear. The intervallic disposition of the basic set points to some elements of a ninth chord (see pitches 4-1-0-5 in Ex. 9-16), a seventh chord (7-6-9-8), and eleventh and thirteenth chords (7-6-9-8-5-10-11). As opposed to Schoenberg, who generally avoided any chordal or tonal implications in the arrangement of a basic set, Paz utilizes octaves and chords such as triads, sevenths, and ninths in a deliberate manner, and he repeats notes of the row or presents them out of order. The clarinet being the solo instrument, the row is quite often treated as a motivic unit in its part. This is particularly true of the second section, "Tema con variaciones," which presents some variety in the manipulation of the basic set. The four-measure theme in the clarinet is a self-contained motivic state-

EXAMPLE 9-16　Juan Carlos Paz, *Tercera composición en los 12 tonos:* basic tone row.

ment of P_0 with successive repetitions of tones 1 and 11 and holdings of tones 0, 1, 5, 10, and 11 for purposes of phrasing. The piano accompaniment is built on R_0, also with repetitions of tones—8, 9, 1, and 2 (Example 9-17). In the eleven variations and coda that follow, the row appears only in its P_0 or R_0 forms. The length of each variation varies from two to fourteen measures.

EXAMPLE 9-17 Juan Carlos Paz, *Tercera composición en los 12 tonos*, second movement ("Tema con variaciones"), mm. 1–7. Copyright 1943 by New Music.

The variation procedure involves not only the pitch outline of the theme, either in its retrograde form or through changes of octave placement, but also (and especially) its rhythmic structure. Variation I (measures 5-7), for example (Example 9-17), consists of R_0 in the clarinet part, with different rhythmic figuration, although measures 4 and 7 are related rhythmically. In each variation the piano accompaniment makes free use of row components, either by frequent repetition of tones or by omission of several tones. Continuity of row material is assured, however, between the theme and Variation I, and among the variations. Thus, as opposed to the clarinet part, which supplies a full statement of the row in whatever form, the piano part often consists of bits of row statement. Both parts are then treated quite independently. An interesting aspect of this work is its overall structure, reminiscent of the Baroque dance suite. The short, fast toccata functions as an introductory prelude, while the gigue, with characteristic rhythmic patterns in 6/8 meter and wide intervallic skips, concludes the work. The third *andante* section, "Canción," in three short parts, is reminiscent of an *aria* of a Baroque suite in its clearly melodic (motivic) character.

Another facet of Paz's musical style can be seen in a work such as *Rítmica Ostinata*, Op. 41 (1942), for orchestra. Written in a bravura style, this work abounds in virtuoso contrapuntal and rhythmic writing. It appears to be primarily an essay in rhythmic polyphony. The title itself indicates the repetitive nature of the work, which has the character of a large toccata by virtue of the fast tempo that prevails throughout, the constant sixteenth- and eighth-note figurations, the numerous pedal points and ostinatos, and the brilliant orchestration. Though Paz does not resort to a twelve-tone series in this work, the harmonic idiom is wholly chromatic and dissonant—with, however, suggestions of temporary tonal centers resulting from the constant pedal points that appear in various parts of the rich, thick orchestral texture. The rhythm is organized motivically, and the various rhythmic motives are combined contrapuntally, as are the melodic motives. A fairly complex counterpoint results. The whole orchestra is treated in a virtuoso manner, with constant participation of all the instruments.

Other Argentine composers representative of the "international" trend in musical composition are Roberto García Morillo, the Spanish-born Julián Bautista, and the Austrian-born Guillermo Graetzer, among others. García Morillo (b. 1911) began writing in the 1930s in a modernistic non-nationalist, personal style. Although quite eclectic in his esthetic attitude, only his works of the 1950s reveal a clearer orientation towards neo-Classicism. The Third Piano Sonata, Op. 14 (1944–1945), in three movements, exhibits a characteristic linear chromaticism, reinforced in numerous passages through unisons and contrasting registers. Dissonances resulting often from false relations and quartal harmony prevail. Repetitions of melodic material are almost always accompanied by subtle rhythmic variants. No extended developmental techniques are found, but thematic materials appear motivically fragmented and generally rhythmically extended. With very simple means, García Morillo creates great rhythmic vitality and an ever-engaging melodic progression. In other works of the period, such as *Las pinturas Negras de Goya* (1939), *Tres Pinturas de Paul Klee* (1944), and the cantata *Marín* (1948–1950), he cultivated an increasingly complex language which includes an intensified, dissonant and often atonal harmony and an original treatment of rhythm. At the same time, many of his works show a clear empathy for Hispanic musical culture.

Julián Bautista (1901–1961), who studied composition under Conrado del Campo in Spain and settled in Buenos Aires in 1939, belongs to the Spanish neo-Classic school of the 1920s to the 1940s, and the Spanish tradition constitutes his primary source of ideas and techniques. His style is predominantly contrapuntal, harmonically advanced, and formally traditional. The formal musical training of Guillermo Graetzer (b. 1914) was in Austria and Germany under von Knorr, Hindemith, and Paul Pisk; it oriented him towards the new tonal style developed by Hindemith. Graetzer's musicological work in choral music and late Baroque music reinforced his affinity with neo-Classicism, as can be heard in the String Trio of 1948–1951. After moving to Buenos Aires in 1930 he taught in various schools and at the National University of La Plata and was influential in the field of music education.

Uruguayan music in the 1940s began to show signs of maturity and to achieve an international reputation which gradually increased during the next two decades. The composers most in evidence during the period under discussion were Carlos Estrada, Héctor Tosar (Errecart), and, to a lesser extent, Guido Santórsola. Estrada (1909–1970), who studied in his native city of Montevideo and at the Paris Conservatoire, cultivated a sober neo-Classic style based on materials and forms inherited from the classical tradition. His incidental pieces for Claudel's *L'Annonce faite à Marie* (1943) and Verlaine's *Les uns et les autres* (1950) and his numerous settings of French poems indicate his long association with and empathy for French culture. He won recognition in Paris, in fact, where several of his works were published and where his First Symphony received its première (1951). His Sonatina No. 1, Op. 45, in three movements, exhibits a predominantly two-part contrapuntal writing (first and third movements), chromatic harmony, and dynamic, syncopated rhythmic patterns, in quintuple meter throughout the first movement.

Héctor Tosar (Errecart) (b. 1923) wrote his most significant works during the 1950s and 1960s, yet his precocious talent was much in evidence in Uruguayan musical life in the 1940s. He studied piano, harmony, and composition in Montevideo. A Guggenheim fellowship took him to the United States (1946–1948), where he studied under Aaron Copland, Arthur Honegger, and Darius Milhaud. He undertook further studies of composition with the latter two in Paris, where he also studied orchestral conducting with Jean Fournet and Eugène Bigot. One of his earlier works, the *Toccata* for orchestra (1940), was premiered by the OSSODRE (the Uruguayan State orchestra) that same year. A characteristic work of his early period is the *Sinfonía* No. 2, for strings (1950). In it Tosar cultivates a decisively modernistic style of enormous rhythmic vitality, rich harmonic resources (often in quartal harmony with dissonant clashes), and original string and dynamic effects. The texture is predominantly polyphonic, with a great deal of imitation. Formal designs follow classical models. The work reveals a certain spontaneity in the constant flow of musical ideas and in the formidable driving force of its rhythms.[15]

After having lived in Brazil for many years, the Italian-born Guido Santórsola (b. 1904) settled and worked in Montevideo. He was particularly influential as a conductor and string player (violin, viola), having founded the orchestra of the Uruguayan Cultural Association and the Kleiber Quartet of Montevideo. As a composer he cultivated a style partly based at first on Brazilian, and later on Uruguayan folk music. Only in subsequent works did he turn to atonality and serial techniques.

A very dynamic figure active in Montevideo during the 1930s and 1940s was the musicologist Francisco Curt Lange (b. 1903). Born and trained in Germany, Lange emigrated to Uruguay in the late 1920s and soon became the major champion of the Latin American composer. He rendered invaluable services to Latin American music not only through his own research work in Argentina, Uruguay, and Brazil but through his indefatigable promotion of music and musicians of Latin America. He founded both the Inter-American Institute of Musicology, which supported the publication of the monumental series *Boletín Latino-Americano de Música* (1935–1946), and the unique *Editorial Cooperativa Interamericana de Compositores*, which published numerous piano, choral, and chamber music works by composers of the Americas. Most important were his basic concept of *americanismo musical*, for which he campaigned in his various publications, and his organization of music performances throughout the hemisphere.

BRAZIL

The major innovating movement in musical composition in Brazil during the 1930s and 1940s emanated from the Música Viva group, which appeared in 1931 under the leadership of the German composer Hans-

[15]Interesting analytical comments are found in Gustavo Becerra Schmidt, "Sinfonía no. 2 para cuerdas de Héctor Tosar," *Revista Musical Chilena*, no. 55 (October–November 1957), 5–23.

Joachim Koellreutter. In its manifesto of 1946 the group declared its opposition to folkloristic nationalism: "In its essence [it] exalts feelings of nationalist superiority and stimulates egocentric and individualist currents which divide man, creating disruptive forces."[16] In a period of strong nationalism in the country, such a dictum appeared very threatening. It symbolized for the majority of Brazilian composers a strong disruption of national values and a foreign intrusion into the country's musical world. Thus, the Música Viva aims were viewed by many as an anti-national campaign. The musical technique that became associated with this campaign was dodecaphony, championed by Koellreutter.

Koellreutter (b. 1915) lived in Brazil from 1937 to 1963 and again since 1974 and taught many Brazilian composers, introducing them to new techniques of composition, especially serialism. In Berlin and Geneva he had studied under Hindemith and Scherchen, among others, but he favored Schoenberg's methods in his works of the 1940s and 1950s. At first rather dogmatic in his treatment of atonality and twelve-tone techniques (as in *Música*, 1941, *Noturnos*, 1945, and *Hai-Kais*, 1942–1945), he used them in a more personal manner in later works. His influence as a teacher of composition was felt in the three most important Brazilian centers for future development of new music: Rio de Janeiro, São Paulo, and Salvador (Bahia). Among his students who cultivated a non-nationalist style in the 1940s were Cláudio Santoro and César Guerra Peixe.

Santoro (b. 1919) has been a rather eclectic composer. After graduating from the Conservatory of the Distrito Federal (1936), he studied with Koellreutter, who introduced him to twelve-tone techniques. In 1946 he went to study with Nadia Boulanger in Paris. There he was also a student of orchestral conducting under Eugène Bigot at the Conservatoire. In 1948 he was the Brazilian delegate to the Prague Congress of Progressive Composers, and the congress's condemnation of dodecaphony as "bourgeois decadence" influenced his development in the 1950s, during which he embraced a nationalist style. His earlier music, however, written between 1939 and about 1947, was oriented towards atonality and a pragmatic twelve-tone technique. Almost all of his early works are abstract, with the exception of the semi-programmatic *Impressões de uma fundição de aço* ("Impressions of a steel foundry") for orchestra (1942). The Sonata for solo violin and the First Sonata for Violin and Piano (both 1940) brought adverse reactions from critics and concertgoers when they were first performed in Rio de Janeiro. The solo work is written in an atonal style but maintains the structure of the Baroque sonata. Two-part counterpoint prevails except in the second movement, which develops a single melodic line. Though the writing is consistently atonal, the sonata is not organized according to the twelve-tone method.

[16]"Manifesto 1946," *Música Viva*, no. 12 (January 1947), 3.

The beginning of the second movement, for example, presents a theme which commences with all twelve tones, but they do not function as a basic set for the movement (Example 9-18). In the First Sonata, however, Santoro adheres to serial techniques. Its second movement, for example, uses the basic row in its four different forms. In other works such as the Second Violin Sonata and the Sonata for flute and piano, both of 1941, the composer applies the essential aspects of the method in a free manner, but motivic repetition and rhythmic periodicities are on the whole maintained.

EXAMPLE 9-18 Cláudio Santoro, *Sonata* for solo violin, second movement, beginning (unbarred). Copyright 1941 by Instituto Interamericano de Musicología. Used by permission.

Santoro relies in a few of his vocal works on the technique of *Sprechstimme*. The song on Alvarenga's poem *Asa Ferida* (1944), for example, calls for cadential glissandos on diminished octaves (recalling Schoenberg's *Pierrot lunaire*) and includes a passage in *Sprechstimme*-like recitation with the indication that it should be interpreted as a "spoken song" and that the accidentals should be observed.

Several works by Santoro written in the 1940s have been labeled "twelve-tone nationalist"; these include the *Sonatina a três* (flute, viola, cello, 1942), the First String Quartet (1943), the Second Symphony (1945), *Música para Cordas* (1946), and the Third Symphony (1947–1948). They might better be described as eclectic in orientation, with their Classic structures, Baroque contrapuntal devices and extensive polyphony, alternation of atonality with pantonality, rhythmic drive reminiscent at times of national music, and original tone-coloring effects. Only in the mid-1960s did Santoro utilize a qualified serialism and other new techniques of composition.

If the label "twelve-tone nationalism" is unsuitable for Santoro's style of the 1940s, it applies well to that of César Guerra Peixe (b. 1914), a decided apologist of atonality and twelve-tone music in Brazil at that time. Under Koellreutter's instruction and guidance, he wrote several works based on serial techniques, the first one being the *Sonatina 1944* for flute and clarinet. Soon, however, he began to write what he himself called a "curious sort of music" which could conceivably unite two apparently irreconcilable musical trends—twelve-tone and nationalist music—and thus create a new, modern expression of musical nationalism. Such a compromise, which demanded some distortion of both serial technique and typically national music traits, proved indeed untenable. Nevertheless, Guerra Peixe was able to produce original, well-conceived works which need no theoretical justification or classification. One such work is the Trio for flute, clarinet, and bassoon (1948), in which the writing is atonal, motivically organized, texturally linear, contrapuntally well-balanced (imitation predominates), and rhythmically isometric.

Another composer associated with the Música Viva group who turned to non-national sources in his last few works was Luiz Cosme (1908–1965). Although he had cultivated a subjective nationalist style in his earlier works, from 1946 on he attempted to avoid the tonal system (in such works as *Três Manchas* and *Madrugada no Campo*) and to adopt freely the twelve-tone method—without, however, concealing his interest in national subjects (as in his ballet *Lambe-Lambe*, 1946). His last work, *Novena à Senhora da Graça* (1950), based on a poem in nine sections by Teodomiro Tostes and scored for string quartet, piano, narrator, and female dancer, makes unorthodox use of some dodecaphonic techniques and appears free of national implications. One of the basic sets which appears at the beginning of the work serves as the expressive thematic idea of various subsequent sections. With this work Cosme proposed to "unite the contents of the poem to music, word, and gesture," but chose a simple rhythmic line for the narration of the poem rather than setting it in a Schoenbergian *Sprechstimme*, as he had thought of doing at first.

For Heitor Villa-Lobos, the period under consideration, which can be extended to the end of his life (1959), represented a less experimental phase in his production, with perhaps the exception of the *Bachianas Brasileiras* (see Chapter 7). Within a definite neo-tonal style he wrote many choral works, some of which, such as the *Missa São Sebastião* (1937), have no nationalist implication whatsoever. Likewise, his numerous instrumental works of this period—symphonic poems, symphonies, ballets, concertos, chamber pieces, solo pieces—exhibit a more generalized tendency towards an abstract character. As opposed to the first seven symphonies, his last five symphonies, for example, written between 1950 and 1957, do not bear any subtitles indicative of extramusical ideas. Often the result of commissions, many works produced after 1945 show a marked concern for virtuosity. The last few years of Villa-Lobos's life saw the production of several solo concertos (Guitar Concerto, 1951, the last three piano concertos, and the violin, harp, and harmonica concertos) and several concertante orchestral and chamber works. It has often been said that these and other works of the period offer nothing new within Villa-Lobos's total creative output. There are undoubtedly many conventional, banal pieces, but also some of unquestionable merit and originality, of which we would mention two contrasting examples, the ballet *Emperor Jones* (1956) and the String Quartet No. 17 (1957).

Emperor Jones, based on Eugene O'Neill's play, was commissioned for the Empire State Music Festival. This work epitomizes the quintessence of Villa-Lobos's eclecticism. Some of his best qualities as melodist, contrapuntist, inventor of rhythms, and masterful orchestrator are displayed in the ballet. At the same time, the various influences on him early in his career (French Impressionism, early Stravinsky) reappear here. Some of the elements of the orchestral language described in the *Choros* (see Chapter 7) reappear in the last part of the ballet, particularly the alternating contrast between the high and low registers of woodwind and brass, the sliding effect of the trombones, the octave doublings, the use of the human voice as a coloristic component, and the various parts of polytonal block chords distributed among contrasting timbres and reinforced by numerous percussion instruments.

The String Quartet No. 17, Villa-Lobos's last (and one he never heard in performance), is an exception to the general statement that his late works merely recapitulate earlier achievements. On the contrary, the work reveals a clear orientation towards an austere simplicity. As opposed to his earlier natural expansiveness, Villa-Lobos cultivates here a rather terse and abstract style characterized by prevailing short, motif-like melodic phrases, frequent isometric patterns, fairly wide melodic ranges, alternation of chromatic and diatonic passages, emphasis upon sonority and timbre especially through the use of unison passages between pairs of instruments, a structural simplification that discards developmental and imitative techniques, and frequent tonal ambiguity resulting from numerous chord alterations. The beginning measures of the first movement (Example 9-19) illustrate some of these stylistic traits. Particularly characteristic are the wide range of the melodic line, the contrary motion between violin 1 and cello line, the alterations, and the unexpected clash in the first measure of the altered ninth chord distributed through almost four octaves.

EXAMPLE 9-19   Heitor Villa-Lobos, *String Quartet No. 17*, first movement, mm. 1–3. Copyright 1959 by Editions Max Eschig. Used by permission.

In summary, the period of the 1930s and 1940s saw the beginning awareness of some Latin American composers of a need to adhere to new methods of composition without concealing their Latin cultural identity. Though these composers remained in the minority, they were able to liberate themselves in most cases from the yoke of musical nationalism. The resulting individualism had its full impact during the next two decades, which evidenced the maturity of the Latin American composer.

BIBLIOGRAPHICAL NOTES

General factual data for this chapter can be found in the various national histories of music mentioned in the bibliographical notes of the previous chapters. Although quite biased, Juan Carlos Paz offers interesting opinions on most musical developments discussed in this chapter in his book *Introducción a la música de nuestro tiempo* (Buenos Aires: Editorial Nueva Visión, 1955).

Carlos Chávez's *La Hija de Cólquide* is analyzed by Jesús Bal y Gay in his article, "'La Hija de Cólquide' de Carlos Chávez," *Nuestra Música*, no. 19 (1950), 207–16. Chávez's own "50 años de música en México," *México en el Arte*, nos. 10–11 (1951), 201–38, is quite informative. A historical summary of 20th-century Mexican music is also provided by Luis Sandi in "Cincuenta años de música en México," *Nuestra Música*, no. 23 (1951), 222–38. On Rodolfo Halffter, see José Antonio Alcaraz, *La música de Rodolfo Halffter* (Mexico: Unam, Difusión cultural, Cuadernos de música, 1977). A very revealing interview with José Ardévol is available in "Entrevista," *Unión*, X/4 (December 1971), 103–6; Julián Orbón provides good comments on Cuban music and his own works in "Diálogo con Julián Orbón," *Exilio* (New York), no. 2 (1969), 5–13.

On Roque Cordero, see Gilbert Chase, "Composed by Cordero," *Inter-American Music Bulletin*, no. 7 (September 1958), 1–4, and Ronald R. Sider, "Roque Cordero, the Composer and His Style Seen in Three Representative Works," *Inter-American Music Bulletin*, no. 61 (September 1967), 1–17.

Domingo Santa Cruz's writings illustrate the development of Chilean musical life; see especially his "Mis recuerdos sobre la Sociedad Bach," *Revista Musical Chilena*, no. 40 (1950–1951), 8–62, and "Nuestra posición en el mundo contemporáneo de la música," *Revista Musical Chilena*, no. 64 (1959), 46–60, no. 65 (1959), 31–46, no. 67 (1959), 39–55. Issue no. 109 (October–December 1969) of *Revista Musical Chilena* is dedicated to the works of Alfonso Letelier. Domingo Santa Cruz has written on Orrego-Salas's Piano Concerto in "El Concierto para piano y orquesta en la obra de Juan Orrego Salas," *Revista Musical Chilena*, no. 39 (1950), 33–53.

On Juan Carlos Paz, the most important writings are: Hector I. Gallac, "La obra musical de Juan Carlos Paz," *Boletín Latino-Americano de Música*, I

(April 1935), 33–42; Francisco Curt Lange, "El compositor argentino Juan Carlos Paz," *Boletín Latino-Americano de Música*, IV (1938), 799–829; Jacobo Romano, "Juan Carlos Paz: un revitalizador del lenguaje musical," *Revista Musical Chilena*, no. 95 (1966), 26–44; and Jacobo Romano, *Juan Carlos Paz: tribulaciones de un músico* (Buenos Aires, 1970). Good analyses are provided by David Sargent in his unpublished D.M.A. thesis, "Juan Carlos Paz: Self-taught 12-tonalist and Innovative Argentine Composer" (University of Illinois, 1975). For the other Argentine composers discussed here, see Alberto Ginastera, "Notas sobre la música moderna argentina," *Revista Musical Chilena*, no. 31 (1948), 21–28. On Julián Bautista, see the special issue of *Revista Ars* (1961) and Roberto García Morillo's study, "Julián Bautista," *Revista Musical Chilena*, nos. 35–36 (1949), 26–43.

Uruguayan composers are treated in Susana Salgado's *Breve historia de la música culta en el Uruguay* (Montevideo: Aemus, 1971). The work of Francisco Curt Lange has been reviewed by many musicologists and critics; among others, see Gilbert Chase, "Francisco Curt Lange and 'Americanismo Musical'," *Inter-American Monthly* (Washington), II/5 (1943), 33ff; Fritz Bose, "Südamerikanische Musikforschung," *Acta Musicologica*, XXIX (1957), 43–45; Gilbert Chase, "An Anniversary and a New Start," *Yearbook*, Inter-American Institute for Musical Research, I (1965), 1–10; and Pola Suárez Urtubey, *Las obras colectivas de Francisco Curt Lange* (Buenos Aires, 1974).

Composers from Brazil discussed here (Koellreutter, Santoro, Guerra Peixe) are the subject of special chapters in Vasco Mariz's *Figuras da música brasileira contemporânea* (Brasilia: Editôra Universidade de Brasilia, 1970). For biographical data on Brazilian composers, see also Marcos Marcondes, ed., *Enciclopédia da Música Brasileira, erudita, folclórica*, popular (São Paulo: Art Editora, 1977).

TEN

COUNTERCURRENTS: SINCE 1950

Musical composition in Latin America since about 1950 has undergone profound transformations that have led to a healthy variety of styles and a diversity of esthetics. The decade of the 1950s represented in some ways both the end of an era and the point of departure of another. In general, the musical nationalism that had been cultivated for decades tended to disappear. The social and intellectual conditions before World War II had reflected a clear dependence on Europe and North America; the resulting need for national identity had pointed to musical nationalism as a path often considered inescapable. But, although political and economic dependence continued during the 1950s and 1960s, cultural dependence lessened considerably. Beginning around the mid-1950s Latin America oriented herself, at least in the larger cities, towards a more cosmopolitan world. Foreign cultural elements continued to prevail but were deliberately assimilated within a new frame of reference. Numerous composers felt that in the process of assimilation a natural qualitative selection would take place, followed by an imitation, re-creation, and transformation of the foreign models according to prevailing local conditions and individual needs. The progressive Latin American composer of the period began then to look at his own cultural environment in an all-inclusive manner. Progressive and avant-garde European or North American "new-music" compositions became well known in a relatively short period of time and were soon considered an integral part of the Latin American composer's cultural milieu. Thus, although the models were foreign in origin, they were to a great extent integrated into the new cosmopolitan cultural world of Latin America.

The decade of the 1960s saw the emergence of new, experimental musical currents in most Latin American countries. Composers espousing such currents, however, had a difficult time finding official support, whether for performance of their music by national orchestras or other ensemble associations or for its publication and commercial recording. The lack of official incentive in the form of commissions or promotion of new-music concerts and the general lack of opportunity for earning a living as composers of new music led several prominent Latin American figures to look elsewhere in the hope that their creative interests would be better served. Thus, some composers settled in Europe (especially Germany, England, France, and Italy), the United States, and Canada, convinced that their own countries could never offer them suitable conditions for their creative activities. Yet conditions for new music did improve in the 1960s, especially in Argentina, Chile, Brazil, Mexico, and to a lesser extent Venezuela. Several societies were formed, generally in cooperation with the International Society for Contemporary Music; a few electronic music studios appeared; some universities provided relatively good training; state broadcasting systems began to give some support to contemporary music; and several state and private institutions funded festivals of new music for which commissions were granted. The Organization of American States organized and sponsored nine Inter-American Music Festivals which took place in Washington, D.C., in April 1958, April 1961, May 1965, June 1968, May 1971, May 1974 (with performances in New York and other cities), May 1976, May 1977, and May 1978; they included over a hundred world premières of Latin American works. The same organization promoted Latin American new music through the Festivals of Music of the Americas and Spain (three events between 1964 and 1970), which took place in Madrid and included twelve world premières of Latin American works. Over the years the O.A.S. also published a series of scores, including some works by young composers. Thus, the isolation of the majority of composers of Latin America in the previous decades diminished considerably. Yet even by the late 1960s a distinct Latin American art-music expression could hardly be said to exist outside the limits of the Latin American continent. Some have even questioned whether such an expression exists within the continent. This chapter provides some facts that may help to answer such a question.

MEXICO AND THE CARIBBEAN

Although Carlos Chávez continued to be quite active as a composer, conductor, and lecturer during the 1950s and 1960s, Mexican musical life no longer centered around him, as it had since the 1920s. In 1948 he resigned as director of the Orquesta Sinfónica de México and in 1953 as director of the Instituto Nacional de Bellas Artes; thereafter, he dedicated himself almost exclusively to composition. He received numerous commissions and was granted a Guggenheim fellowship for composition in 1956. His interest in teaching was unabated: he delivered the Charles Eliot Norton lectures at Harvard University in 1958–1959, out of which came his book *Musical Thought*; and in 1960 he opened a workshop in composition ("Taller de Composición") at the Mexico City Conservatory, which he directed until 1964. Several young Mexican composers benefited greatly from the workshop.

Chávez's production of the period is dominated by four symphonies (the last, no. 6, 1961–1962, being commissioned by the New York Philharmonic); the opera originally titled *Love Propitiated* but renamed *The Visitors* (1953–1956); the cantata *Prometheus* (1956); *Resonancias* (1964) for orchestra; *Clio*, a symphonic ode (1969); the ballet *Pirámide* (1968); several chamber pieces, such as *Invención II* for string trio (1965); and several piano pieces, such as *Invención* (1958) and the sonatas no. 5 and no. 6 (1960 and 1961). *Sinfonía No. 3* (1951–1954) is written in a style akin to *Antígona* and *La Hija de Cólquide* (see Chapter 9). *Sinfonía No. 4* (subtitled *Romántica*), commissioned by the Louisville Orchestra, is, in contrast to earlier works, lyrical and quite emotional in character. It is largely tonal and rather classical in formal designs. Its contrapuntal texture, with frequent imitations and short ostinatos, reminds one of the style of the Piano Concerto. The Fifth Symphony was commissioned by the Koussevitzky Foundation and completed in 1953. Written for string orchestra, this work confirmed Chávez's affinity for neo-Classicism, with a general observance of classical forms, dissonant polyphonic textures, and frequent polytonal harmonies. The third and last movements reveal an unusual structure. The exposition of the last— *Allegro con brio*—presents six major motifs, all interrelated. The sixth motif functions as the keystone of the exposition since the first five reappear in mirror fashion (reminding one of the overall formal design of the Violin Concerto) in original or retrograde forms.[1] The movement does not develop any material as such; the middle section is a short bridge-like passage.

The cantata *Prometheus*, for solo voices, chorus, and orchestra, received its world premiere during the Cabrillo Music Festival in California

[1]Cf. Roberto García Morillo, *Carlos Chávez, Vida y Obra* (Mexico: Fondo de Cultura Económica, 1960), pp. 169–70.

(1972). Chávez himself characterized its music as simple, melodic, lyrical, and reflecting his own feelings towards the Aeschylian Prometheus—"the forethinker, the kind god who champions mankind, who protects the feeble, and who, heroically, rebels against tyranny and injustice." (In most of Chávez's subsequent works, he ceased to rely on such extramusical themes.)

Among Chávez's most significant works of the period are *Soli II, III,* and *IV* (respectively 1961, 1965, and 1966). *Soli III* calls for bassoon, trumpet, timpani, viola, and orchestra, *Soli IV* for French horn, trumpet, and trombone, and *Soli II* for wind quintet. The titles are justified by the appearance of each instrument as soloist in each movement: in *Soli III* the same principle is applied to the four solo instruments. *Soli II,* consisting of a prelude, rondo, aria, sonatina, and finale, shows the composer's masterly technical command of contrapuntal writing, harmonic invention, rhythmic variety, and timbre blendings. Nowhere had Chávez's concern with clarity, terseness, and novelty of instrumental timbre combinations found a better expression than in these works. Chávez has explained that the directing principle in these pieces is that of non-repetition—the avoidance of standard sequence, symmetry, and recapitulation and of the "repetitive procedures implicit in the Viennese serial technique." In their place is a "continuous unfolding of successively new musical ideas—the element of renewal rather than repetition." This guiding principle affects the melodic writing. Wide-range, disjunct, chromatic, ejaculatory motifs establish the general improvisatory character of *Soli II* (Example 10-1). The continuous unfolding of ideas and the autogenetic nature of melodic designs produce the unusual impression of never reaching a terminal point. The harmonic language, while still based on tonal centers, avoids any traditional tonal functionality through the insistent presence of harsh dissonances. The principle of non-repetition is observed almost

EXAMPLE 10-1   Carlos Chávez, *Soli II:* "Preludio," mm. 1–16. Copyright by Mills Music, Inc. Used by permission.

throughout, even in the rondo section, in which there is only one literal repetition of the opening oboe motif (mm. 46 and 92), and one abbreviated presentation of the "ritornello" (mm. 141–45). Characteristic rhythmic patterns help to delineate the formal structure. Virtuoso writing is evident, especially in wide intervallic skips and frequent sudden running figures. Example 10-2 illustrates the abrupt changes of registers characteristic of the melodic writing, here a twelve-tone row presented in retrograde at measures 193–94.

EXAMPLE 10-2   Carlos Chávez, *Soli II:* "Aria," bassoon melodic line, mm. 190–97. Copyright by Mills Music, Inc. Used by permission.

Twelve-tone and other serial procedures gained the attention of several Mexican composers during the period of the 1950s and 1960s, at first primarily under the guidance of Rodolfo Halffter, who fostered these techniques as a teacher of composition at the National Conservatory and himself turned to dodecaphony in works of the early 1950s (*Tres Hojas de Album* for piano, 1953, and *Tres Piezas* for string orchestra, 1954). While Halffter resorts to the inherent chromaticism of the series, he applies the technique so loosely that none of the technical and esthetic implications of Schoenberg's method are present. One could rightly argue that Halffter's writing is anything but dodecaphonic, since he does not explore twelve-tone set-operations very often. The *Tres Piezas* for string orchestra are a case in point. The three pieces—"Sonata," "Arioso," "Rondo"—reveal a style not unlike that of Halffter's previous neo-Classic works. Largely tonal, they are characterized by repetitions of melodic motifs, rhythmic patterns, and harmonies. The progression of the bass line, through repeated or adjacent notes, octaves, or intervals such as fifths and fourths, reinforces the feeling of tonal centers. The final cadence of each of the pieces stresses a tutti unison, each time introduced by a lower semitone which seems to function as a leading tone. Although the thematic material is quite (sometimes wholly) chromatic, it is not ordered in a dodecaphonic manner. Melodic motifs are rarely based on twelve successive tones, as the beginning theme of "Rondo" reveals (Example 10-3). When they are so based, the melodic shape of the series often resorts to melodic sequences. There are, of course, exceptions. For example, the beginning measures of the first of the three pieces present a full twelve-tone motif (with repetitions of a few groups of tones). In *Tripartita*, Op. 25 (1959), the exposition of the last movement—"Sonata"—presents the basic set without repetition of tones, immediately followed by an inverted version (transposed, beginning in the viola part) of the series. The traits described in *Tres Piezas*, however, prevail in later works such as the Third Piano Sonata (1967) and *Pregón para una Pascua Pobre*, for chorus, trumpets, trombones, and percussion (1968). The Spanish rhythmic elements noted in Halffter's works of the 1940s reappear occasionally in these works.

Among Halffter's students who have adhered to serial techniques somewhat more systematically is Jorge González Avila (b. 1926), primarily a composer of piano music. In general, however, González Avila does not follow a strict twelve-tone procedure but, contrary to his teacher, uses his sets as precompositional elements. Besides a collection of twenty-four Inventions for piano (1961–1964), in which twelve-tone methods are applied quite freely, he has written several dozen piano études for didactic purposes, some of which illustrate dodecaphonic techniques.

Strict twelve-tone composition has not attracted the attention of young Mexican composers. Atonality and serialism (i.e., the serialization of more than one parameter) have found more acceptance. Joaquin Gutiérrez-Heras (b. 1927), for example, has cultivated a free atonal style. A student of Galindo and Halffter in Mexico City, Rivier and Messiaen at the Paris Conservatory, and Bergsma and Persichetti at the Juilliard School, Gutiérrez-Heras is well informed and up to date on the various contemporary styles. Yet he professes independence from any style or school. He has declared that almost all of his compositions reflect a "voluntary lack of complexity." His *Variations on a French Song* (1960) for harpsichord and his *Sonata Simple* (1965) indeed reveal a melodic simplicity quite unusual in music since 1950. His symphonic scene *Los Cazadores* ("The Hunters") (1962) has been found to contain some typical Mexican overtones in its rhythmic aspect, but his *Trio* for woodwind (1965) has a distinct atonal expression.

Another student of Halffter, Mario Kuri-Aldana (b. 1931), has developed a wholly individual style based on traditional procedures but expressed in a contemporary language, if sometimes mixed with reminiscences of neo-nationalist/neo-Classic elements. He studied piano at the Academia J. S. Bach, then composition at the National University of Mexico (1952–

EXAMPLE 10-3 Rodolfo Halffter, *Tres Piezas:* "Rondo," Violin 1, mm. 1–6. Copyright by Ediciones Mexicanas de Música. Used by permission.

1960). Igor Markevitch and Jean Giardino were his teachers of conducting at the National Institute of Fine Arts in Mexico City; he also studied privately with Halffter and Luis Herrera de la Fuente. In 1963–1964 he was in Buenos Aires, studying at the Torcuato Di Tella Institute under Alberto Ginastera. Besides his activity as a composer and a teacher, Kuri-Aldana has conducted research in folk music. His first works (of the mid-1950s) were influenced by the styles of Revueltas and Chávez, and to a certain extent by that of Halffter. He has also cultivated a semi-popular style (e.g., the *canción ranchera María de Jesús*, 1968, and the choral piece *Peregrina agraciada*, 1963). His suite for double wind orchestra, *Los Cuatro Bacabs* (1960), is at times reminiscent of the early style of Blas Galindo in its continuous repetitive rhythmic patterns and its mestizo folk polyphony in parallel thirds. His cultivated style (e.g., *Candelaria*, 1965, a suite for wind quintet) calls for clarity of texture, contrast in timbres (reinforced by extreme instrumental ranges), dissonant harmonies (widely spaced quartal chords), and great rhythmic variety.[2]

One of Galindo's students at the Mexico City National Conservatory was Leonardo Velásquez (b. 1935), who cultivated a neo-nationalist style in his early works, such as the *Siete piezas breves* for piano; their pentatonicism betrays the influence of his teacher. His ballets *Gorgonio Esparza* (1956) and *El brazo fuerte* (1959) and the symphonic poem *Cuauhtemoc* (1960) confirm his interest in developing a modern style rooted in national sources.

Avant-garde techniques and esthetics had their followers in Mexico during the 1960s. Foremost among them were Manuel Enríquez, Héctor Quintanar, Eduardo Mata, Manuel de Elías, and Mario Lavista. Enríquez (b. 1926) became the avant-garde composer most in evidence in Mexico during the 1960s. He studied violin in Guadalajara and theory in Morelia (under Miguel Bernal Jiménez). He was a student of Peter Mennin at the Juilliard School in 1955–1957, but also during that period in New York came under the influence of Stefan Wolpe, who oriented him to serial techniques. Since that time he has kept up with all avant-garde music developments, participating in European and United States new-music festivals. In 1971 he worked at the Columbia-Princeton Center for Electronic Music. Since about 1960 he has written atonal (neo-expressionist), serial, and aleatory music. His first serial work was *Preámbulo* (1961) for orchestra. His *Tres Invenciones* (1964), for flute and viola, exemplify Enríquez's concentrated musical thought. He has termed them the culmination of his admiration for Webern. They are miniature pieces reduced to minimum materials, in which all musical parameters are equally important. Expressionist influences are reflected especially in the tiny melodic cells which replace traditional thematic material. Enríquez does not resort to twelve-tone writing here, but his melodic motifs

---

[2]Kuri-Aldana's view of contemporary Mexican music is eloquently expressed in his article "Jóvenes compositores mexicanos," *Música* (Havana, Cuba), no. 49 (November–December 1974), 14ff.

EXAMPLE 10-4   Manuel Enríquez, *Tres Invenciones*, I, mm. 1–9.

tend to be wholly chromatic (Example 10-4). Certain instrumental effects (use of harmonics, tremolos, sul ponticello, and col legno in the viola and flutter-tonguing in the flute), affecting only a few notes at a time, remind one of Webern's early techniques. The work is characterized by a constant fluctuation of expressive moods, with static and energetic passages alternating.

Chance operations appear more frequently in Enríquez's works after 1964. His *Reflexiones* (1964), for solo violin, and his Sonata for violin and piano (1964) were his first works to use aleatory techniques. Such techniques involve composition through chance operations (with random procedures) and often call for free improvisation; a certain degree of unpredictability in the actual realization of works using these techniques results. The term "indeterminacy" is often used as a synonym for "aleatory." Freedom of choice can also be applied to musical structure, resulting in variability of the sequence of sections in a work; this is often referred to as "open form." In relation to his later *Ambivalencia* (1967), Enríquez explained his purposes:

My greatest concern when I write music—regardless of the language of each work—is to achieve an expressive equilibrium. I do not experiment per se.

Ambivalencia cost me many months of reasoning and analysis. All factors are compensated: I request the performer that he play what is determined and that he [then] act with freedom. Everything is calculated and foreseen so as to be integrated into the whole of the work.[3]

In the piano piece *A Lápiz* (1965) Enríquez organizes his material in five units or structural modules, each combining fixed and free elements. For this he uses both traditional pitch notation and proportional notation. In later pieces, such as the Second and Third String Quartets (1967 and 1974, respectively), *Díptico I* (1969) for flute and piano, *Díptico II* (1971) for violin and piano, *Móvil I* (1969) for piano, and *Móvil II* (1969), in three different versions for any bowed string instrument, he identified more readily and fully with the esthetic concepts of indeterminacy. Increasingly, he has relied on graphic notation, a type of nonspecific notation in which different symbols, drawings of different sizes and shapes, are intended to give general directions to the performer, who can, in extreme cases, choose at random any of the numerous combinations of possibilities. *Díptico I* provides an illustration (Example 10-5). Each shape or sign is generally explained by the composer.

EXAMPLE 10-5 Manuel Enríquez, *Díptico I*, section Ⓔ, flute part.

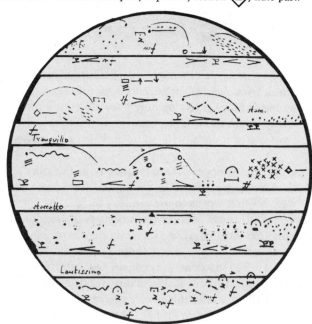

[3]As quoted in Otto Mayer-Serra and José Antonio Alcaraz, "La obra de Manuel Enríquez," *Espejo*, V (1968), 221.

The most common devices include tone clusters, direct manipulation of the piano strings (struck with the fingers or nails, or open hands), continuous glissandi following approximately the indicated design, sounds of indefinite length, and notes with free rhythm and meter.

Enríquez has indicated that 1967 was a decisive year for him because he once again changed his concepts, esthetic attitude, language, and technique. The Second String Quartet, of that year, illustrates a turning towards open form as a result of his adherence to indeterminacy, a principle first set forth by John Cage in the 1950s. "The Quartet," said Enríquez, "has an open technique almost totally, which impelled me to free myself from the·clichés specific to the writing for four instruments and to force the performers to contribute with me to new quests. I thought of different means of expression and a different sonorous world."[4] These means consist above all of juxtaposing fixed sections (fixed, that is, in pitches, durations, rhythms, and dynamics) and free sections (in which each performer is invited to choose at random any of the indicated alternatives and play according to the approximate visual representations of pitch, rhythm, and dynamic curves—as in Example 10-6). Each of the six lines of sequence Ⓝ in Example 10-6 presents different

EXAMPLE 10-6 Manuel Enríquez, *String Quartet No. 2*, third movement, sequence Ⓝ .

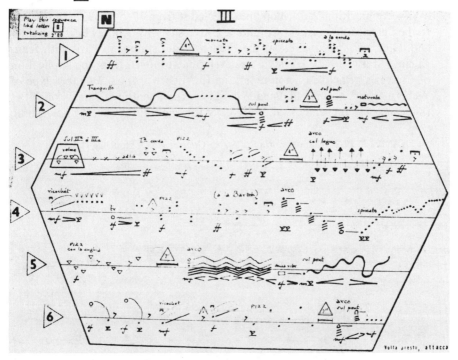

[4]As quoted in ibid., 227.

materials, the only one of which consistently determined by the composer being the succession of dynamics; pitch, rhythm, overall duration of a line, and specific tone color remain undetermined. With the Third String Quartet, the outcome of chance operations becomes even less predictable as the alternatives for random choice increase in number. Sequence ⌷L⌷ of that work, for example (Example 10-7), offers to each of the four performers a free choice among nine segments. In addition, in most of the segments the materials are graphically less precise, since the space between horizontal lines represents the whole register of the instrument and the sounds to be produced are only suggested approximately by the locations, within the space, of the notational signs.

The total production of Enríquez, including his orchestral works since 1961, reveals an experienced composer who has reached rather soon an unusually high degree of self-confidence. His composition entitled *Él y Ellos* ("He and Them") (1975), for violin ("Él") and chamber ensembles ("Ellos"), is conceived in a highly virtuosic and free style, relying on open form in certain sections. In these the soloist selects and arranges at random his own segments and those of the musicians that accompany him.

Another dynamic Mexican composer of new music who has gone through a metamorphosis is Héctor Quintanar (b. 1936), a student of Galindo, Halffter, Jiménez Mabarak, and Chávez. He assisted the last-named in the Composition Workshop and directed it from 1965 to 1972. In 1964 he studied electronic music at Columbia University with Andrés Lewin Richter and, later, *musique concrète* at the French Radio studios in Paris with Jean-Etienne Marie (1967). His stylistic development moved from the application of Chávez's principle of non-repetition (in such works as *Soli*) to a type of Webernian serialism and Penderecki-like experiments with new sonorities (his *Galaxias*, for orchestra, 1968, calls for such aural effects as whistling

EXAMPLE 10-7   Manuel Enríquez, *String Quartet No. 3*, sequence ⌷L⌷.

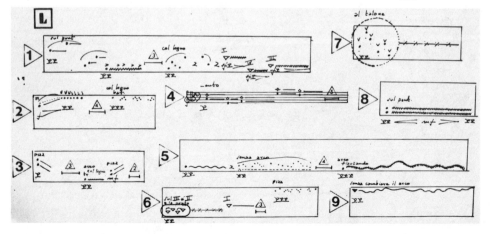

through horns, trumpets, and trombones), then to electronic music, aleatory techniques, and mixed media. The latter currents appear in his works after about 1967, such as *Aclamaciones* for chorus, tape, and orchestra; *Sideral I*, on tape (1968); *Símbolos* (1969) for chamber ensemble, tape, slides, and lights; and two electronic-music pieces, *Ostinato* (1971) and *Sideral III* (1971). Quintanar pioneered in the composition and study of electronic music in Mexico. In 1970 he became founding director of the electronic music studio at the Mexico City Conservatory. The studio, which includes a Buchla synthesizer, became operative in 1971. During that year concerts of live electronic music were organized. However, relatively few Mexican composers have felt at ease with electronic techniques: besides Quintanar, only Mata, de Elías, and Lavista have used them, and these only occasionally.

Eduardo Mata (b. 1942), also a student of Halffter at the Conservatory and of Chávez at the Workshop in the early 1960s, has developed a musical language since the mid-1960s which combines freely aspects of serial and aleatory techniques. The special sound qualities of a work like *Improvisaciones No. 2* (1965), for strings and two pianos, reveal the composer's great concern for timbre. Piano I is treated as a percussion instrument, with the piano strings being played on directly with mallets, sticks, fingers, and hands. Other percussion instruments (two woodblocks, two cowbells, a suspended cymbal) hang inside the piano, forming with it a single unit of the ensemble. The piano soundboard is divided into four registers, indicated notationally by four staves. The work itself has the character of an improvisation by virtue of its pitch and duration approximations, freedom in the treatment of form, contrasting moods, and changeable sonorities. Considering Mata's clear, meticulous, and subtle handling of tone colors, it is curious that he has written only one major work of electronic music, the ballet *Los Huesos Secos* (1963).

Manuel Jorge de Elías (b. 1939) gives further evidence of a progressive outlook in Mexican contemporary music. In his works of the 1960s he cultivated a serial style mixed with aleatory procedures and also paid some attention to the electronic medium. He studied piano and composition first at the School of Music of the National University of Mexico and at the National Conservatory, and later in Europe with Stockhausen and Jean-Etienne Marie. Luis Herrera de la Fuente and Huber-Contwig were his teachers of orchestral conducting. His most significant works are *Vitral No. 2* (1967) for chamber orchestra and tape; *Experiencia No. 3* (1968), for five performers, called a "graphic for improvisation"; Sonata No. 1, for solo violin, involving aleatory procedures; *Pro Pax*, a short piece on tape; *Nimyé* (1969) for solo flute and Sonata No. 2 (1969) for solo violin, both aleatory works; and *Vitral No. 3* (1969), for orchestra. *Vitral No. 3* calls for some of the typical performance gestures of new music, such as rhythmic patterns produced by tapping the mouth pieces of brass instruments with the palm of the hand, and it combines counterpoints of discontinuous, unrelated lines (traditionally notated) with various series of clusters, rhythmically free and functioning as drones.

Mario Lavista's small production (his first works date from 1965) projects an extremely inventive and engaging personality. He represents the extreme left wing of the Mexican avant-garde. Born in 1943, he studied with Halffter and Quintanar and participated in the Composition Workshop at the Conservatory (1963–1967). He also studied in Europe with Jean-Etienne Marie, Henry Pousseur, Iannis Xenakis, and Stockhausen. In Darmstadt, while attending the International Course of New Music, he became acquainted with the Hungarian composer Gyorgy Ligeti, who exerted some influence on his esthetic development. In the early 1970s he studied electronic music in Tokyo. He has also taught music theory at the Mexico City Conservatory. More than his compatriots, Lavista is a bona fide experimentalist. He relies on improvisation and chance operations in the most unconfined manner, explores new sonorous possibilities (including undetermined ones), combines electro-acoustic and visual elements, and attempts to expand the concepts of musical time and space. Random organization both in details and larger structures appear in *Divertimento* (1968), which exists in two versions. The first version includes a woodwind quintet, five woodblocks, three transistor radios with short-wave bands, five microphones, five loudspeakers, four amplifiers, three potentiometers, and a mike mixer. The second version calls for the additional participation of the audience, whose members are provided with noise-producing objects. As the score indicates (Example 10-8), the elements more or less predetermined by the composer are hardly more than certain color blendings, durations, and levels of dynamics, in an obvious application of John Cage's most extreme concept of indeterminacy and non-self-expression. This concept underlies several works of the period by Lavista, particularly *Pieza para un(a) pianista y un piano* (1970) ("Piece for a pianist and a piano"), which has the alternative title *Pieza para dos pianistas y dos pianos* ("Piece for two pianists and two pianos") in a second version. This second version adds a second pianist and a second piano; they are to remain completely silent throughout the piece, but the pianist is required to "communicate this silence to the listeners." The esthetic implications of a piece without performance are well known. Silence in the Cagean concept—that is, the absence of sounds or noises intentionally made—becomes an integral part of the activity of performers and involves the attention of listeners. Lavista here applies the concept but dramatizes it by demanding an apparent contradiction (performance versus non-performance) in one and the same situation. Lavista is also concerned with time, which is evident in a work like *Kronos* (1969), which calls for a minimum of fifteen alarm clocks, three microphones, three loudspeakers, and three potentiometers; its duration is indeterminate but is to be within a range of from 5 to 1,440 minutes. A broad variety of procedures producing new sounds within a sequence of strict meters and predetermined pitches and

EXAMPLE 10-8 Mario Lavista, *Divertimento*, beginning section.

rhythms appears in one of Lavista's recent works, *Quotations* (1976), for cello and piano.

In sum, Mexican music since 1950 shows clear signs of a dynamic development which includes not only the growth of older composers such as Chávez, Galindo, and Halffter but a sensitivity to various international currents that brings it to a truly contemporary maturity.

In Cuba, most of the members of the Grupo de Renovación Musical (established in 1942) continued to be very active during the period after 1950. The leader of the group, José Ardévol, began to pay attention to atonality and serialism in works after about 1957. His *Música* (1957), for chamber orchestra, and the Third String Quartet (1958) indicate that new trend. During the first few years of the Cuban Revolution (1959), Ardévol played a major role as National Director of Music in the reorganization of the country's musical life. Thanks to him, Cuba has enjoyed a remarkable freedom of artistic expression, conveyed not only through his own stylistic development but through that of other members of the Grupo Renovación (Gramatges, Martín, León) and of younger composers like Natalio Galán, Juan Blanco, Carlos Fariñas, Leo Brouwer, Roberto Valera, and Sergio Fernández.

Since about 1965, Ardévol has combined a post-Webernian serialist style with a few aleatory techniques (e.g., in the cantata *La Victoria de Playa Girón*; *Música para guitarra y pequeña orquesta*; the cantata *Che Comandante*, on a text by Guillén; *Hasta su sol sangrando*, subtitled *Cantata de cámara No. 1*; and several chamber music works).

Gramatges has followed suit in such works as *La muerte del guerrillero* (1968), on a text by Guillén, and *Cantata para Abel* (1974), for narrator, mixed chorus, and ten percussionists. Martín, on the other hand, has maintained his early interest in a modern Cuban expression. He practically ceased to compose during the period 1953–1959 because he joined the Fidel Castro movement participating in the fighting against the Batista regime. Several of his works of the 1960s reflect his political convictions. The songs *Cuatro Cantos de la Revolución* (1962), *Así Guevara* (1967), the cantata *Canto de héroes* (1967) for soprano, baritone, and orchestra, and *Cinco Cantos de Ho* (1969) for soprano, flute, viola, and piano (on texts by Ho Chi Minh) reveal an eclectic language. Some serialist procedures, however, permeate his abstract works of the period (e.g., his two string quartets of 1967 and 1968). Martín has been quite influential in post-Revolutionary Cuba as music educator and critic.

Argeliers León studied for a time in the mid-1950s with Nadia Boulanger and, as a result, seems to have developed an interest in serialism.[5] He continued also to cultivate a distinctly Cuban modern style in such works as *Akorín* (1956), subtitled *Cantos negros para piano*; *Danzón No. 3* (1957), also for piano; and *Cuatro danzas cubanas* (1959), for string orchestra. *Akorín* is a transcription and adaptation of Afro-Cuban cult songs in which a two-part counterpoint prevails, with effective imitation of Afro-Cuban overlapping call-and-response practice. In the String Quartet No. 2 (1961) and the Quintet No. 2 (1963) a more modern idiom surfaces. The quintet (for flute, oboe, clarinet, bassoon, and guitar) is one of the most significant works of the composer. León writes a twelve-tone row at the very outset of the work but does not treat it as a strictly serial set. He does rely, however, on melodic inversion, variation techniques, and an almost total chromaticism. This work reveals also an original blending of unusual timbres. León writes very idiomatically for the guitar, as the quintet and the *Tres canciones lentas* (1959), for guitar solo, corroborate. During the 1960s León occupied important administrative posts, including the directorships of the Music Department of the National Library "José Martí" and the Institute of Ethnology and Folklore of the Academy of Sciences (both in Havana). His reduced activity as a composer was balanced by an increased production as an ethnomusicologist.

---

[5] José Ardévol, *Introducción a Cuba. La Música* (Havana: Instituto del Libro, 1969), p. 104.

During the 1950s a younger group of progressive composers began to appear in Cuba. Those most in evidence included Juan Blanco, Aurelio de la Vega, Carlos Fariñas, and Leo Brouwer. Blanco (b. 1920), a student of Ardévol and Gramatges, began cultivating some aspects of musical nationalism in the early 1950s (as in his *Quinteto No. 1*, 1954, for flute, oboe, clarinet, bassoon, and cello) but soon rejected it. In a few years he became one of the most radical experimentalists in Cuban music. He learned on his own the techniques of *musique concrète* and electronic music, which he was among the first Cubans to explore. His works of the 1960s and early 1970s involve either electronic media, aleatory procedures, or mixed media. His *Música para danza* (1961) and *Estudios I-II* (1962–1963) are electronic pieces; chance operations appear in *Texturas* (1963–1964), for orchestra and tape, and *Episodios* (1964), for orchestra. *Contrapunto espacial I* ("Spatial counterpoint I") (1965–1966), for organ, three wind groups, and four percussion groups, initiates a series of five major works belonging to so-called spatial music, i.e., music in which the actual location of the sound sources, live or recorded but generally transmitted through loudspeakers, is integral to the structure of the work. The impression of sound moving through space is accomplished by recording sounds on different channels so as to be able to transfer them rapidly from one speaker to another or, more traditionally, by dividing the performing forces (voices or instruments) into broadly separated units. Blanco experiments with these techniques in *Poema espacial No. 3* (subtitled *Viet-Nam*), dating from around 1968, which incorporates sound and light and includes four tape tracks distributed to thirty-seven loudspeakers during the actual performance. In *Contrapunto espacial II*, also known as *Erotofonías* (1968), Blanco divides sixty string instruments into twenty groups and reinforces them with five percussion groups, guitar, alto saxophone, and three tape tracks based on recited passages from the Song of Solomon. In 1969 and 1970, he went one step further with *Contrapunto espacial III* and *Contrapunto espacial IV*, respectively subtitled *Si, no: y qué?* and *Boomerang*, and combined the spatial concept with that of theater music. These works call for ten to twenty actors, five to twenty-four instrumental groups dispersed over the performance area, and tapes. The more recent *Erotofonías II* (1974), on two tape tracks, is much less ambitious.

Aurelio de la Vega (b. 1925) is, together with Julián Orbón, the best known Cuban composer of his generation. He first studied law at the University of Havana, then music at the Instituto Musical Ada Iglesias in Havana (1950–1955), under Gramatges. While in Los Angeles as cultural attaché to the Cuban Consulate he took private lessons in composition with Ernst Toch. From 1953 to 1959 he directed the music department at the University of Oriente (Santiago de Cuba). Since 1959 he has been living in California as professor of composition at San Fernando Valley State College (later renamed California State University, Northridge). After an early affiliation with post-Impressionism and the modernistic Romanticism of Szymanowski as in the song cycle *La fuente infinita* (1944), de la Vega turned in the early 1950s to a highly chromatic language combined with a strong rhythmic drive. He also developed some technical concerns that were to remain important to him, particularly a virtuoso style of writing for traditional instruments (and consequently a special attention to timbre) and a strong reliance on structural principles. Although he voiced his opposition to musical nationalism, he used typical Cuban melodic and rhythmic traits in some of his early works, for example, his *Leyenda del Ariel Criollo* (1953), for cello and piano. The chromatic harmony of this work, however, dilutes considerably its nationalist character.

Together with such chromaticism, de la Vega cultivated free atonality (e.g., *Elegy*, 1954, for string orchestra, and *Divertimento*, 1956, for violin, cello, piano, and string orchestra). In 1957, he began developing a style of unconventional twelve-tone technique with the String Quartet "In Memoriam Alban Berg." With this style came an increasing use of polyphony, which culminated in the Symphony in Four Parts (1960). Around the mid-1960s, de la Vega gradually abandoned serialism for electronic means, open forms, and aleatory procedures and graphic scores. One of the earliest works indicating that direction is *Structures* (1962), for piano and string quartet, which presents serialism in three of its movements and improvisatory structures in the other two. At the same time, de la Vega continued to explore new sonorities. The early electronic piece *Vectors* (1963) was followed by *Segments* (1964), for violin and piano, *Variants* (1964), for piano, and *Interpolation* (1965), for solo clarinet with or without prerecorded sound elements. The instrumental resources called for in these works include microtonal vibrato for the violin, tone clusters and various types of manipulation of the piano strings, and use of clarinet keys as sound sources. In addition, *Interpolation* requires different types of embouchure positions (meticulously notated and explained), the fingering of a note without sounding it, breath sounds without specific pitch, and even the use of a specially devised mute for the clarinet. Nowhere has de la Vega been so successful, however, in terms of expressive color blendings and structural organization as in *Tangents*, for violin and prerecorded sounds, and *Para-Tangents*, for trumpet and the same prerecorded sounds. Both works (1973) explore the timbres and the expressive aspects of the solo instruments in a dialogue with the electronic sounds. Both are virtuoso pieces covering the most extreme ranges of the instruments and requiring many different types of articulations, attacks, and phrasing. In both instrumental and electronic parts, motivic elements are presented and developed. In *Tangents* these motifs have the character of abrupt and exclamatory utterances whose expressiveness emanates especially from chromaticism and wide range (Example 10-9). Particularly effective is the treatment of the timbral possibilities of the violin. Trills, tremolos, wide vibrato, glissandos, mutes, harmonics, and other devices often suggest an

EXAMPLE 10-9 Aurelio de la Vega, *Tangents*, beginning. Copyright 1973 by Aurelio de la Vega. International copyright secured. Used by permission.

"electronic" manipulation of the instrument. Aleatory procedures are employed in these works, but de la Vega really committed himself to indeterminacy only in the later *Olep ed Arudamot* (1974) (the retrograde form of "Tomadura de pelo," or "Pulling one's leg"), for nonspecific instrumentation (first realization in 1976), and *The Infinite Square* (1974); both are graphic scores.

Carlos Fariñas (b. 1934) and Leo Brouwer (b. 1939) also show avant-garde stylistic development. Most of their early works (middle to late 1950s) stemmed from nationalist musical interests; these were followed by a penetration into serialist esthetics. Fariñas's Sonata for violin and cello derives from twelve-tone techniques, while his *Tientos* for small instrumental ensembles are aleatory. Brouwer is one of the most talented composers of the Cuban avant-garde. His early nationalist concern is well expressed in the guitar pieces *Danza característica* (1958) and *Tres apuntes* (1959) (he is an excellent guitar player) and in the Trio (1960) for two violins and viola, in five sections. Rhythmic patterns involving syncopations, often set against regularly pulsating figures, constitute the most obvious national trait of the Trio. After the Cuban Revolution, Brouwer's contacts with the contemporary Polish avant-garde (Penderecki, Lutoslawski) and with Luigi Nono prompted him to adopt more readily new-music techniques; the music and ideas of Cage and Xenakis have also been influential. Since about 1962 he has written in a post-serialist and aleatory manner. His *Sonograma I* (1963), for prepared piano, is generally acknowledged as the first piece of aleatory music in Cuba. *Conmutaciones* (1966), for prepared piano and two percussionists, is written entirely in graphic notation. In the late 1960s Brouwer began cultivating mixed media, first with *Cantigas del tiempo nuevo* (1969), which includes actors, children's chorus, piano, harp, and percussion.

Other Cuban composers who have studied in Poland or Czechoslovakia, such as Roberto Valera (b. 1938) and Sergio Fernández (b. 1946), have contributed to the dynamic development of the Cuban avant-garde, but few of their works have been heard outside Cuba and Eastern Europe.

Since about 1946 the Panamanian Roque Cordero has written his most significant works in an almost exclusively serialist idiom. He first used the twelve-tone method of composition in his Sonatina for Violin and Piano (1946). The basic set utilized in all three movements of the work (expressed thematically as in Example 10-10) consists of major and minor thirds, minor

EXAMPLE 10-10   Roque Cordero, *Sonatina*, first movement, mm. 1–5. Copyright 1962 by Peer International Corporation. Used by permission.

seconds, and their inversions; it is used freely, i.e., with melodic and harmonic repetitions and many octave doublings. Characteristic of Cordero's style is the frequent melodic and harmonic occurrence of the seventh.[6] The basic forms of the set are used, with occasional transpositions, the pitches frequently distributed between the two instruments. Example 10-11 illustrates the simultaneous use of various aspects of the set: R_3 (retrograde transposed down a major third) and R_0 in the violin part, partial versions of R_0 in the piano accompaniment.[7] The parallel thirds that result from the two parallel rows are not distinguishable to the ear because the parts move independently of each other.[8] Contrapuntal texture in which the parts are built from several forms of the set appears quite often. The formal designs of the Sonatina's movements are traditional—respectively, sonata-allegro, binary, and rondo. Some passages of the first and third movements contain rhythmic patterns associated with Latin American folk music, such as the habanera rhythm, the syncopation ♪♩♪, the Cuban *tresillo*, and the simultaneous or successive combination of 6/8 and 3/4 meters.

Cordero's Second Symphony (1956) exemplifies his mature serialist writing. Complete in one movement, the symphony is based on three related tone rows, which are freely treated, and follows a compound sonata form. One trait of this work typical of Cordero is its frequent ostinatos, one of which is derived from the rhythm of the Afro-Panamanian and Colombian dance known as *cumbia*.[9] During the 1960s Cordero refined his serialist techniques, while retaining the same general characteristic traits, with the exception of an increased concern for timbral effects and rhythmic intricacies. In more than one respect the First String Quartet (1960), the Violin Concerto (1962), the Sonata for cello and piano (1963), and the Third Symphony (1965) show analogous treatment of rhythm, with the previously mentioned Latin flavor of hemiola, but also a new irregularity of punctuation and phrasing.

The Violin Concerto is a truly virtuoso work, with a technically very demanding solo part which pauses rarely. The orchestra is also treated in a virtuoso manner, particularly in the last two movements. In the second (slow) movement, it is reduced to a chamber ensemble; it emphasizes short solo passages for winds and blends unusual colors, such as violin harmonics and clarinet in low register at the end of the movement. The third movement opens with effective ostinato solos by the timpani. The concerto is based on a twelve-tone set that opens with a major seventh, an interval characteristic of

---

[6]Ronald R. Sider, "Roque Cordero, the Composer and his Style Seen in Three Representative Works," *Inter-American Music Bulletin*, no. 61 (September 1967), 6.

[7]After Sider, "Roque Cordero." Sider's analysis of Cordero's music derives from the composer himself.

[8]Ibid.

[9]For more detailed analytical comments, see ibid., pp. 8–17.

EXAMPLE 10-11   Roque Cordero, *Sonatina*, first movement, mm. 87–95. Copyright 1962 by Peer International Corporation. Used by permission.

Cordero's previous music. (See the violin part in Example 10-12). The first theme of the first movement, based on the original form of the row, stresses the sevenths by repeating the appropriate tones of the series. The theme appears throughout the movement in various forms and various transpositions of the set, such as O_6 at measures 24–27 of Example 10-12. The development section exhibits much contrapuntal texture and rhythmic variety. The retrograde form of the set (R_0), presented first by the flute, makes up the

EXAMPLE 10-12 Roque Cordero, *Concerto* for Violin and Orchestra (reduction for violin and piano), first movement, mm. 20–29. Copyright 1969 by Peer International Corporation. Used by permission.

second theme (mm. 116–121) of this sonata-form design. Cordero's later works (Symphony No. 3, 1965; String Quartets nos. 2 and 3, 1968, 1973; Concertino for viola and string orchestra, 1968; *Permutaciones*, 1974; Variations and Theme for Five, 1975) consolidate his strong individuality in handling the serial technique while retaining a Latin accent without being nationalist.

Most other Central American composers have cultivated a style often based on indigenous, mestizo, or Black musical expressions of their countries, often mixed with a Romantic idiom or an Impressionistic language. The first generations of composers following this trend include Jesús Castillo (1877–1946), the dean of Guatemalan professional composers, Ricardo Castillo (1894–1967), Salvador Ley (b. 1907), and Enrique Solares (b. 1910)—all from Guatemala—and the Nicaraguan Luis A. Delgadillo (1887–1964). Other trends, however, have not been neglected. José Castañeda (b. 1898), for example, was an early experimenter in polytonality, microtonality, and serialism in Guatemala. Younger composers throughout the Central American area have paid attention to non-nationalist currents. To mention but a few, Jorge Sarmientos (b. 1933), a Guatemalan who studied at the Di Tella Institute of Buenos Aires, has used serial techniques; Bernal Flores (b. 1937), from Costa Rica, a graduate of the Eastman School of Music, has written in an atonal style; and Gilberto Orellana (b. 1942), from El Salvador, has experimented with serial techniques.

Up to about the mid-1960s Venezuelan music generally followed the nationalist trend, combined with some neo-Romantic or neo-Classic elements. With the establishment of the Instituto Nacional de Cultura y Bellas Artes (INCIBA), which promoted national prizes for composition and commissioned works, the appearance of the Caracas Music Festivals, and the creation of a laboratory of electronic music, together with the publication of a bulletin (under the direction of the music critic Eduardo Lira Espejo), music in Venezuela found a suitable atmosphere for the development of contemporary techniques of composition. The composers most in evidence during the late 1960s were Antonio Estévez (b. 1916), who, after an early nationalist period (e.g., his *Cantata Criolla*, 1954), turned to the electronic medium in such works as *Cosmovibrafonía I* and *Cosmovibrafonía II*, both of 1970; Rhazes Hernández López (b. 1918), who adhered to serialism and free atonality; José Luis Muñoz (b. 1928), who used aleatory techniques in such a work as *Móviles* (1967); and Alexis Rago (b. 1920), who wrote in a neo-tonal, chromatically linear style (*Cinco Instantes para orquesta*, 1968; *Mítica de Sueños y Cosmogonías* for wind quintet, 1968). A younger composer, Alfredo del Mónaco (b. 1938), has cultivated electronic music successfully (*Cromofonías I*, 1967; *Tres Ambientes Coreográficos*, 1970) and has tried his hand at electronic music through computer (*Synus-17/251271*, 1972). Since 1969 the Greek composer Yannis Ioannidis (b. 1930) has been in

Caracas as the director of the INCIBA Chamber Orchestra and as professor of composition at the Institute Intermusica. His influence in exposing young Venezuelan composers to contemporary music has been very beneficial. He received his own training in composition at the Vienna Hochschule für Musik and has cultivated primarily an atonal style.

The Puerto Rican Héctor Campos-Parsi, who began as a nationalist composer (see Chapter 5), turned to neo-Classicism in the 1950s and to atonality and serialism in the 1960s. His Sonata in G for Piano (1952–1953) is an example of the transition from a nationalist to a neo-Classic idiom. Later works by him include the two vocal pieces *Columnas y círculos* (1966 and 1967), *Kolayia* (1963) for orchestra, percussion, and tape, *Dúo trágico* (1965) for piano and orchestra and *Petroglifos* (1966) for string trio. The Puerto Rican composer of the 1930s generation who adhered most firmly to new-music techniques in the 1960s was Rafael Aponte-Ledée (b. 1938). A student of Cristóbal Halffter at the Madrid Conservatory and Alberto Ginastera and Gerardo Gandini at the Buenos Aires Torcuato Di Tella Institute, he has followed several trends including serialism, electronic music, and indeterminacy (*Presagio de pájaros muertos*, 1966, for actor and tape; *Impulsos . . . in memoriam Julia de Burgos*, 1967, for orchestra; *La Ventana abierta*, in two versions, 1968–1969; and *SSSSSS²*, for solo double bass, three flutes, trumpet, and percussion, 1971).

THE ANDEAN AREA

With the exception of Chile and to a lesser extent Peru, the Andean countries have not been able since 1950 to develop musical institutions capable of sustaining a flourishing creative activity in contemporary music. The institutions of musical learning, such as the Bogotá and Quito National Conservatories, have not provided training in composition conducive to innovative attitudes. For this reason the few progressive composers from Colombia and Ecuador who emerged in the 1960s have studied, and in some cases settled, abroad.

Colombian representatives of contemporary techniques include Fabio González-Zuleta, Luis Antonio Escobar, Blas Emilio Atehortúa, and Jacqueline Nova. González-Zuleta (b. 1920) has cultivated the classic forms together with polytonal, atonal, and serial elements (Violin Concerto, 1958; Third Symphony, 1961; and *Quinteto Abstracto* for woodwinds, 1961). Although Escobar (b. 1925) drew on national sources in many of his works of the 1950s (see Chapter 6), he later appeared primarily as a neo-Classicist (*Pequeña Sinfonía*, 1960, and the opera for solo voices, chorus, and percussion *Los Hampones*, 1961). Atehortúa, a student at the Torcuato Di Tella Institute of Buenos Aires in 1963–1964 and 1966–1968, was recognized by the mid-1960s as one of Colombia's foremost avant-garde composers. His music combines a rich rhythmic imagination with effective color blendings, especially those involving percussion (as in *Concertante* for timpani and string orchestra, 1968). He writes only occasionally for voices (*Cántico delle creature*, for bass, two choruses, winds, string basses, percussion, and tape, 1965) and uses serialist techniques freely in some of his works (*Cinco Piezas Breves*, 1969; *Partita 72*, 1972). The Belgian-born Nova (b. 1938), also a student of Ginastera at the Torcuato Di Tella Institute, represents the most radical trend in Colombian new music. Although she has not written a great deal, her works (such as *12 Móviles* for chamber ensemble, 1966) have gained fairly wide recognition.

The only Ecuadorian composer since 1950 who has developed along lines of experimental esthetics is Mesías Maiguashca (b. 1938). After an early training at the Quito National Conservatory, he studied at the Eastman School of Music, then at the Torcuato Di Tella in Buenos Aires. He worked in close contact with Stockhausen (1968–1972) as a collaborator at the Electronic Music Studio of the German Broadcasting System in Cologne. His first European sojourn made such an impact on him that he decided to reside in Germany permanently as a free-lance composer. His discovery at that time of electro-acoustic techniques and his experiments in the Cologne Electronic Studio led to such major works as *Hör Zu* (1969) on tape, *A Mouth Piece* (1970) for amplified voices, and *Ayayayayay* (1971) on tape. Other works written by him in Germany include the Second String Quartet (1967), with live electronics, and *Dort wo wir leben* (1967), a documentary film score. Besides his successful *Übungen für Synthesizer* (1972), he has been working also in mixed media, as in *Oeldorf 8* (1973) for four instrumentalists and four-track tape.

In Peru, while Holzmann refined the neo-Classic style that he had developed in the 1940s (e.g., in Partita for strings, 1957) and eventually tried his hand at twelve-tone writing, some of his students gave Peruvian music a truly contemporary character during the 1960s. Particularly significant in this development have been Enrique Iturriaga, Celso Garrido Lecca,[10] Enrique Pinilla, Francisco Pulgar Vidal, Leopoldo La Rosa, José Malsio, and especially César Bolaños and Edgar Valcárcel. Born in the 1920s and 1930s, these composers advocate a clear anti-nationalist attitude but are also conscious of the need to assert a Latin American personality in their new music by reflecting the special conditions in which this music is created. Admittedly rather subjective and vague, this attitude has nevertheless motivated them to a cultivation of contemporary styles treated in a unique

---

[10]Because he has been a resident of Chile, he is often considered an exponent of Chilean contemporary music. See Roberto Escobar, *Músicos sin pasado* (Santiago de Chile: Editorial Pomaire, 1970).

manner. Iturriaga (b. 1918) exemplifies this. A student of Holzmann at the National Conservatory and of Arthur Honegger in Paris, Iturriaga displays in his works an attempt at integration of native and European elements. For example, the major-minor modal effect of several of his works resulting from the use of successive parallel major and minor thirds has been shown to be characteristic of the popular music of Arequipa (known locally as "terceras arequipeñas"); yet such an effect is also common in neo-Classic works of the 1930s. The *Suite para Orquesta* (1957), which won first prize in the Caracas Inter-American Music Festival in 1957, exhibits polytonal writing and an original rhythmic vitality. In the 1960s, Iturriaga turned his attention to serialism. *Vivencias* ("Cuatro Fragmentos para orquesta") of 1965 shows Webernian influences, not only in its serialist construction but in the treatment of timbres. As a teacher of composition, Iturriaga has had a powerful influence in Peru.

A student at the conservatories of Lima (under Holzmann and Sas) and Santiago, Chile (under Free Focke and Santa Cruz), Garrido Lecca (b. 1926) developed a style in which contemporary European musical practices (quartal or quintal harmonies, atonality) and locally derived musical traits (use of pentatonic scales) converge—for example, in his Suite for woodwind quintet (1956) and his *Música para seis instrumentos i percusión* (1956). After about 1960 he turned to some aspects of the twelve-tone method, concentrating on orchestral writing (*Sinfonía*, 1960; *Laudes*, 1962). In the 1960s he also wrote several works evoking Peruvian history and culture but without utilizing any national musical material (*Elegía a Machu Picchu*, 1965, for orchestra; *Apu Inca Atahualpaman* for soloists, narrator, three choruses, and orchestra, setting an anonymous Quechua text from the colonial period; *Intihuatana*, 1967, for string quartet; and *Antaras*, 1969–1970, for double string quartet and double bass).

A student of Holzmann and Sas in Lima, then of Nadia Boulanger in Paris, Conrado del Campo in Madrid, and Boris Blacher in Berlin, Enrique Pinilla (b. 1927) has put into practice his conviction that the modern composer should try his hand at all techniques available to him. Thus he has cultivated a polytonal and atonal language and, later, serialist and electronic music procedures. A special concern of his, developed after his studies with Blacher, has been the careful treatment of variable meters, i.e., the systematic shifting of meters (2/4, 3/4, 4/4, 5/4, etc.). He effectively explores rhythmic and metrical variations in *Estudio sobre el ritmo de la marinera* ("Study on the rhythm of the *marinera*"), for piano (1959). His works of the 1960s reveal further elaborations of complex rhythms (e.g., Three Movements, for percussion and piano, 1961) and complex orchestration, which includes the superimposition of contrasted and at times unrelated textures (*Canto para Orquesta, No, 1*, 1963; *Festejo*, 1966; and *Evoluciones No. 1*, 1967). In 1966–1967, Pinilla worked with Vladimir Ussachevsky at the Columbia-Princeton

Electronic Music Center. However, this interest in the electronic medium, which resulted in the work *Prismas* (1967), does not seem to have been maintained in subsequent years. Pinilla also adhered for a time to serialism but tended to restrict the use of the method to pitch. He also exploited Alban Berg's device of *Hauptrhythmen* ("principal rhythmic motives") but treated the basic rhythmic motives as if he were developing conventional melodic material (e.g., in his Four Pieces for Orchestra, 1961).[11]

Francisco Pulgar Vidal (b. 1929) and Leopoldo La Rosa (b. 1931) have written in a neo-nationalist vein but also have cultivated freely twelve-tone and other techniques. Pulgar Vidal's inspiration in native sources takes the form of microtonal discoveries in Indian instruments or of new sonorities achieved by treating traditional instruments (e.g., the Inca panpipes known as *antaras*) in unusual, massive combinations. Abstract evocations of Peruvian themes form the substance of several later works, such as *Chulpas* (Seven Symphonic Structures) (1968), *Eleven Choral Pieces* on traditional Peruvian motifs (1968), and the cantata *Apu Inqa* (1970). La Rosa, in the early 1970s, used aleatoric devices in some of his works.

Pantonality and polytonality appear in the works of the 1950s of José Malsio (b. 1924), a student of Hindemith at Yale University and of Schoenberg in Los Angeles. His early neo-Classic language (as in the Concerto Grosso of 1945 and *Preludio y Toccata*, 1952, for piano) was followed by some experiments in atonal writing and electronic music.

César Bolaños (b. 1931) represents, together with Edgar Valcárcel, the progressive avant-garde of Peruvian music. Bolaños studied under Sas at the Lima Conservatory and went on to New York to study electronic music at the RCA Institute of Electronic Technology (1958–1963). He continued his studies with Ginastera at the Torcuato Di Tella Institute in Buenos Aires, where he collaborated in the Laboratory of Electronic Music (founded in 1964). There he was responsible for the seminar on composition by electronic means, and until 1970 he gave a course on audio-visual theory and practice at the Institute. Since that year he has carried out experiments, at Honeywell Bull Argentina, in the application of computers to music composition. (Works created through that process have been referred to generically as ESEPCO, from "Estructuras Sonoro-Expresivas por Computación.") Thus, from the very beginning of his career Bolaños oriented his activity as a composer towards experimental music in the electronic medium and towards indeterminacy. His first electronic piece—*Intensidad y Altura*, on tape, based on a poem by César Vallejo—was elaborated at the Di Tella Institute in 1964. Subsequently he produced various works for dance, theater, and film calling for live electronics, such as *Lutero, Yavi* (1965), *Dos en el Mundo*

---

[11]Cf. Juan Orrego-Salas, "Serialism in Latin American Music," paper presented at the thirty-fifth Annual Meeting of the American Musicological Society (St. Louis, Missouri, December 1969), kindly communicated by the author.

(1966), and *Espacios I, II,* and *III* (1966–1968). The computer applications in some of his works include the use both of computers as generators of electronic sounds and of precompositional structures, for example, in works such as *Sialoecibi* (ESEPCO I), for piano and a narrator-mime-actor, and *Canción sin Palabras* (ESEPCO II), subtitled "Homage to non-pronounced words," for piano with two players and tape. In these and other works Bolaños put into practice the avant-garde concept of music theater in which the stage action is an integral part of the instrumental performance. This is true, for example, of *Divertimento III* (1967), for flute, clarinet, bass clarinet, piano, silent harp, and percussion. The action has been described in the following terms:

> [*Divertimento*] . . . turned out to be a sort of burlesque concerto in motion for the piano-percussionist, who first belabors a defenseless Steinway inside out, top to bottom, then walks to the sidelines, stuffs a pipe with tobacco, rotates a harp 180 degrees, and then—forgetting both pipe and harp—returns to the attack on the piano with increased vigor. Meanwhile, the other three artists are adding piquant sounds, including occasional vocalized syllables, to the general furore. At a certain point, the three walk off stage à la Haydn's Farewell Symphony and cluster in front of the conductor, who is busy directing the piano-percussionist.[12]

Bolaños was also among the first Peruvians to use mixed media—which, in his case, involve a range of activities from performance-theatrical actions to abstract audio-visual environmental movements. Works of this nature include *Alfa-Omega* (1967) on biblical texts, calling for a theatrical mixed chorus, among other performing forces, and *I-10-AIFG/Rbt-1* (1968), with visual materials, in which the performers (three narrators, horn, trombone, electric guitar, two percussionists, and two operators of electronic instruments) are directed through light signals previously programmed and synchronized by an automatic system. Multiple layers of sound produced in an aleatory manner by twenty-one or more instrumentalists, and of words taken from Ernesto "Che" Guevara's diary of his guerrilla campaign in Bolivia, constitute the basis of Bolaños's *Ñacahuasu* (1970).

One of the most creative personalities of the Peruvian avant-garde is Edgar Valcárcel (b. 1932), who studied at the Lima National Conservatory, Hunter College in New York, and the Torcuato Di Tella Institute. He also studied electronic music under Ussachevsky and Alcides Lanza at the Columbia-Princeton Laboratory (1966–1968). His development as a composer is symptomatic of the Latin American composer of new music in general, in its assertion of the composer's intellectual freedom and its attempts to con-

---

[12]Irving Lowens, "The Fourth Inter-American Music Festival. Pianos and Ping-Pong Balls," *Inter-American Music Bulletin*, no. 66 (July 1968), 2.

tribute unique features to new music expressions. Valcárcel has cultivated various contemporary techniques, from dodecaphony to electronic and aleatory procedures. Among his most significant chamber works of the 1960s are *Espectros I* (1964) for flute, viola, and piano; *Espectros II* (1966) for horn, cello, and piano; *Dicotomías III* (1966) for twelve brass and string instruments; and *Hiwaña Uru* ("Day of the Dead" in Aymara) (1967), for eleven instruments. His orchestral works include *Aleaciones* (1966) and *Checán II* ("Love" in Mochica) (1970); among numerous vocal works, the *Canto Corral a Túpac Amaru II* (1968) is considered the most successful of those calling for mixed media. Valcárcel's electronic pieces, such as *Invención para sonidos electrónicos* (1966) and *Antaras* (1968), for flute, percussion, and electronic sounds, were elaborated at the Columbia-Princeton Laboratory.

Few composers in Bolivia have cultivated non-nationalist styles. The Bolivian art-music scene has lagged a great deal because of the lack of suitable institutions for the support of music-making. Thus, most Bolivian composers who developed an interest in contemporary music studied abroad and often felt alienated upon returning to their native country. The La Paz composer Jaime Mendoza Nava (b. 1925) got his training in Europe and North America and cultivated a neo-Classic style in which appear some elements of native music of the Bolivian plateau (pentatonicism and characteristic rhythms). Gustavo Navarre (b. 1932), a student at the Paris Ecole Normale de Musique, has created a neo-Romantic language combined at times with characteristic traits of Bolivian folk music. Atiliano Auza León (b. 1928) wrote at first in a neo-Classic vein but, following a year of study at the Di Tella Institute in Buenos Aires (1965), turned to twelve-tone technique. (His *Preludio, Invención, Passacaglia y Postludio* of 1966 is based on a row by Dallapiccola.) The most talented of the younger Bolivian composers is Alberto Villalpando (b. 1940). He studied composition in Buenos Aires under García Morillo and under Ginastera and others at the Di Tella Institute (1963); in 1971, he worked with Stockhausen at the Cologne studio. He began using serialism in his First String Quartet (1964) and *Variaciones Tímbricas* (1966), for soprano and chamber ensemble. Electronic and aleatory techniques penetrate his later works (*Danzas para una imagen perdida*, a ballet for orchestra, 1970; *Mística No. 3*, for instruments with contact microphones and tape, 1970; and *Mística No. 4*, for string quartet, piano, and tape, 1970).

A wide range of genres and styles has characterized Chilean composition since about 1950. The development of a flourishing musical life, especially in Santiago, since the 1920s encouraged dynamic activities which remained unrivaled in the Andean area. The University of Chile continued to be the main pillar supporting the country's musical vigor. As early as 1954 the first experiments in electronic music were initiated by the composers Juan Amenábar and José Vicente Asuar, who created in 1955 the Taller Experimental del Sonido (Experimental Sound Workshop) at the Catholic University in Santiago. Together they devised a project for a laboratory of electronic music in 1958. With the foundation of the Philharmonic Orchestra of Chile in 1955 (later renamed the Municipal Philharmonic), the establishment of several chamber ensembles at the Catholic University, and the introduction of commercial recordings of Chilean music and a series of score publications by the Instituto de Extensión Musical (1959), musical composition was strongly stimulated. Quantitatively and qualitatively, the production of Chilean music since 1950 has been extraordinary. The stylistic development of most composers incorporates several countercurrents. Only a few characteristic examples can be sketched here.

Domingo Santa Cruz continued to cultivate his neo-Classic style, characterized by contrapuntal textures and linear chromaticism. He did not write as much, however, as during the previous decades. His Opus 28 (*Seis Canciones de Primavera*) dates from 1950, Opus 32 (*Endechas*) from 1960, and Opus 37 (*Oratio Jeremiae Prophetae*) from 1970. Although he maintained the tonal foundation of his previous works, he wrote in an increasingly dissonant harmony and textural complexity. At the same time his dramatic and highly expressionist sense seemed to be reinforced during this period. His String Quartet No. 3 (Op. 31, 1959), for example, bears witness: the total chromaticism in some passages seems to obliterate a strong sense of tonality, yet traditional compositional techniques (imitation, melodic inversion, harmonic pedals, variation techniques, and others) are present. The complex textural density of this quartet (Example 10-13) reappears in later works such as the Symphonies No. 3 and No. 5, of 1965 and 1968, respectively.

The period after 1950 was a very productive and successful one for Juan Orrego-Salas. A brief examination of a few of his works will illustrate his stylistic development. The neo-Classic elements we observed in previous works (see Chapter 9), such as a preference for Baroque and Classic genres and forms, modal linear writing, and rhythmic drive, remain the underlying basis of his style. But the early uniform and orderly melodic quality gives way to more disjunct and rhythmically irregular organization, and quartal harmony, altered chords, added-tone formations, and clusters make the tonal relationships less obvious. With his adoption of twelve-tone procedures (restricted, however, to pitch selection, without application of serial techniques as such) atonality prevails in Orrego-Salas's later works. The rhythms remain energetic but become less regular. Variable meters and occasionally free-metered passages occur frequently. The Symphony No. 2 (1954), Op. 39 ("To the Memory of a Wanderer") is not a programmatic work, despite the circumstances of its composition—the tragic death of a friend of the composer in the mountains of Machu-Picchu in Peru. In the first movement Orrego-Salas intended to express rhythmically and melodically "what could appear as a synthesis of Latin American folk dances." Indeed, syncopated

EXAMPLE 10-13   Domingo Santa Cruz, *Cuarteto No. 3*, Op. 31, first movement, mm. 180–85. Copyright 1970 by Peer International Corporation. Used by permission.

patterns often contrasted with regular pulsations, and isometric-ostinato passages throughout the movement suggest that intention. The first motif of the slow introduction displays the typical syncopation which epitomizes so much Latin American dance music (Example 10-14).

EXAMPLE 10-14 Juan Orrego-Salas, *Symphony No. 2*, Op. 39, first movement, mm. 1–4. Copyright 1977 by Peer International Corporation. Used by permission.

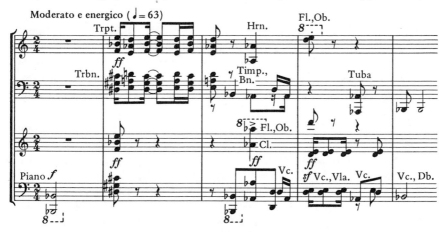

The second movement—Maestoso—is written in the spirit of a funeral march and presents extended lyrical melodies (entrusted to the French horn) and a development section worked out in the style of a chorale-prelude. Particularly characteristic of Orrego-Salas's style is the perpetual motion of the third movement, which also reveals a highly virtuosic and imaginative orchestration. That motion is assured by an ostinato figure in sixteenth-note values. This symphony is in many respects a summary of the composer's achievements up to 1954. Harmonically it is still very tonal, rhythmically very regular. Technical craft is evident in the classical procedures of thematic development (fragmentation, sequence, canonic imitations), formal structures (sonata form, rondo-sonata form), and harmonic practices (chorale-like harmonizations).[13]

Orrego-Salas's *Sonata A Quattro*, Op. 55 (1964), reveals well the maturity of his musical thought. The "Baroque" instruments implied by the title are flute, oboe, harpsichord, and double bass; the movements are "Intrada," "Aria," "Perpetuum Mobile," and "Cadenze e Varianti." In each, formal clarity and balance are maximized. Each part is treated soloistically, with the woodwinds imitating or complementing each other; even the bass part is given prominent passages. Neo-Baroque traits include prevailing polyphonic textures and use of ostinatos, figurations, and ornamentations. Of special interest are the achievements involving rhythm and timbre. Irregular rhythmic aggregates become almost the rule here. The first move-

---

[13]For an analysis of another work of the same period, see María Ester Grebe, "Sexteto de Juan Orrego Salas, para clarinete en Si Bemol, cuarteto de cuerdas y piano," *Revista Musical Chilena*, no. 58 (March–April 1958), 59–76.

ment, for example, derives some of its stimulative appeal from its 5/8 meter, which divides the main motif into units of three plus two. Similarly, a well-timed shift to triple meter, interrupting the constant sixteenth-note ostinato in duple meter of the third movement (Example 10-15), adds much excitement to the *perpetuum mobile*. Variable meters occur in the last section of the last movement, together with the alternation of 6/8 and 3/4 that is found also in Orrego-Salas's earlier works. Artful handling of timbres with original instrumental effects, a special concern of the composer, is apparent in the sonata. Several harpsichord stops are called for. Flutter-tonguing generally occurs on tremolos. The double-bass range is considerably extended through the use of harmonics which, in some passages, are applied to tremolos and glissandi. Quite unusual is the blending of the harpsichord's low register with the double bass. In the "Cadenze e Varianti movement," the lack of sustained tone by the harpsichord is compensated for by wide arpeggiations. Other works of the same period by Orrego-Salas stress tone color equally. An extreme example is found in the last few measures of the Piano Sonata, Op. 60 (1967), in which the pianist is directed to stop the F♯ string with the left hand inside the soundboard and to strike the key with the right hand: five such F♯s, each with a different dynamic (*p, meno, pp, meno, ppp*) complete the sonata.

Orrego-Salas also writes skillfully for voices. The monumental *Missa* "In Tempore Discordiae," Op. 64 (1968–1969), for mixed chorus, tenor, and orchestra, exhibits a well-balanced choral writing in which homophonic texture predominates. Effects such as free-metered recitatives for the soloist and the chorus (in unison) and quasi-*parlando* and murmuring techniques reinforce the dramatically refined character of this work. Some aleatory procedures appear in it, although sparingly. *Palabras de Don Quijote*, Op. 66 (1970–1971), for baritone and chamber ensemble, in four scenes, can be performed as a pantomime or monodrama. The vocal line is particularly disjunct and chromatic, at times even atonal. Only occasionally (for instance, in the third scene, "A Sancho") do we find the arabesque type of Spanish melody of Orrego-Salas's early vocal works. A neo-Baroque coloristic orchestration is conveyed by blending harp, harpsichord, and guitar, as in the scene "A Dulcinea" (mm. 46 ff). Another monumental choral symphonic work is the oratorio *The Days of God* (1975), for mixed chorus, vocal soloists, and orchestra.

In more recent works, Orrego-Salas tends to write in an atonal vein but continues his experiments with sound coloring. *Presencias*, Op. 72 (1972), for example, for flute, oboe, clarinet, harpsichord, violin, viola, and cello, begins with a twelve-tone row and in some passages calls for finger-tapping on the string instruments' soundboards. In addition, isolated short motifs, notes, or sparse chords are given their own timbres, articulations, and dynamic levels. The whole work is written, however, in a most economical manner and reveals the fruition of Orrego-Salas's considerable maturity.

EXAMPLE 10-15. Juan Orrego-Salas, *Sonata a Quattro*, Op. 55: "Perpetuum Mobile," mm. 80–87. Copyright 1967 by Peer International Corporation. Used by permission.

Among the Chilean composers of the 1920s generation Gustavo Becerra-Schmidt (b. 1925) has been one of the most successful and articulate. He received his training at the University of Chile and at the Santiago National Conservatory (studying composition with Allende and Santa Cruz). Since 1947 he has taught composition at the University of Chile. Between 1953 and 1956 he visited several European conservatories to learn about various methods of teaching composition. He was the director of the Instituto de Extensión Musical at the University from 1958 to 1961; he also acted as Secretary of the Facultad de Ciencias y Artes Musicales. He has served for some time as cultural attaché of the Chilean Embassy in Bonn. His works cover a wide range of genres and styles. He began in the early 1950s by cultivating a neo-Classic idiom, with traditional Classic forms, modal harmonies and melodies, and regular rhythmic groupings. Examples of this style are the Violin Concerto (1950) and the First String Quartet (1950). The second movement of the latter, however, is based on a twelve-tone row used in imitation, as can be seen in Example 10-16.[14]

Yet, occasional atonal passages such as this do not seem unsuitable within the main neo-Classic context of Becerra-Schmidt's music. From about 1955 he adopted the serialist method of composition; this resulted in an atonal harmony, but he maintained classical formal concepts. To compensate for the lack of tonal structural elements, Becerra stressed thematic relationships and highly condensed form. Webernian influences are felt in his works of the mid-1950s such as the Third String Quartet (1955) and the Symphony

EXAMPLE 10-16   Gustavo Becerra-Schmidt, *String Quartet No. 1*, second movement, mm. 20–26.

[14]Cf. Luis Merino, "Los Cuartetos de Gustavo Becerra," *Revista Musical Chilena*, no. 92 (April–June 1965), 48. See also Tomás Lefever, "Lo Neoclásico en la obra de Gustavo Becerra," *Revista Musical Chilena*, nos. 119–20 (July–December 1972), 36–48.

No. 1 (1955–1958); pointillistic procedures appear clearly, for example, in the first movement of the quartet and the second of the symphony, while the third movement of the latter exhibits a *Klangfarbenmelodie*—"tone-color melody," a series of timbres used consistently as thematic material. From 1958 to the early 1960s Becerra loosened his previous serial method by combining it with what has been called a "complementary polychordal system."[15] This system also involves the twelve tones of the chromatic scale, which are divided into groups or "polychords" in such a manner as to obtain two polychords of six tones each, three of four tones each, and so forth. In addition, in the case of two polychords of six tones, the pitch organization of each can be varied according to the factorial of 6, making 720 possibilities available. Further variants include the alternation of both polychords according to the factorial of possibilities of each of them, thus providing a very wide spectrum of workability with pitch materials. Becerra felt that such a system was less restrictive than dodecaphony.[16]

Other characteristic traits of Becerra's music in this period are the use of melodic formulas from Jewish biblical cantillation (in his slow movements), an increased importance attached to counterpoint, a generally effusive character of first movements as opposed to the introspective nature of second movements, an overall summary content in last movements, and a deliberate attempt to reach a compromise between traditional and contemporary techniques. The quartets nos. 4, 5, and 6 and the Symphony No. 2 illustrate these traits. At the same time, Becerra showed a new concern for writing a less esoteric, more easily accessible type of music, although without concession. For this he tried to combine a traditional idiom (including aspects of European music, Chilean folk music, Javanese music, among others) with modern technical devices of composition. His Quartet No. 6 (1960), for example, begins with a stylization of some elements of Javanese gamelan music. In the presentation of the first theme, an eighth-note figure in the cello part represents the gamelan's percussion, each time on a different beat of the measure, at each repetition of the five-beat motif of the viola, which simulates the winds and strings of the Javanese orchestra; the second violin with its wide improvisatory line represents a woodwind solo passage (Example 10-17). A formal procedure that recurs frequently in this and other works of this period by Becerra is the formation of a second section of a given structure by making a retrograde of the first, or, in a sonata form, making the recapitulation the retrograde of the exposition.

During the 1960s Becerra introduced aleatory techniques in his works, as in the Third Symphony (1960), the Concertos nos. 1 and 2 for guitar (1964, 1968), the String Quartet No. 7 (1961), and the oratorio *Macchu*

[15]Luis Merino, "Los Cuartetos de Gustavo Becerra," p. 55.
[16]Ibid., p. 58.

EXAMPLE 10-17 Gustavo Becerra, *String Quartet No. 6*, first movement, first theme. From Luis Merino, "Los Cuartetos de Cuerda de Gustavo Becerra," *Revista Musical Chilena*, no. 92 (April–June 1965), 63.

Picchu (1966), on a poem by Pablo Neruda. He began by resorting to interchangeable structures (Quartet No. 7), then moved to open forms, controlled chance elements, and interpretative freedom. For this, he developed his own notational system, which he called "open notation" because it allowed several possible performing versions.[17] Example 10-18, from the oratorio *Macchu Picchu*, illustrates the type of frames used for durations and reiteration of materials: the material in the smaller frames is to be performed before proceeding to the next larger frames; an arrow indicates repetitions of the same processes until another arrow cancels the repetitions (Example 10-18).

Becerra's esthetic thought has been molded by his sociopolitical views and concerns. His choice of texts is significant in this respect. Influenced by Marxist philosophy, he has resorted to poems or texts by Chilean poets or writers such as Neruda, Gabriela Mistral, and Nicanor Parra, or to texts on such subjects as Lenin's death, guerrilla warfare, the Guatemalan revolutionary fight, the Vietnam war, and Allende's death (in such a work as *Chile 1973*, for voice and chamber orchestra). His is a modern esthetic philosophy—the result of experiences from the Third World—in which the

[17]See Hernán Ramírez, "Introducción a la grafía de Gustavo Becerra," *Revista Musical Chilena*, nos. 119–20 (July–December 1972), 60–81.

artist is conceived as a humanist and art as a form of superstructure, following Marx and Luckacs.[18]

The Chilean composers born in the 1930s and most representative of the musical avant-garde are León Schidlowsky and Fernando García. Schidlowsky (b. 1931) studied at the Santiago National Conservatory and the University of Chile. He also studied composition with Adolfo H. Allende and Free Focke in Santiago, and in Detmold, Germany (1952–1954). In 1955 he became a member of the Agrupación Tonus, a private musical association for new music, of which he became the director in 1957. He also directed the Instituto de Extensión Musical from 1963 to 1966 and was professor of composition at the University of Tel Aviv in the early 1970s. He has been influential as a composer conscious of his social function and deeply devoted to questions of a sociopolitical and religious nature. He has shown a particular concern for the misfortune of the Jewish people throughout the world, which accounts for the pronounced mysticism of many of his works. His profuse output reveals a phase of expressionist and dodecaphonic style (1952–1956) followed by one of adherence to total serialism (1959 to about 1963), then, since about 1964, one of utilization of aleatory procedures.[19] His first works, dating from 1952 (*Tres Trozos* and *Seis Miniaturas* for piano), were written under the influence of Schoenberg's and Webern's atonal expressionism. His early stylistic orientation was also towards irregular and asymmetric phrasing, predominant use of continuous variation and microstructures, formal freedom, and special attention to timbre and

EXAMPLE 10-18   Gustavo Becerra, *Macchu Picchu*, open notation. From Hernán Ramírez, "Introducción a la grafía de Gustavo Becerra," *Revista Musical Chilena*, nos. 119–20 (1972), 74.

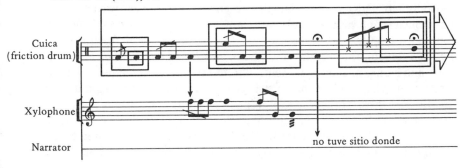

[18]See Melikof Karaian and Jorge Vergara, "Algunos aspectos de la posición cultural y estética de Gustavo Becerra," *Revista Musical Chilena*, nos. 119–20 (July–December 1972), 49–59. See also the essay by Becerra himself entitled "Becerra 1972," *Revista Musical Chilena*, nos. 119–20 (July–December 1972), 8–25.

[19]See María Ester Grebe, "León Schidlowsky Gaete. Síntesis de su Trayectoria Creativa (1952–1968)," *Revista Musical Chilena*, nos. 104–5 (April December 1968), p. 11.

dynamics. His studies with Hanns Jelinek, a student of Webern, oriented him towards a Webernian twelve-tone style in which a complex and compact texture and a punctilious observance of timbre variety predominate (as in *Seis Canciones Japonesas*, 1954, for voice and nine instruments). Several works of 1955 show also a pointillistic treatment of twelve-tone material, for example, the *Ocho Estructuras* for piano and the Trio for flute, cello, and piano.

Beginning around 1956, Schidlowsky reassessed his dodecaphonic methods and, while retaining them as a whole, gave new attention to timbre and rhythm. Thus he tried to incorporate polyrhythmic elements and new sonorities in such works as *Nacimiento* (1956), the earliest example of *musique concrète* in Chile, completely elaborated on tape, and *Cantata Negra*, for contralto, piano, and percussion (1957). The period of 1959–1963 saw the production of some works in which twelve-tone writing prevails as before, but with added emphasis on rhythm, and others in which total serialism operates. The latter are well represented by *Amatorias* (1962), for tenor and nine instruments, in which not only pitches are serialized but durations and dynamics also. The first eight measures of the first section (Example 10-19) illustrate the application of this process. Measures 1-5 present the serialization of pitches (RI_0) and durations (also in RI form), while measures 6-8 repeat the same serialization but this time in RI_4. Particularly significant is the different, independent serialization applied to dynamics, in a symmetrical arrangement of opposite levels (Ex. 10-19; qf and qp mean "quasi forte" and "quasi piano.")[20] Some aleatory techniques appear, for the first time, in three of the seven sections of the work.[21]

Schidlowsky's reliance on aleatory procedures was confined at first to the free juxtaposition of controlled elements; pitches and durations were generally left undetermined, but timbre and dynamics were predetermined. Tone clusters appear more frequently in works such as *Invocación* (1964), for soprano, narrator, and orchestra, and *Llaqui* (1965), for orchestra. *Cuatro Episodios* (1966), for narrator and piano, and *Estudiante Baleado* (1967), for voice and piano, introduce elements akin to new-music techniques, including direct manipulation of the piano strings and a mixture of singing and shouting. Both of these works also exhibit popular-music components in the form of rhythmic traits of the Chilean *cueca* (the national folk dance), the American twist, and the Argentine tango.[22] Schidlowsky used graphic notation for the first time in *Imprecaciones* (1967), for a cappella mixed chorus. Since then,

---

[20]Cf. ibid., p. 28.

[21]The use of aleatory procedures should not be construed as a contradiction to the concept of total serialism, since the latter rarely involves the total predetermination of all music parameters. Moreover, there is in the serial system an inherent factor of unpredictability—for example, in chord formations.

[22]María Ester Grebe, "León Schidlowsky," p. 36.

he has elaborated a complex system of notation, both explicit and free, corresponding to the varying problems inherent in each work.

Fernando García (b. 1930) and Miguel Aguilar-Ahumada (b. 1931) are among the many Chilean composers who have expressed themselves in a serial language. García studied trombone at the National Conservatory in Santiago and composition with Orrego-Salas, Botto, and Becerra. Like Becerra and Schidlowsky, he reveals a deep concern for sociopolitical conditions in the Third World. Several of his works of the 1960s use texts by

EXAMPLE 10-19 León Schidlowsky, *Amatorias*, first movement, mm. 1–8. After María Ester Grebe, "León Schidlowsky Gaete. Síntesis de su Trayectoria Creativa (1952–1968)," *Revista Musical Chilena*, nos. 104–5 (April–December 1958), 28.

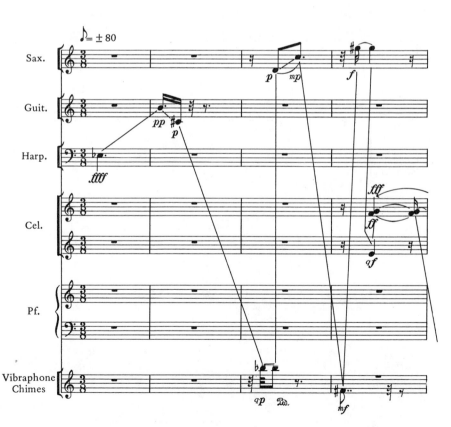

Pablo Neruda (*América Insurrecta*, 1962; *La Tierra Combatiente*, 1965) and other revolutionary writers (as in *Los Héroes Caídos Hablan*, 1968, which makes use of texts by Soviet fighters). His serial works reflect special care in treating tone color. Percussion and other timbral resources abound in such works as *Estáticas* (1963), for orchestra, and *Sombra del Paraíso* (1963), for tenor, clarinet, bassoon, violin, cello, and percussion.

Aguilar-Ahumada, who studied composition at the Santiago National Conservatory and conducting at the Cologne Hochschule für Musik (1963–1965), has been a rather eclectic composer. Up to about 1954 his music showed the influence of Hindemith, Bartók, and Stravinsky, mixed with the early expressionism of Schoenberg and Berg; next he cultivated a post-Webernian serialist style (*Microscopía No. 2*, for piano, 1957; *Umbral y Ambito*, for chamber ensemble, 1962). In 1965 he began to use aleatory procedures combined with electronic sounds. *Texturas* (1965), for example, calls for piano and concrete sounds on tape, while *Composición sobre tres sonidos* ("Composition on three sounds") (1965) is strictly an electronic piece; the three sounds are obtained from glasses containing liquid, from balloons, and from a tape synthesis of the sounds of a cow. His full-fledged interest in indeterminacy is seen in *Música aleatoria 1969*, for orchestra.

Chilean electronic music has had two major exponents: Juan Amenábar and José Vicente Asuar. Amenábar (b. 1922) has been active as a teacher and a composer of electronic music. He first experimented in the medium while he was working for Radio Chilena (1953–1956). He was responsible for the creation of the Experimental Workshop at the Catholic University in Santiago. His piece *Los peces* (1957)—generally considered the first tape composition in Latin America—was produced at this workshop. Later electronic works by him include *Klesis* (*Invitación*) (1969), the ballet music *El Vigía del Personal* (1968), *Música Contínua* (1969), and *Ludus Vocalis* (1971). He has also written many works in more traditional media and styles.

José Vicente Asuar (b. 1933) has been influential in the establishment of electronic music studios in several Latin American cities. A trained acoustic engineer, he came to music composition with a natural interest in sound experimentation. He studied with Urrutia-Blondel at the Santiago Conservatory, with Boris Blacher at the Berlin Hochschule für Musik, and privately with Meyer-Eppler. While in Germany (1960–1962) he attended the Darmstadt summer courses taught by Boulez, Stockhausen, Maderna, and Ligeti. After directing the electronic music studio of the Santiago Catholic University (1958–1959), he mounted and organized the electronic studio at Karlsruhe (1960–1962) and later (1965–1968) that at Caracas (which was called the "Estudio de Fonología Musical"). Since 1968, he has taught sound technology at the University of Chile. Asuar wrote his first electronic work, *Variaciones Espectrales*, in 1959 and continued to pay attention to the electronic medium during the 1960s, either by working exclusively on tape or by incorporating electronic sounds in works for instrumental ensembles. He generally treats the various electronic techniques with great freedom and flexibility, but he is very careful in structuring his materials. The piece *Preludio La Noche*, elaborated at the Karlsruhe electronic laboratory in 1961, uses pure sinusoidal signals and follows a well-defined formal scheme. In later works (*Estudio Aleatorio*, 1962; *La Noche II*, 1966; *Catedral*, 1967; and *Kaleidoscopio*, 1967) a larger range of signals, with the many signal modifiers and other apparatus available in electronic music technology, is put into action, always with a very sensitive approach to timing, timbral variety, and structure. In 1970, on a Fulbright grant, Asuar studied computer music with Lejaren Hiller at Buffalo. Since then he has elaborated computer scores programmed for traditional instrumental ensembles (such as *Formas I-II*, 1970–1972, for orchestra), and for complete electronic sound synthesis.[23]

ARGENTINA AND URUGUAY

There is no doubt that in Argentina (and especially the nation's capital, Buenos Aires) there developed after 1950 the most flourishing musical life in Latin America. This was due to the renewed vitality of previous institutions such as the Teatro Colón and the Asociación Wagneriana, the numerous state symphonic orchestras and concert-promoting associations, the upsurge of new-music activities in national and private universities, and the generally improved level of music instruction in both public and private institutions. Among the latter, the Latin American Center for Advanced Musical Studies at the Di Tella Institute of Buenos Aires was unique. Established in 1962 and directed by Alberto Ginastera, the Center offered two-year fellowships biannually to twelve composers from Latin America, contracted with world-renowned composers (e.g., Messiaen, Xenakis, Nono, Copland, Dallapiccola, and Ussachevsky) to conduct composition seminars, established an electronic music studio (directed by Francisco Kröpfl), and sponsored concerts and festivals of the faculty members' and fellows' works. Until it ceased to function in 1970, the Center promoted the most advanced techniques of composition of the time. It was unable to open its doors to all interested in new music, yet it made possible the gathering together of some of the most promising young composers of Latin America, thereby reducing the isolation in which they had previously found themselves.

Provincial music centers also developed in Argentina during the

---

[23]See José Vicente Asuar, "Música con computadores: ¿cómo hacerlo?," *Revista Musical Chilena*, no. 118 (April 1972), 36ff, and by the same author, "Haciendo música con un computador," *Revista Musical Chilena*, no. 123–24 (July–December 1973), 81ff.

1960s. The Instituto Superior de Música at the Rosario Universidad del Litoral initiated seminars and courses in new music, and in Córdoba a group for experimental music was incorporated into the School of Fine Arts (through the efforts of the composer Horacio Vaggione); it organized a remarkable series of concerts of new music of the Americas as part of the Third American Art Biennial of Córdoba (October 1966).

Buenos Aires saw the creation of several groups for the dissemination of new music. The Asociación de Jóvenes Compositores de la Argentina, founded in 1957 with such composers as Mario Davidovsky and Alcides Lanza as members, has given over seventy-five concerts of Argentine contemporary music and has also helped in its publication and recording, particularly in association with the publishers Editorial Argentina de Música, Ricordi Americana, and the Club Internacional del Disco. The Agrupación Euphonia (later known as Agrupación Música Viva) was established by Gerardo Gandini and Armando Krieger in 1959 with the aim of promoting the study and performance of contemporary music. To ensure the official representation of professional musicians in Argentine governmental institutions and in international music organizations, the Unión de Compositores de la Argentina was created in 1964 through the initiative of the composer Rodolfo Arizaga. Together, these and other previously established music associations afforded Argentine composers and performers an unprecedented degree of professional organization.

Since 1950, three generations of composers have been active in Argentina. A few born prior to 1920 continued to be productive; many more, born in the 1920s, represented the most varied stylistic currents; and numerous younger figures born in the 1930s and 1940s entered the scene with new ideas, some of them contributing substantially to twentieth-century music.

Among the first generation, Alberto Ginastera and Juan Carlos Paz retain our attention. Ginastera's second phase, which we have called one of "subjective sublimation" of musical nationalism (see Chapter 7), lasted until about 1954, the year of the composition of *Pampeana No. 3*. Between that work and the String Quartet No. 2 (1958), Ginastera wrote only one major work, the Harp Concerto (1956); it anticipated the new orientation of his most recent creative period. This period—one of neo-expressionism—began precisely with the Second String Quartet, first performed by the Juilliard String Quartet at the 1958 Inter-American Music Festival in Washington. Although Ginastera employed twelve-tone techniques extensively in this work, he maintained the strong rhythmic drive of his earlier ones and continued to favor traditional formal structures. According to him,

> the first movement, marked *allegro rustico*, is in sonata form, having two main themes, one harsh and the other tranquil. The second movement, *adagio angoscioso*, is a song in five sections: A B C B' A'. It consists of a broad crescendo and diminuendo, with a climax in the dramatic middle section. The third

movement, *presto magico*, is a scherzo, with two trios. Played with muted strings throughout, it brings out unusual sonorities of the quartet. The fourth movement, *libero e rapsodico*, is a theme with three variations, in which each part is written as a cadenza for the different instruments of the quartet. The fifth and last movement, marked *furioso*, has a three-part structure, resembling a toccata in its rhythmic persistence and its nervous and energetic character.[24]

The basic set is not treated according to strict twelve-tone method but simply provides the thematic and harmonic material. In this work, and later ones, twelve-tone techniques are often combined with other procedures—microtonal, polytonal, non-serialist, or atonal.

This is true, for example, of the *Cantata para América Mágica* (1960), for soprano and a large percussion ensemble (with fifty-three instruments, including two pianos, divided into sixteen different groups). Here serialization is applied to pitches, rhythms, timbres, dynamics, and orchestral textures, and it is often coupled with microtonality, polyrhythms, and even aleatoric rhythms.[25] In six sections ("Prelude and Song of Dawn," "Nocturne and Love Song," "Song for the Warriors' Departure," "Fantastic Interlude," "Song of Agony and Desolation," and "Song of Prophecy"), the *Cantata* sets poems of pre-Columbian origin (transmitted by Christian missionaries working in Aztec, Mayan, and Inca cultures) and is conceived in homage to pre-Columbian civilization. The evocation of this primitive world is all the more successful because it is achieved through contemporary musical means. Besides the serial techniques, the work reflects the intricacies of timbral blending and rhythmic structure of much twentieth-century music. Polyrhythms and irregular rhythmic units built up by additive figures are at times reinforced by the introduction of what Ginastera has called "irrational values,"[26] that is, indivisible values within a given metric unit, such as gruppetti of seven or nine thirty-second notes equalling the usual eight (as in the "Prelude and Song of Dawn"). From such "irrational values" to undetermined values was only a step, and Ginastera took it in "Song of Prophecy" (mm. 111 ff). The melodic and harmonic materials follow the basic set, which is made up of two hexachords, the first F♯, G, C♯, C, B, F, the second (a retrograde inversion of the first) A♭, D, E♭, E, B♭, A. From this set, secondary sets are derived but are treated freely, as may be seen in Example 10-20, in which the melody exposes only one row, but with tones repeated. Harmonies often result from a vertical arrangement of the row, thus creating total-chromatic and atonal chord formations. Texturally, the *Cantata* pre-

[24]Program Book, First Inter-American Music Festival (Washington: Organization of American States, 1958), pp. 46–47.

[25]See Pola Suárez Urtubey, "La 'Cantata para América Mágica' de Alberto Ginastera," *Revista Musical Chilena*, no. 84 (April–June 1963), 29.

[26]Ibid.

EXAMPLE 10-20 Alberto Ginastera, *Cantata para América Mágica:* "Song of Agony and Desolation," mm. 7–11. Copyright 1961 Barry y Cia. Used by permission.

V. Canto de Agonía y Desolación

sents dense, block-like passages (often associated with ritual dance, as in the "Song for the Warriors' Departure") and highly elaborated counterpoint—as in, for example, the canonic web of the "Nocturne and Love Song" created by the two pianos, celesta, and glockenspiel. Quite characteristic of Ginastera's style is the expressionist vocal writing in the work, which re-appears subsequently in his operas. The voice is treated in an angular manner, with wide intervallic skips (elevenths, thirteenths), chromaticism, and micro-tonal inflections; and both recitative in *parlando* style and *Sprechstimme* are employed. The vocal part demands great virtuosity and reveals Ginastera's previously undisclosed dramatic skills.

Another work of this period that shows Ginastera's striking origi-nality is the Piano Concerto of 1961, written under a commission from the Koussevitzky Foundation and premiered at the Second Inter-American Music Festival. Individual treatment of twelve-tone technique and masterly and varied orchestration are some of the marks of this originality. In four movements, the concerto is cast in traditional formal schemes, but the first movement is made up of a cadenza and ten micro-structures referred to as "varianti," each of a different character. The basic set is presented in the form of a "rotating polychrome chord," the intervals of which (fourth, fifth, seventh, and octave, all chromatically altered as a result of serial procedures) form the basis of the atonal idiom of the movement (Example 10-21). A melodic transposition of the row serves to introduce the piano in a virtuoso, cadenza-like manner (Example 10-21b). Quite typical of Ginastera's twelve-tone music is the alteration of row material, as is found in this concerto. Another persistent trait is a kaleidoscopic and multicolored orchestration, which admirably projects Ginastera's expressive intensity. Although in the first movement soloist and orchestra alternate in violent contrasts (calling for dense orchestral sonorities), in the second ("Scherzo allucinante") a soft dynamic level, combined with a transparent, individualistic, and pointillist orchestration, is maintained. In contrast again to that, the finale (a "Toccata

EXAMPLE 10-21 Alberto Ginastera, *Piano Concerto* (1961), (a) basic set; first movement, mm. 1–3; (b) basic set: first movement, mm. 4–5. Copyright 1964, 1975 by Barry Editorial, Com., Ind., S.R.L. Used by permission of Boosey & Hawkes, Inc. Sole agents.

concertata") is reminiscent of earlier examples of Ginastera's last-movement orchestration in its percussive effects of orchestral tutti, which match the bravura style of the movement.

Later orchestral and instrumental works by Ginastera, such as the Violin Concerto (1963), the Piano Quintet (1963), the *Estudios Sinfónicos*

(1967–1968), the Cello Concerto (1968), the Piano Concerto No. 2 (1972), and *Serenata* (1973), for cello, baritone, and chamber ensemble, continue to explore new-music techniques and new sonorities. Most are virtuoso works. The *Estudios Sinfónicos*, for example, stress individual instrumental groups, except in the last study, which displays tutti forces. The work also explores colorful clusters and combines microtonal and aleatory structures. Sonata form and variation form remain favorite designs for Ginastera. The second movement of the Second Piano Concerto consists of an ingenious set of thirty-two variations on a chord (F-A-D-C♯-E-G-B♭) from the fourth movement of Beethoven's Ninth Symphony.

Ginastera's esthetic ideals since about 1960 have been equated with Romantic surrealism. The predilection for the supernatural, the fantastic, and the ritualistic that is apparent in his orchestral and chamber works finds no better expression than in his dramatic works of the 1960s. The operas *Don Rodrigo* (1963–1964), *Bomarzo* (1966–1967), and *Beatrix Cenci* (1971) are typically expressionistic works in both esthetic philosophy and musical technique. They all involve tragic situations emerging from the neurotic states of morbid and pathological characters. Two themes specifically relevant to contemporary Western society—sex and violence—are overtly emphasized.[27] The extraordinary success of these operas in Buenos Aires, New York, and Washington resulted not only from their timely libretti but also from the large spectrum of musical means put into action to express their intense dramas. Such means include a combination of atonality, serial techniques, and aleatory procedures, a reliance on structural symmetry, and an array of uncommon vocal and instrumental effects. The success of Ginastera as an opera composer is also due to his ability to correlate musical and dramatic elements. The three acts of *Don Rodrigo*, for example, conform dramatically to exposition, crisis, and dénouement. The same dramatic sequence is applied to each act (each with three scenes). The scenes are separated by instrumental interludes and organized in an overall arch form. Ginastera has revealed the palindromic structure of the nine scenes, with each pair having opposite emotional meaning (see Figure 10-1)[28] and with scene V (the violation of Florinda by Rodrigo) the climax. Each scene follows a specific musical form such as rondo, suite, or aria; this organization is clearly derived from Alban Berg's *Wozzeck*, as is the vocal writing, although to a much lesser extent. The vocal resources include simple speech with prosodic rhythm, speech with musical rhythm and relative pitch, *Sprechstimme*, recitatives ranging from slow to fast delivery of syllables, and regular singing. Scene V illustrates the expressive effectiveness of these techniques, as

---

[27]The production of *Bomarzo* at the Colón Theater in Buenos Aires scheduled for August 1967 was banned by the mayor on moral grounds. A critic of the *Neue Zeitschrift für Musik* called the work "Porno in Belcanto."

[28]See John Vincent, "New Opera in Buenos Aires," *Inter-American Music Bulletin*, no. 44 (November 1964), 3.

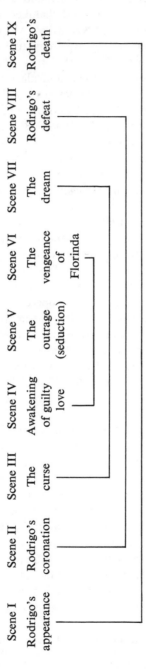

FIGURE 10-1. Relationship of the scenes in Ginastera's *Don Rodrigo*

Florinda begs for mercy and her voice loses strength: from the short sung motifs (measures 406–407), she shifts to *Sprechstimme* (m. 408), then to speech on relative pitches (m. 410), and finally, when overcome, to low-pitched speech (m. 411). Besides Ginastera's customary original treatment of timbres, we find two unusual examples of spatial music (the illusion of sound in motion). The first occurs in the first scene of Act II, where eighteen horns brilliantly sound hunting calls from all around the hall. The second, at the end of the opera, involves twenty-four bells divided into three groups and spread in multiple positions around the hall. The bells (one group playing a chromatic scale, the other two sounding pitches derived from a twelve-tone row) are sounded in an unsynchronized way; they are joined by the strings, reinforcing them through a total-chromatic chord with added microtones, and by the woodwinds and brass, giving forth a chord based on the same series as that of the bells. The resulting impression is overwhelming and effective, for this closing section represents the miracle of bells that augurs Spain's eventual recovery.

Bomarzo and *Beatrix Cenci* likewise indicate Ginastera's unique talent as a dramatic composer. In them he elaborates further his first experiments but maintains the same concern with form and organization. Yet he goes beyond his earlier achievements in the treatment of contemporary techniques of composition. At the same time, he remains attached to the tradition of grand opera.

Ginastera's choral symphonic work *Turbae ad Passionem Gregorianam* (1975) is a highly dramatic, at times even theatrical, setting of the Passion. Besides relying on older devices of Passion music (including clear evocations of Bach's St. Matthew Passion), he also resorts to some of the vocal techniques of his operas (shouts, whispers, whistles, and the like). A very effective dramatic contrast is established between the soloists, who sing in Gregorian chant (and are thus minimized), and the chorus (representing the *turba*, or crowd, the main protagonist of the setting). The choral writing in this work represents a real vocal tour de force in its overpowering virtuosic demands. The orchestra, with a large percussion section, organ, and piano, enhances the dramatic intensity by means of carefully placed massive effects.

During the 1950s Juan Carlos Paz wrote only a few works. He found himself, as he said, at a dead end as a composer. With the development of avant-garde techniques—which, he felt, opened the doors to the most extreme individualism—composition became a challenge to him again, perhaps because of the renewed freedom of choice that music of the 1960s could offer. During that decade he wrote two orchestral works (*Continuidad 1960* and *Música* for piano and orchestra, 1963) and a few chamber and instrumental works (*Invención* for string quartet, 1961; *Concreción* for woodwind and brass, 1964; *Galaxia* for organ, 1964; and *Núcleos* for piano, 1962–1964). These works reveal a free atonal, intuitive style open to all sorts of rhythmic and timbral experiments. Although it has been assumed that Paz had abandoned the dodecaphonic method as such after the 1950s, he used it as late as 1960 in the first movement of *Continuidad*. His language of the 1960s retained a post-Webern quality, especially in the pointillist treatment of timbre and the high concentration of thought, as can be seen in the five *Núcleos* for piano. In these pieces, he also experimented with some aleatory techniques,[29] and his *Música*, for piano and orchestra, even resorts to open forms.

Among the numerous Argentine composers born in the 1920s, only Roberto Caamaño, Hilda Dianda, Francisco Kröpfl, and Alcides Lanza can be considered here. Together with García Morillo, Caamaño (b. 1923) is the most significant neo-Classic composer of the period since 1950. Although he has written some orchestral works (a Suite for strings, 1949, *Música* for strings, 1957, and a Piano Concerto, 1958), his major contributions have been in sacred and secular choral music. His *Magnificat* for chorus and orchestra (1954) and *Cantata para la Paz* for soloists, chorus, and orchestra (1966) reveal his thorough knowledge of compositional techniques of the common-practice period, especially counterpoint.

Dianda (b. 1925) cultivated a modernistic style in her early works of the 1950s (*Concertante* for cello and orchestra, 1952), but after about 1960 she developed an earnest interest in new-music techniques. From 1958 to 1962 she lived in Europe, where she worked with the Groupe de Recherches Musicales in Paris and at the Electronic Music Studio in Milan; she attended the Darmstadt summer courses in 1960 and 1961. Her search for new sonorities is evident in works for chamber ensembles and for orchestra, in which a virtuoso writing prevails (*Núcleos*, 1963; *Ludus I*, 1968; *Ludus II*, 1969). She has also paid attention to percussion timbres and to electronic music; her work *a 7* (1966), for cello and five tapes, was produced at the electronic laboratory of San Fernando Valley College in California.

The Hungarian-born Kröpfl (b. 1928) has been one of the most successful Argentine composers of electronic music. A student of Paz, he became a member of the Agrupación Nueva Música in 1950 and its director in 1956. His early adherence to new techniques was motivated by his teacher. The piece *Dos Estudios* (1953) is written for prepared piano. In 1959, Kröpfl organized the Estudio de Fonología Musical at the Buenos Aires National University, and he later directed the Electronic Music Laboratory at the Di Tella Institute. He has written numerous instrumental pieces, and his electronic music discloses his original treatment of the medium. Each work addresses itself to some technical problem—for example, *Exercise in textures* (1960), *Exercise with impulses* (1961), *Exercise in motions* (1962), and *Exercise with colored noise* (1962). In the series of works called *Diálogos* (1964–1968),

---

[29]For some analytical comments on these pieces, see Jacobo Romano, "Juan Carlos Paz: Un Revitalizador del Lenguaje Musical," *Revista Musical Chilena*, no. 95 (January–March 1966), 26–42.

Kröpfl explored further the large range of electronic sound possibilities, from the use of simple filters to complex sound synthesis.

Alcides Lanza (b. 1929) has also been attracted to the electronic medium and other new methods of composition. A former student of Julián Bautista in Buenos Aires and at the Di Tella Institute (1963–1964), he is considered one of the most prominent composers of the Argentine avant-garde. From 1965 to 1971 he lived in the United States, working and teaching at the Columbia-Princeton Electronic Music Center. In 1971 he became a teacher of composition at McGill University in Montreal. Lanza's early works, such as the *Concierto de Cámara* (1960), are based on a free atonal idiom. At about the same time, he began experimenting with timbre, as *Plectros I* (1962), for one or two pianos, bears witness. Whether on one or two pianos, this work must be performed by two players, as it calls for a plethora of effects obtained through direct manipulation of the strings (for which a plectrum, eight thimbles, two timpani mallets, and two side-drum sticks are used); random choice of pitches occurs within each of the four sections into which the piano frame has been divided. In the *Three Songs* (1963) for soprano and chamber ensemble, a pointillistic treatment of timbre, dynamics, and articulation effectively complements the athematic vocal line.

Beginning around 1965, Lanza developed a major interest in electronic music out of his association with the Columbia-Princeton Center. In the resulting works, electronic sounds tend to be incorporated with those of traditional instruments (e.g., *Plectros II* for piano and tape, 1966; *Interferencias I* and *II*, respectively for winds and tape, and percussion ensemble and tape, 1966 and 1967) or are associated with mixed media (*Penetrations III*, *V*, *VI*, and *VII*, 1969–1973). Lanza also uses synthesizer with traditional instruments, as in *Plectros III*, for piano and synthesizer (1971). Although he relied increasingly on indeterminacy in many of his works of the late 1960s and early 1970s (e.g., *Ekphonesis I*, *II*, and *III*, 1968 and 1969), those calling for traditional instruments disclose at times electronically conceived aleatory.[30]

Of the Argentine composers born in the 1930s and 1940s, Mauricio Kagel has certainly been the most influential, in both Argentina and Europe. Born in 1931, he studied music privately with Juan Carlos Paz, who initiated him in contemporary composition. He worked for a few years as a choral coach and conductor at the Teatro Colón before settling permanently in Germany (1957). Some of the works written before his leaving Argentina were structured in a controlled fashion (such as the *String Sextet* of 1953, revised in 1957, which includes polymetric patterns and microtones and gives some choice of timbre and in the performance of dynamics and articulation); others were more experimental and freely structured (such as *Musique de*

---

[30]For an example, see the reproduction of the notation of *Eidesis III* (1971) in *Composers of the Americas*, 17 (Washington: Organization of American States, 1971), 83.

Tour [Tower Music], 1954, for prerecorded concrete sounds, with light pro-
jections). Kagel's most significant works were written in Europe after 1957.
His major impact has been in mixed media and particularly music theater,
which he has in many ways revolutionized. Theatrical elements first appeared
in his works *Sur scène* (1959–1960) and *Pandorasbox* (1960–) and culminate
in *Ludwig Van* (1969) and *Staatstheater* (1971), the latter being the anti-opera
par excellence of the twentieth century.

Antonio Tauriello, Mario Davidovsky, Gerardo Gandini, and
Armando Krieger were some of the major figures of Argentine new music to
appear in the 1960s. Tauriello (b. 1931), a student of Ginastera for composition and Walter Gieseking for the piano, began his activities in the late 1950s
as a conductor at the Teatro Colón. He later acted as assistant director at
the Chicago Lyric Opera (1965), the New York City Opera, and the American
Opera Theater. He also appeared as conductor at the Inter-American Music
Festivals in Washington, where some of his works were performed. With
the exception of two operas (*Escorial*, 1966, and *Les guerres picrocholines*,
1971), Tauriello's major works are for orchestra or smaller instrumental
groups. In them he draws upon many contemporary orchestral and instrumental techniques. He utilizes a post-Webernian serialism, microtonalism,
total chromatic, and aleatory forms in which sound-blocks are his working
elements. His musicality and freedom of thought are particularly evident in
Música III (1966) for piano and orchestra, *Canti* (1967) for violin and
orchestra, a Piano Concerto (1968), and *Mansión de Tlaloc* (1969) for
orchestra. According to the composer, in the Piano Concerto

> the soloist is independent from the orchestra and has before him a part that
> suggests a musical texture where a succession of sounds and their intensity is
> given, while the duration of each note depends on the value the performer
> wishes to give it in the context of quantities of space. There exist, however,
> certain points of synchronization that the soloist must follow. The work con-
> sists of eleven structures, divided into three parts, which are performed with-
> out solution of continuity, and where poetic conception prevails over the
> techniques employed.[31]

Davidovsky (b. 1934) is another major composer who has made his
career abroad. A student of Guillermo Graetzer in Buenos Aires, he developed early an atonal, abstract lyric style (First String Quartet, 1954;
Noneto, 1957; *Pequeño Concierto*, 1957; and *Série Sinfónica*, for chamber
orchestra). Under a Guggenheim fellowship (1960), he moved to the United
States, where he worked with Varèse, Babbitt, Ussachevsky, Luening, and

[31]From Program Notes, Fourth Inter-American Music Festival (Washington,
1968).

Sessions. His association with the Columbia-Princeton Electronic Music Center in New York (of which he was assistant director) stimulated further his interest in electronic music. His first work exclusively in this medium (*Study No. 1*) dates from 1961. He has, however, given more attention to the investigation of timbres resulting from a combination of electronic materials and traditional instruments. This resulted in a well-known series of seven works (1963–1974) entitled *Synchronisms*, for various instruments and tape.

Gandini (b. 1936), a pianist-composer, has developed a very coherent style based on a free utilization of serial techniques and a keen treatment of timbres. A student of Ginastera and Caamaño, he worked for several years in the United States (1964–1966) and Italy (1966–1967). He then taught at the Buenos Aires Catholic University and at the Di Tella Institute, and in 1970 joined the American Opera Center at the Juilliard School. He has been an active performer of new music in South America, the United States, and Europe. His early works, such as *Pequeñas elegías* (1959) for piano and *Cinco Poemas de Quasimodo* (1963) for soprano, clarinet, viola, harp, and celesta, already revealed some of the features that were to become prominent in later ones: a serial and atonal organization of pitches, an extreme manipulation of dynamics and timbres, and, above all, a rigorous economy and concentration of musical ideas and means. *Música Nocturna* (1964), for flute, violin, viola, cello, and piano, is an outstanding example of Gandini's expressive power. The work is non-thematic and appears to be a study in new-sonority perception. The expressive devices in this "night music" include numerous instrumental effects, contrasts between static parts or passages and fast, elusive, and delicate figures, and an acute pointillistic treatment of the minute materials at work. *Contrastes* (1968), for two pianos and chamber orchestra, further exemplifies Gandini's compositional means. Contrasts between soloists and orchestra involve the whole spectrum of elements (texture, dynamics, density, timbre, and others); aleatory procedures become an integral part of the composition. A very sharp, if reserved, sense of humor enters into some of Gandini's works, either through titles (*A Cow in a Mondrian Painting*, 1957) or through musical resources, as in *L'adieu* (1967), for piano and percussion, and the *Fantaisie Impromptu* (1970) for piano and orchestra. The latter work—an "imaginary portrait of Chopin"—fragments, superimposes, and transforms elements of Chopin's B minor Mazurka in an amusingly clever manner.

Armando Krieger (b. 1940), also a student of Ginastera at the Di Tella Institute, has been active, together with Tauriello and Gandini, as a performer and a conductor in concerts of new music in Argentina. As a permanent conductor at the Teatro Colón, he has conducted modern operas and symphonic concerts. He has also taught at the Catholic University and at the Instituto Superior de Arte of the Teatro Colón. He first wrote in a largely post-Webernian vein but soon turned to aleatory procedures in his search for new sonorities with classical instruments. He has written considerably for the piano, his own instrument as a performer. An early work, *60 para piano*, subtitled "Study of sonorities" (1960), seeks out new sound possibilities for the instrument; particularly striking in it are experiments with registers, dynamics, and timbre, including harmonics and sonorities extracted from clusters. Among Krieger's most substantial compositions are *Elegía II* (1962) for contralto, flute, piano, and percussion, *Cinco Nocturnales* (1964) for chamber ensemble, *Métamorphose d'après une lecture de Kafka* (1968) for piano and fifteen instruments, and the organ piece *Constelaciones* (1969).

Another composer from Argentina who has won recognition abroad is Luis Jorge González (b. 1936). He graduated from the Universidad Nacional de Cuyo and completed his master's and doctoral degrees in composition at the Peabody Conservatory of Music in Baltimore. He has received many awards, from the Fondo Nacional de las Artes of Argentina, the International Henryk Wieniawski Competition (1976), and the Guggenheim Foundation (1978), among others. His early works, such as *Visiones de la Pampa* (1963–67), for orchestra, display a neo-nationalist orientation. In a few years, however, he moved to free atonality and non-serial twelve-tone techniques, as seen in *Voces II*, for nine instruments (1973), and the series *Soledades Sonoras* (1974–76). Besides a search for new sonorities, González's music reveals a clear interest in melodic writing supported, for the most part, by non-triadic harmony in the form of polychords. He has, on occasions, resorted to open forms and has tried his hand at the electronic medium.

Dynamic composers have appeared in Uruguay during the period under examination. However, several of the most promising talents had to look to the outside for support and stimulation, especially during the 1960s, when most musical institutions faced serious financial difficulties. The composers who have followed some of the most advanced styles are León Biriotti, Antonio Mastrogiovanni, José Serebrier, and Sergio Cervetti.

The music of Biriotti (b. 1929) developed from a language imbued with considerations of craftsmanship (e.g., the *Suite Concertante*, 1963, for violin and orchestra, and *Sinfonía Ana Frank*, 1964, for strings) to a total serialist style and the use of electronics. He has been particularly concerned with questions of set theory, which he refers to as a system of structures through permutations ("Sistema de Estructura por Permutaciones") of ordered sets. For him, a set comprises not only the usual possible transformations of a twelve-tone row, applied both horizontally and vertically, but a series of internal, numerical relationships and interactions among the various forms of the rows.[32] This combinatorial-like method was applied in his *Espectros* (1969) for three orchestras, *Permutaciones* (1970) for chamber

[32]See León Biriotti, "Técnica del Sistema de Estructuras por Permutaciones," *Yearbook for Inter-American Musical Research*, X (1975), 138–69.

orchestra, and *Laberintos* (1970) for five instruments, among others. In *Espectros*, for example, ordered sets involve the construction of eleven forms of the series in such a manner as to provide eleven different inversions of the vertical complex of the twelve tones. In other words, the series is presented simultaneously in horizontal and vertical relationships twelve times in both original and retrograde versions without repetition. The result produces a total chromatic cluster, each time different, with internal timbral variety. In *Simetrías* (1970), for nine instruments, Biriotti applied the system not only to pitches and durations but to dynamics and to special instrumental effects (including some undetermined), all in a rigorous, symmetrical overall structure. While this is essentially a technique of composition that allows the most varied diversity of esthetic and stylistic idioms, it also provides one of the most cohesive means of internal structure.

Mastrogiovanni (b. 1936) studied composition with Héctor Tosar in Montevideo, then at the Di Tella Institute with Gandini and Kröpfl. There he also studied electronic music and produced *Secuencial II* (1970), on tape. Most of his works, however, call for traditional instruments, either in solo pieces or in ensembles. A free serial style dominates his compositions of the mid-1960s (e.g., the *Sinfonía de Cámara*, 1965). In later works, such as *Reflejos* (1970), for seven instruments, and *Secuencial I* (1970), for orchestra (both winners of the Dutch Gaudeamus Foundation prize), he turned to new procedures involving especially sound textures and timbres.

More than any other composer of his generation, Serebrier (b. 1938), a resident of the United States for many years, has attempted to instill a characteristic Latin American flavor in some of his works, particularly through an intricate and clever treatment of rhythm (as in *Partita*, 1956–1958, for orchestra). He studied composition and conducting at the Curtis Institute, the University of Minnesota, Tanglewood, and the Pierre Monteux School. He has been very active in the United States and South America as a conductor. In some of his works of the 1960s he gives evidence of a preoccupation with tone color through the unorthodox instrumental ensembles he calls for (*Variations on a Theme from Childhood*, 1964, for trombone with string quartet; *Passacaglia and Perpetuum Mobile*, for accordion and chamber orchestra) and with the exploitation of cluster effects and orchestral sound-blocks. Mixed-media techniques, serialism, and the concept of spatial music are combined in a work like *Colores Mágicos* (1971), subtitled "Variations for Harp and Chamber Orchestra with 'Synchroma' Images." (The Synchroma is a light-producing machine which responds directly to sound; the composer can, therefore, control through sound the motion and patterns of the light.) This work was premiered with immediate success at the Fifth Inter-American Music Festival.

Another Uruguayan composer who settled in the United States is Sergio Cervetti (b. 1941), a student of Stefan Grove and Ernst Krenek at the Peabody Conservatory. As a composer-in-residence in the Berlin Cultural

EXAMPLE 10-22   Sergio Cervetti, score of *Cocktail-Party*.

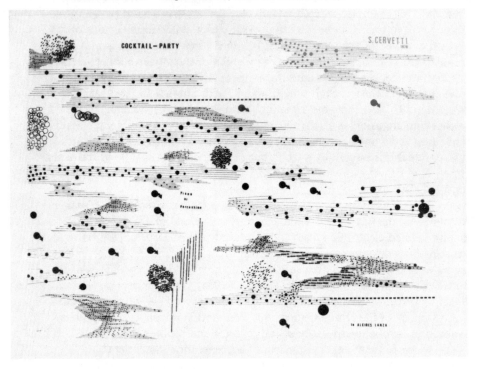

Exchange Program (1969–1970), he became interested in music for the stage from his association with the dancer Kenneth Rinker, with whom he founded the Berlin Dance Ensemble. In 1970 he worked at the Princeton-Columbia Electronic Music Center and taught at Brooklyn College. He represents the left wing of the Uruguayan avant-garde in his works of the late 1960s and early 1970s. After an early interest in serialism he became attracted to experimental techniques, particularly electronic music (*Studies in Silence*, 1968; *Oulom*, 1970; *Raga III*, 1971), chance operations, and mixed media in the form of theater music in such works as *Peripetia* (1970) and *Cocktail-Party* (1970). The latter, calling for "a certain number of amplified instruments (piano obbligato) and a variable number of guests" resorts to visually intricate and provocative graphic notation (Example 10-22).

BRAZIL

As opposed to the other major Latin American countries, Brazil has developed since about 1960 important musical activities in several major cities (not only in Rio de Janeiro), such as São Paulo, Recife, Salvador, and, to a lesser extent, Belo Horizonte, Brasilia (the new capital), and Curitiba. The musical scene during the 1950s did not bring about any significant change. The composers active previously (Mignone, Guarnieri, Siqueira, Lacerda) continued to dominate the scene, with little stylistic innovation. Even such composers as Cláudio Santoro and César Guerra Peixe, who had adhered to twelve-tone techniques earlier (see Chapter 9), embraced musical nationalism during the 1950s. Only after 1960 do we witness a radical change. Several groups of dissenting composers were founded to promote new music, such as the Grupo Música Nova in Santos and São Paulo, the short-lived Grupo Musical Renovador in Rio de Janeiro, and the very active Grupo de Compositores da Bahia in Salvador. Several festivals of avant-garde music took place: two festivals in Rio (1962, 1966) under the promotion of conductor Eleazar de Carvalho, who also supported Santoro's initiative in organizing the First Inter-American Festival of Rio de Janeiro (1967), and the two Guanabara Festivals (1969, 1970), organized through the initiative of the composer Edino Krieger, which had wide repercussions throughout the continent. In 1971 the composers Krieger, Guerra Peixe, Marlos Nobre, Aylton Escobar, and others (all of quite different stylistic tendencies) formed in Rio the Brazilian Society of Contemporary Music, later to be affiliated with the ISCM. Few institutions of higher learning, however, paid attention to new music, and most conservatories and private music schools neglected it altogether. Among the exceptions have been the Universities of São Paulo, Brasilia, Bahia, and, since about 1974, Campinas.

Among the older Brazilian composers, the development of Cláudio Santoro during the 1960s claims our attention. After some incursions into musical nationalism in the 1950s (see Chapter 7), his music underwent a profound stylistic transformation first revealed in the Symphony No. 8 (1963), which represents a return to serialism and a major concern for more freedom of sound organization. By the time of this work, Santoro had definitely freed himself from folk rhythmic formulas and other local idioms in favor of what he called a "universal form and language." This language is illustrated in such works as the string quartets no. 6 and no. 7 (1963, 1965), the Piano Sonatina No. 2 (1964), and the orchestral works *Cinco Esboços* (1964–1965) and *Interações Assintóticas* (1969). The last-named marks a departure from Santoro's earlier conventional orchestral writing, with its use of micro-tuning combined with static sound-blocks, clusters, and random noises of scraping instruments. His first experiments with aleatory procedures and the use of graphic notation date from 1966. Among these, *Intermitências II* (1967), for piano and chamber orchestra, calls for microphones and loudspeakers to amplify the performing forces, as well as the use of the fists and closed hands for cluster production on the piano and direct manipulation of the piano strings. Random percussive elements and limited improvisation are also part of the work's organization (Example 10-23). In the later *Cantata Elegíaca* (1970) for two choruses and orchestra, on a poem by the sixteenth-century

EXAMPLE 10-23. Cláudio Santoro, *Intermitências II*, mm. 60–67. Copyright 1967 by Société des Editions Jobert. Used by permission.

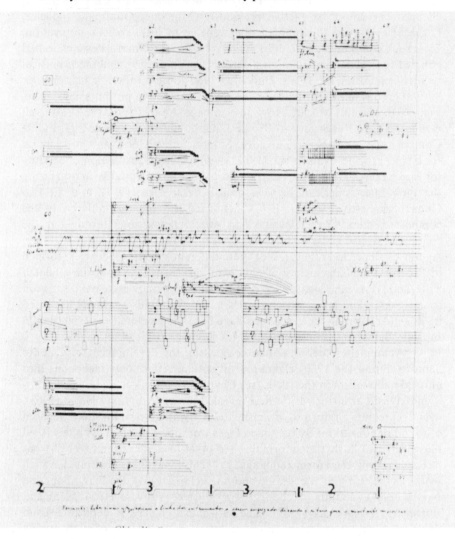

Portuguese poet Luiz de Camões, improvised choral and instrumental sections occur, together with fragmentation of the text *ad libitum* and with contrast between singing and whispering, murmuring, and speaking. Santoro has also exploited successfully the combination of electronic music with traditional instruments and indeterminacy. In the series of six *Mutationen* (1968–1972), each performer is required to make his own tape.

Edino Krieger (b. 1928), who studied at the Brazilian Conservatory of Music in Rio, then privately with Koellreutter and later at Tanglewood with

Copland and the Juilliard School with Mennin, began by writing in a post-Romantic and Impressionist vein. Koellreutter's influence led him to turn to dodecaphony during the late 1940s (Woodwind Trio, 1945; *Música 1947*, for string quartet), but he abandoned it around 1952 in favor of a slightly nationalist neo-Classic language, as seen in such works as *Chôro* (1952) for flute and string orchestra, *Abertura Sinfônica* (1955), the First String Quartet (1955), and especially *Brasiliana* (1960) for viola or alto sax and strings. Since 1965, Krieger has utilized freely some serialist organization and other more advanced techniques together with characteristic elements of Brazilian popular music (*Ludus Symphonicus*, 1966). Aleatory processes appeared for the first time in the incidental music, called *Fanfarras e Sequências*, written especially for the Second Guanabara Music Festival (May 1970).

Among the members of the São Paulo Música Nova Group, Gilberto Mendes, Rogério Duprat, and Willy Corrêa de Oliveira have been the most in evidence. Mendes (b. 1922), a native of Santos and a student of Santoro and Olivier Toni, frequented the Darmstadt Summer Course for New Music in 1962 and 1968, where he studied with Boulez, Pousseur, and Stockhausen. He visited on several occasions the electronic music studios of Cologne, Karlsruhe, and Paris. Essentially an experimentalist, Mendes has created highly original works in his settings of concrete poems by Brazilian avant-garde poets such as Décio Pignatari and José Lino Grünewald. His work *Beba Coca-Cola* ("Drink Coca-Cola") (1966), called "Motet in D minor," on a poem by Pignatari, explores the sonic structure of individual syllables, which provide the sound source of the work. Microtonal effects are mixed with talk, chanting, howling, and shouting. The final section of the piece calls for a theatrical scene during which the singers display a strip bearing the word *Cloaca* (which looks like an altered form of "coca-cola" but actually means "sewer" in Portuguese), in an obviously critical, anti-advertising gesture. This piece has achieved an unprecedented popularity for an experimental work, most likely because of its entertaining and shocking elements.[33] Mendes has been strongly motivated by Satie, the pop artists Rauschenberg and Lichtenstein, the writers Pound, cummings, and Kafka, and the movie director Godard. These influences have stimulated his interest in exploring the visual aspects of the music world. His works *Cidade* (1964), *Blirium c-9* (1965), *Vai e Vem* (1969), *Son et Lumière* (1968), *Asthmatour* (1971), and *Pausa e Menopausa* (1972) exhibit a clear affinity for Cage's concept of indeterminacy and music theater. From the Brazilian avant-garde poets Mendes has inherited the quest for a new artistic language aiming at integrating all musical materials and means of expression available through modern technology. Thus mass communication has become an important element of his artistic credo.

[33]See Gilberto Mendes, "Musica Nuova Brasiliana: Dati e Problemi," in *Aut Aut*, nos. 109–10 (Milan 1969), 206ff.

The Música Nova Group's manifesto appeared in print in 1963.[34] It called for total adherence to avant-garde philosophies and techniques. Together with Mendes and Corrêa de Oliveira, Rogério Duprat (b. 1932) has been the major spokesman for the group. He studied cello and composition in São Paulo and took the Darmstadt summer courses in 1962. Beginning as an atonalist and serial composer, he later cultivated electronic music and mixed media. *Antinomies I* (1962), for chamber orchestra, combines a post-Webern instrumental style with some random procedures. At about the same time as he completed that work, Duprat explored the application of a computer to electronic music in *Experimental Music* (1963). In collaboration with Damiano Cozzella, another member of the São Paulo group, he elaborated on tape the pieces *Ludus Mardalis 1-2* (1967). Since about 1965 Duprat has worked mainly as an arranger of urban popular music, particularly with the Tropicália group, utilizing very effectively his knowledge of electronic music. He has also organized mixed-media events for television: his *Concêrto Alimentar* ("Feeding Concerto") (1969), for example, for kitchen and bathroom fixtures and utensils, electric appliances, food, and beverages, was an event for television with anticipated home-audience participation.

Willy Corrêa de Oliveira (b. 1938) has also been interested in mass communication and its implications for new-music creation. He studied with Olivier Toni and worked as music director of several São Paulo publicity firms. Since 1969 he has taught at the University of São Paulo. A native of Pernambuco, he applied some elements of Northeastern folk music to his early works but turned to serial techniques in the early 1960s (*Música para Marta*, 1961). His numerous scores for plays utilize the electronic medium, but since about 1965 he has been stimulated by aleatory techniques applied to sonic collage of borrowed materials from Western music and combined with controlled passages (*Divertimento*, 1967). His association with Brazilian concrete poets has also resulted in several original works, such as *Um Movimento Vivo* (1962) for chorus, *Três canções* (1970) for voice and piano, on texts by Augusto de Campos, *Und wozu Dichter in Durftiger Zeit* (1971–1972)—two songs for soprano, string quartet, bass, and guitar, on a poem by Haroldo de Campos—and *Cicatristeza* (1973) for female voice. The last-named is a tour de force of imagination in the various effects it demands of the voice and its treatment of theatrical elements.

In the five piano pieces titled *Kitschs* (1968), Corrêa de Oliveira suggests very clearly the implications of his esthetics. The first four pieces are carefully structured (based on a series of pitches and a derived series of chords). The last one, however, consists of fragments from the previous pieces recorded on tape by the performer. Eight strips of different sizes from the score of each *Kitsch* are cut and the performer is supposed to edit them at random (or not at all), then step down from the stage and look for a seat

[34]Gilberto Mendes, Rogério Duprat, et al., "Manifesto música nova," *Revista de Arte de Vanguarda Invenção*, no. 3 (June 1963), 5–6.

among the audience, to listen to the tape. Finally the pianist must applaud frenetically, shout "Bravo," and induce the audience to join in. Particularly indicative of the composer's critical attitude is *Kitsch No. 3*, subtitled "Make it yourself." The composer supplies a series of pitches and a number of chords which constitute part of the materials for the piece, which is to be "composed" by the performer; the other materials are models taken from the standard piano repertoire (Mozart, Debussy, and others). The resulting score should simulate the various styles of the composers proposed, through a selection from the series of pitches and chords provided. The ridiculing of "do-it-yourself" manuals is evident, but the composer's view of traditional concepts of value and expertise—as insignificant!—is also apparent.

Other young composers who have worked in the São Paulo area include José Antonio de Almeida Prado, Raul do Valle, and many others, all students of composition of Camargo Guarnieri, who exerted on most of them a dogmatic influence in favor of musical nationalism. Almeida Prado (b. 1943), a graduate of the Santos Conservatory, succeeded in freeing himself from that influence around the mid-1960s. He undertook further studies in Paris from 1969 to 1973, working with Nadia Boulanger and Olivier Messiaen. In 1974 he was appointed professor of composition at the State University of Campinas. The *Variações sobre um Tema do Rio Grande do Norte* (1963), for piano, illustrates the early neo-nationalist trend of his compositions. Written in an atonal language, the variations rely on typical traits (primarily melodic and rhythmic) of folk-music genres. Since around 1965, however, Prado has cultivated a style in which a post-Webern serialist character (rather than strict technique) often prevails, together with highly individualized harmonic and timbral effects (in which the human voice has an important part) and rigorous formal structures. His *Pequenos Funerais Cantantes* (1969), for solo voices, mixed chorus, and orchestra, which won the first prize at the First Guanabara Music Festival, displays a dazzling imagination in instrumental and vocal effects involving tone color, rhythm, and texture, with an unusual economy of means. This work and later ones also reveal the mystic temperament of the composer. *Livro Sonoro* ("Sound Book") (1973) for string quartet, for example, is a work whose expression is meant to be imparted with the same characteristics as a text, that is, thought, language, and narration. Thus, the work includes six miniature sections: "Thought," "Discourse," "Anti-Discourse," "Sonnet," "Period," and "Memory." Within an athematic, atonal language, varying moods are created, primarily through rhythmic and timbral exploration. A more recent work, *Thérèse, L'Amour de Dieu* (1975), an oratorio for vocal soloists, narrators, chorus, and orchestra, also shows the composer's mystic bent and some technical affinity with Messiaen's *La Transfiguration de Notre Seigneur Jésus Christ*.

Raul do Valle (b. 1936), a colleague of Almeida Prado at the State University of Campinas, has also developed a highly original language based on atonality and exploration of new sonorities. He too was a student of

Nadia Boulanger in Paris and studied privately with Alberto Ginastera in Geneva. Among his most successful works are *Rabiscaduras* (1969) for brass and percussion, the Mass *Da Nova e Eterna Aliança* (1974), and *Cambiantes* (1974) for percussion, which was awarded a prize in Geneva in 1975.

Among the composers active in Rio de Janeiro during the 1960s, Marlos Nobre (b. 1939) came to occupy a prominent position within the Brazilian avant-garde. A student of Koellreutter and Camargo Guarnieri and of Ginastera at the Di Tella Institute in Buenos Aires (1963–1964), where he familiarized himself with the most advanced techniques of composition (including electronic techniques with José Vicente Asuar), Nobre moved stylistically from a nationalistic concern mixed with the dissonant style of Milhaud to twelve-tone techniques. Beginning about 1964, he attempted to create a new language based on free serialism, akin to those of Dallapiccola and Berio rather than to that of the Viennese school. Since 1967 he has worked with aleatory procedures and proportional notation, but with nativistic overtones. Many of his works have the natural exuberance found earlier in Villa-Lobos's, particularly in their dramatic intensity, projected through special timbral effects and highly contrasting dynamics. Among some of his most characteristic works are *Variações Rítmicas* (1963) for piano and percussion; *Ukrinmakrinkrin* (1964) for soprano, wind instruments, and piano; *Canticum Instrumentale* (1967) for flute, harp, piano, and timpani; *Rhythmetron* (1968) for percussion; *Concêrto Breve* (1969) for piano and orchestra; and *Mosaico* (1970) and *In Memoriam* (1973), both for orchestra. *Ukrinmakrinkrin* combines an atonal-serial language with some native ritualistic flavor. The text, in Xucurú Indian dialect, is a ritual incantation of tribal origin. Nobre uses it, however, primarily for sonorous effects, as the vocal line shows no connection with Indian traditional music. The second movement, subdivided into various partially aleatoric structures, displays a free and delicate treatment of materials, without fixed pulsations. The atonal style is limited primarily to intervals of seconds, sevenths, and ninths. The first vertical structure utilizes only two pitches of the series, the second increases to four, and so on until the sixth structure, with all twelve pitches. In three parts—"Densidades," "Ciclos," and "Jogos"—the work *Mosaico* displays its composer's sophisticated command over new techniques, particularly in its clusters covering the total sound-space of the orchestra, its treatment of sound-blocks, its deep sense of engineering, and its violent contrasts derived from a complex and brilliant orchestration. Especially noteworthy is its use of percussion instruments, which include many typically Brazilian instruments treated soloistically.

Only in recent years has the University of Brasilia succeeded in gathering together a dynamic group of composers. Santoro attempted in 1963 to implement an ambitious music program, but he did not remain in Brasilia. Later, the composer Rinaldo Rossi promoted the instruction of new-music composition and was able to attract such promising composers as Nicolau Kokron (1937–1971) and Fernando Cerqueira. The composer most in evidence in Brasilia in recent years, however, has been Jorge Antunes (b. 1942). A student at the Rio de Janeiro School of Music and at the Faculdade Nacional de Filosofia, where he took a degree in physics (1965), Antunes later went to the Di Tella Institute, where he worked particularly in electronic music. He continued his studies of electronic music at the University of Utrecht and with the Parisian Groupe de Recherches Musicales. Since 1973 he has been a professor of composition at Brasilia, where he directs the electronic music laboratory of the University and *GeMunB* (Group of Musical Experimentation of the University of Brasilia). In the late 1960s, Antunes appeared as one of the most representative composers of experimental music in Brazil. He pioneered in electronic-music composition in his country, and from about 1965 he cultivated what he calls "integral art," or mixed media including not only sounds and colors but also odors and flavors (for example, *Ambiente I*, 1965). In his orchestral and chamber-music works (*Cromoplastofonia*, 1967–1968; *Concertatio I*, 1969; *Isomerism*, 1970; *Bartokollagia*, *MCMLXX*; and *Music for Eight Persons Playing Things*, 1970–1971), he relies a great deal on aleatory procedures. His early electronic pieces *Valsa Sideral* (1962) and *Contrapunctus Contra Contrapunctus* (1966) utilize simple structures, such as repetitions of given cells (although in distorted rhythmic patterns), but also anticipate special effects such as mirror shapes through the use of ostinatos, tape loops, and feedback systems; these came to be referred to as "hypnotic music" and were standardized later by the United States composer Terry Riley, among others. Antunes's subsequent electronic pieces, such as *Auto-Retrato sobre Paisaje Porteño* (1969) and *Historia de un Pueblo* (1970), reveal a more subtle and more mature treatment of their media.

The Seminários Livres de Música (later renamed Escola de Música e Artes Cênicas of the University of Bahia) were founded in 1954, under the direction of Hans J. Koellreutter, and became during the 1960s a dynamic center for new music. Various performing ensembles, including a trio and an experimental percussion ensemble, were established there, and in 1966 the Grupo de Compositores da Bahia was organized. This group consisted of several faculty members and several students of the school. Their aims and purposes were the stimulation and dissemination of contemporary music through exchange and research programs, concerts, festivals, publications, and the gathering of materials on twentieth-century music. Courses and festivals each year bring together composers and students from various Brazilian states and from abroad. The person largely responsible for this development has been the Brazilian composer of Swiss birth, Ernst Widmer (b. 1927), who settled in Bahia in 1956. A graduate of the Zurich Conservatory in composition, piano, and music education, he went to the University of Bahia as a teacher of composition, orchestration, and music literature, and conducted the University Madrigal Group (1958–1967). For many years he directed the university's School of Music and was very influential as the teacher of a whole generation of local composers. From his teacher Willy Burkhard at the Zurich Conservatory, he learned the educational value of fostering maximum independence from his students. His own output, however, shows him to be an eclectic. Before the age of twenty-one Widmer had what he later described as a "reactionary attitude" in musical composition, from which he moved to a moderate modernist style when he had fully assimilated the lessons of Stravinsky, Bartók, and Hindemith. Then, in the 1960s, he developed intermittent and often unexpected interests in avant-garde music. His creative activity can be considered as a gradual convergence of intuition and intellect, naiveté and sophistication, originality and traditionalism. This complex of attitudes has resulted in what he has called "progressive" and "regressive" phases, often in coexistence. Among his works exemplifying the latter tendency are the *Chinesische Lieder* (1948), the Suite for orchestra (1953), *Hommages à Stravinsky, Frank Martin et Béla Bartók* (1960) for oboe and string orchestra, and *O Homem Armado* (1967) for band or wind orchestra. The "progressive works" include the Wind Quintet (1954), *Ceremony after a Fire Raid* (1962–1963), *Pulsars* (1969), *Sinopse* (1970), *Quasars* (1970), *Rumos* (1972), *Convergencia* (1973), *ENTROncamentos SONoros* (1972), and a series of eight works (only four completed) that form the cycle of *Morfoses* (1973–1975).

Pulsars, for violin, bass, clarinet, bassoon, trumpet, trombone, and percussion, alternates aleatory sections (undetermined in durations, phrasing, and articulation) with totally controlled passages. *Sinopse*, for soprano, chorus, violin, cello, piano, and orchestra (which won first prize at the Second Guanabara Music Festival), is a product of a creative imagination. With varying resources (in tonal, modal, polytonal, and serial idioms) Widmer maintains effectively the character of the poem (Jorge de Lima's sonnet *A Torre de Marfim*, "The Ivory Tower"), which refers to the gradual transformation of things apparently immutable. Exploration of new timbral blendings (often through chromatic clusters) appears to be one of the fundamental concerns in this work. Aleatory techniques and spatial-music effects occur in *ENTROncamentos SONoros*, for piano, five trombones, strings, and tape.

Widmer has also explored very efficiently the various vocal techniques exploited in new music. *Rumos*, for example, for narrator, mixed chorus (of more than fifty singers), orchestra, Smetak instruments (see page 352), and tape, calls for humming, shouting, blowing, whispering, hissing, and whistling in addition to regular speech and rhythmic articulation of consonants. The composer also anticipates the active participation of the audience and gives detailed instructions to that effect: to the expected laughters, whistles, jeers, and the like from the audience, elements of the orchestra are supposed to respond spontaneously. In case of total and uncontrollable chaos, the composer has supplied an emergency ending (Example

EXAMPLE 10-24 Ernst Widmer, *Rumos*, "emergency ending." Reproduced with the kind permission of the composer.

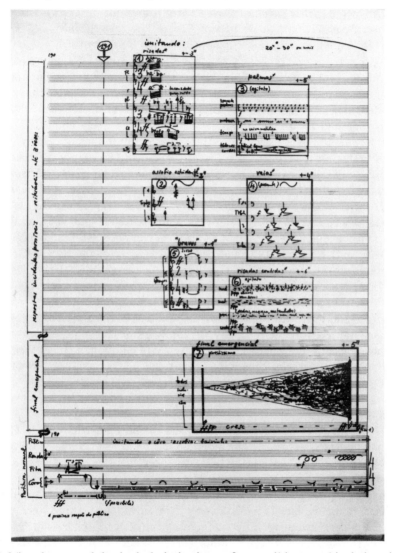

10-24), whose modules include imitations of a possible anarchical situation. Such an attitude is relevant to Widmer's continuous interest, not in creating works as such, but in offering propositions: to involve and captivate the listener, and, at the same time, to deny him a feeling of adjustment.

Among the founding members of the Bahian Group, Milton Gomes and Fernando Cerqueira were recognized as prizewinners at the First Guanabara Music Festival. Gomes (1916–1974), a physician by profession, studied with Koellreutter and Widmer at the Bahia University. Although he wrote his first work (*Integração*) only at the age of forty-six, he has cultivated a very expressive personal and advanced style, combining new sonorities through percussion (*Estrutura para nove instrumentos de percussão*, 1964; *Study of Sound Variations on Plastic Expressions of Schizophrenics*, 1965), serial techniques, and formal strictness. The later work *Primevos e Postrídios* (1969), for chorus and orchestra, displays a special concern for sound experimentation, within an unusually static harmony and almost motionless rhythm. Fernando Cerqueira (b. 1941), a student at the Bahian School, has been teaching at the University of Brasilia since 1971. He has followed twelve-tone and serialist methods, which he applies freely and mixes with other techniques such as microtonality and some random operations. His works best known in Brazil are *Elegia* for chorus, brass, and percussion; *Transubstanciação* for orchestra (1968); *Heterofonia do Tempo ou Monólogo da Multidão* (1969) for solo voices, chorus, and orchestra; *Trio Metamorfose* (1970) for piano, violin, and cello; and *Decantação* (1970) for chorus and orchestra. The last work is a study in new orchestral and vocal timbres.

Walter Smetak (b. 1913), a Swiss-born composer who established his residence in Salvador in 1957 and became a member of the Bahian Group, represents an interesting case of heterogeneous experimentalism. He has developed a series of instruments for sound experiments; these have been used in most of his and other group members' scores, for both their acoustical properties and their theatrical-gesture possibilities. The calabash appears as a fundamental constituent of many of Smetak's instruments, which often operate by means of ingenious kinetic systems. In addition, many of them are truly pop-art-like works, reminding one of the "objets trouvés" art movement. His works for these instruments include *Pesquisas*, *M2005*, *serVIR A SERv*, *Um Sol Realizado*, and others; all stress improvisation and aleatory techniques.

The most creative younger members of the Bahian Group of Composers are Rufo Herrera, Lindembergue Cardoso, and Jamary Oliveira. The Argentine-born Herrera (b. 1935) has been living in Brazil since 1963. He was first trained at the Buenos Aires National Conservatory and continued his studies of composition later in Brazil under Olivier Toni and Ernst Widmer. Since the late 1960s he has lived in Salvador as a free-lance composer. His deep awareness of contemporary music developments in Europe and North America is reflected in his works. Besides exploring new timbres (through new treatment of traditional instruments or electronically generated and altered sounds) in such works as *Engramas*, for ten instruments, and *Enantiodromia*, for five instruments, he has also experimented with aleatory procedures and collages (*Ámbitus Mobile I* and *II*, 1970). Herrera was one of the first in the Bahia area to organize mixed-media events, particularly in conjunction with the Dance Department of the University of Bahia.

Another eclectic composer who has nevertheless created a typical avant-garde local style is Lindembergue Cardoso (b. 1939). A student of composition at the University of Bahia, he learned from Widmer techniques of the various trends of contemporary music. Since 1966 he has been first bassoonist of the University Symphony Orchestra and a member of the university's woodwind ensemble; later, he became professor of theory and composition. His first works reveal some concern for nationalistic esthetics (*A Festa da Canabrava* and *Missa Nordestina*, both 1966), but he subsequently turned to more abstract ideas and reached a more frankly contemporary style, including a combination of aleatory processes with fixed elements (String Trio, 1967; *Via Sacra*, 1968; *Captações*, 1969; and *Pleorama*, 1971). Several of his works (e.g., *Espectros*, 1970; Wind Quintet, 1970; *Kyrie Christe*, 1971; Piano Toccata, 1972; and *Sedimentos*, 1973) evidence his successful treatment of carefully planned timbral effects.

The musical thought of Jamary Oliveira (b. 1944) has, like that of Cardoso, been shaped by his teacher Widmer. Perhaps more than his Bahian contemporaries, he has shown an extreme freedom of thought that is clearly revealed in his non-dogmatic approach to music composition. By the late 1960s he cultivated an unorthodox twelve-tone technique, after some earlier incursions into neo-nationalist atonality. He prefers to write for small chamber ensembles and soloists and for the voice. Aleatory processes occur alongside any other techniques, tonal or atonal, that he believes might help to express a given idea. Among his most significant works are a Piano Trio (1967), *Conjunto II* (1968), *Tonal-A-Tonal* (1969), *Conjunto III* (1969) for Smetak instruments, *Interações* (1970), *Congruencias* (1972), and *Ludus* (1973).

We have provided ample evidence of the vitality of Latin American music development since 1950. Yet many critics have raised questions concerning the likelihood of an original contribution of Latin America within established contemporary compositional techniques. Such questions result from the presumed universality of musical creation in the Western art-music tradition, which congealed during the nineteenth century as a prominent and enduring case of cultural ethnocentrism. Contemporary sociocultural conditions in Latin America have shaped new societies resulting from the blending of several cultures, including the prevailing Western European culture. However, sources of musical creation need not originate only from a single traditional area of musical activity; they reflect, in fact, perhaps unconsciously, the cultural renaissance that the continent has undergone since about 1960. No doubt many Latin American composers have suffered from what is called the "terrorism of the avant-garde," but in following international models the Latin American composer has automatically transformed them in order to authenticate them. Here is the nature, it seems, of what Gustavo Becerra refers to as the Brazilian *sotaque* ("local, regional accent") in contemporary music, which can be extended to all Latin American countries.[35] Admittedly, it is difficult to point out accurately where and how the *sotaque* manifests itself in the considerable music production since 1950, but its existence can hardly be questioned. Given the uniqueness of the cultural context in which his music is created, the Latin American composer cannot escape revealing some aspects of that context. At the same time, in our age of swift communication, new processes of composition in any part of the world can be readily assimilated anywhere. According to Becerra, "the melting pot in which the music of the future is taking shape is nothing less than the whole world."[36] Latin America is undoubtedly contributing her own developing esthetics to this process.

BIBLIOGRAPHICAL NOTES

Latin American music during the period since 1950 has not been studied extensively or adequately. Much of the data gathered in this chapter have been supplied by many of the composers mentioned in it. A few bibliographical items, however (in addition to the references in footnotes), may be indicated.

Aurelio de la Vega gives an overview of Latin American music since 1950 in "New World Composers," *Inter-American Music Bulletin*, no. 43 (September 1964), 1–16, and in "La música artística latinoamericana," *Boletín Inter-americano de Música*, no. 82 (1971–1972), 3–33. See also de la Vega's assessment of music in Latin America in the 1960s in his article, "Avant-Garde Music at the American Art Biennial of Córdoba," *Yearbook*, Inter-American Institute for Musical Research, III (1967), 85–100. Juan Orrego-Salas surveys the contemporary trends and personalities in "The Young Generation of Latin American Composers: Backgrounds and Perspectives," *Inter-American Music Bulletin*, no. 38 (November 1963), 1–10. Several interesting papers by Latin American composers on various questions of "new music," first presented at the First Inter-American Composers Seminar (Indiana University, April 1965), are available in *Music in the Americas*, ed. George List and Juan Orrego-Salas (The Hague: Mouton & Co., 1967). Several entries on individual composers and summary articles on Argentina, Brazil, Chile, and Mexico are included in *Dictionary of Contemporary Music*, ed. by John Vinton (New York: E. P. Dutton, 1974).

In addition to the series *Composers of the Americas*, which includes several biographies of composers active since 1950, see the periodical *Heterofonía* for short biographical sketches of Mexican composers. In his *Introduction to Twentieth-Century Mexican Music*, Dan Malmström covers the period since 1950 in his last chapter. The bulletin *Música* from the Casa de las Américas of

---

[35]Gustavo Becerra Schmidt, "Modern Music South of the Rio Grande," *Inter-American Music Bulletin*, no. 83 (March–June 1972), 5 (reprinted from *The World of Music.*)
[36]Ibid., p. 2.

Havana keeps us up to date on Cuban music activities. A selection of José Ardévol's writings from 1932 to 1963 was published in his book *Música y revolución* (Havana: Ediciones Unión, 1966). Leo Brouwer gives a general assessment of the Cuban musical avant-garde in "La Vanguardia de la música cubana," *Sonda* (Madrid), 1970. Aurelio de la Vega's works are analyzed in Alice B. Ramsay, "Aurelio de la Vega: his Life and Works" (unpublished Master's thesis, San Fernando Valley State College, 1963), and in John R. Schortt, "Aurelio de la Vega, un compositor de las Américas," *Revista Musical Chilena*, no. 84 (1963), 62–88. Further discussion of Roque Cordero's works and those of other Central American composers is provided in Ronald R. Sider, "The Art Music of Central America, its Development and Present State" (unpublished doctoral thesis, Eastman School of Music, University of Rochester, 1967).

Broad overviews on contemporary Colombian and Peruvian music appear, respectively, in Guillermo Espinosa's short article, "Colombian Music and Musicians in Contemporary Culture," *Inter-American Music Bulletin*, no. 27 (1962), 1–4, and Enrique Pinilla's "La música contemporánea en el Perú," *Fanal* (Lima), no. 79 (1966), 17–23. Edgard Valcárcel has also written on Peruvian music in "Estado actual de la composición musical en el Perú," *Cultura y pueblo* (Lima), nos. 7–8 (1965–67), 44–45.

Samuel Claro gives a general introduction to experimental music in Chile in his article, "Panorama de la música experimental en Chile," *Revista Musical Chilena*, no. 83 (1963), 110–17. The issues nos. 119–20 (1972) of the same periodical are dedicated to the works of Gustavo Becerra. Becerra himself is a prolific author of articles; see especially the series of nine articles on "Crisis de la enseñanza de la composición en Occidente," *Revista Musical Chilena*, nos. 58–65 (1958–1959). Among the many writings of José Vicente Asuar which shed light on his own development as a composer, the following are outstanding: "Y . . . sigamos componiendo," *Revista Musical Chilena*, no. 83 (1963), 55–99; "Mi fin es mi comienzo," *Revista Musical Chilena*, no. 89 (1964), 43–78; and "Recuerdos," *Revista Musical Chilena*, no. 132 (1975), 5–22.

Argentine musical life and institutions are discussed in Hilda Dianda's book, *Música en la Argentina de hoy* (Buenos Aires: Edición Proartel, 1966). For specific biographical information and lists of works of Argentine composers, Rodolfo Arizaga's *Enciclopedia de la música argentina*, mentioned in the notes for Chapter 4, should be consulted. Ginastera's *Don Rodrigo* is the subject of Orrego-Salas's article, "An Opera in Latin America: *Don Rodrigo* by Ginastera," *Artes Hispánicas*, no. 1 (1967), 94–133. Pola Suárez Urtubey's study on Ginastera is *Alberto Ginastera en cinco movimientos* (Buenos Aires, 1972). Alcides Lanza wrote about his own music development; see his "Selbstportrait" in the Program Booklet of the *Donaueschinger Musiktage 1972*, 13–15. As part of the German new-music scene Kagel's music has been studied fairly extensively; see especially Ulrich Dibelius, *Moderne Musik, 1945–65* (Munich, 1966); Dieter Schnebel, *Das musikalische Theater des Mauricio Kagel* (Cologne, 1968); and also by Schnebel, *Denkbare Musik. Schriften 1952–1972* (Cologne: Verlag M. DuMont Schauberg, 1972).

The works of some of the Brazilian composers mentioned in this chapter are discussed by Caldeira Filho in his book *A aventura da música* (São Paulo: Ricordi Brasileira, 1970). For Santoro's music of the late 1960s, see the review-essay by Edwin London, "Four scores by Claudio Santoro," *Yearbook for Inter-American Musical Research* (University of Texas at Austin), VII (1971), 51–58. Paul Earls reviews critically Nobre's *Ukrinmakrinkrin* and *Mosaico* in *Yearbook for Inter-American Musical Research*, VIII (1972), 178–80. On the São Paulo Música Nova Group, see Rogério Duprat, "En torno al 'Pronunciamento'," *Revista Musical Chilena*, no. 86 (1963), 33–38, and M. Lozano, "El grupo brasileño música nova," *Sonda* (Madrid), no. 1 (1968), 37ff. An informative tribute to the Group of Bahian Composers is given by León Biriotti in his booklet *Grupo de compositores de Bahía: reseña de un movimiento contemporáneo* (Montevideo: Instituto de Cultura Uruguayo-Brasileño, 1971). A short pamphlet in English, entitled *Music in Brazil: Now*, contains four articles by Osvaldo Lacerda, Jamary Oliveira, Sergio Vasconcellos Corrêa, and Edino Krieger; it was published by the Cultural Department of the Brazilian Foreign Relations Ministry in 1974. The same department has issued, between 1975 and 1978, complete catalogues of works by some thirty-five Brazilian living composers. These can be obtained by writing to Ministério das Relações Exteriores, Departamento de Cooperação Cultural, Científica e Tecnológica, Brasilia, D.F.

INDEX